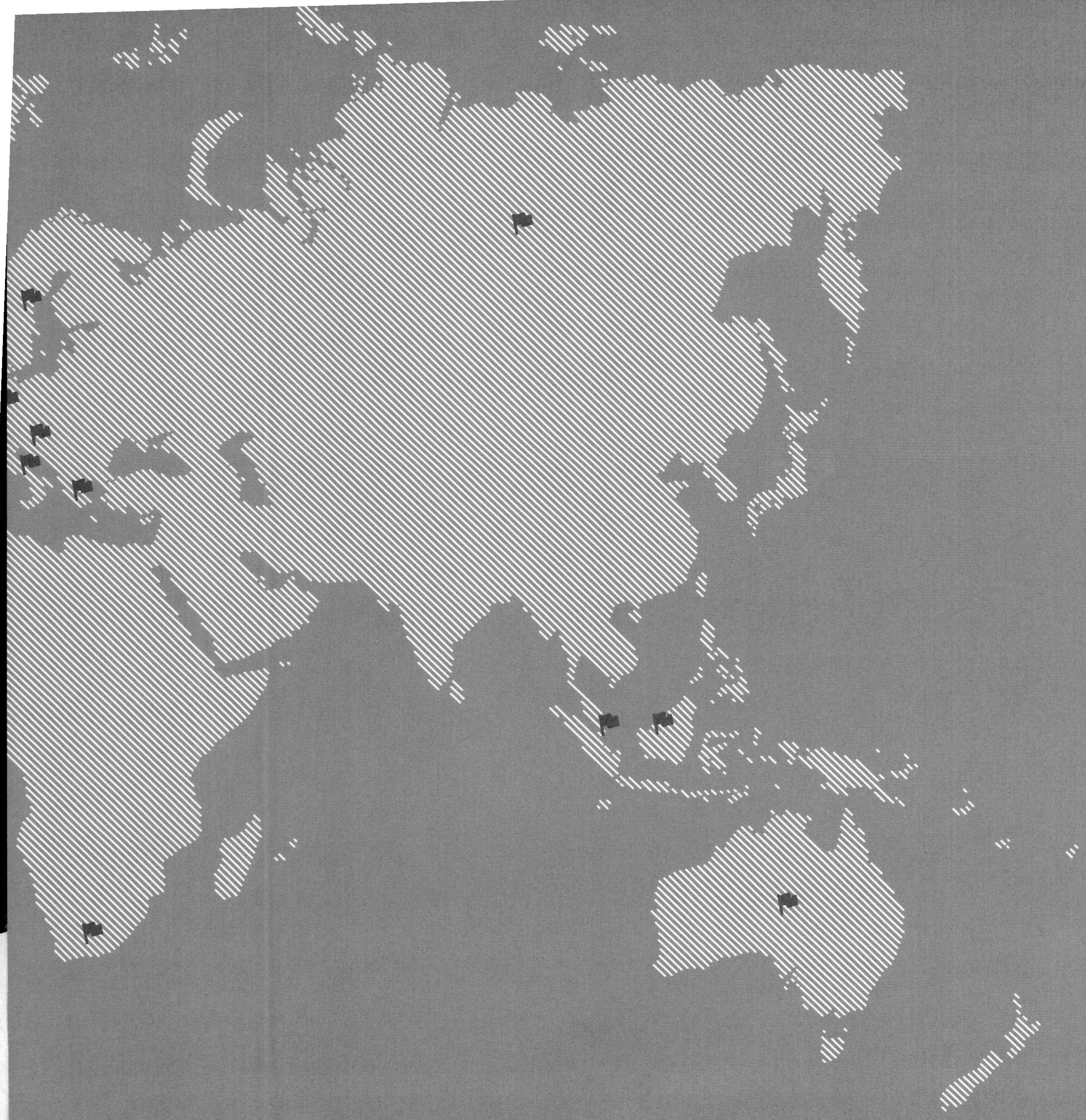

AF334723

The DISTINGUISHED GENTLEMAN'S RIDE

A DECADE OF DAPPER

FOREWORD BY CHARLEY BOORMAN

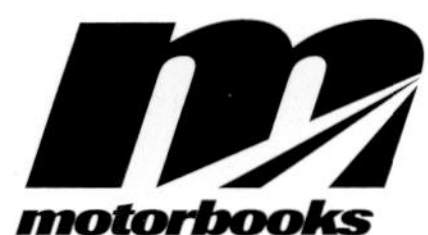

motorbooks

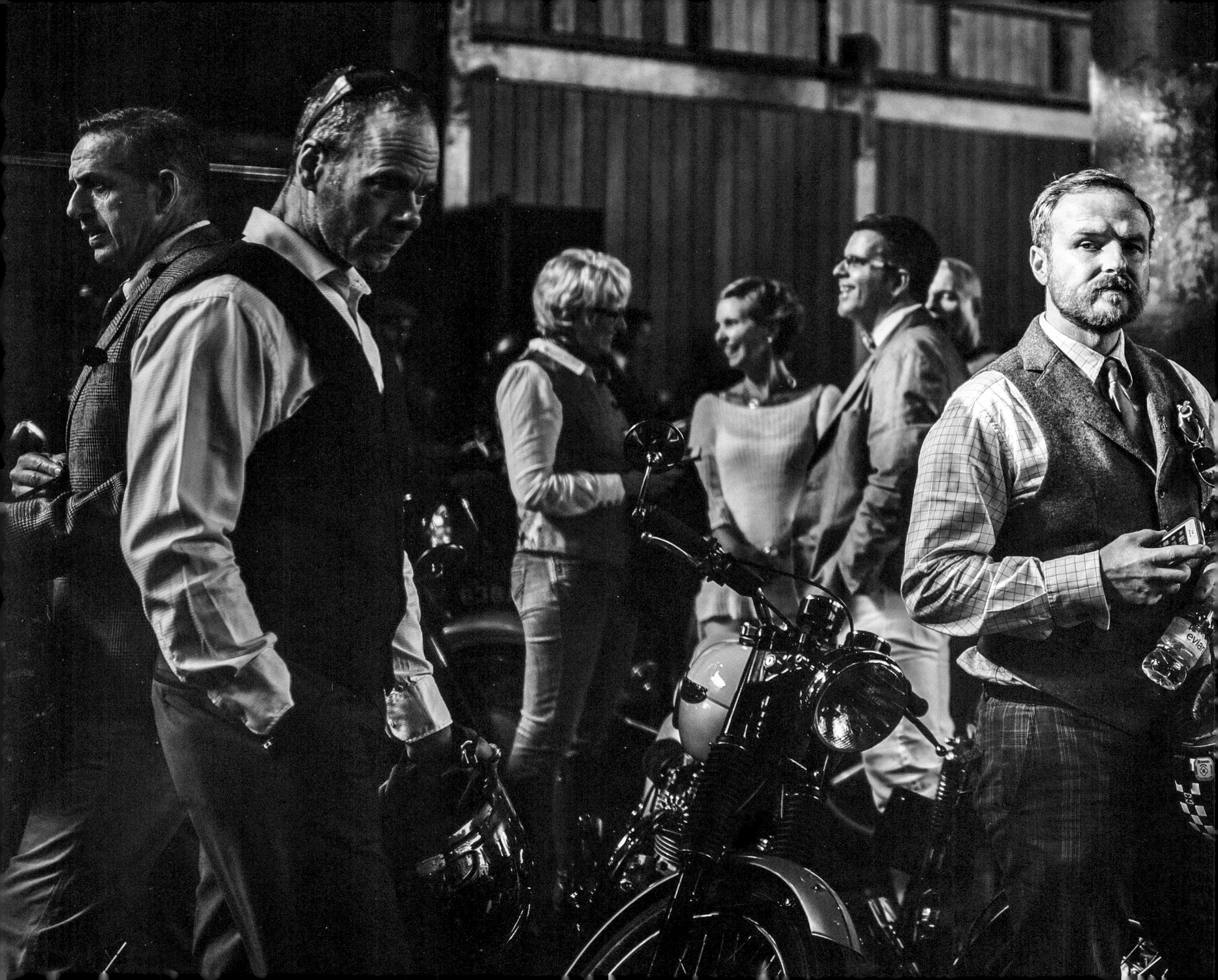

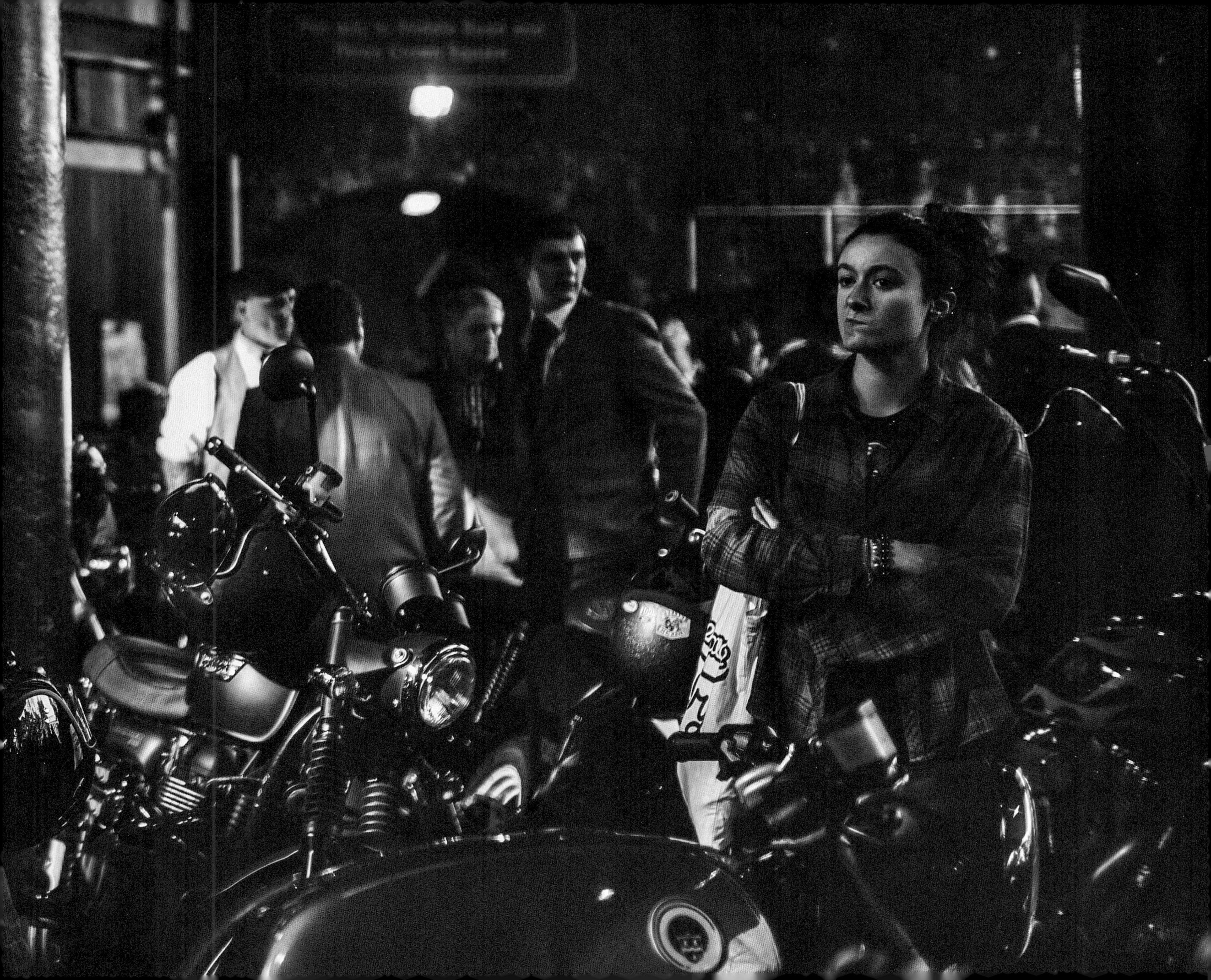

To all the Distinguished Gentlefolk
who are no longer with us.

Ride in Peace.

...ENTS

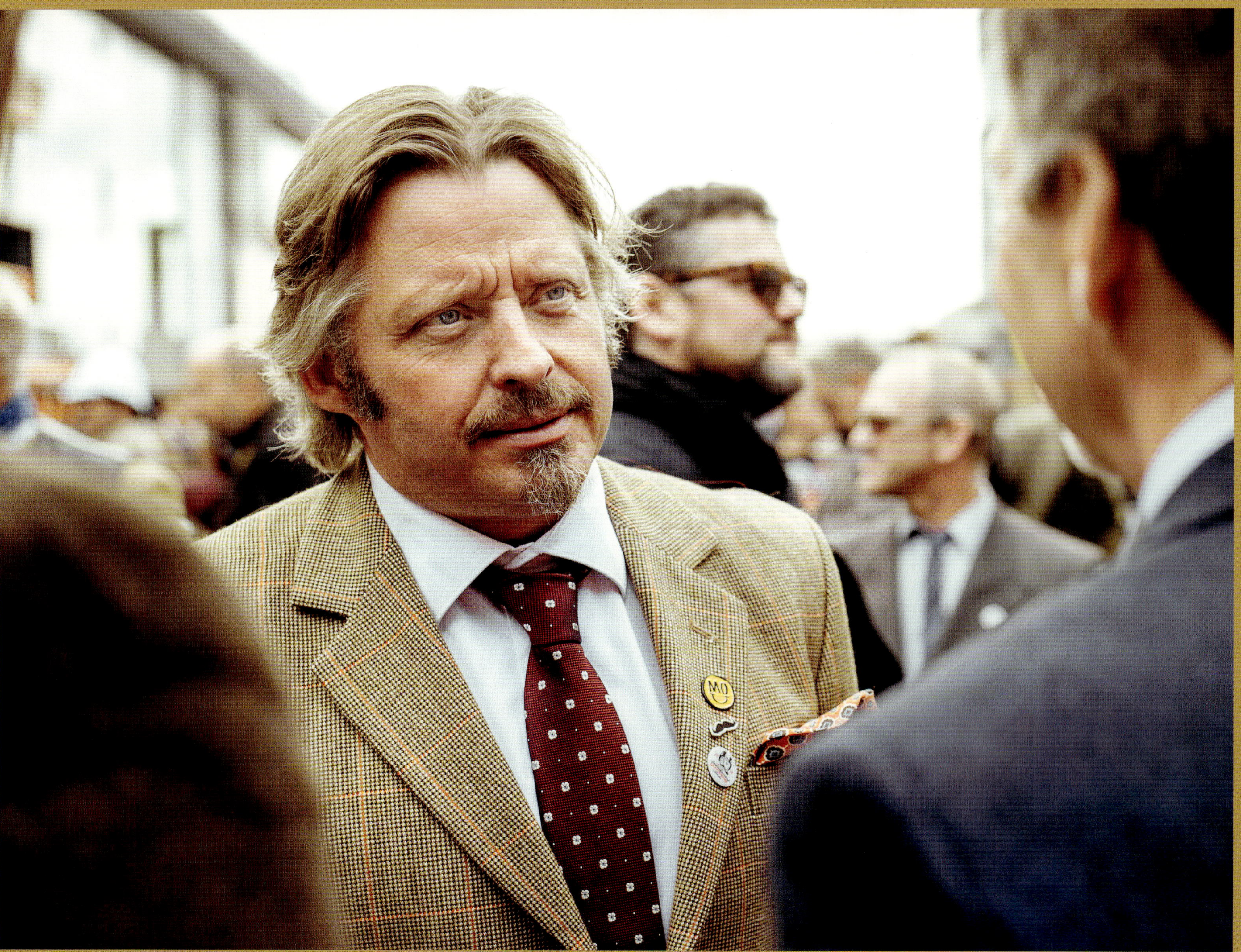

FOREWORD

I remember the first time I came on a Distinguished Gentleman's Ride in London. I was super excited about what to expect. I headed to the start with a great friend of mine, Roy, as it's all about friends and like-minded people.

I remember pulling into a petrol station and there were a whole bunch of people getting ready for the ride. I remember how so many people made such a big effort to dress as a Distinguished Gentleman. In particular, there was one guy who was in full horse riding gear. Jodhpurs, riding boots, jacket and a whip tucked down the side of the boot.

He walked over to his motorbike: an old Harley. He had replaced his seat with an English horse saddle. I reckon that is the whole tone for The Distinguished Gentleman's Ride for me. I've been to every one since and I now go to the one in Surrey.

It's funny. I'm just sitting here in my garage on a bike trying to remember the day when I met Mark Hawwa for the first time. I remember him bounding up to me with the most infectious enthusiasm for the ride. The whole idea of getting people together from all over the world and dressing up. Getting together and sharing stories about riding motorcycles and friendships.

I've spent a lot of time with Mark over the years, a lot of times in Australia. And he's always planning something awesome. I have to say he's one of the nicest men I know. I really recommend taking a good look at this book to see what he's achieved and how many people have been touched by his enthusiasm.

The money that's been raised has saved people's lives. Whether sitting on the beach in Sydney or getting ready to ride in London, it's always a pleasure to be on The Distinguished Gentleman's Ride.

Charley Boorman
DGR Ambassador
Adventurer, Writer & Entertainer

INTRODUCTION

It's the last Sunday in September 2016 and I'm standing in The Bike Shed, London, in a brand new suit. In front of me is a man I've never met before. He is crying and he comes in for a hug. Not just quietly sobbing or with a few tears in his eyes, but *properly* crying.

It's the kind of public display of emotion you rarely see outside of people's homes or movie theaters. This gentleman is tall and broad, a real staunch kind of guy, and here he is as brittle as the rest of us. But the truth is that when you strip away the layers of The Distinguished Gentleman's Ride, this is what is at its core. Mates talking honestly to each other, even if they are mates you've only just met.

I'd love to be able to tell you that these last ten years were some grand plan of mine that I came up with in a giant moment of inspiration. But the truth is a whole lot more chaotic, unplanned and is made up of many moments of sheer dumb luck. In fact, it's not a story about me at all. Instead, it's more of a story about the connection that everyone who's silly enough to jump on a motorcycle and ride it feels when they see someone else who's silly enough to do the same.

When I turned 25, I woke up and out of nowhere thought to myself, "I want to get a motorcycle." I don't know where the idea came from but like much of the last decade, it was just one of those strange, beautiful moments that life throws at us all. I bought a Honda VTR250 and practiced in the backstreets near my house while hiding it from my parents.

Riding it was cool, but I quickly realized that I needed friends with me to fully enjoy the experience. I needed a group of mates around me to learn from and share stories with. So Sydney Cafe Racers was born with the sole purpose of bringing riders together and having fun.

Then in 2011, after seeing a photo of *Mad Men*'s Don Draper on a classic bike in a suit posted in Perth Cafe Racers, the trajectory of my life changed. What if there was a bigger, more meaningful reason for riding together than just shits and giggles? What if all the world's riders came together on the same day to break stereotypes, celebrate motorcycles and do some good, too?

I ended up spending the next 10 years of my life living, breathing and sleeping it; much of it while living with my parents, unable to pay board and with them constantly telling me I should go to university instead. Adding the men's health cause to an already successful event in 2013 also gave it a second wind, setting it on a course that would take it from a 'cool moto event' to something that changes people's lives.

And so we're back at The Bike Shed. The bawling biker standing in front of me tells me that he'd be dead without The Distinguished Gentleman's Ride. His story was the most profound I had ever heard. He'd decided he was at the end of his life and he had given up hope. Then while sitting in a hospital bed ready to depart, he sees a story about the DGR and finds the motivation to not give up and to join us.

I still feel insecure, inept and totally overwhelmed by the way things have turned out. Sometimes it feels like someone else could have done a better job than me, but it's hard to doubt the value of what you're doing when strangers tell you that you saved their life. And while it's impossible to know exactly, to date we estimate that the event has saved more than 1000 fathers, sons, brothers and uncles from taking their own lives or dying from cancer. Just let *that* sink in for a moment.

So to anyone who's ever taken part, helped organize, documented an event, donated money or just been a fan, this book is a testament to what we've all achieved just by getting dressed up and riding together once a year.

Happy 10th Anniversary, Distinguished Gentleman's Ride.

Mark Hawwa
DGR Founder

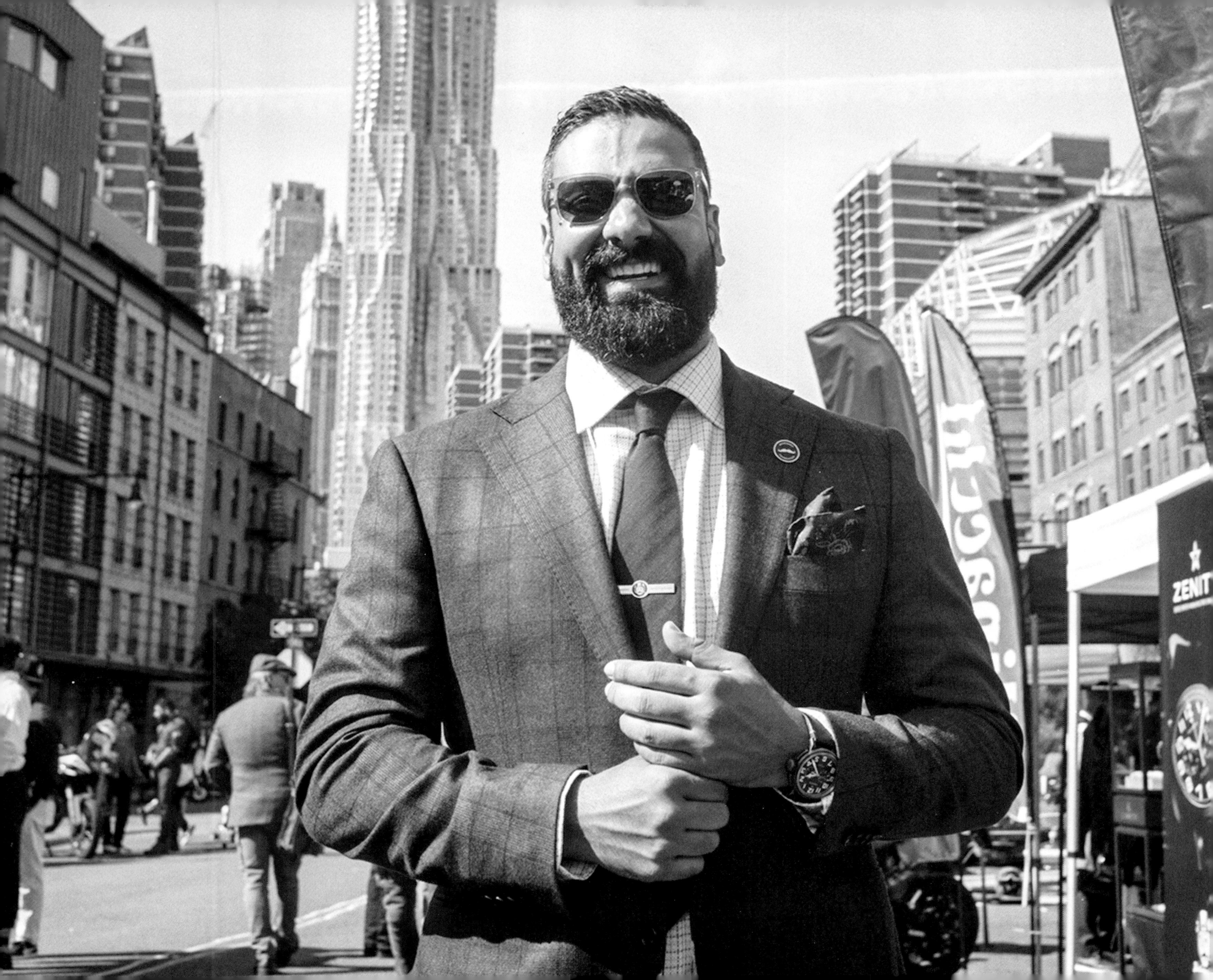

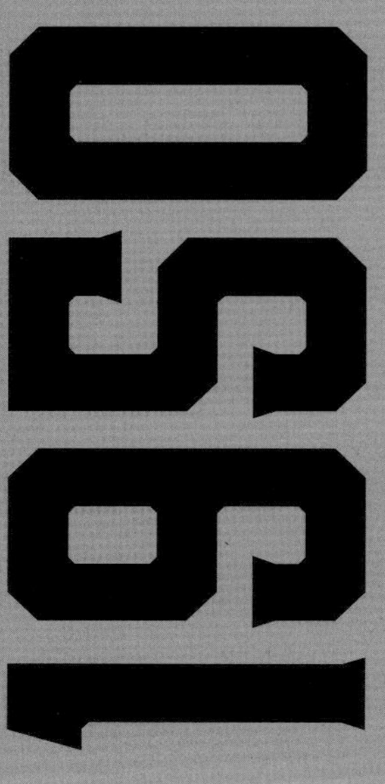

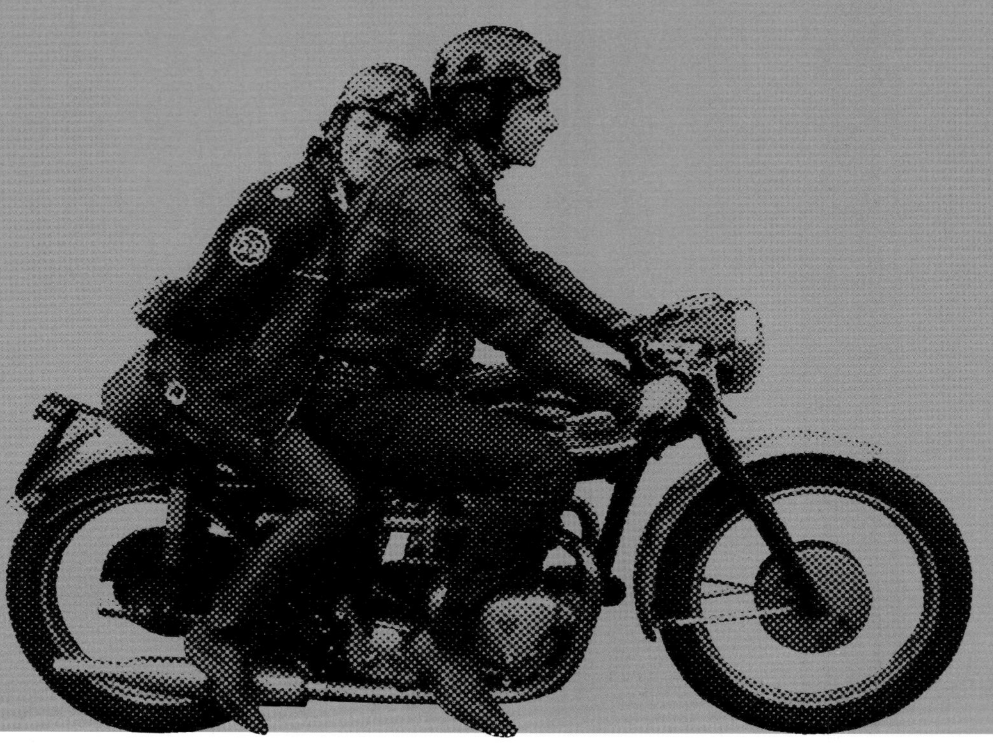

BEFORE DGR

It's July 2001 and a humid Tokyo summer is in full swing. New York's terror attacks are only a few months away, but the world remains blissfully unaware and a little more innocent. If you are into motorcycles and you spend any time in the city's cooler inner suburbs like Harajuku and Omotesando, you'd be noticing something kind of interesting. More specifically, you'd be noticing a new style of custom bike. Bikes that were only being built in Japan.

More often than not, you'd be looking at modded Yamaha TW125s, with their balloon-like tires and extended swingarms. They've been popular here for ages, and while they were fun as hell and they did look cool, they were destined to remain "big in Japan" and they won't make much of a splash elsewhere.

Alongside the TWs, keen-eyed bikers would also be noticing something newer and a little cooler. The same bike customizers who were modding the TWs had now turned their attention to another Yamaha mainstay; a single-cylindered, "Universal Japanese Motorcycle" the company called the SR400.

A seemingly vanilla bike that had been on sale in Japan for over 30 years, some bright spark had realized that with some simple mods and a few budget aftermarket parts, these bikes could be made to look a whole lot cooler. Suddenly the streets of Tokyo were having a cafe racer revival, fueled by the country's fanatical love of Western Rock 'n' Roll culture and all things British.

Over the next few years, a long list of Aussie moto fans would pass through this 'ground zero' of 21st century cafe racer culture and go on to bigger and better things. Dare Jennings of Deus Ex Machina fame would use it

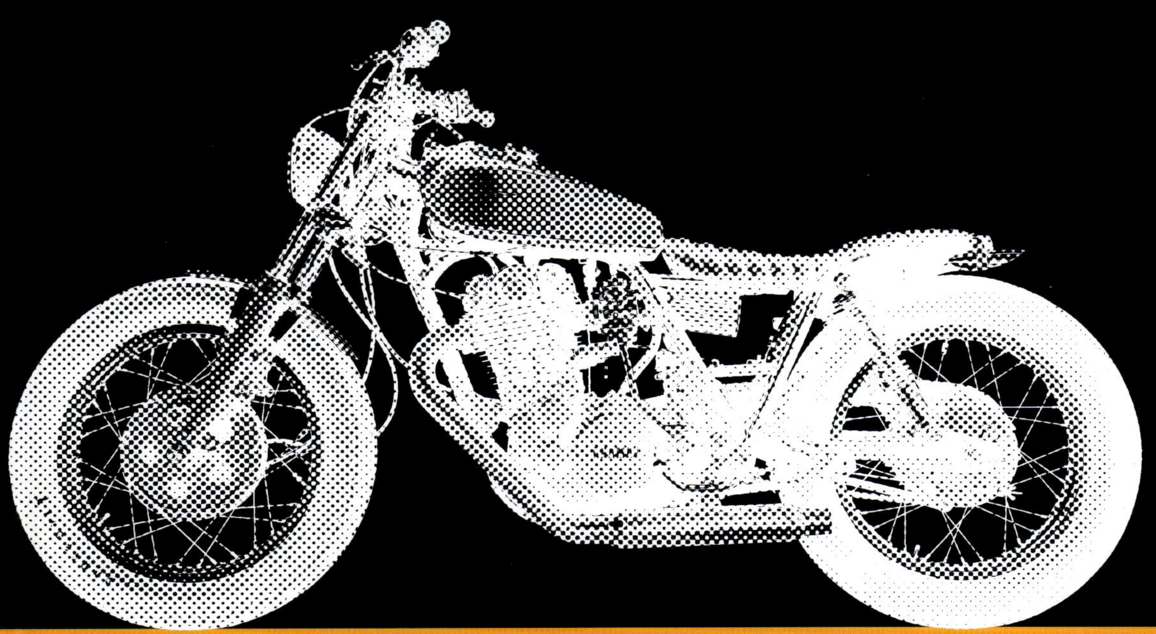

as a template for his new clothing and cafe business venture in Sydney. Andrew Jones would spend two years living here and then go on to help Scott Hopkin develop the Pipeburn.com custom bike blog. Chris Hunter from Bike Exif and Geoff Baldwin from Return of the Cafe Racers would be inspired enough to start their own online homages that would spread the cafe racer word globally.

But most importantly for our story, a young Mark Hawwa would spend four weeks on holiday in Japan and return to Sydney inspired enough to buy his own custom Yamaha SR500 to recreate what he'd seen and fallen in love with half a world away.

For many bike-curious Sydneysiders, a real chord was struck. They'd been attracted to the idea of riding a motorcycle for a long time, but the fact of the matter was that up until this point, the dominant moto culture favored garish sportsbikes that were both uncomfortable and dated in their '90s fluro-racing looks.

But this new moto style that was now showing its face locally was different. It wasn't just now cool. It wasn't just this season cool. It was more timelessly, effortlessly cool. Cool like Marlon Brando and Steve McQueen. It connected many historical moto dots, and suddenly it was clear to many who'd toyed with the idea of riding a motorcycle that this was what they'd been waiting a lifetime for.

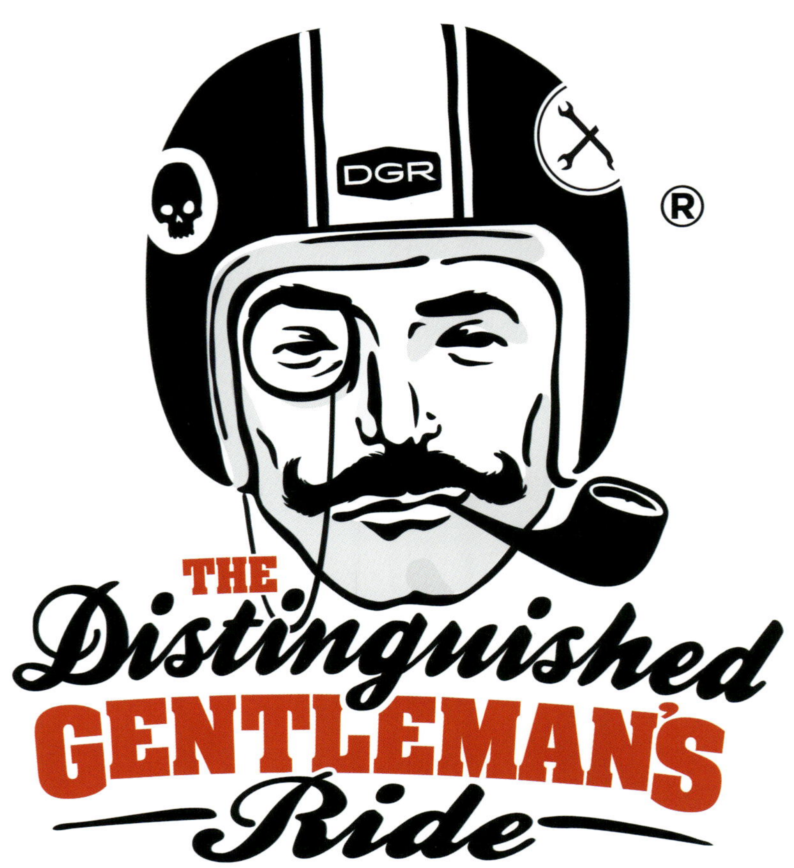

"Plans, meetings, late nights, hours of looking through old ads, vintage art, sports mascots and 70's counter-culture and we got to this. A strong-chinned, mustachioed, archetypal gentleman. Every designer's dream is to create something that takes on a life of its own; I think we did that here."

Tom Wall
Sir Remington Designer

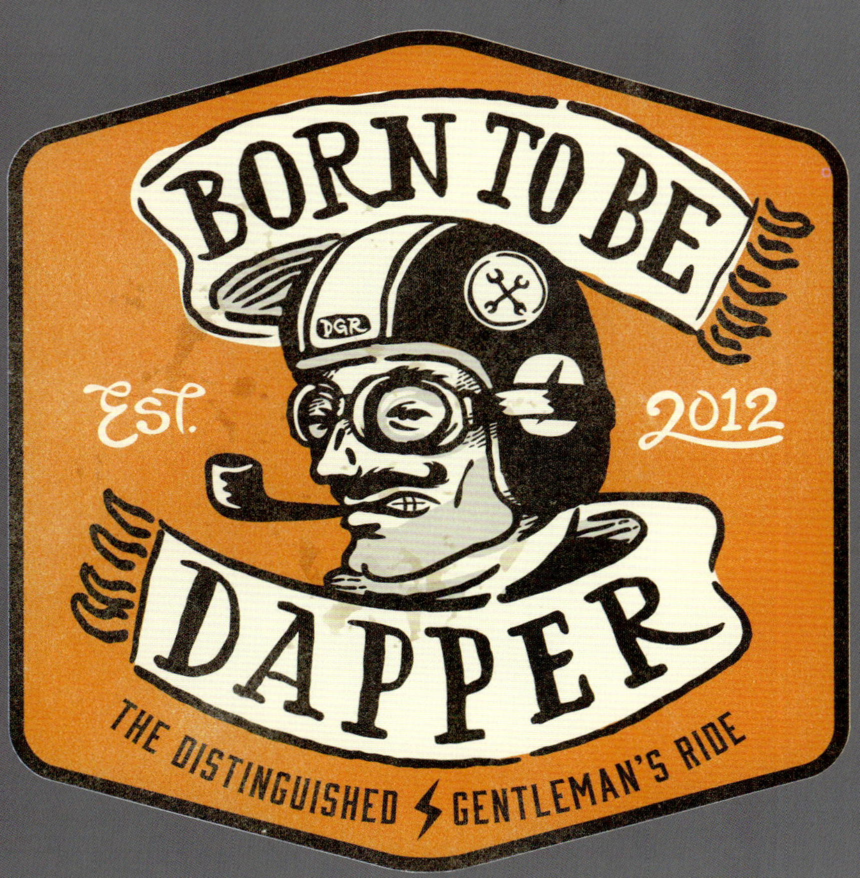

"This happened in my first year of hosting a DGR ride in 2013 and I think I pulled – or maybe stole – inspiration from the 80's TV series 'Remington Steele'. My initial name was actually 'Sir Remington Snarlbucket III' but only Sir Remington was kept, as the rest may have been a little over the top."

Niklas Borg
DGR Ride Host & Sir Remington Namer

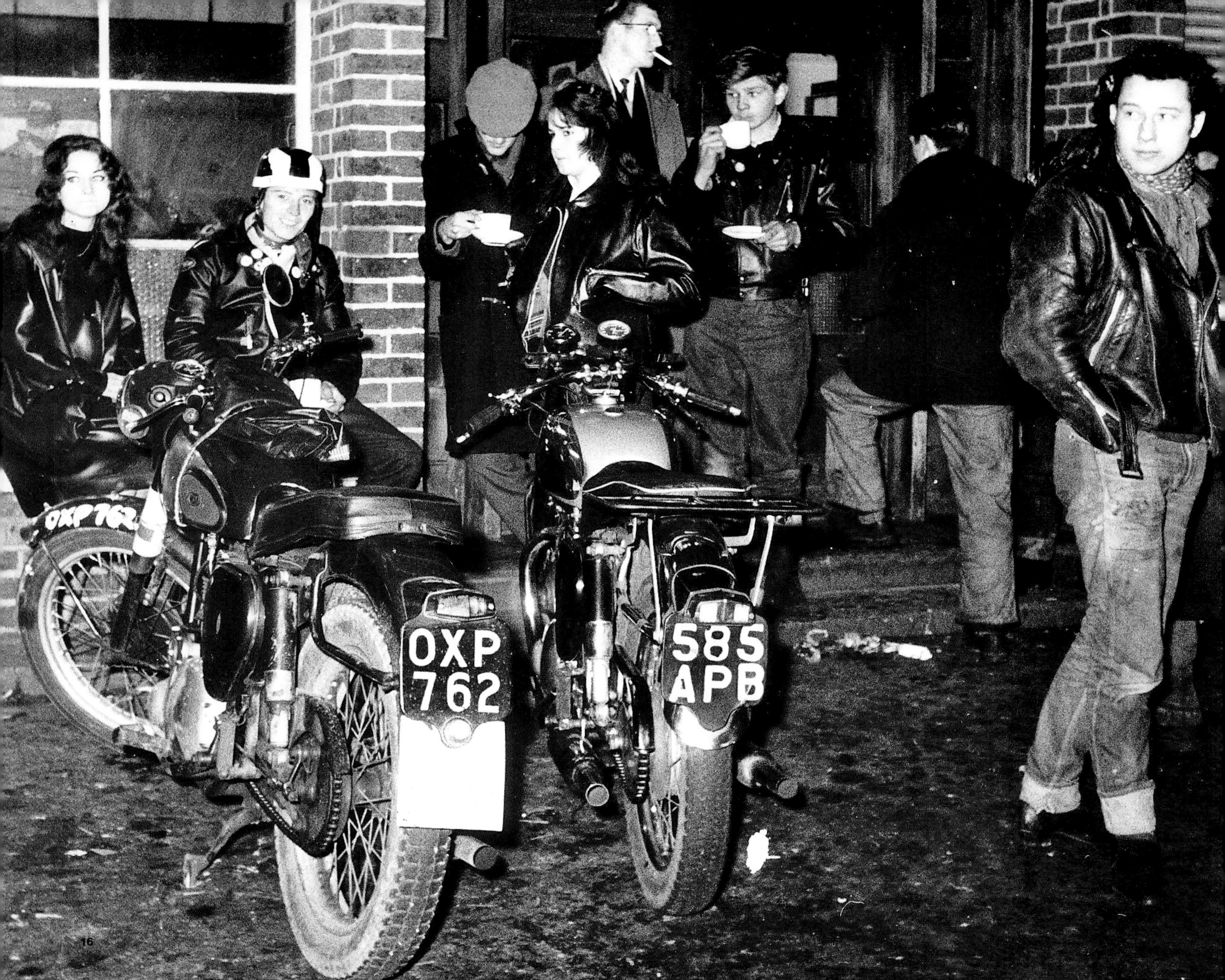

OXP 762
585 APB

CAFÉ RACERS:
THE NEED FOR SPEED, WITH STYLE

You've gotta dig deep for the real history of the social phenomenon called café racers. It's a trend with a hundred names because its motivating impulse is as old as humanity: the need for speed. Aldous Huxley called speed 'the one genuinely modern pleasure,' but the urge was inside us long before motors.

The Romans had speed limits for horses two thousand years ago, because they needed them: people like to go fast. The first pedal-cycles of the 1860s were exalted as 'akin to flying' when coasting downhill: a motor was attached to the bicycle to extend that feeling indefinitely, making that thing we love, the motorcycle. And as they say, when the second motorbike was built, the race was on.

There have always been cults of speed: people who race this or that, or each other, or time itself. The café racer belongs to a particular group of arch-enthusiasts who embraced a dangerous pastime: racing on the road.

And they clumped: in the 1910s at the Red Lion pub in Hatfield, in the 1920s at Southend Pier, in the 1930s at the Tram, and the 1950s at the Ace Café or Busy Bee or at similarly seedy locations in nearly any big city around the world. The riders were called various names over time: speed merchants, speed kings, promenade percys, etc., but the one that stuck (because of a newly globalized postwar media) was café racer. It was hurled as an insult ('you only race from café to café'), but was quickly embraced as great branding.

Was the café racer the bike or the rider? For a while (the 1950s-60s) the café racer was both, much like the centaur we become when straddling a motorcycle. But a funny thing happened on the way to the marketplace: factories stole the term. It started slowly in the early 1960s, when certain British companies labeled their hottest models 'CR,' wink wink.

By the early 1970s the term 'factory café racer' was in general parlance, and in 1977 even Harley-Davidson got in on the act with their XLCR, explicitly built to compete with the all-conquering Italian (900SS, V7 Sport, SFC), British (Commando, Trident), and even German factory café racers (R90S) of the day. It was the 1970s, not the '50s, that was the apex period of café racers, because the factories responded to popular demand.

And then, everything went plastic. Café racers became sportbikes in the 1980s, and while some riders went along with the plan, a post-Punk subculture didn't like the flavor, preferring rotten old school original café racers over new bikes. This was the beginning of the end for the motorcycle industry's relevance to youth culture, as hip riders went retro instead of new, and started making their own café racers.

This trend for home-customizing remained strong into the 2000s, outliving the horrors of the fat-tire TV chopper scene, and flourishing with the arrival of Internet custom bike blogs. The motorcycle industry was in the doldrums but finally pulled its head out of the sand in the 2010s, once again building factory café racers, along with trackers, street scramblers, and bobbers, all styles that had originally come from the hands of home builders. A new generation of web-savvy riders, who care little about the scene in the 1950s.

Londoners have latched onto the café racer purely for the aesthetics. Which makes sense, because naked bikes built for speed have always looked amazing, and always will.

Paul d'Orleans
Moto Historian

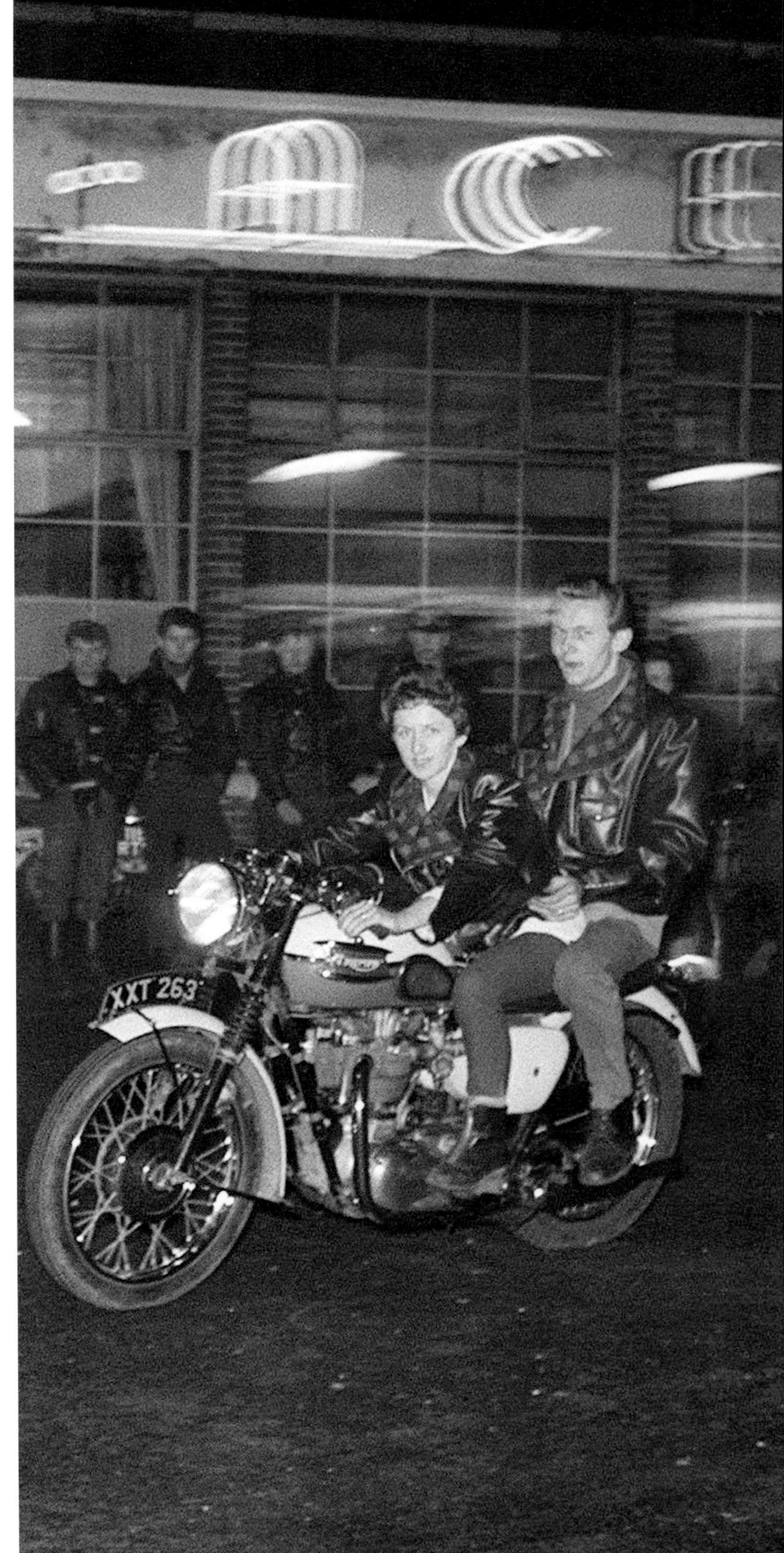

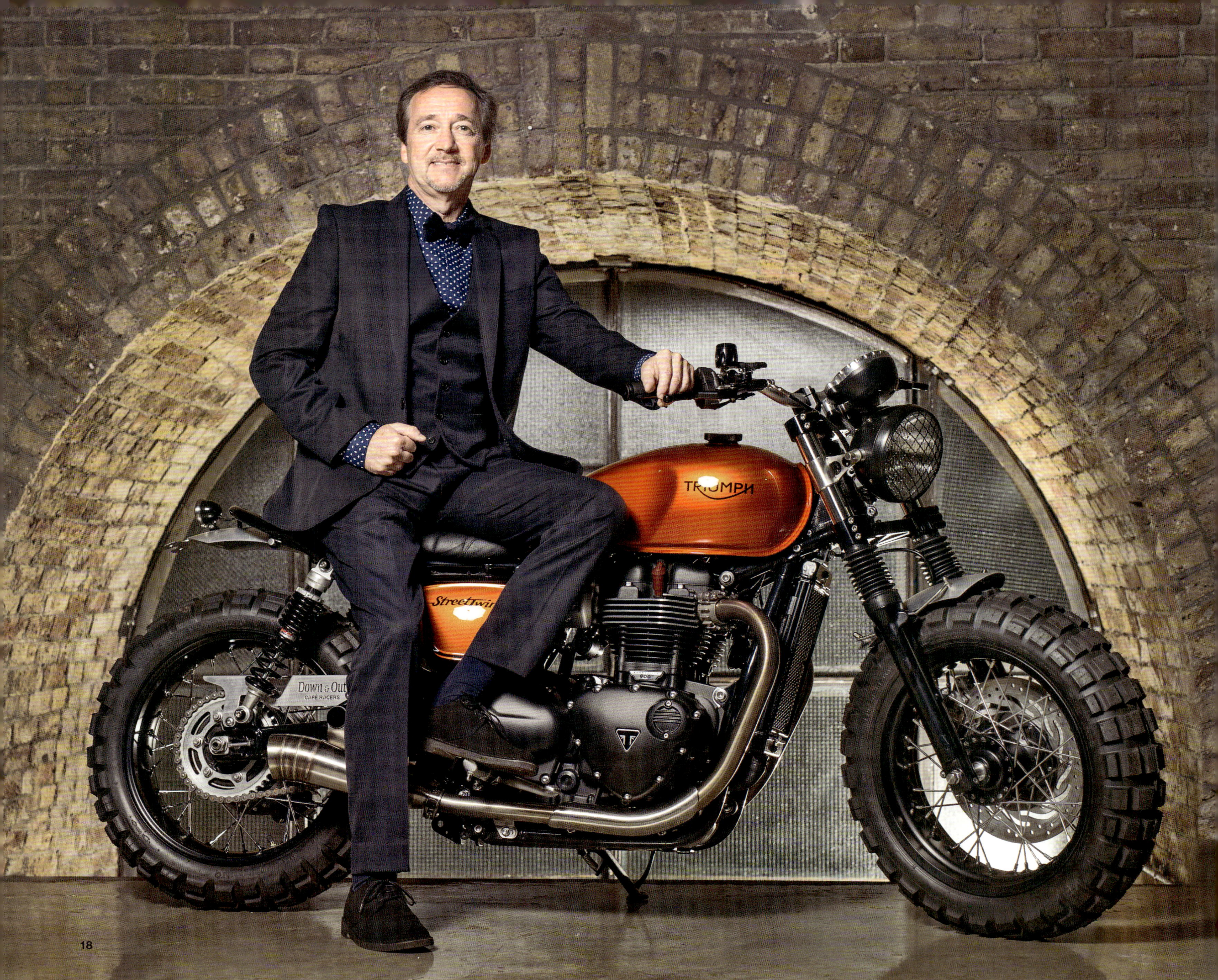

A SOUTHERN GENTLEMAN

I was born in a little town in Northwest Louisiana called Shreveport. Motorcycling is not a very popular sport in the state of Louisiana. I'm in the Louisiana state Hall of Fame and I'm the only motorcycling person in there, to give you some perspective.

But my family was a racing family. They raced go-karts in the 1950s and by the time I came along in 1961 they were into motorcycling. My sister dropped her passion for sport to chase boys. I started riding at three years old relentlessly in my yard, in the wet and in the sunshine.

I was very fortunate as I grew up in the country. We had about two acres of land so I was able to ride on the property in between the trees and was able to hone my skills. One thing I've realized is that motorcycling gave me the awareness of paying attention and to trust in my own abilities. Years later I came to understand that riding in my yard also helped me heal some life scars that occurred when I was just a kid.

I bring all of this up because it is the foundation of my life, of what I recognize, what I sense and feel and what I see in others. That's racing for me, even if it's only a small part of it. Racing is certainly my heritage and it has given me a foundation of trusting but it's also given me the perspective as I grew and became an adult as to what really matters in life.

One of the things that I'm most thankful for – besides my racing success – is the people that I met on my journey. When I signed for Honda in the fall of 1979 to race in the United States, it was to start their superbike program. When they started the Honda Racing Corporation, I won that first 500cc World Championship in 1983. One of the most amazing experiences for me was after I won, I traveled to Japan to meet Mr Honda at his home in Tokyo. I walked in and he put his hands on my shoulders and said, "Thank you." It made me think back to when I was about six-years-old and I was in a small Honda dealership in Shreveport. Mr Gorman who owned the dealership, had a picture on the wall of him and a Japanese man. I remember so clearly him telling me, "Little Freddie, that's Mr Honda."

And so after I met Mr Honda, I thought what an amazing thing life is. We get those little glimpses of moments and then someday they all make sense. So it is through motorcycling that I've got to see the world, meet some incredible people and understand why I had those moments and what they really mean.

My relationship with the DGR is very similar to that. My wife Alexandra and I were in Australia for a classic event in 2015 and again in 2016, and while we were there we got invited to a ride through Sydney one evening. It's how we met Mark Hawwa.

It was an incredible evening. Riding through Sydney was absolutely beautiful and to meet people that had such a love for motorcycling was amazing. It was not about racing, but it definitely was about motorcycling and its community.

See, I believe we are all in this together and the DGR is one of the most important experiences I had, because it's about bringing people from different cultures, backgrounds, countries and beliefs together for a great cause. Not only for motorcycling, but more importantly for men's health.

One of the things I enjoyed when we lived in London was going to the Bike Shed Motorcycle Club where we met Dutch and Vikki, the organizers of the DGR ride in London. I got asked to be an Ambassador.

We dressed up, got on a Triumph and rode through the streets of London representing the DGR and what motorcycling has represented to me ever since I was a little kid; the gift to open my eyes and really see the world and all its incredible experiences. To allow me to have my dreams come true from when I was a kid, imagining myself winning a World Championship in my bed at night. And then one day I was in Mr Honda's house, the same man I saw when I was a little kid. He gave me my dream which then allowed me to give him his.

My true belief in motorcycling, my opportunity to meet my wife Alexandra, for us to go on the DGR ride together and to meet some incredible people from all walks of life is what DGR is for me. That's why I'm so incredibly proud to be a part of it.

Freddie Spencer
DGR Ambassador
World Champion Racer

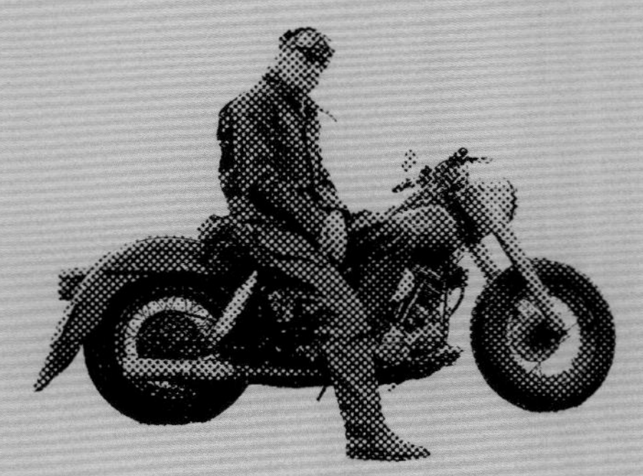

2012

- RIDE ONE -

OUR INAUGURAL EVENT STARTED IN SYDNEY. IT QUICKLY MADE ITS WAY AROUND THE WORLD WITH **58 CITIES** AND OVER **3,000 RIDERS** TAKING PART IN THE FIRST EVER DISTINGUISHED GENTLEMAN'S RIDE.

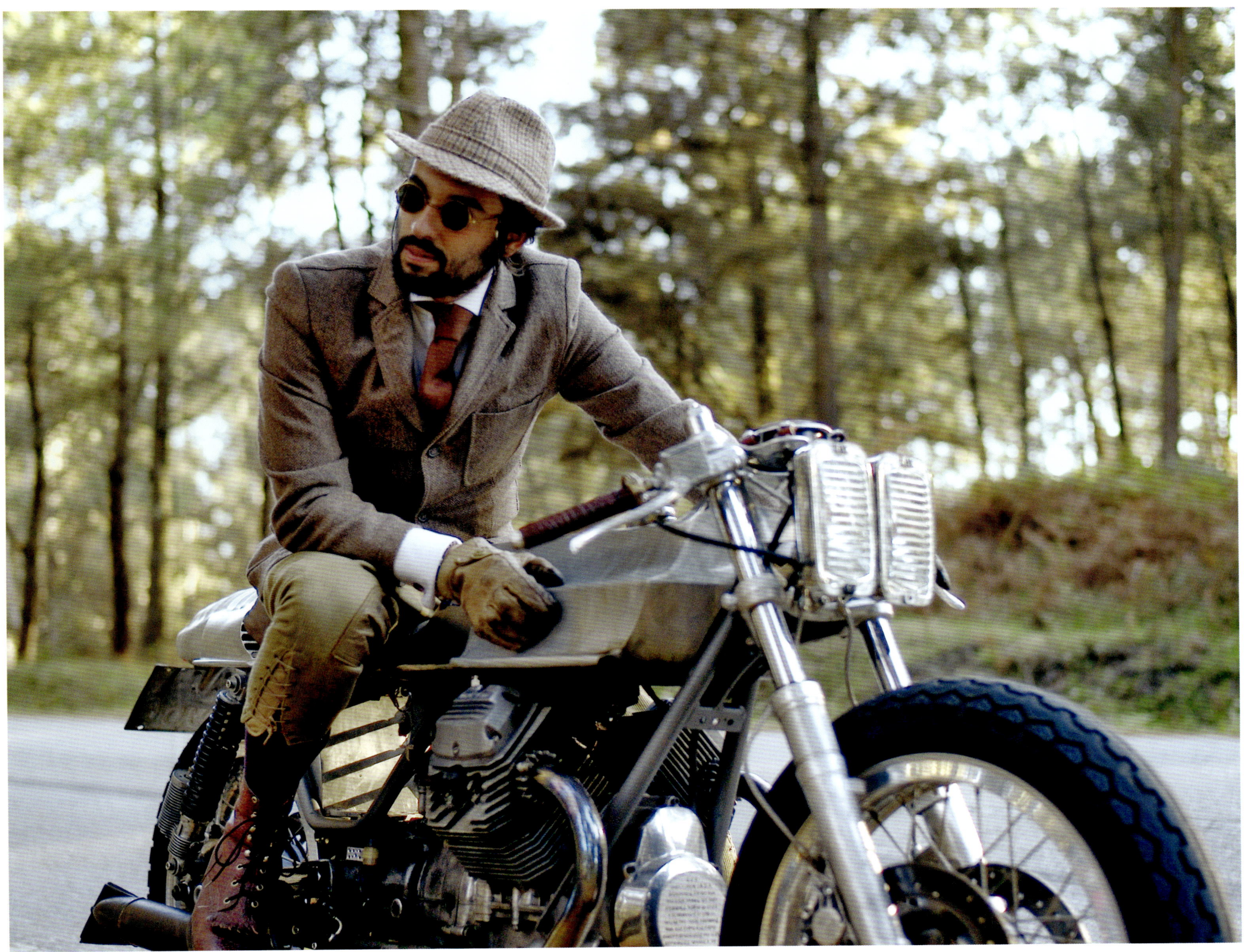

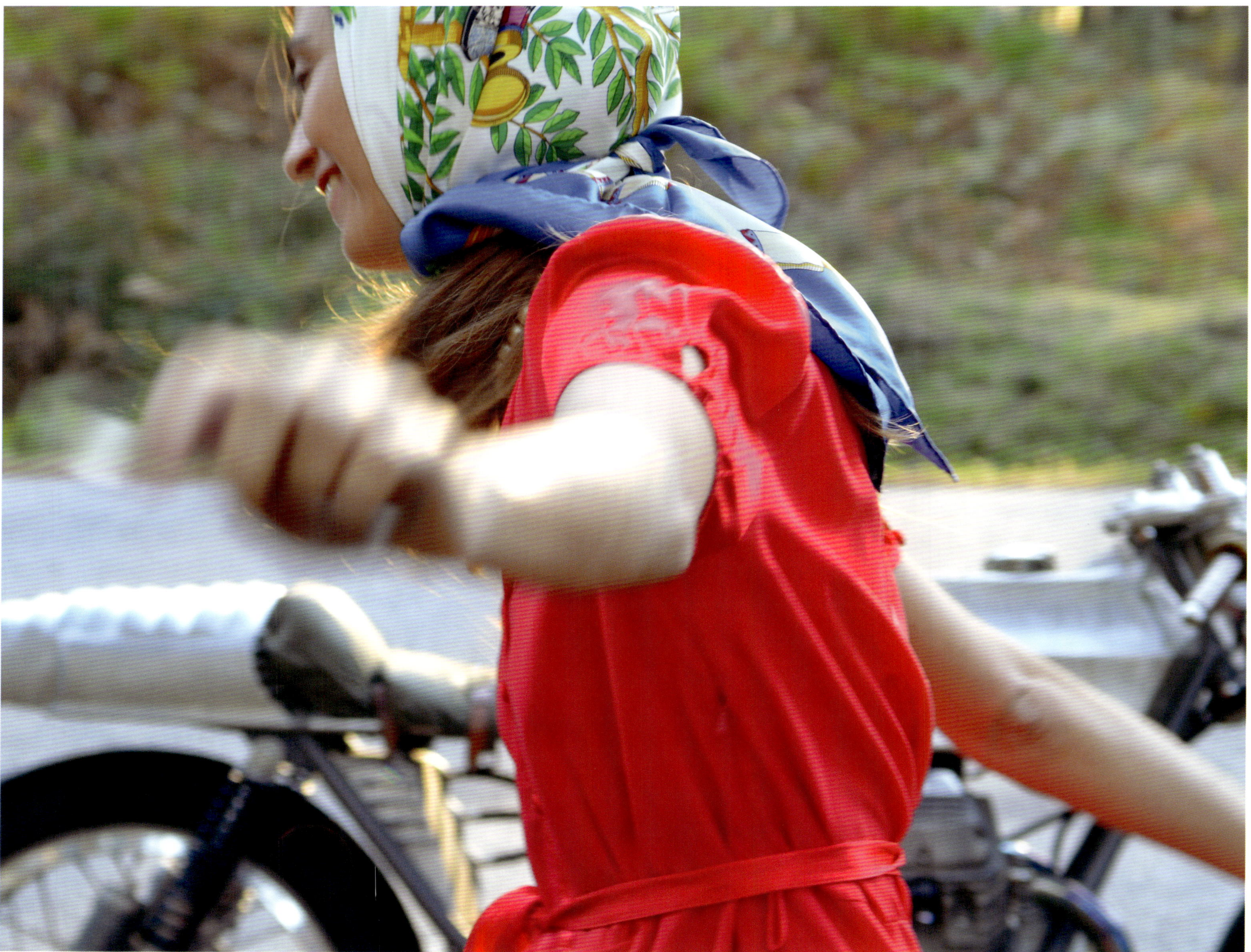

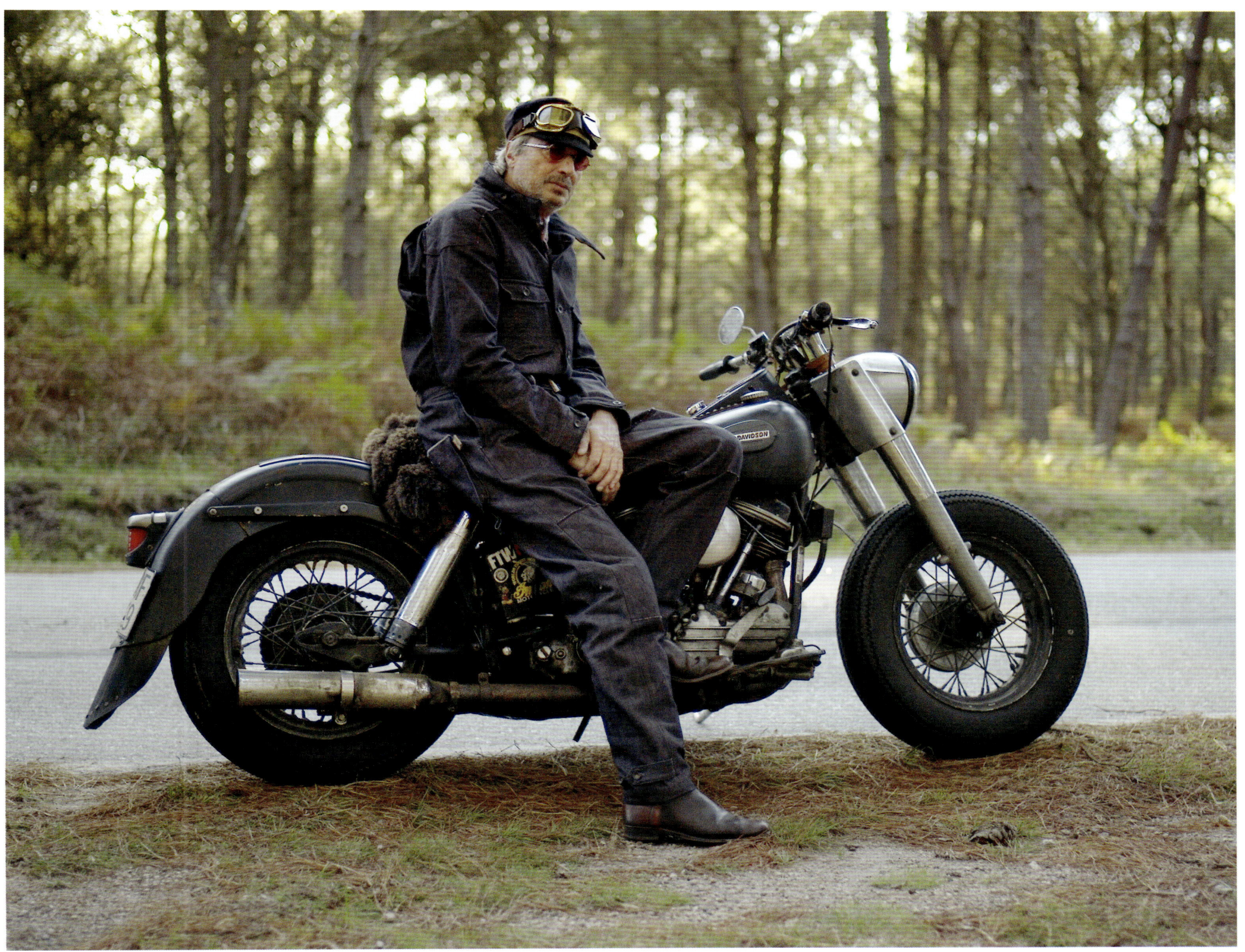

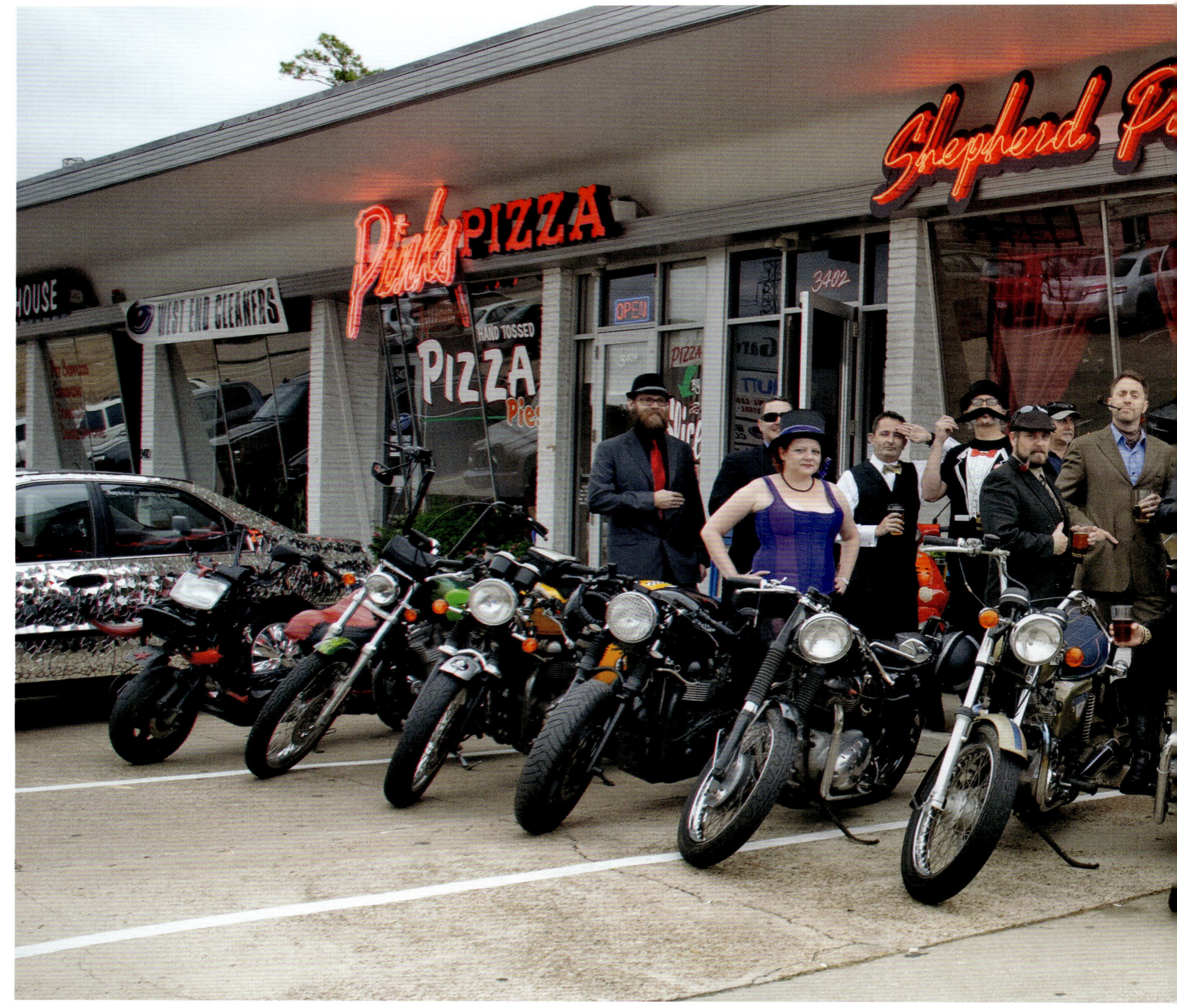

Pinky PIZZA
Shepherd P
WEST END CLEANERS
HARD TOSSED
PIZZA
Pies
OPEN
3402

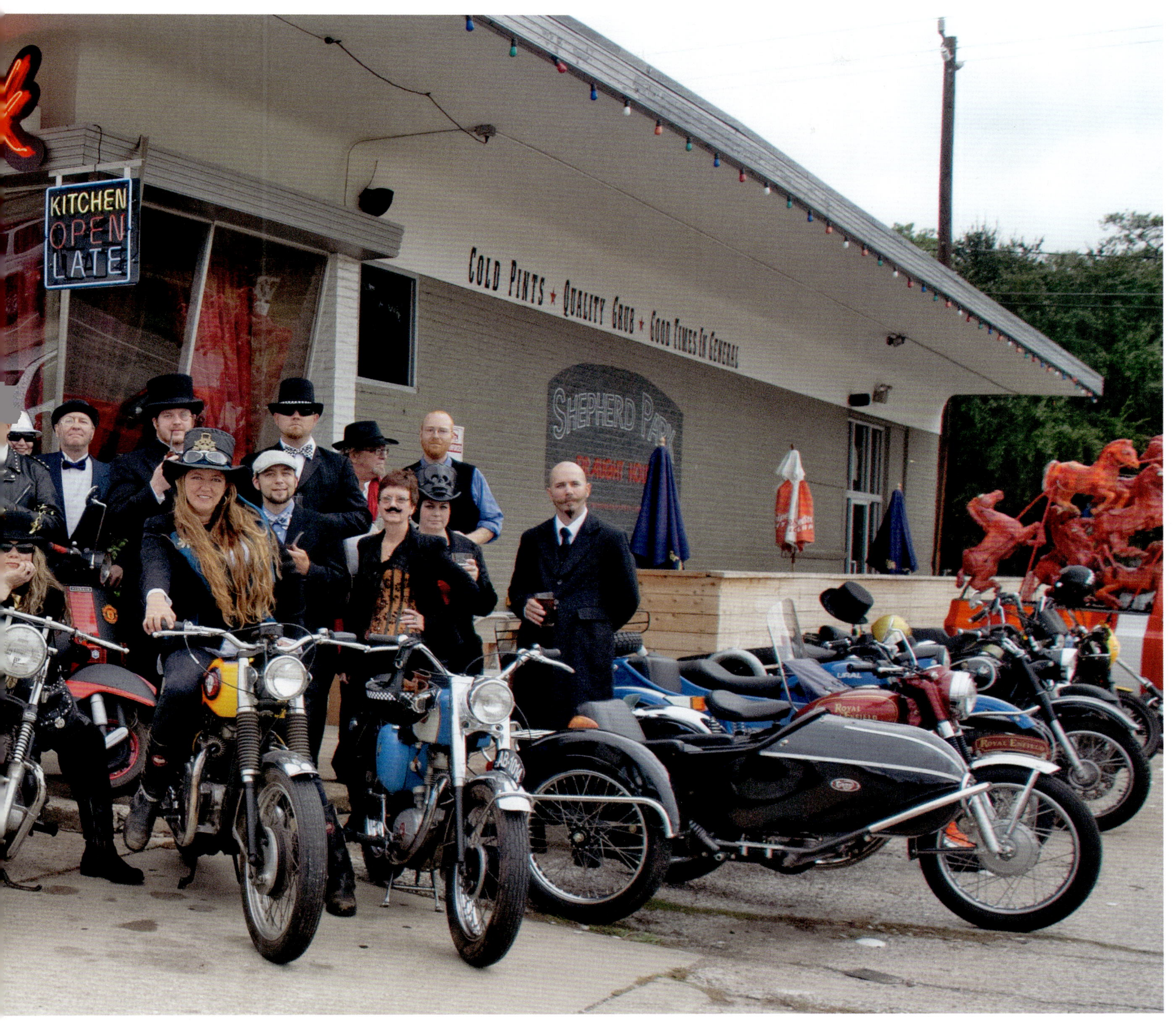

KITCHEN
OPEN
LATE
COLD PINTS ★ QUALITY GRUB ★ GOOD TIMES FOR GENERAL
SHEPHERD PARK

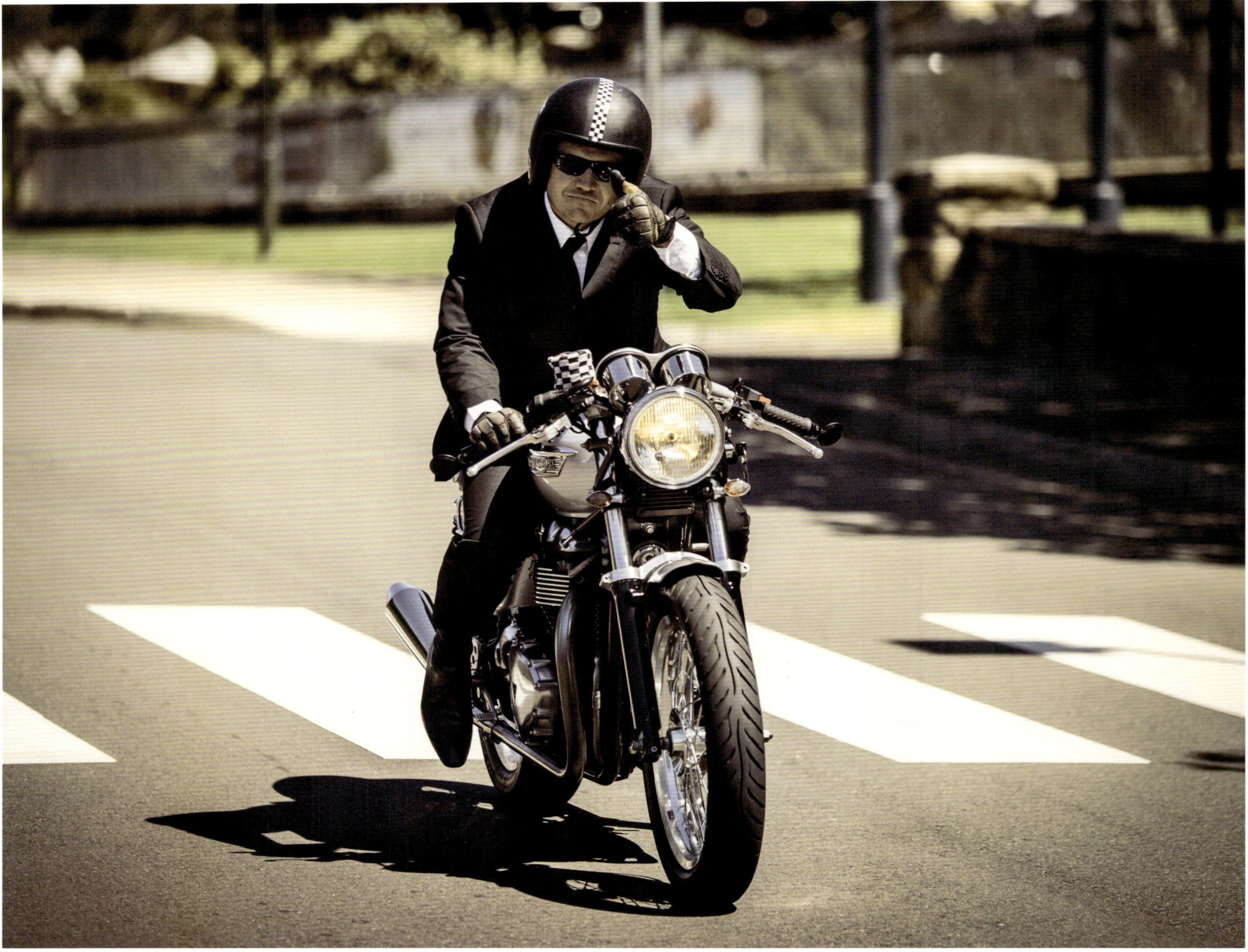

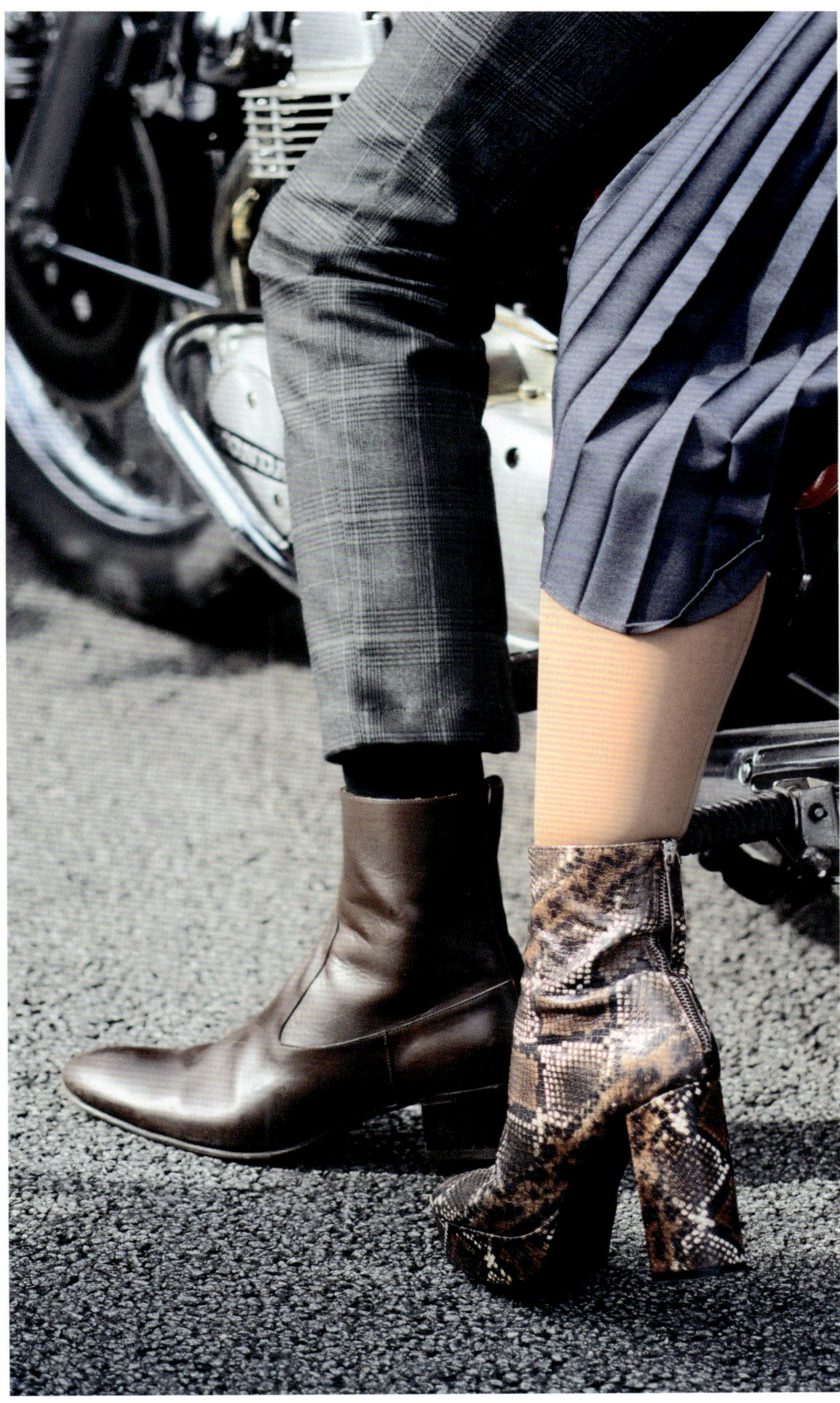
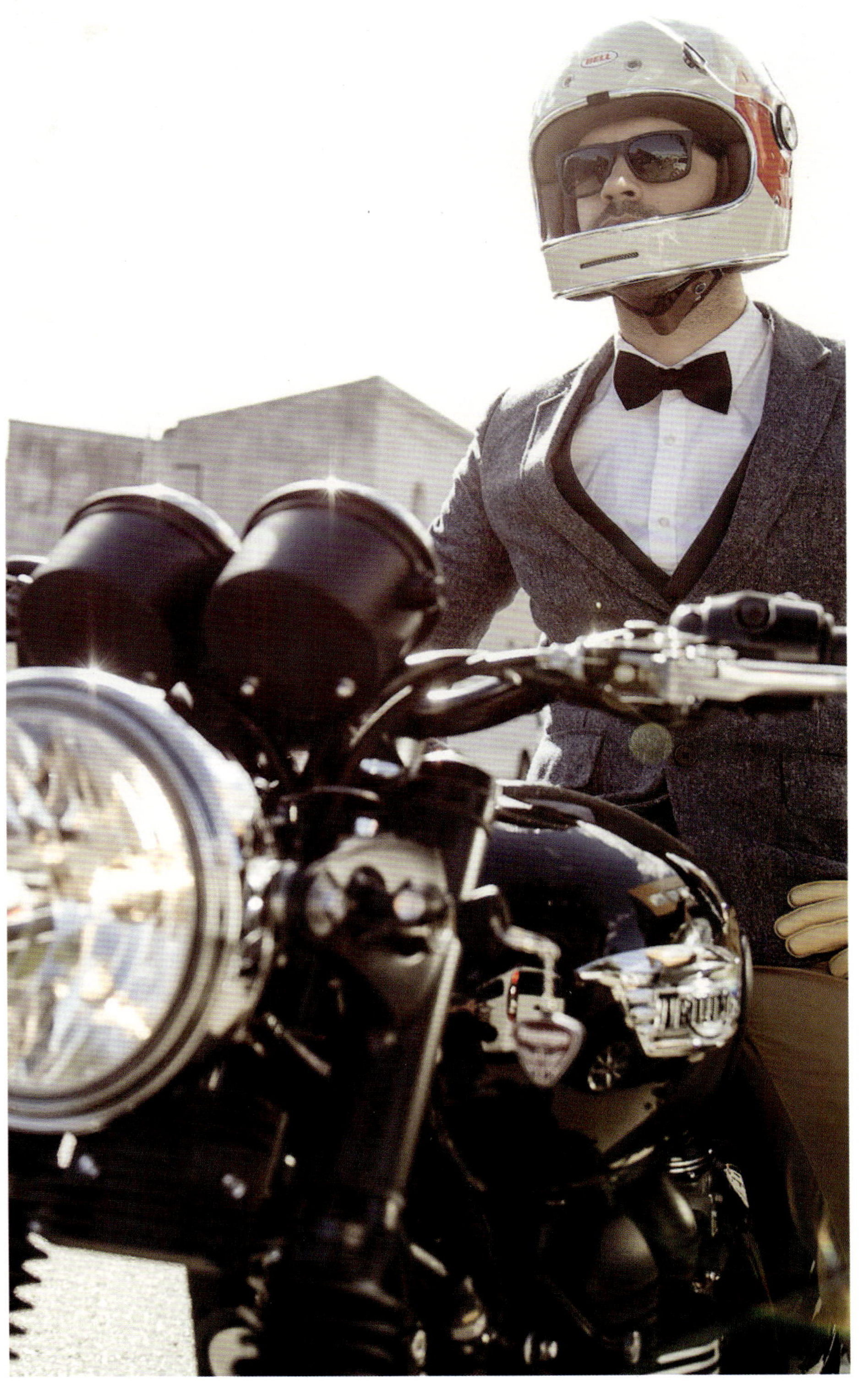

Movember-DGR Challenge Award
A DGR-FUNDED PROJECT

The Movember—DGR Challenge Award funds large scale, transformational prostate cancer research projects with a focus on "first in field" discoveries that have a high probability of reducing the chances of death and suffering due to recurrent advanced prostate cancer. Funding new research since 2016, together with Movember, we have enabled pioneering research into world-leading cancer research institutions.

2017
Dr Douglas McNeel

Dr. Douglas McNeel's research looks at treatments that activate the immune system to target cancer as a promising new way of treating men with prostate cancer. This project builds on previous work and aims to provide an effective new therapy for men with metastatic, castration-resistant prostate cancer.

The trial is open for recruitment at the Washington University Siteman Cancer Center and Carbone Cancer Center, with 60 men to be recruited by December 2022.

2018
Dr Susan Halabi

Developing cancer treatment takes many years, partly due to the length of time it takes to determine the safety and efficacy of the treatment. This project aimed to speed up this process so that new treatments could be available to men up to two years earlier.

The team showed that the length of time that a man lives without his cancer progressing can reasonably be used to predict how long he will eventually live.

2019
Dr Charles Drake

New strategies are needed to harness the power of the immune system as an effective treatment for men with prostate cancer. Dr Drake and his team initiated a clinical trial combining a well-tolerated and effective IL-8 blocking antibody with an anti-PD-1 drug for men with castration-sensitive prostate cancer.

The phase I/II trial is currently recruiting across three sites in the US and is expected to complete the study in August 2023.

2020
Dr Phuoc Tran

Oligometastatic prostate cancer is when the disease has begun to spread outside the prostate and is still thought to be potentially curable. Results from Dr Tran's previous research have demonstrated that targeting sites of this cancer with stereotactic ablative radiation prolongs progression-free survival.

In this project, the team is analyzing samples from men to investigate whether the levels of circulating tumor cells and DNA are associated with patient outcomes.

2020
Dr Arul Chinnaiyan

This project investigates how two gene mutations called SMARCA2 and SMRCA4 drive disease progression in metastatic, castration-resistant prostate cancer. They will search for biomarkers used to identify those who are more likely to benefit from treatment with SMARCA2/4 degraders.

If successful, the team will initiate a clinical trial to test the safety and efficacy of the degraders alone and in combination with enzalutamide in men with mCRPC.

2021
Dr Matthew Freedman

Associate Professor Freedman's team have identified a set of DNA regulators that may be responsible for the development of treatment-resistant cancer.

The team will be developing new treatments that target these DNA regulators as a means to prevent the development of advanced lethal disease, as well as establishing a prostate cancer research resource that will enable other researchers to uncover novel treatment opportunities for sufferers.

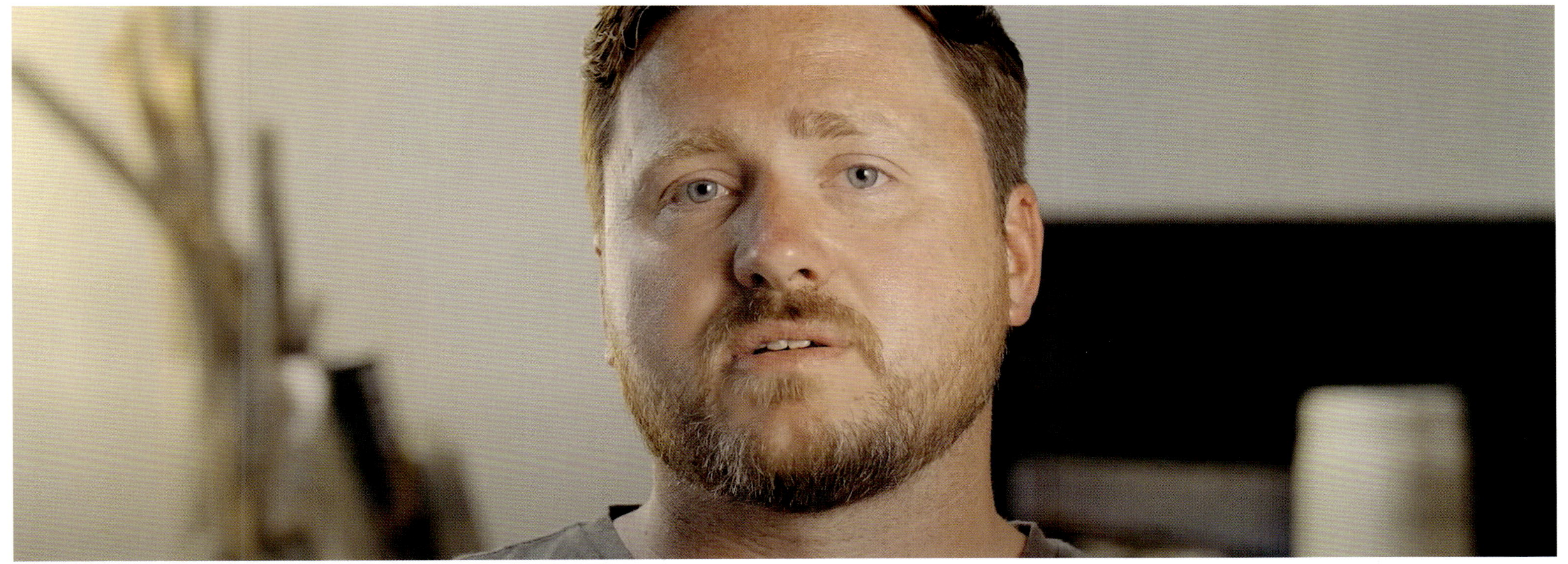

SURVIVOR STORIES: Chris Livett

My depression began as a bit of a slow burn. Work started to get really busy and I wasn't putting my family first. It was a perpetuating spiral of guilt and I started to change, snapping more at my kids. The next thing I know, I wake up one morning and I just couldn't go to work. I said to my wife Lindsay, "I just can't. I can't do it." I realized that I didn't know how to deal with it at all.

The doctor asked me how I felt, and I just fell apart. I remember my first session with a therapist, talking about my life. I started to realize some of the driving factors behind my mental illness.

The first time I remember my Mum being sick, my Dad sat me down in my bedroom and told me she was ill. She had about two years to live, which is tough to hear when you're 11. I was told it was cancer, but no one really talked about what that was. The toughest part was when my Dad told me that I wasn't allowed to tell my brother.

The lowest point I had was when I started thinking that Lindsay would be better off without me. Those kinds of things are quite frightening. Despite being surrounded by people, you still feel totally alone. One of the things I always had in the back of my mind was that at the time,

I was the same age as Mum when she was sick and my daughter Izzy was the same age I was back then. There were so many parallels. They are probably one of the things that stopped me from getting even lower; I didn't want Izzy and Ben to go through not having a dad or only one parent. I didn't want that parallel to continue. They were a big factor in my recovery.

A part of the help I needed to get through my depression and anxiety was a course of antidepressants. Some of the side effects is they make you go to the loo regularly, and I noticed a bit of blood. Feeling something wasn't quite right, I booked in for a colonoscopy. Soon after, the doctors told me I had advanced prostate cancer and that it had already spread. Lindsay and I decided there and then that we'd be honest about it with the kids. I didn't want to repeat what I had gone through with Mum.

I had just come through what I thought was my biggest battle – depression. I'd learned so much about myself going through that. Had I not gone through it and learnt all I had, I don't know how I would have coped with cancer. Being able to be open, honest, and share with family and friends everything I was going through made it easier to cope.

After I went through the chemo and the radio therapy, I told Lindsay that I wanted to get a bike. All this time I had wanted one and she was really supportive of it. I went to my Triumph dealer and saw a DGR t-shirt. The staff asked me if I was going to ride in it this year. I thought it was in London and figured it was too far from me, but she told me there was a local one and that it was a global event.

So when I got home I looked it up and found a ride in Liverpool. I started reading about what DGR did and what it represented; about its founding purpose to support men's mental health and prostate cancer. I thought it just seemed too amazing to come along at that exact time.

Lindsay and I often look back to before we were engaged. We just seemed like very different people. Now we really know how each other feels and thinks. I can't imagine going through that with anyone else and despite it all, it's made us better for it. It's made me a better dad, husband and friend. I'm almost grateful for it. Because of that, it's made me stronger.

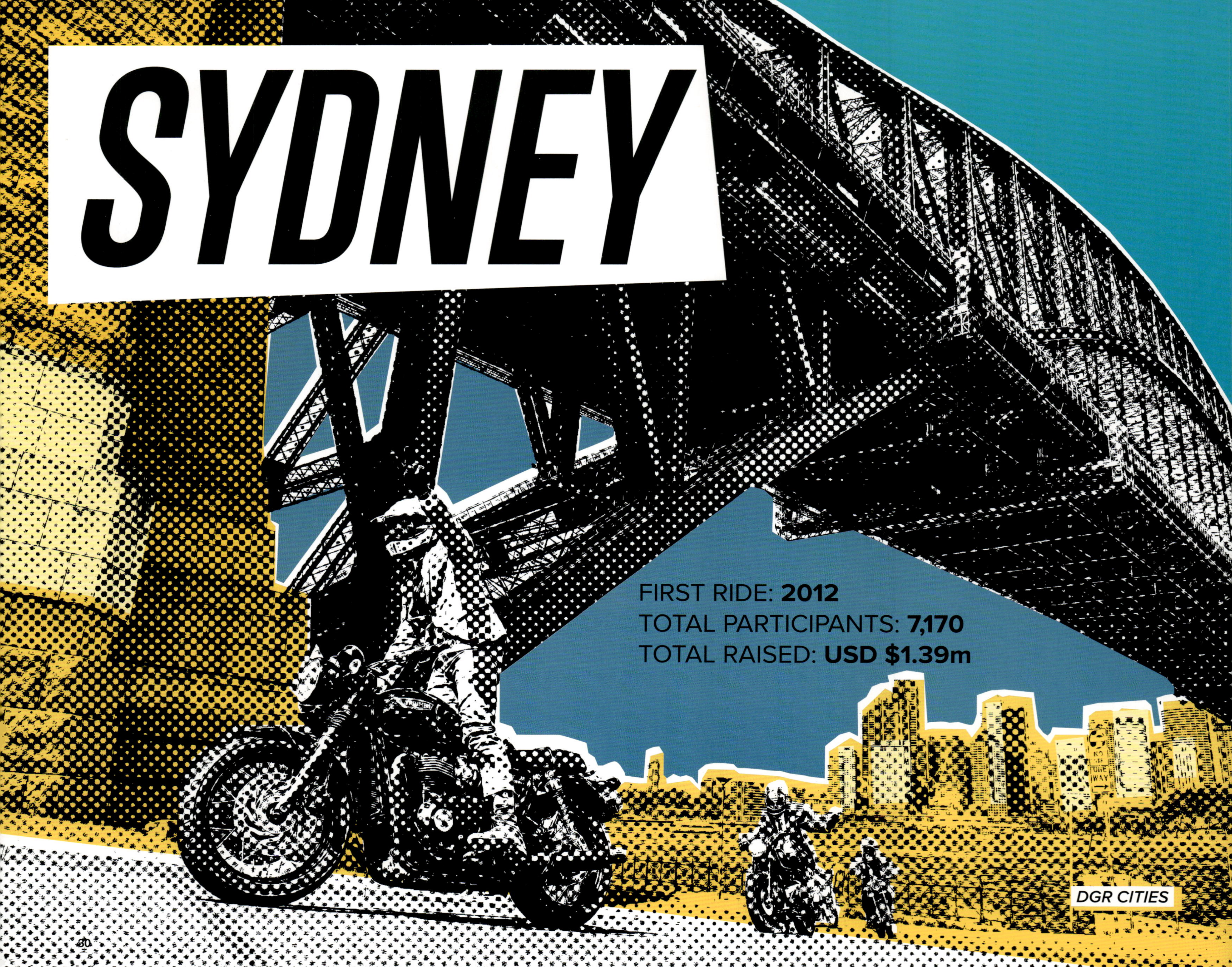

SYDNEY
FIRST RIDE: 2012
TOTAL PARTICIPANTS: 7,170
TOTAL RAISED: USD $1.39m
DGR CITIES

BOBBERS

The 'Bobber' is a tribute to minimalism, keeping only the absolute essentials and featuring shortened fenders and a bobbed, under-sprung seat. The style evolved from a 1920s and 1930s style of motorcycle that was called a 'cut down.' This became known as a 'bob-job' in reference to the bobbed tail or cut-down rear fender.

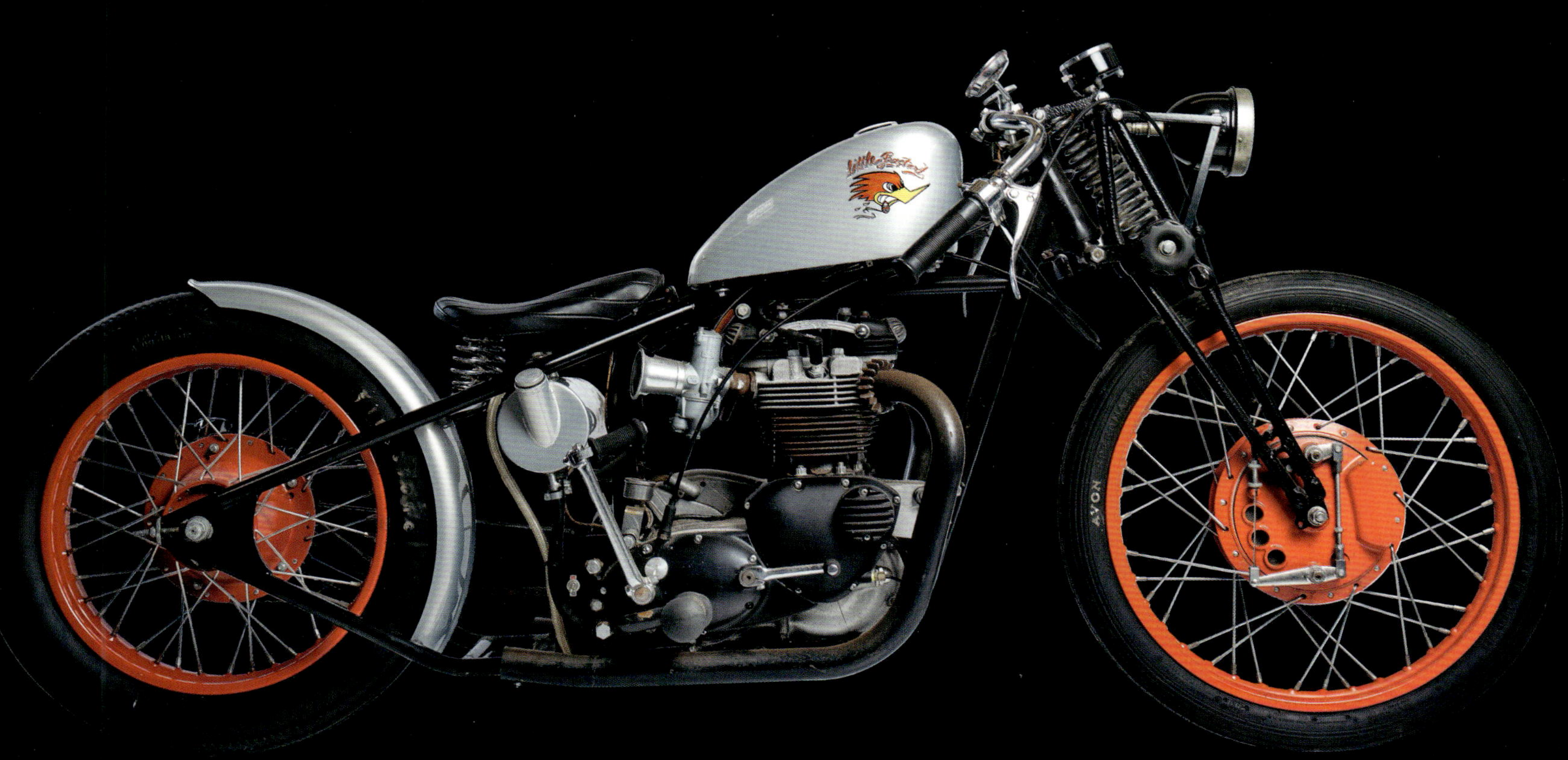

Standout Fundraiser
SIMON WHITTAKER

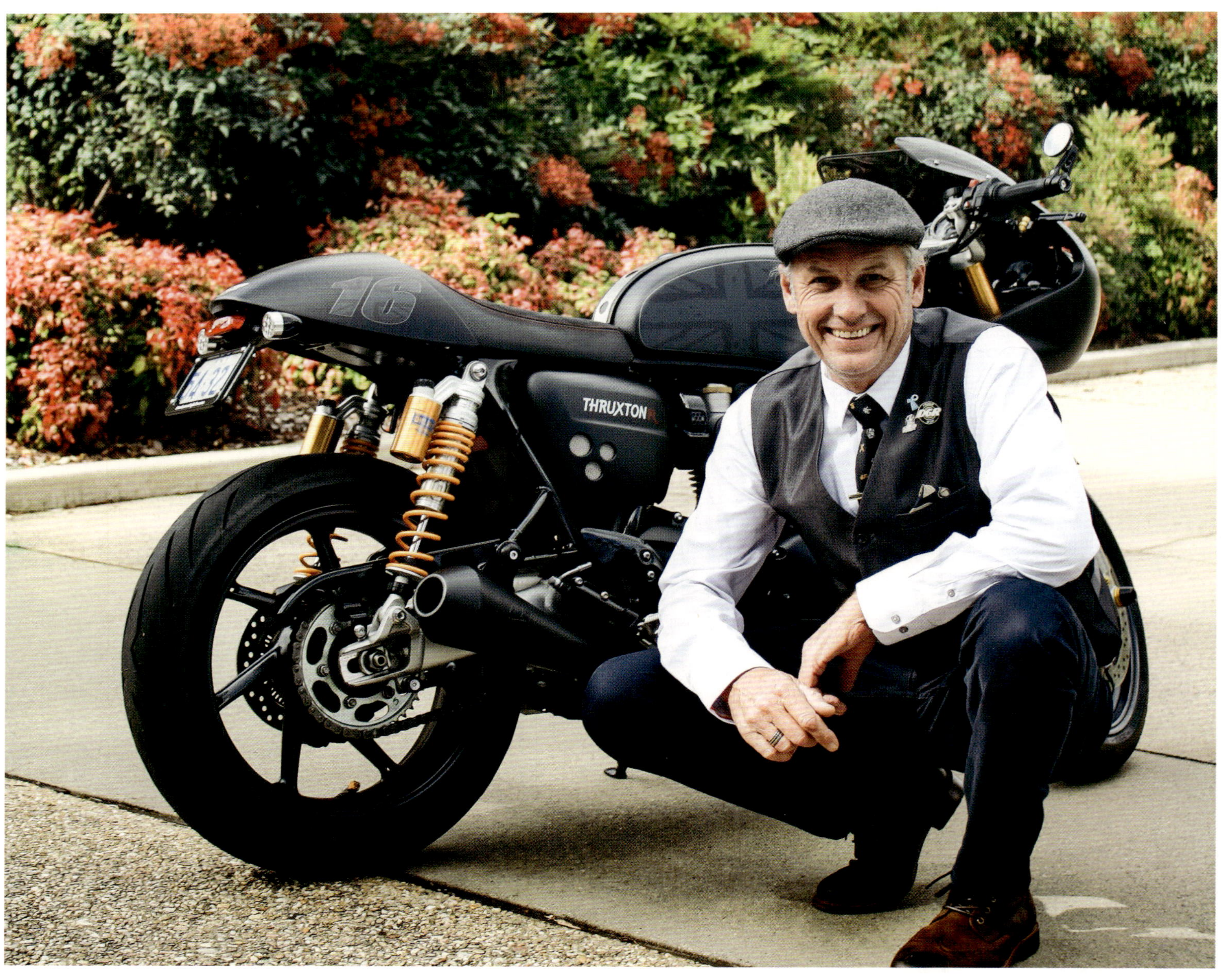

Ride Location
CANBERRA, AUSTRALIA

DGR has always had a positive effect on Canberra riders. It comes around once a year but it also serves as an annual reminder for men to get their PSA test or talk to a doctor about prostate cancer. I also know for a fact this event has encouraged many people to seek help for their mental health, or improved their awareness by just starting a conversation with a mate.

It also encourages men to get involved with DGR organizers to lend a hand or provide support for the event, which helps men to make connections through a shared interest in bikes. I've made a lot of new friends from my involvement in DGR, too. So it's worth getting stuck into the cause and to make a difference.

The small rides are easy as the numbers are manageable. The big ones can be nerve-racking as you have to be really organized and get a lot of help. For the last few I've passed the baton over to someone else to take it on although I'm still involved, just in a smaller role. This hasn't stopped me in my fundraising role, which has continued throughout. Seeing everyone having a great day and supporting the event is incredibly rewarding.

One year I took my CB360 'Cherry Bomb,' a real '70s style Flat Tracker designed and built by me. So in keeping with the theme, I found a flash three-piece denim suit online. 190 bikes in total showed up. I'd always thought it would be awesome to have a traditional barbershop quartet come along and sing. I finally made it happen when 'The Canberra Chordsmen' turned up and started singing.

That was a highlight for me and everyone there. The riders were really into it with some great fashion on display, including street art. All the bikes were in the DGR style and the local TV station, radio and photographers were capturing everything and the place was abuzz. In 2016 we got to meet the Governor General, Sir Peter Cosgrove, which was another highlight.

Since DGR 2013, I decided to get creative with my campaign against prostate cancer. I started building relationships with local businesses to donate raffle prizes and sponsor the event as well as holding fundraiser BBQs at my work and at the local Triumph dealer. I'm blown away by the continued generosity my supporters, friends and family have shown.

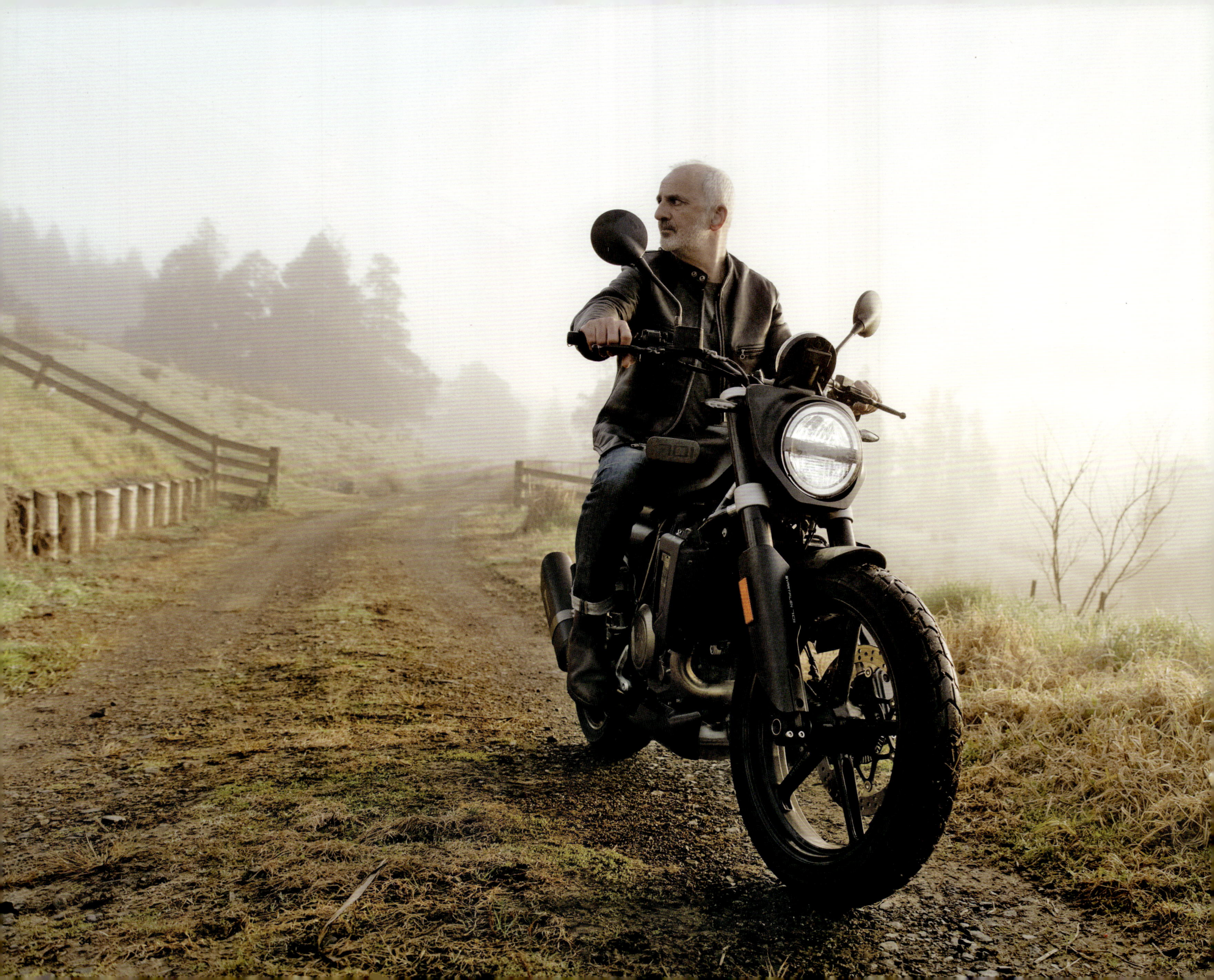

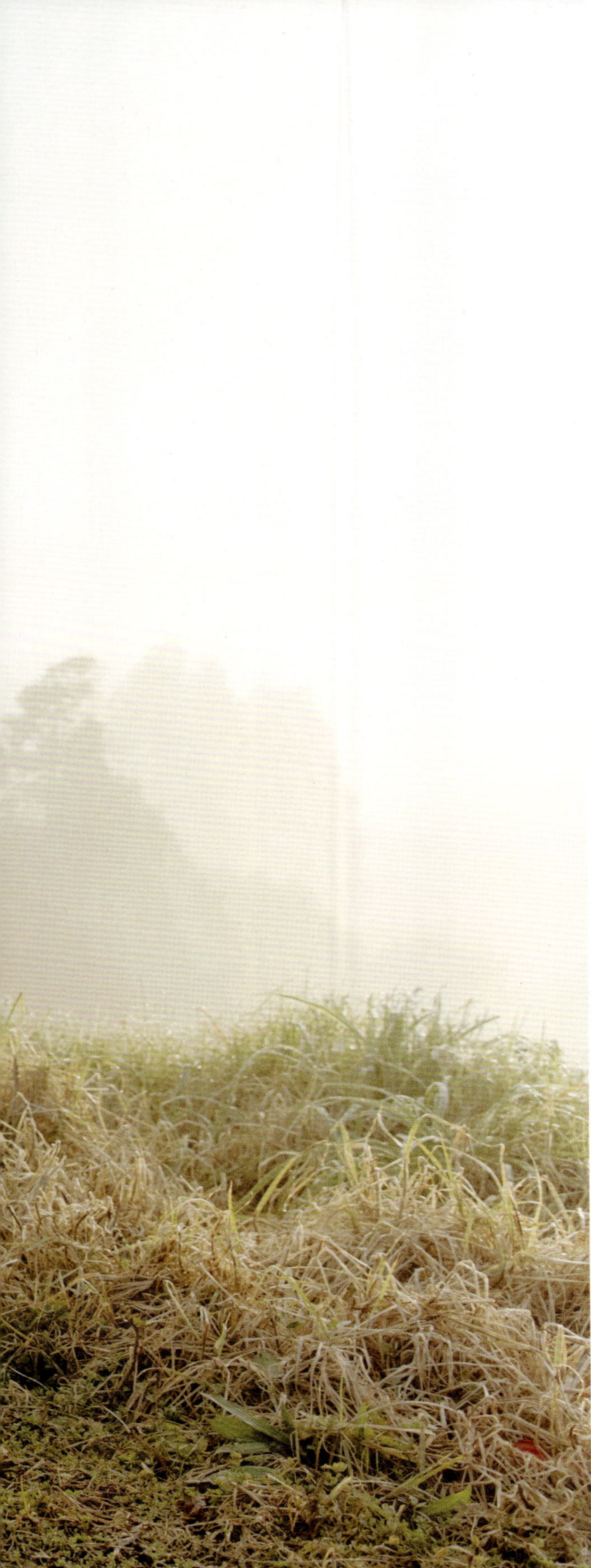

A FIRE HOSE OF STYLE

Motorcycling is essentially a solitary pursuit. Sure, there are clubs and group rides, and folks who like to travel nuts to butts with a pillion, but mostly it's undercover. Just man and machine.

The DGR changed all that. The burgeoning scale of the event thrust motorcycling into the public eye like no other. Even better, it was a beacon of good news; here were stories about bikes that didn't involve crashes or speeding.

But when I first heard about the DGR, I suspected it would fizzle out. After all, motorcycling is very tribal, and motorcyclists are an unusually opinionated bunch. Sportbike guys don't generally hang with chopper guys.

But then the genius of DGR became apparent. The cart was hitched to the genre of motorcycling that appealed most to non-riders: bikes with a classic, custom or retro theme. And the rest? Sorry, not sorry. This laser focus turned out to be critical, and it created a veritable fire hose of style.

The custom scene was a big part of the DGR right from the start. And as the aphorism goes, 'A rising tide lifts all boats.' Customizing is really all about aesthetics and panache, and the DGR provided an outlet for extroverts and style mavens to strut their stuff. It was a springboard for more subdued folk too, who enjoyed the opportunity to dress up for a day and raise a few bucks for a good cause.

I'd call the DGR a celebration at heart, and like most celebrations these days, it spilled onto social media. I always enjoyed seeing customs that had featured on Bike EXIF in the rides: it was confirmation that they weren't locked away in the corner of a garage, or lying idle in someone's living room. You got to see the owners of the bikes too, and sometimes the builders—with grimy jeans and t-shirts swapped out for slick suits, or even plus fours.

More importantly, the DGR helped connect the general public to the joys of motorcycling, and fostered a sense of community around the bike-building scene.

It was more fuel for the custom fire, and played a big part in dragging the art of modifying motorcycles into the mainstream. These days even the man in the street would pause to examine a good custom bike—even if he doesn't know which side the gearshift is on.

And to do all this while raising tens of millions of dollars for men's health? That's a win in anyone's book. Long may it continue.

Chris Hunter
Founder, Bike EXIF
Partner, Iron & Air

In 2009 I bought a Triumph Thruxton because I loved the 50's era British cafe racer and rocker scene, but I didn't have funds for an era-specific machine, or the knowledge to build one. I spent the next three years looking for cafe racer groups, but there weren't any.

Then one day in 2012, I find this Australian Cafe Racer forum that a guy called Mark Hawwa had started, and on there was a thread about a "Distinguished Gentleman's Ride." The thought of it appealed to me and I asked if there was one going in Brisbane, Mark responded with, "There will be when you start one." So I did.

Originally it was just for fun and getting together with like-minded people. When the charity component came in with prostate cancer as the fund recipient, it was a bit more personal as my father-in-law has been through prostate cancer treatment.

Then the introduction of the mental health component moved it right into my ballpark, as suicide prevention is a passion of mine. For me now, it's about the direct personal connections we make on ride day as well as the difference we make outside the riding community with the funding through Movember.

If you've attended, if you've fundraised, or even if you've only just seen it pass by, there is an immediate, inherent joy in a DGR event. It's why so many feel the need to be a part of it. It transcends every boundary you can think of and pulls people together irrespective of their location, life circumstance, or belief systems, and not just locally in each ride, but globally. If you're DGR in Brisbane, then you're DGR in Indianapolis, or Marrakesh, or Istanbul. You're family.

The 2018 wet ride would be one of my faves. Despite some rain, 260 very committed riders rolled the dice and turned up at the start. We gave them the choice to cancel and go home, or ride a revised (and safer) route. Everyone chose to ride. We were soaked and shivering, but man did we laugh. A pack of idiots riding around in the rain in suits. The 260 wore it as a badge of honor after that.

WHEN YOU START ONE

Ride Host: **JEFF GOUGH**

Location: **BRISBANE, AUSTRALIA**

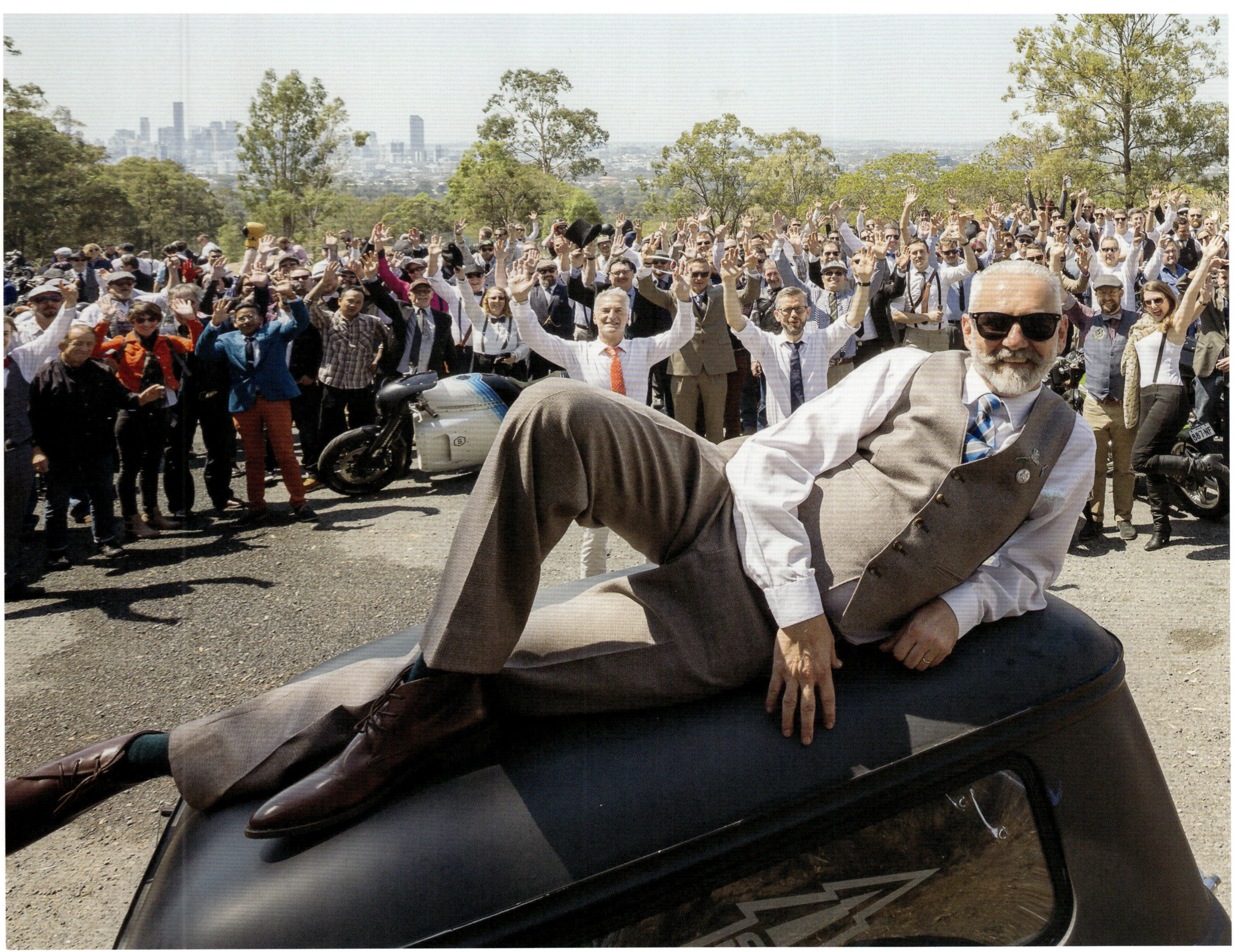

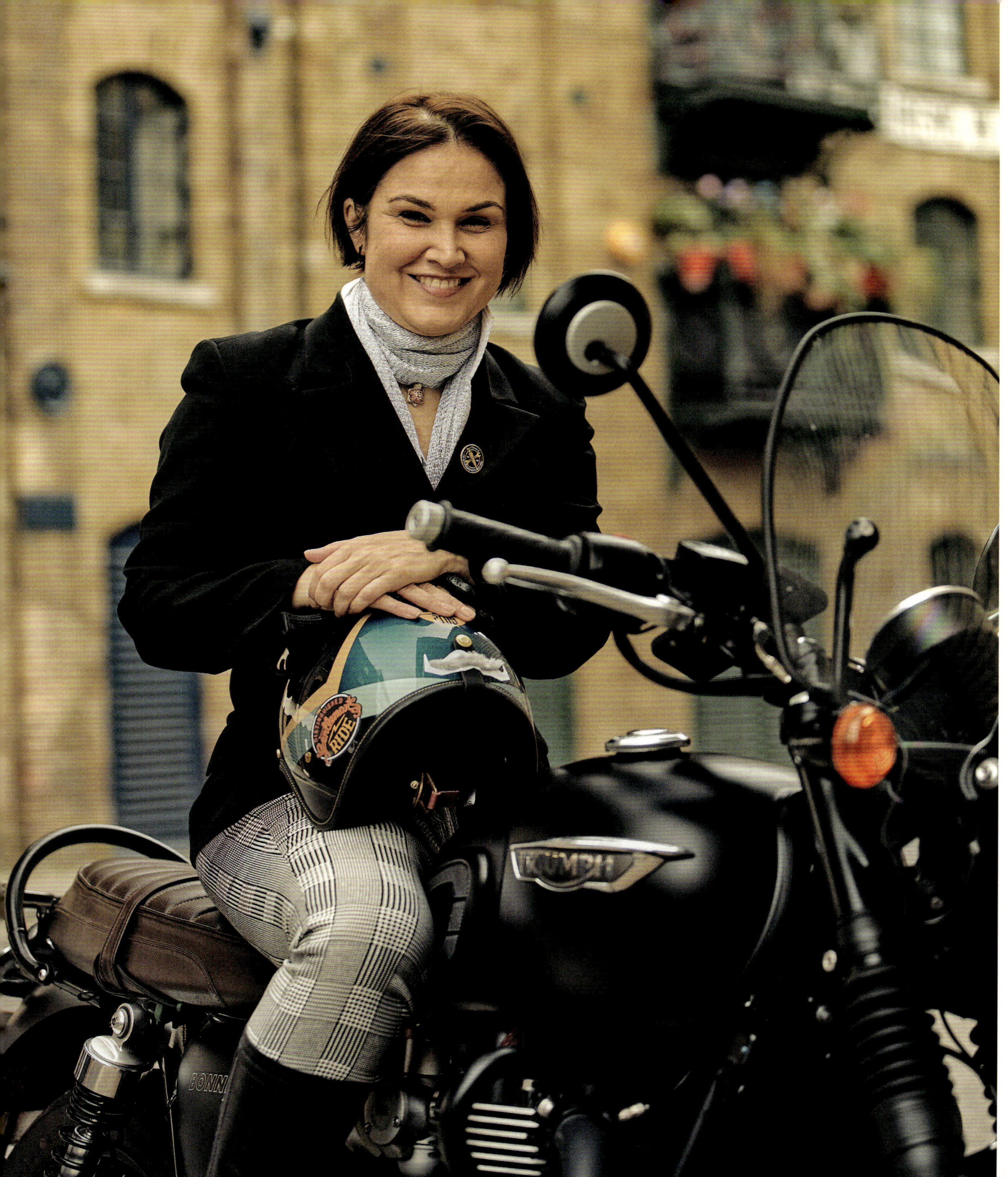

Stefania Schito

*"In April 2017 I lost my Dad to prostate cancer.
Then in September 2017, I saw hundreds of
classic motorcycles and dapper men riding across
Tower Bridge for The Distinguished Gentleman's
Ride. At that moment I thought, "Well, this
would be a much better way to pay tribute to my
Dad than growing a Movember mustache!"*

*My first DGR was in September 2018 and I
was the top female and 5th-highest fundraiser
worldwide. When I was interviewed after the
ride, they asked what I felt. I said, "Love." People
were really kind and respectful. It is a unique
feeling to be part of something so big which unites
people worldwide and builds such solidarity and
support in the community.*

*I love everything about The Distinguished Gen-
tleman's Ride! I love planning and fundraising,
and being a part of the ride. Most importantly
for me, it's a day dedicated to my Dad."*

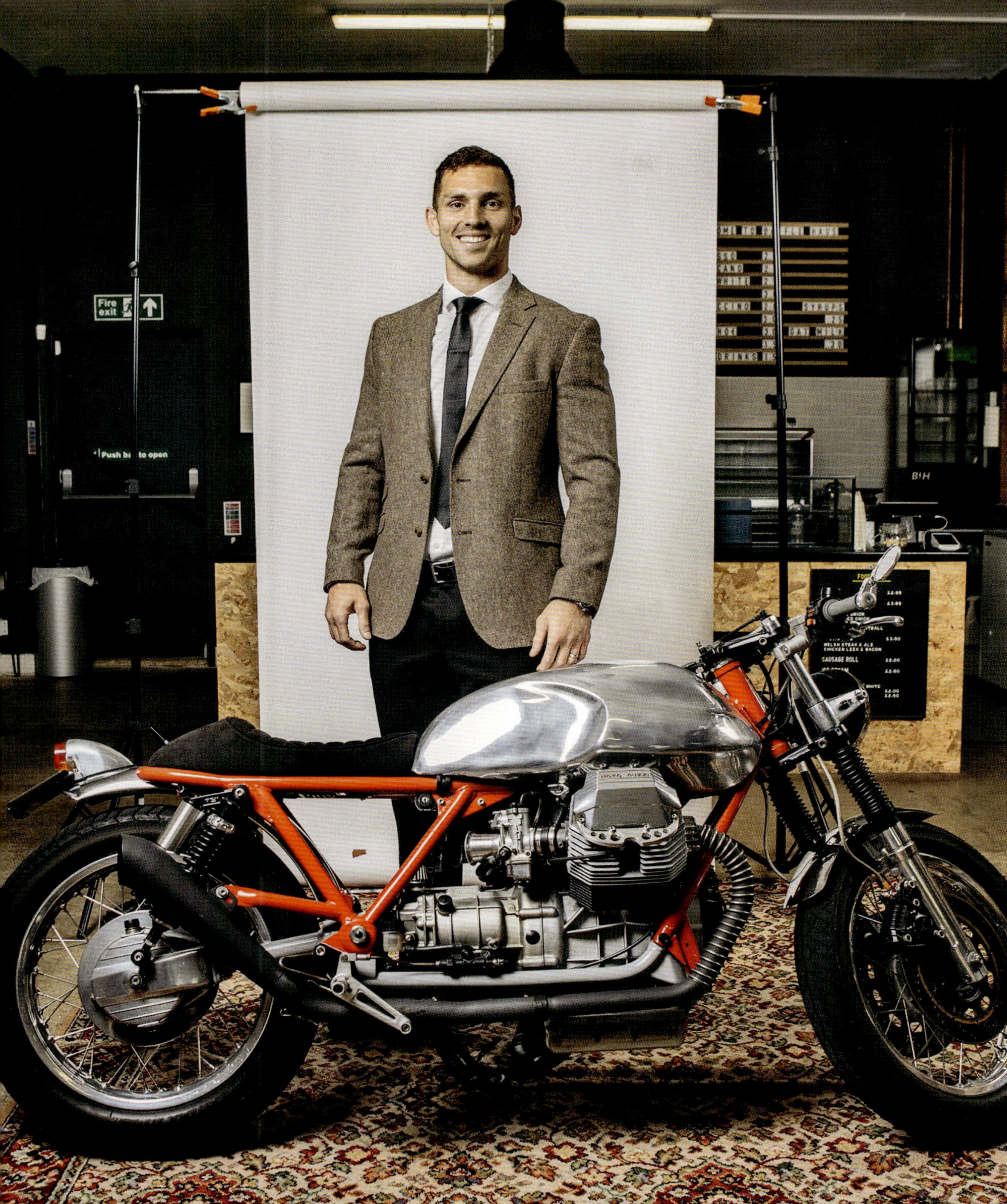

GLOBAL AMBASSADOR

George North

"Where do I start with DGR? I knew of The Distinguished Gentleman's Ride before being asked to be an ambassador. I had done the ride previously with my group of mates, 'The Baffle Boys'. As much as we sound like a really bad boy band, we're just a group of guys that connect with what the DGR stands for. Oh, and who also like riding their motorbikes.

I've have had a few friends and family face mental health challenges. Coming from the macho world of rugby, it's even harder to talk about these things. The main reason I support DGR and Movember is to try and help break down these barriers. I'm very fortunate to have support with the mental side of professional sport, but others do not. If I could help in a small way to break down these barriers or start a conversation to help someone, it's a win for me.

Community, connections and family are huge to me. We need the support of our circle more so than ever these days to lean on in good and bad times. And there is always time to make sure your mates are OK."

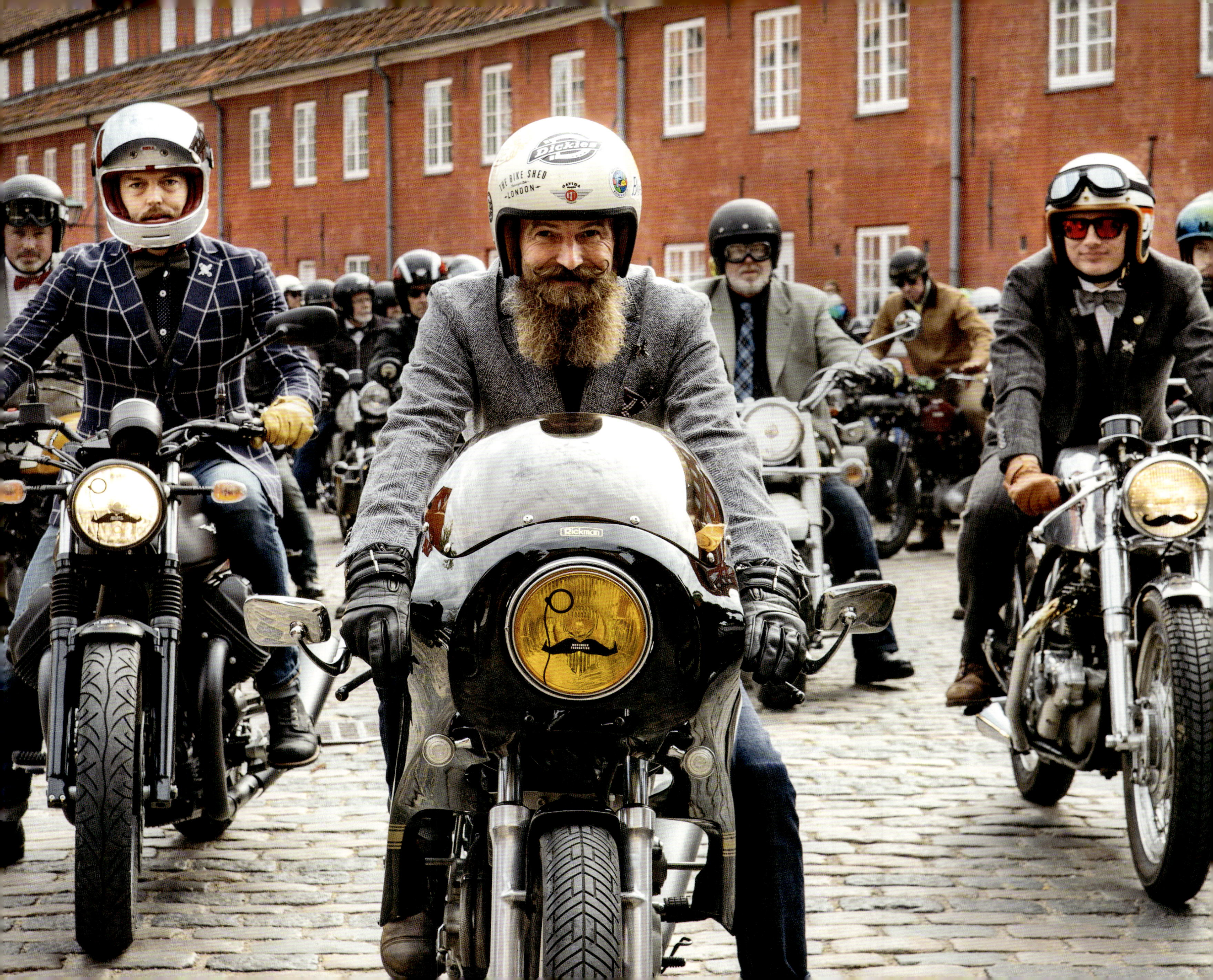

SOCIAL CONNECTIONS CHALLENGE

Standing shoulder to shoulder

Riding can be inherently isolating. Commonly, men experiencing mental health challenges don't ride to talk, they ride to escape. Once the helmet is on, and the visor is down, there's no time to think of anything other than you and the road. After almost 10 years of bringing awareness to our cause areas, it was time for something different.

In 2020, The Distinguished Gentleman's Ride, in partnership with Movember, announced the DGR Social Connections Challenge. The aim was simple, to use funds raised by DGR to invest in programs that tackle social isolation and poor mental health within the motorcycle community. Within The Distinguished Gentleman's Ride are over 300,000 motorcyclists around the world who want to see the mental health of their community strengthened and supported. With that, Movember and The Distinguished Gentleman's Ride released the DGR Social Connections Challenge: a program that encouraged its community of distinguished gentlefolk to come to them with ideas designed to improve the lives of men in motorcycling.

The first phase of The Distinguished Gentleman's Ride Social Connections Challenge funded a total of 18 projects from across Australia, Canada, New Zealand, the UK and the US to help them to develop their ideas. In the second phase, the eight most promising projects were allocated additional funding to enable their program to be delivered in a pilot format.

HARLEYS IN HOLLYWOOD

It's hard to say exactly how I found out about The Distinguished Gentleman's Ride, but it was when I was first getting into motorcycles. These weren't just any run-of-the-mill motorcycles though.

Cafe racers had caught my eye. They were weird and wild. At the time, I was still living in Australia. It was around 2013, and a mate of mine in Sydney had called me after hearing about The Distinguished Gentleman's Ride there. He and I used to ride old Honda cafe racers together. There was something completely alluring about Hondas that were stripped down and built into customs.

I was abroad a lot at the time, but he had told me about it. He wanted me to join him in Sydney and ride together, but the timing just didn't match. From that point on, I knew it sounded cool and that in some way or another I'd get involved.

I ended up hearing from the distinguished gentleman himself, Mark Hawwa, about getting involved as an ambassador for the ride in 2017. We had known friends of friends - you know the old adage that you're only six degrees of separation or fewer from anyone - and he thought to reach out. The ride had really gained momentum by then, we got connected and talked about getting involved and at that time, it all just lined up.

Then I had to come home to Sydney and do a bit of stuff and I had the opportunity to meet the crew and learn a little more about what DGR does. I was pumped to get involved. My style has come a long way from those Hondas. Now, I'm able to ride in DGR with a bit more American grunt on my vintage-style Harley-Davidson chopper; call that the American influence from living in Los Angeles for the last few years.

I've never personally been impacted by mental health or prostate cancer, but I know how hard it can be for those who are. I wanted to get involved in the ride simply because I think it's a cool way to raise funding and awareness for a hugely important issue while being a part of a like-minded global community.

When you can turn a passion like motorcycling into something that brings people together from around the world with the internet, it's a great way to shed light on a cause that we all care about.

Being an ambassador for The Distinguished Gentleman's Ride taught me that I want to do more. I want to get more inspired and to be there for my mates. At the time, I had shared my profile and asked for donations, and they came flooding in. I had messages from people all over saying how much it meant to them to see these issues being brought to light.

Sometimes you underestimate how much something like that will touch people, and it's not a hard thing to do. I hope I can do more in years to come, and even if it's not at an official level, you just might see me chilling at the back of the pack of DGR in LA.

Jai Courtney
Actor & DGR Ambassador

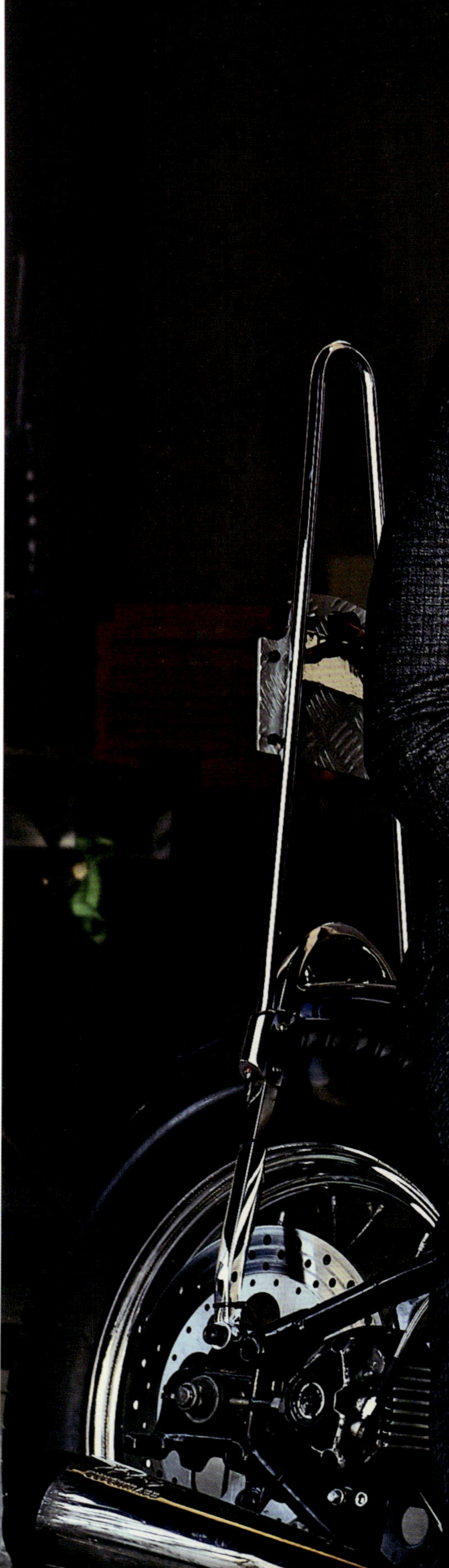

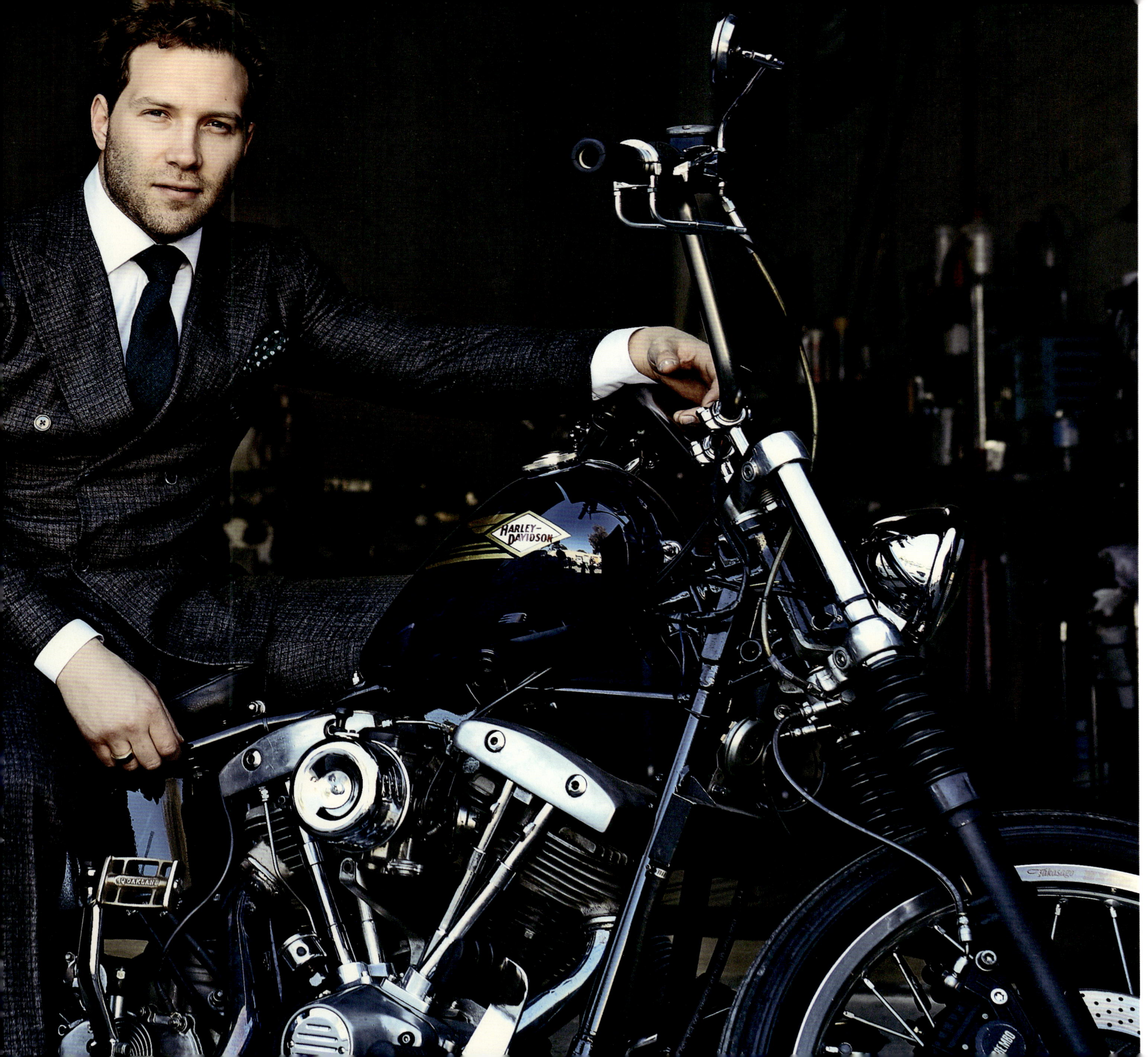

HARLEY-DAVIDSON

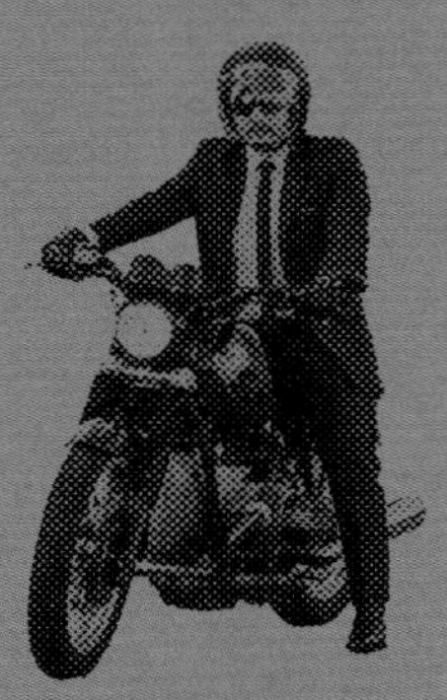

2013

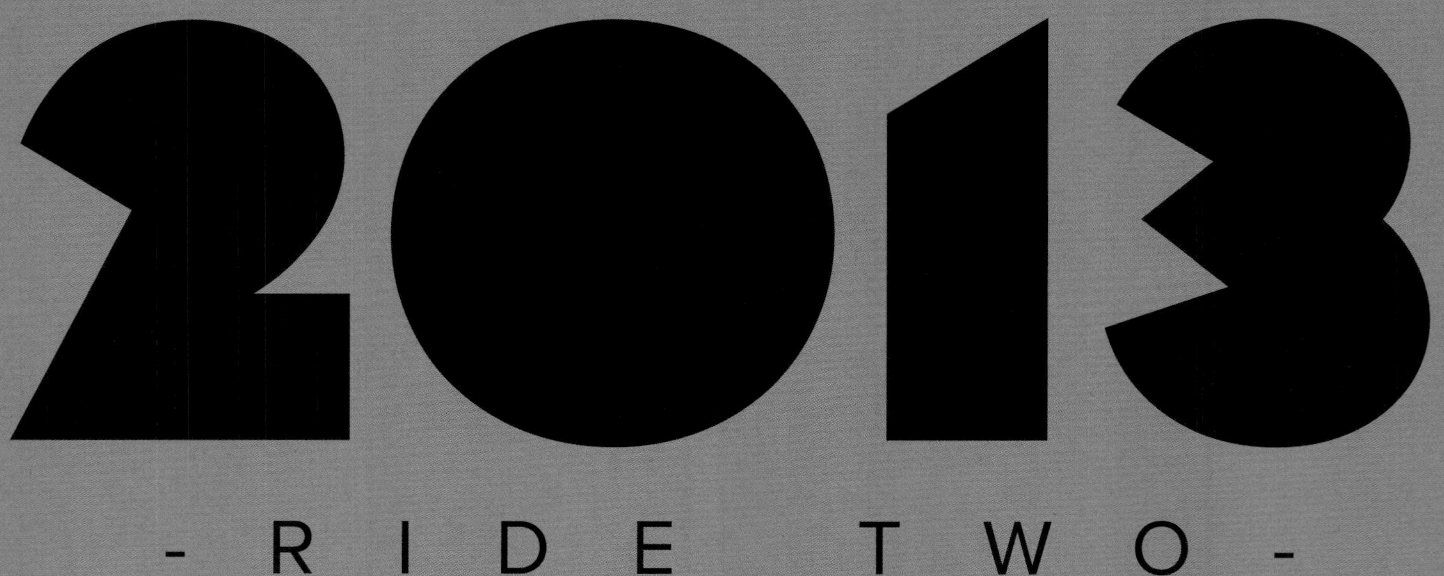

- RIDE TWO -

CARRYING ON FROM THE MOMENTUM OF 2012, 2013 SAW **11,000 RIDERS** AND **145 CITIES** TAKE PART. DGR BEGAN PARTNERING WITH THE PROSTATE CANCER FOUNDATION AUSTRALIA.

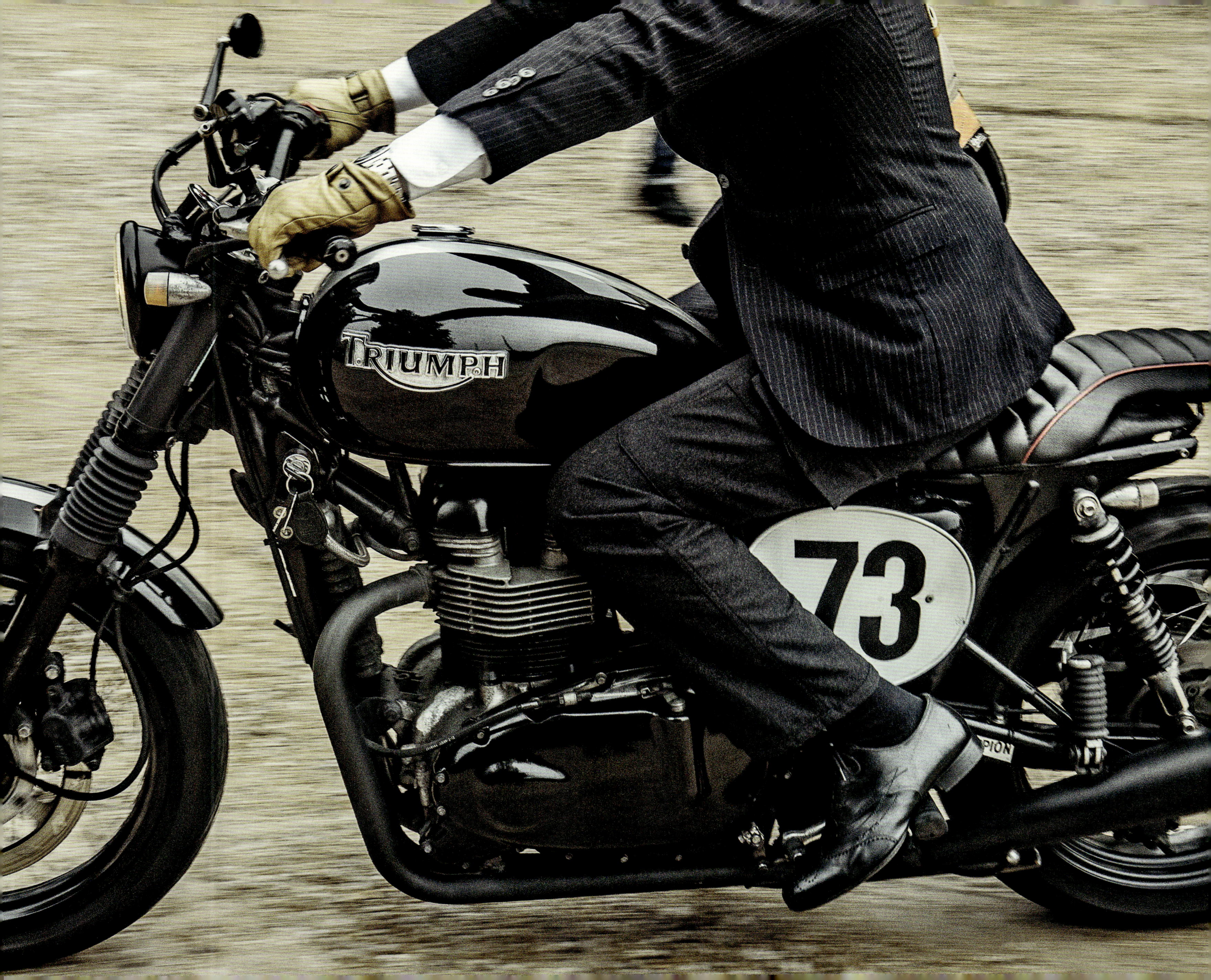
TRIUMPH
73

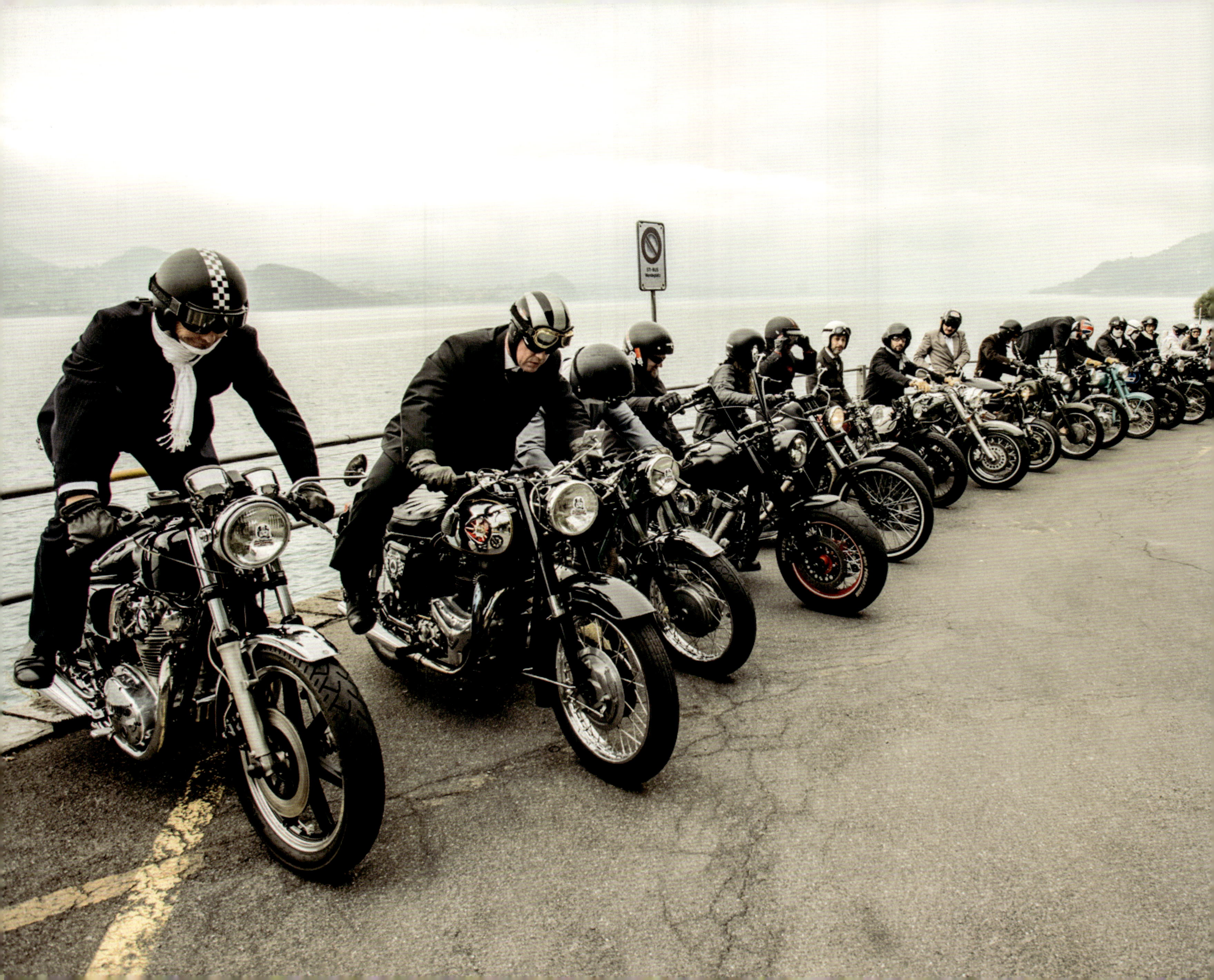
ST-BUS
Vordeplatz

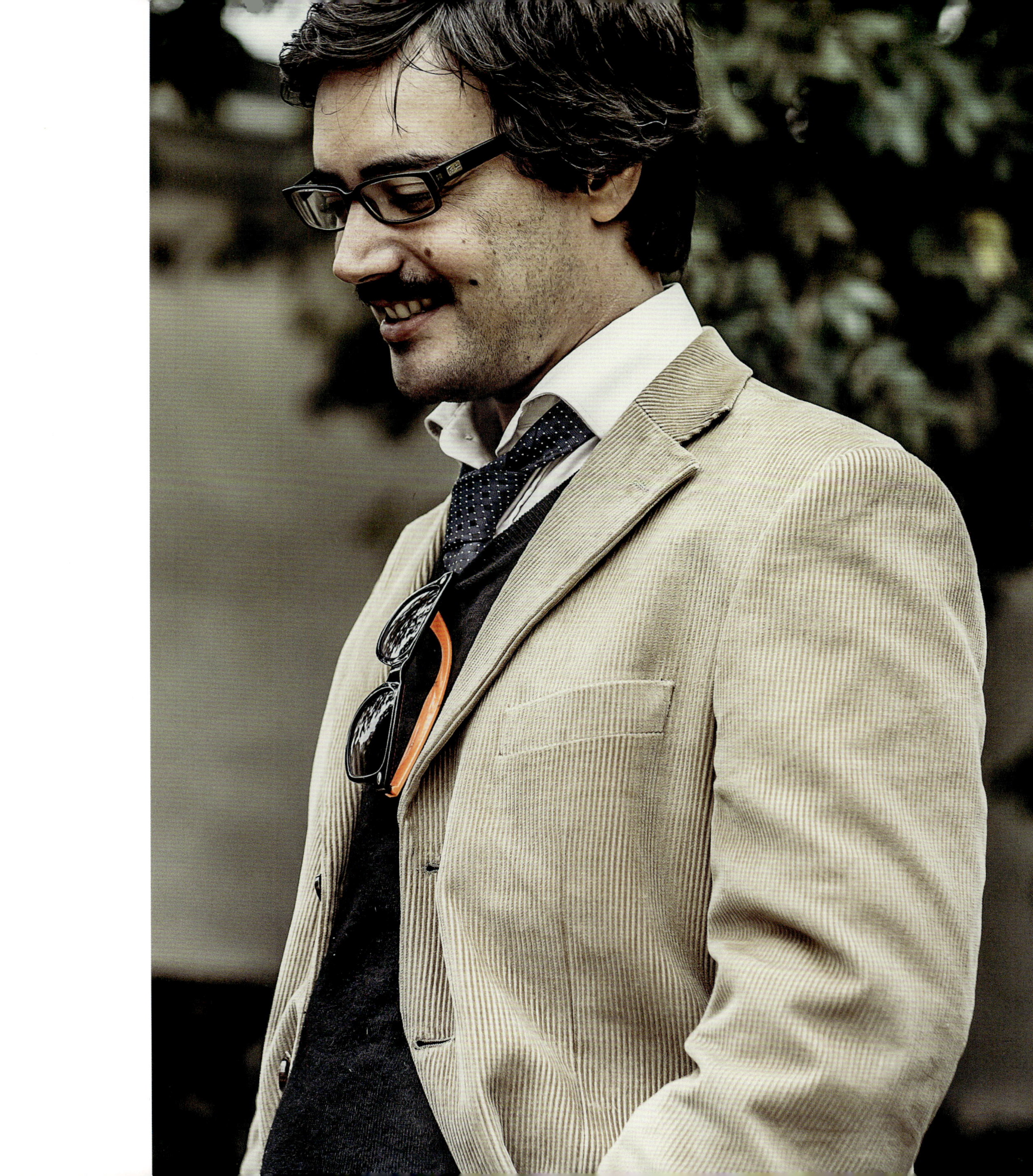

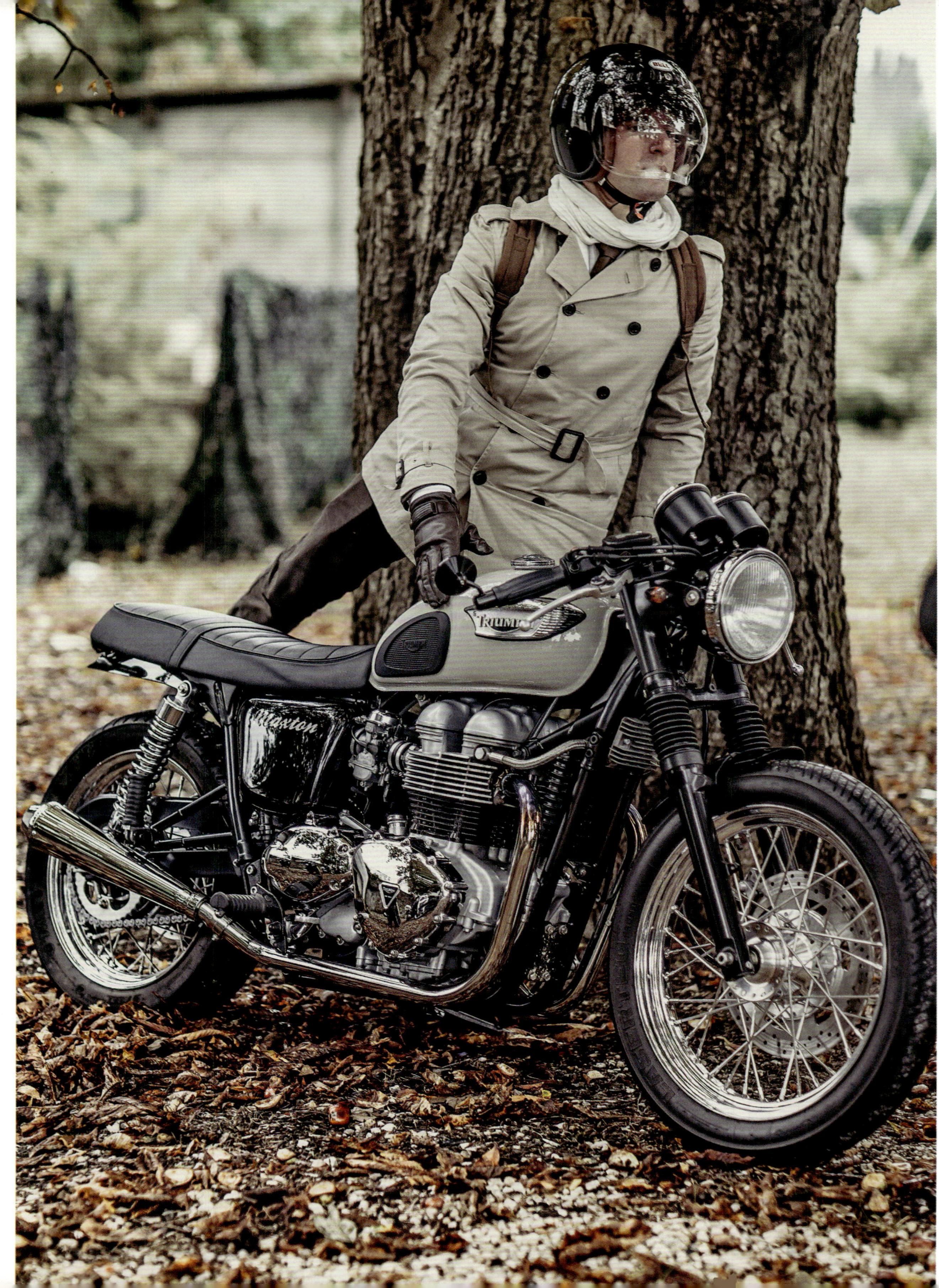

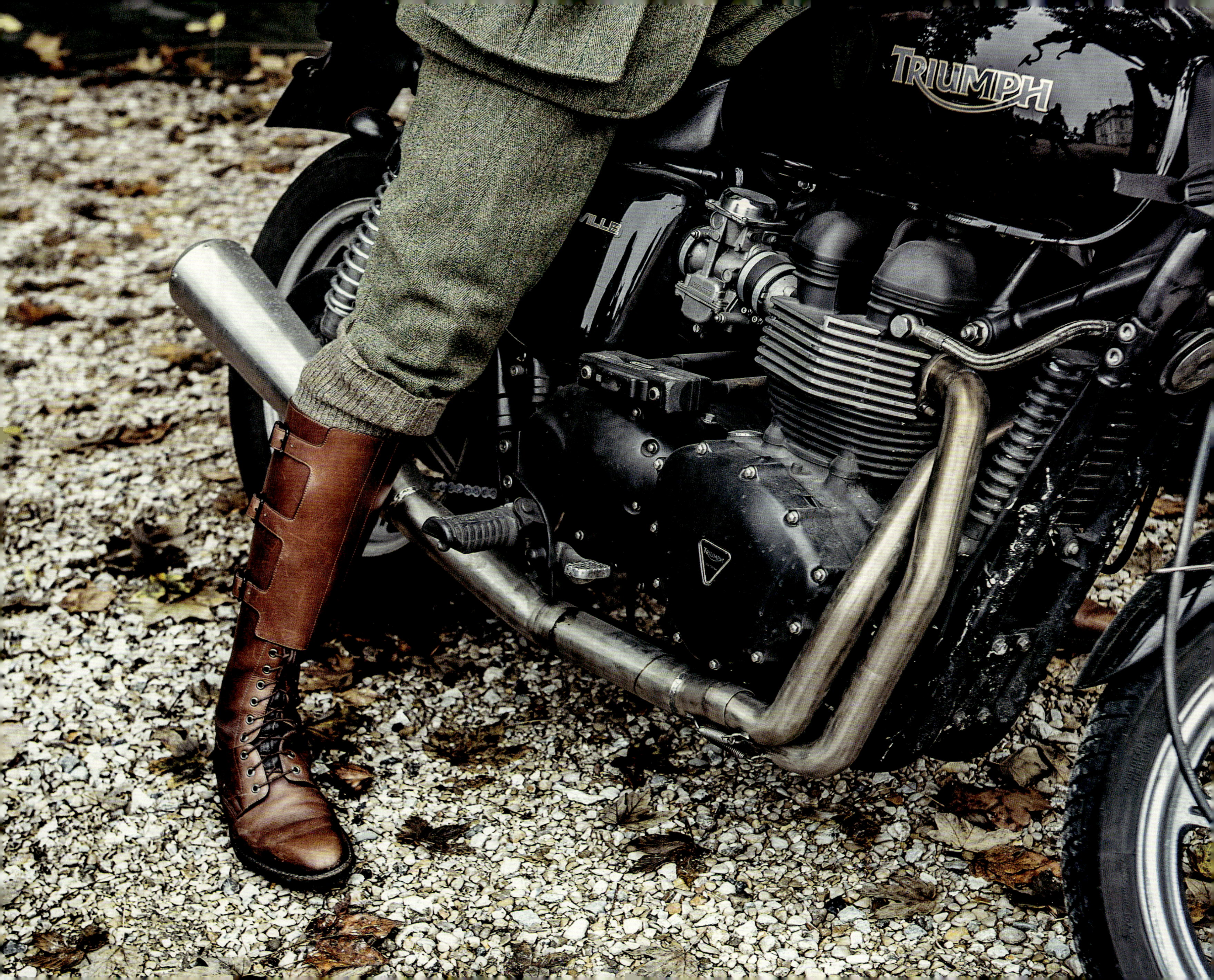
TRIUMPH

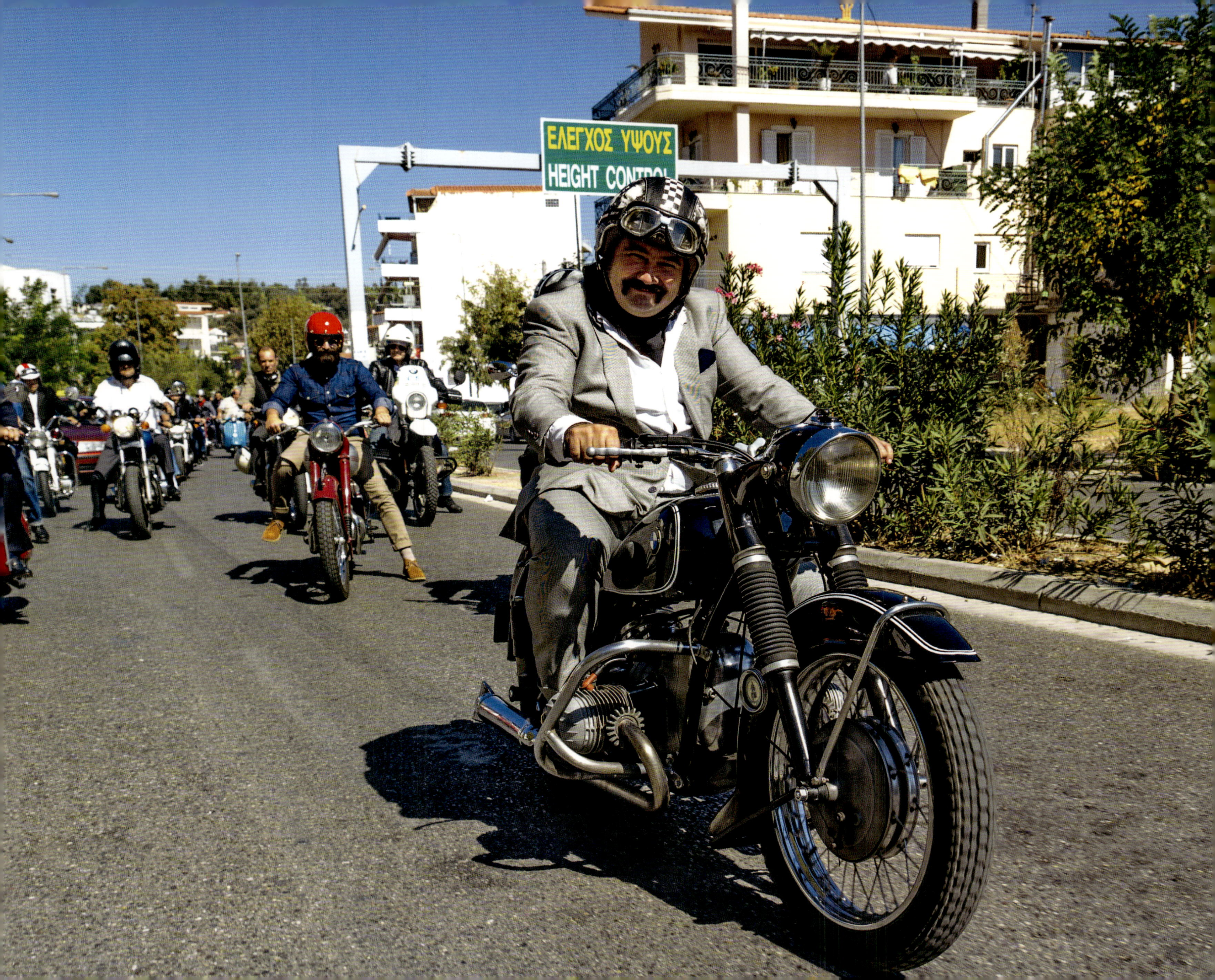
ΕΛΕΓΧΟΣ ΥΨΟΥΣ
HEIGHT CONTROL

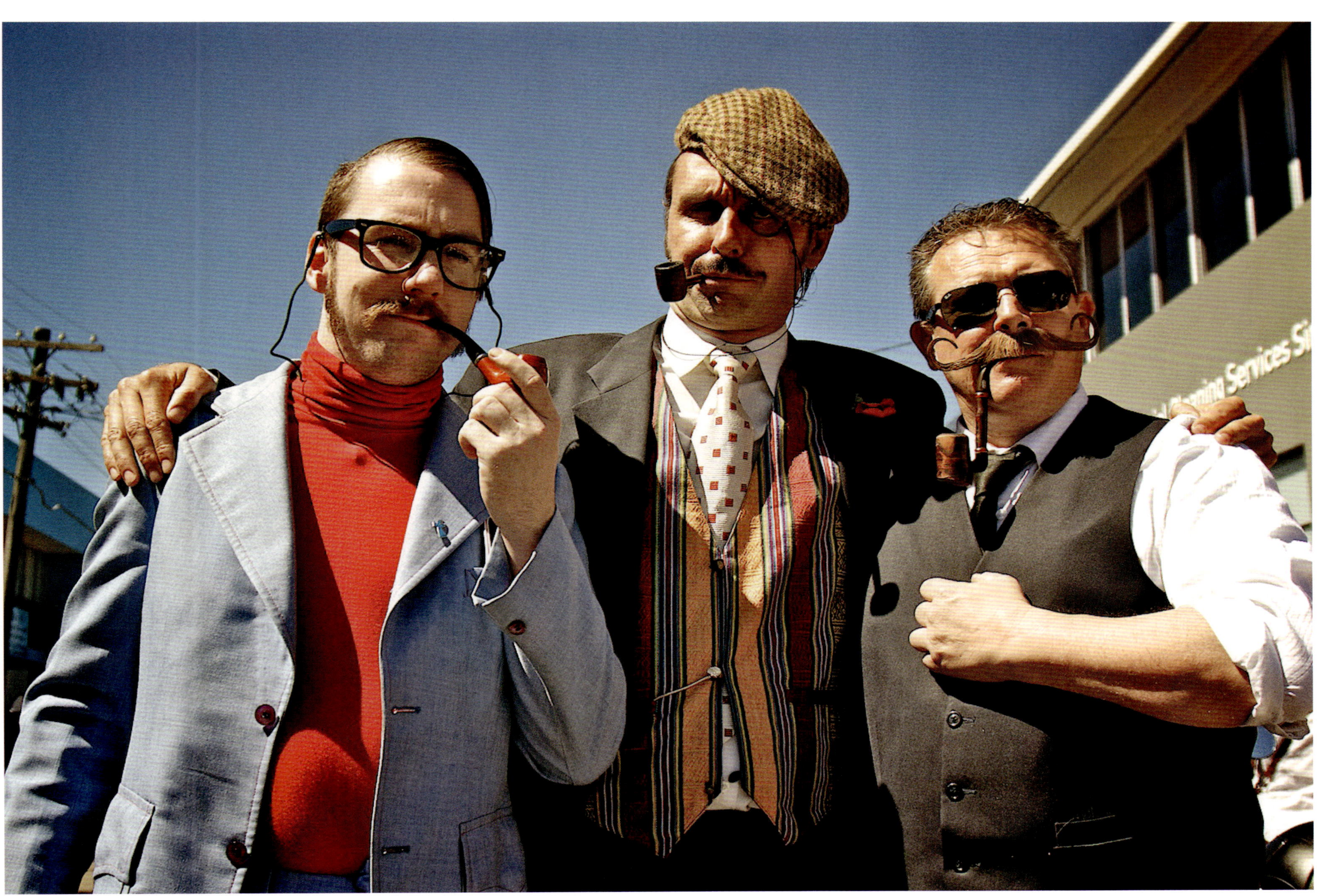

Cleaning Services S

Riding is escapism for me. I have a pretty stressful job, so it's the only time I can get away from emails and phone calls. I can just put my helmet on and find my Zen. I'm connected to nature; I smell and see things I might not have ever been able to see.

I found out about DGR through Instagram, just through posts from local San Diego riders. I decided to go, and knew absolutely nobody. So I gathered up some friends of mine and forced them to join the gentry.

From that first ride, I've made friends that I still keep to this day. It's a true community that has built up around the ride here. It's completely different to what you'd find in other types of motorcycle groups.

I work with a lot of men in the construction industry. I wanted to do something to give back to these guys and to raise awareness because there's not a lot of men's health issues that we talk openly about. It is really nice to be able to do something for these amazing guys and to increase people's knowledge.

I knew all too well about prostate cancer, as one of my really good friends was diagnosed in his early 40s. I learned a lot about it by living through it with him. I wanted to do something for my community, to help bring awareness to them and help encourage them to get checked and take care of their health. And hopefully that's exactly what I have done.

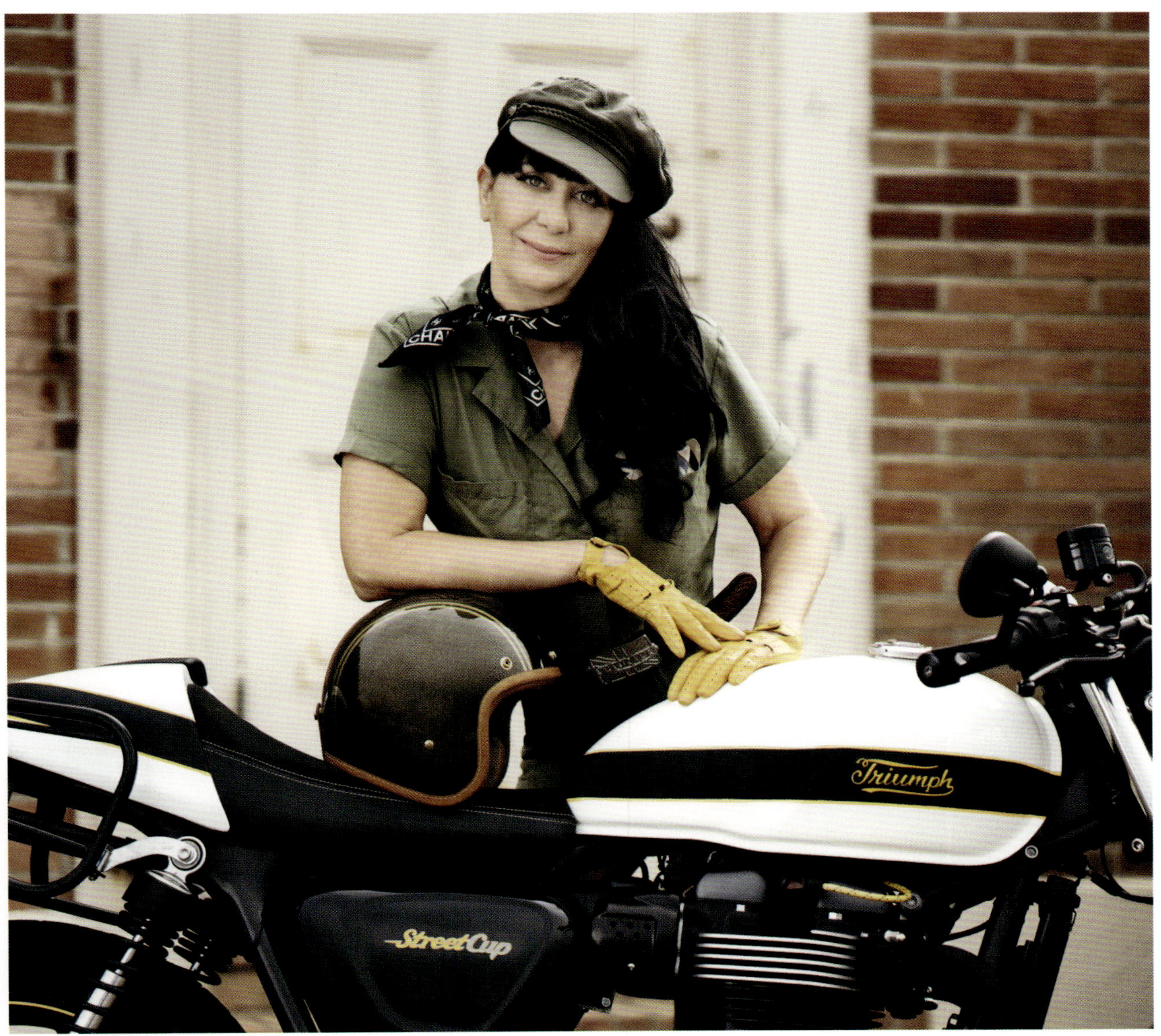

Ride Location
SAN DIEGO, UNITED STATES

CHOPPERS

A chopper is a style of custom motorcycle that emerged from the West Coast of America in the late '50s and early '60s. They commonly feature a large engine, dramatically modified steering angles, very long forks, small tanks and 'ape hanger' handlebars which are often complemented by a tall 'sissy bar' behind the seat.

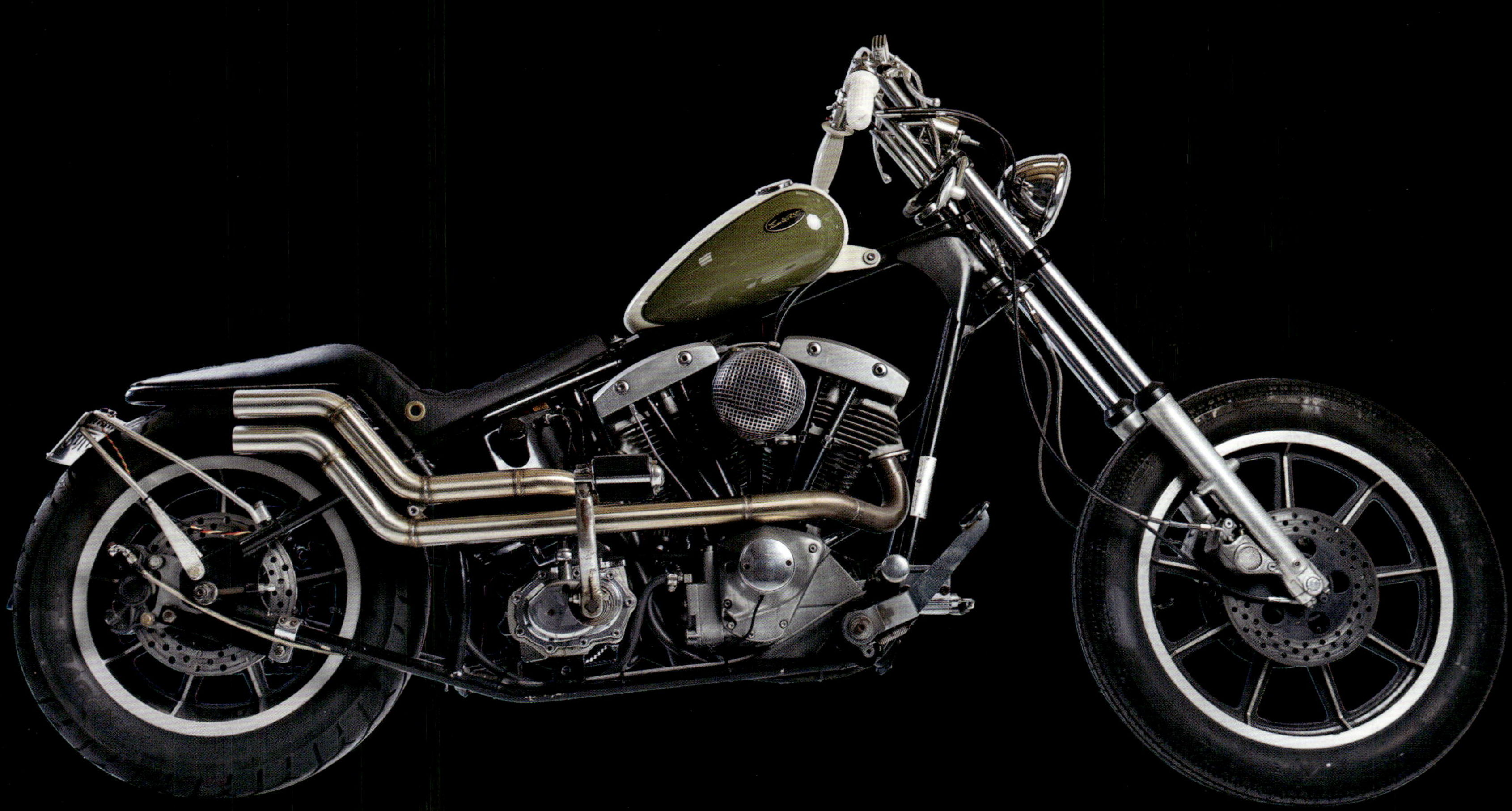

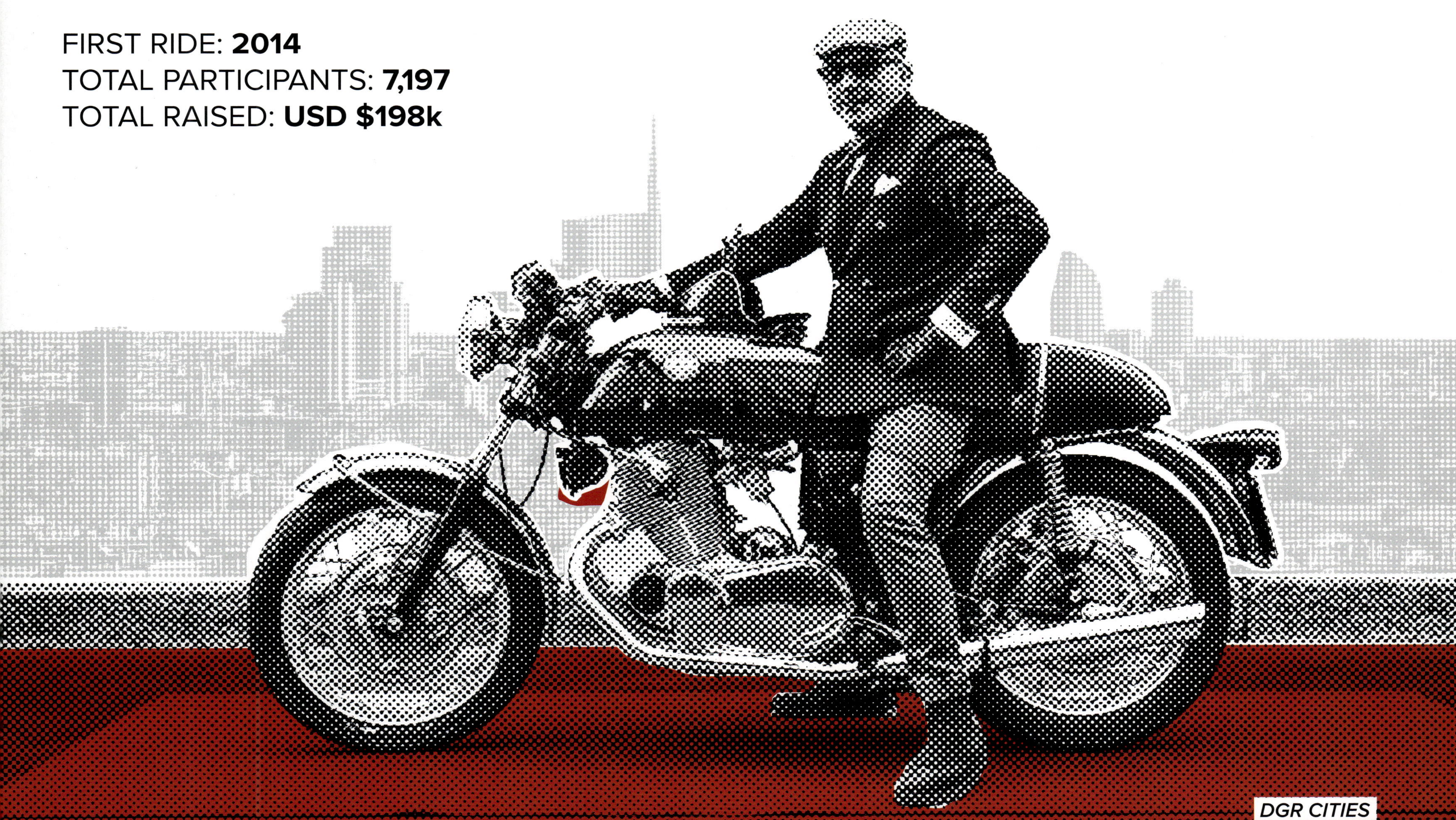

MILANO
FIRST RIDE: 2014
TOTAL PARTICIPANTS: 7,197
TOTAL RAISED: USD $198k
DGR CITIES

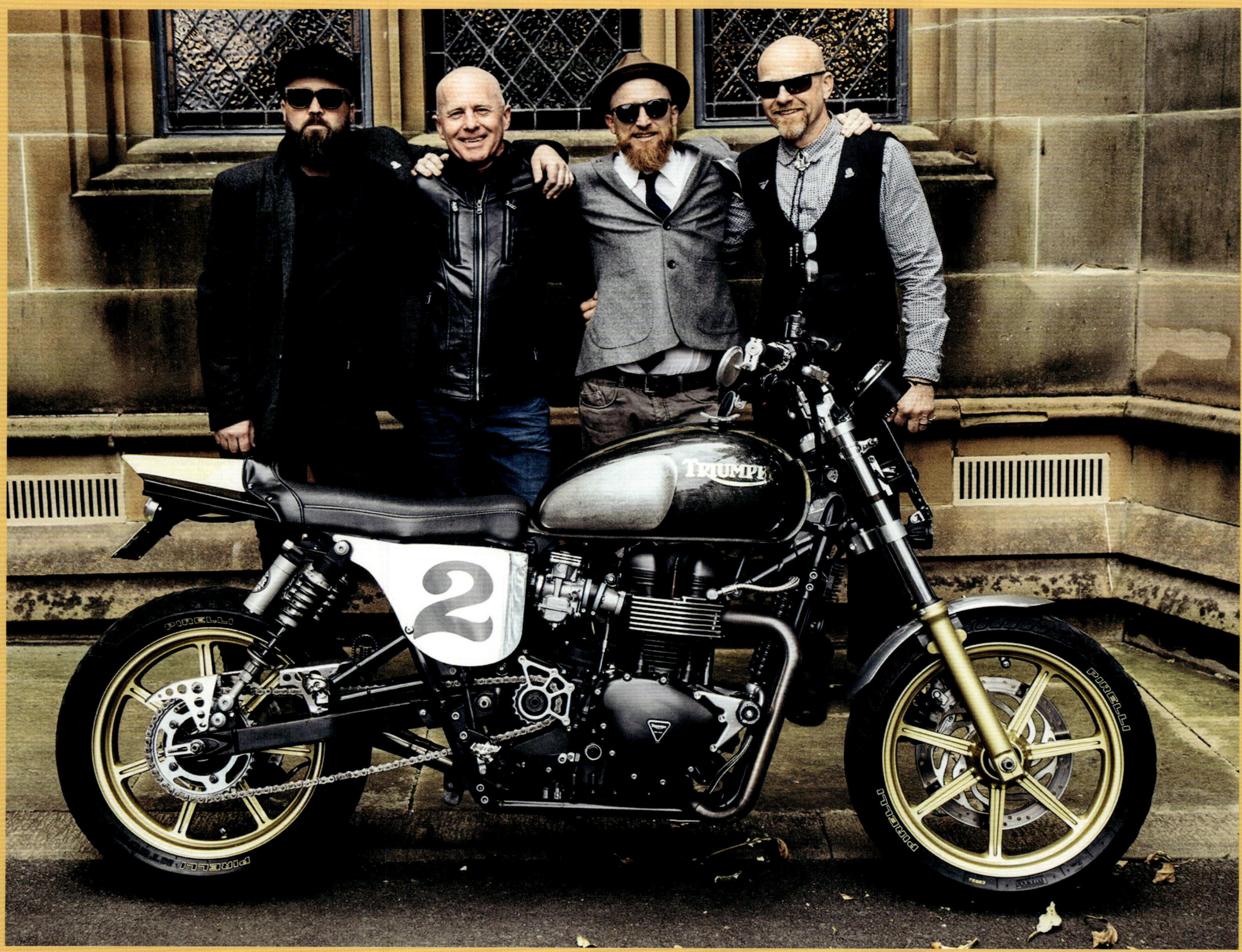

TRIUMPH
2

It's difficult enough going through the trials and tribulations of cancer treatment. But becoming cancer-free is just the start of it, and what gets left behind can result in unexpected effects to you physically and mentally.

For Mark, his surviving cancer resulted in ongoing impacts to his mental health. His story speaks of struggles after his diagnosis, and the toll treatment takes on those who are going through it and beyond.

you do that, the more you retreat. Eventually, you just implode."

The stigma of mental health amongst men is devastating, complex, and prevalent. Shame compounds mental health struggles and for Mark, it led him to completely pack up his life and impulsively drive from Ballarat to see his son in Sydney, over 600 miles away.

Parking at the front door, Mark was so overcome by his anxieties he was unable to walk;

After a distressing phone call from a friend, Mark's family rushed to his side. Spending the time needed to get him back on his feet and find the support he needs; they returned the favor to a strong and supportive dad who'd raised them all those years ago.

Mark broke the cycle when he started sharing what had happened to him with friends and neighbors. Those feelings of loneliness and isolation dissipate when you don't feel the shame weighing you down. Self-acceptance

SURVIVOR STORIES: Mark Atkinson

"That was the hardest thing for me. I never thought
I'd be talking to my old man about suicide."

Mark, his sons Kel and Bon, and his brother Chris, are all members of the DGR Sydney community. The rock of his family and friends, Mark struggled to communicate how he was feeling after his treatment. His daughter, Kate, had caught on to those fleeting comments; the ones that make you wonder whether someone is reaching out for help.

"It took a while for dad to start saying stuff. And when he did, I don't think I really realized how bad it was." Rather than getting help and leaning on those who he held up, Mark isolated himself. "I didn't want to tell anyone what the problem was. With that goes embarrassment and guilt. And the more

eventually having to call Kel from the driver's seat to help him get out. "Then when we went inside and talked about some pretty big things," Kel said. "That was the hardest thing for me. I never thought I'd be talking to my old man about suicide."

Mark knew that he needed a change. Falling in love with the stillness of Tasmania, he decided that a peaceful life there would help him on his journey of healing. But it wasn't quite the end of his struggles.

Mark began suffering from a bout of panic and anxiety attacks as a result of being so far away from his family and support networks.

paved the way for Mark to speak about his journey, and he let people know that his challenges began with a mental illness.

To highlight Mark's struggle and success, DGR funded a short film called "Survivor." It is a must-see for anyone seeking an introspective view of depression and the mental health impacts that often go with prostate cancer diagnosis and treatment.

For Mark, everything began unraveling after his treatment, but luckily he leveraged the support network around him and emerged a survivor.

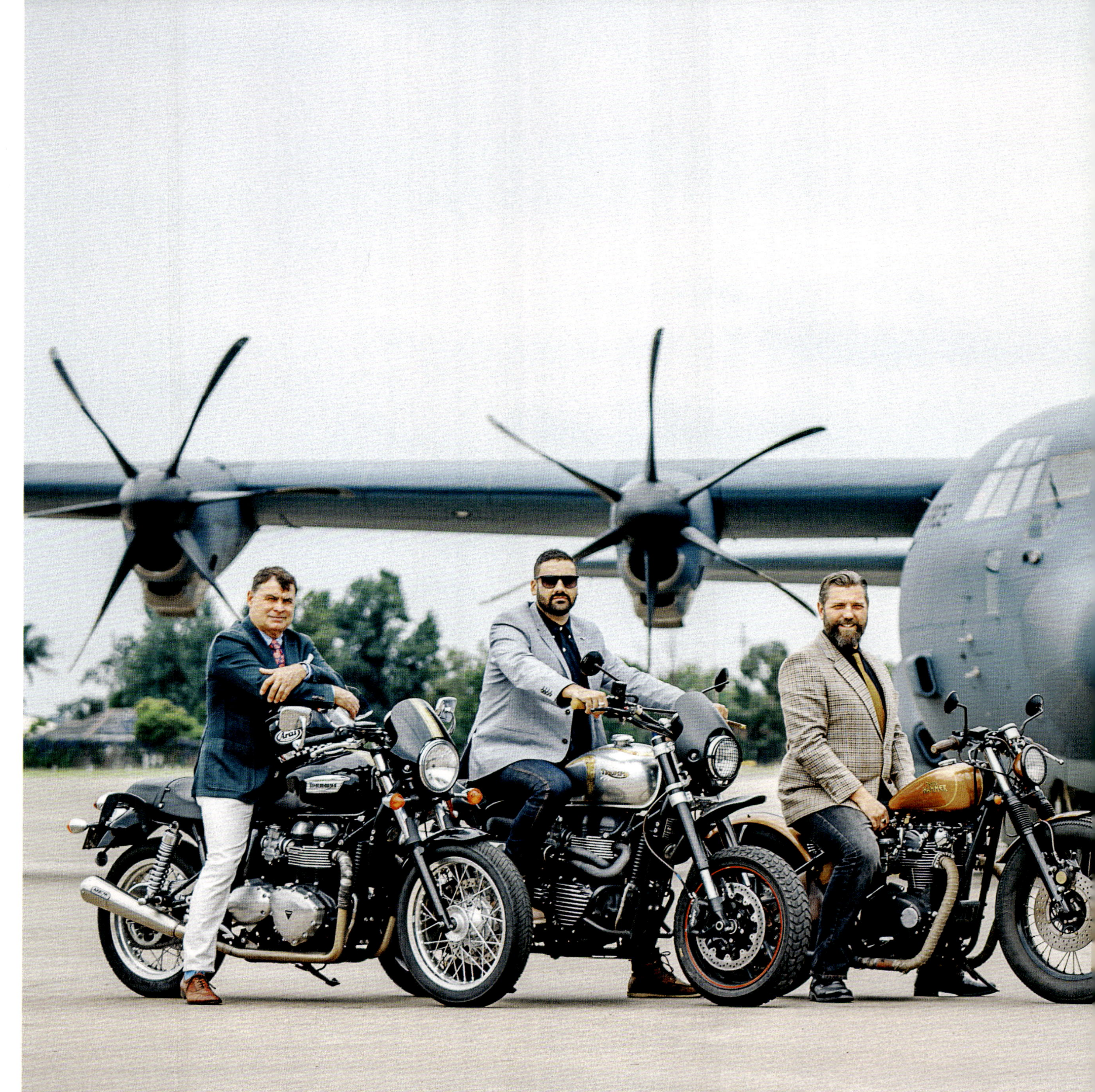

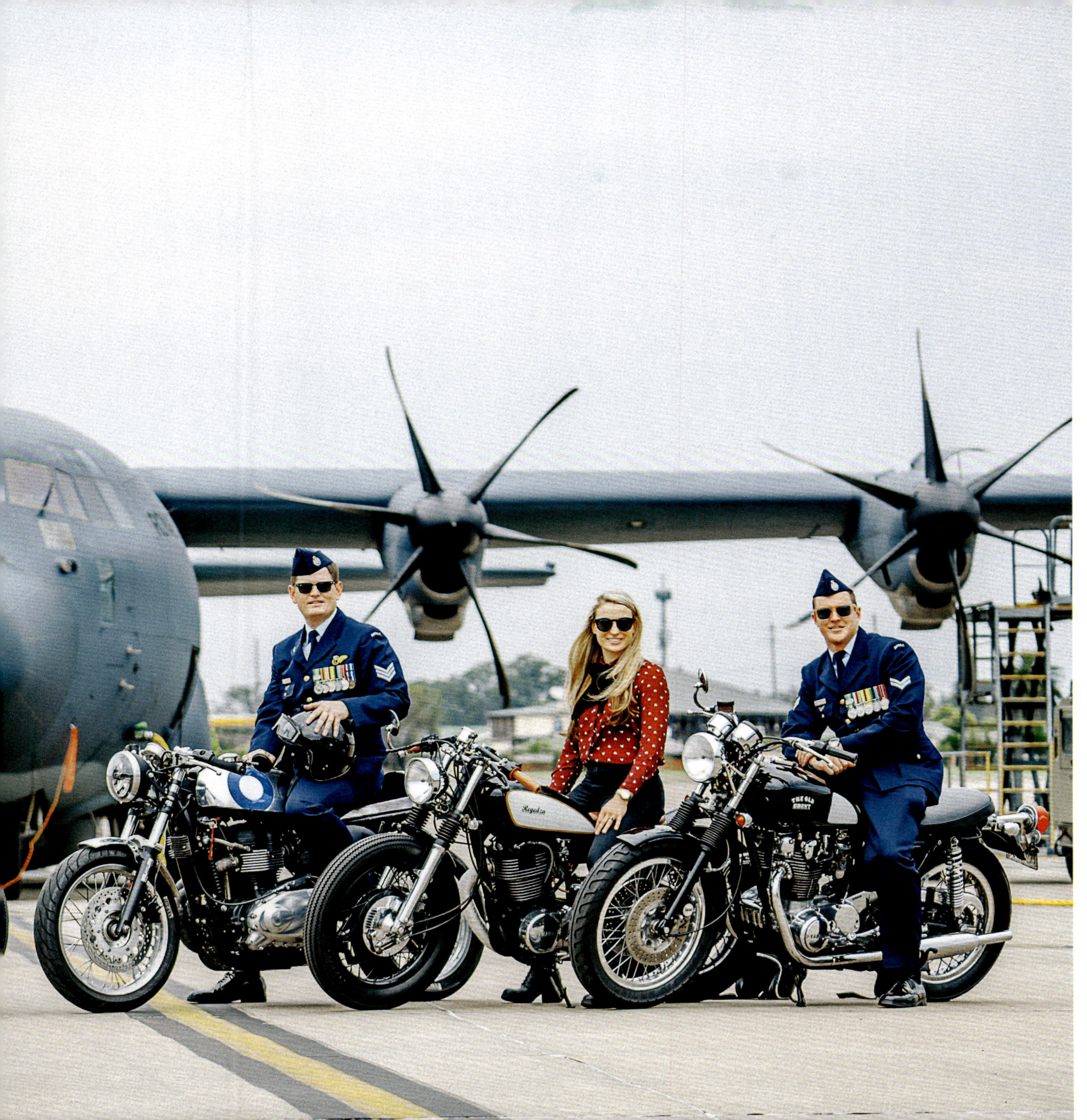

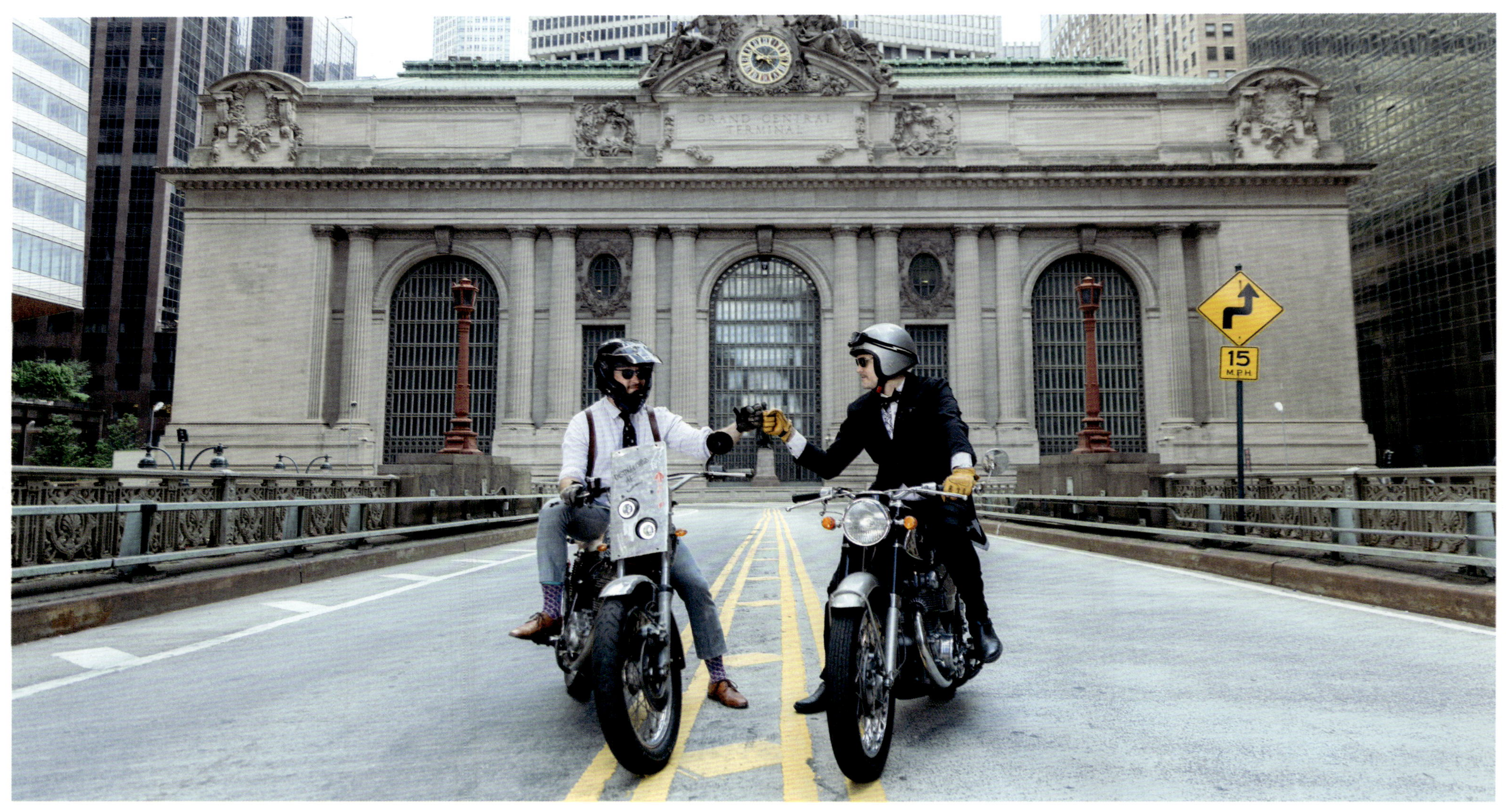

A SUIT SMELLING
LIKE EXHAUST

Ride Hosts: **MIKE HIGGINS & ALLISTER KLINGENSMITH**
Location: **NEW YORK, UNITED STATES**

MIKE: I came across DGR in 2014 the same way so many folks did, on Instagram. Being a vintage moto guy, it piqued my interest. I registered and headed out the next morning, grabbing my tweed jacket and helmet, and stuffing a shop rag into my breast pocket at the last minute. It didn't disappoint; I found myself amongst an eclectic group in lower Manhattan. Making fast friends amidst the gentry, I volunteered to help the following year. I was hooked.

A series of random events thrust me into the lead role as host and organizer of the New York City ride. I embraced the challenge, having met Allister on the 2015 ride I managed to get him to join me. We pulled together a good crew around us and have proudly grown the DGR NYC ride to be one of the premier rides worldwide.

ALLISTER: I happened upon a random DGR post somewhere, cobbled together a suit that I didn't mind smelling like exhaust, grabbed a buddy and prayed that my little CB360 would make it all 20 miles. We ended up at Lincoln Center, were told by the NYPD to disperse because the President showed up and they had better things to do than babysit 250 bikers in tweed. How things have changed. Little did I know how much a part of the next six years it would end up becoming.

MIKE: NYC is a different place on a moto. It geographically shrinks just for the ease of getting around it provides. But psychologically it changes it too. The moto community in NYC is its own small town. Having grown up riding dirt bikes, it was a natural fit to get one once I landed in New York. The change it made in my experience here is pretty profound. It's become so much more than a way to get around. It's the guys at the garage, the weekends wrenching on each other's bikes, the rides out of the city. It's definitely a passion, a hobby and really part of my lifestyle.

ALLISTER: Motorcycles are community. Be it wrenching in the garage, racing enduros on the weekend, moto-camping in the Catskills or taking over the streets of Manhattan with a bunch of well-dressed riders. It's community, camaraderie and communion on two-wheels.

MIKE: The most common outcome of DGR is making new friends. The city can seem big and lonely. Breaking the

ice over a shared enjoyment of motos has led to plenty of lasting friendships. The DGR in NYC just brings together folks. The focus on mental health the last few years has been really positive, too. In many ways the sheer act of joining in to support the cause is therapeutic. We always hear from people that they'd like to get together more often. And then they organize other meet-ups and weekend rides to bridge the gap until the next DGR.

Organizing the ride is a ton of work. But it's also very rewarding. The month leading up to it can be a bit stressful, just trying to line up everything – for the route, the event, and the local fundraising – in time for the big day. But once we go kickstands up, the work is done, and we try our best to just enjoy the heck out of it.

"MIKE AND I JOKE THAT WE PLAN A THOUSAND-PERSON WEDDING ONCE A YEAR."

NYC brings out some pretty gorgeous motos, and the dapper dress is second to none. We've been able to secure access to some iconic NYC landmarks that give the DGR that wow factor you just couldn't experience on a normal ride through the city. All that is the icing on the cake. Seeing the collection of folks gather each year and the relationships it creates is the most satisfying part. That's what DGR is really all about.

ALLISTER: Mike and I joke that we plan a thousand-person wedding once a year. It's certainly an undertaking to manage all the logistics, the people, the sponsors, the food and the band. And sometimes things don't go as planned. We've both gotten fairly decent at rolling with the punches. All that said, it's amazing on the morning of the event watching the first bikes show up. Seeing everybody in their Sunday best, ready to go and excited. Being in a sea of 1000

motorcycles, escorted through the empty streets of NYC by the NYPD with their lights and sirens full bore, the people on the sidewalks gawking. It's a priceless experience and that's a big part of the draw.

MIKE: My favourite DGR moment was a look Allister and I shared the first time we had a full NYPD escort on the ride. As we pulled out onto the FDR Drive, we suddenly saw the vast sprawling roadway usually jammed with cars, completely cleared for us. We'd worked hard to plan it and arrange the highway patrol support but we both had this wild-eyed, "How the hell did we pull this off?" glance, along with an ear-to-ear grin. That'll stay with me forever.

ALLISTER: A small moment that I enjoy every single year is the calm before the storm. I somehow manage to be the first one at the meet up point and seeing my lonely bike sitting there, knowing a thousand more will soon be joining it is pretty amazing. It's a reminder that without people like Mike and the fantastic community, these events just couldn't or wouldn't happen.

MIKE: For fundraising, I do the basics for my personal ride. I push stuff to Facebook, post on Instagram, and hit up a few of the regular folk. As a host, I want to lead by example, so I make sure I get a respectable few hundred bucks each year. We also push to get local sponsorship for the ride, so our efforts tend toward driving that number up instead. If that corporate support and our planning work can help us throw a bigger, better event, we feel that translates to riders embracing their own fundraising much more.

ALLISTER: I fundraise the same way any self-respecting fundraiser does. I grovel and play the guilt card. A little competition with other DGR rides – and fellow ride hosts – also goes a long way.

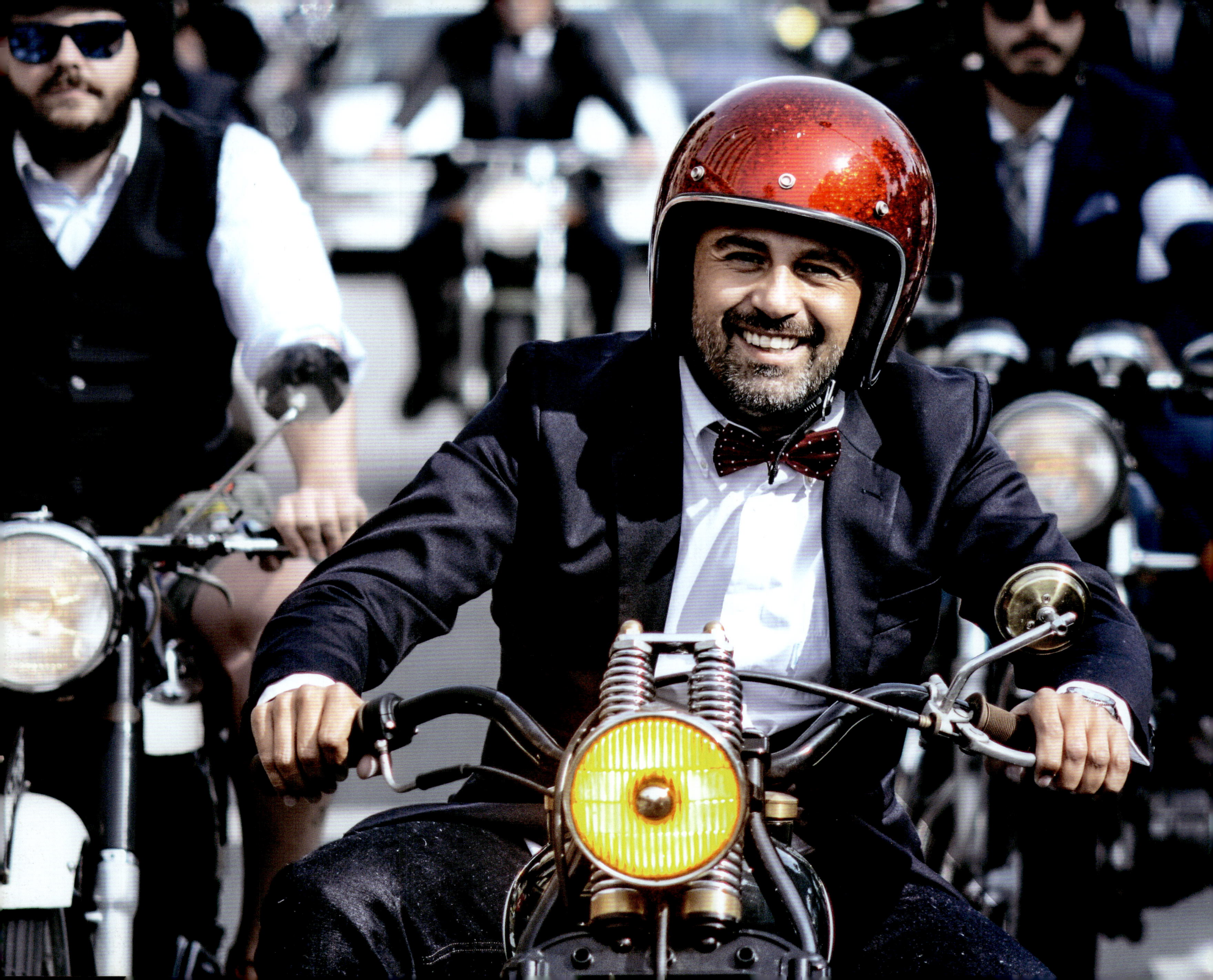

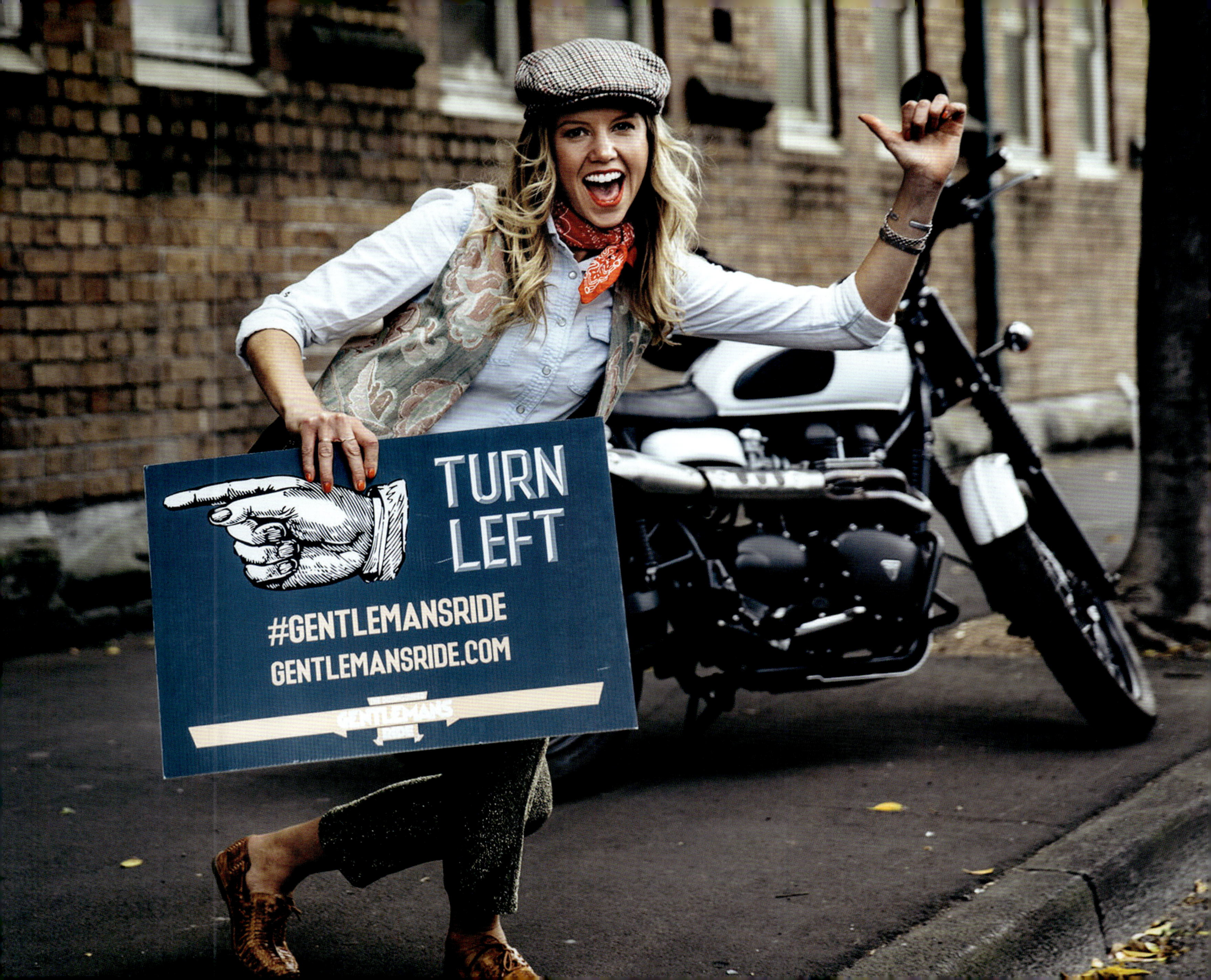

TURN
LEFT
#GENTLEMANSRIDE
GENTLEMANSRIDE.COM
GENTLEMANS

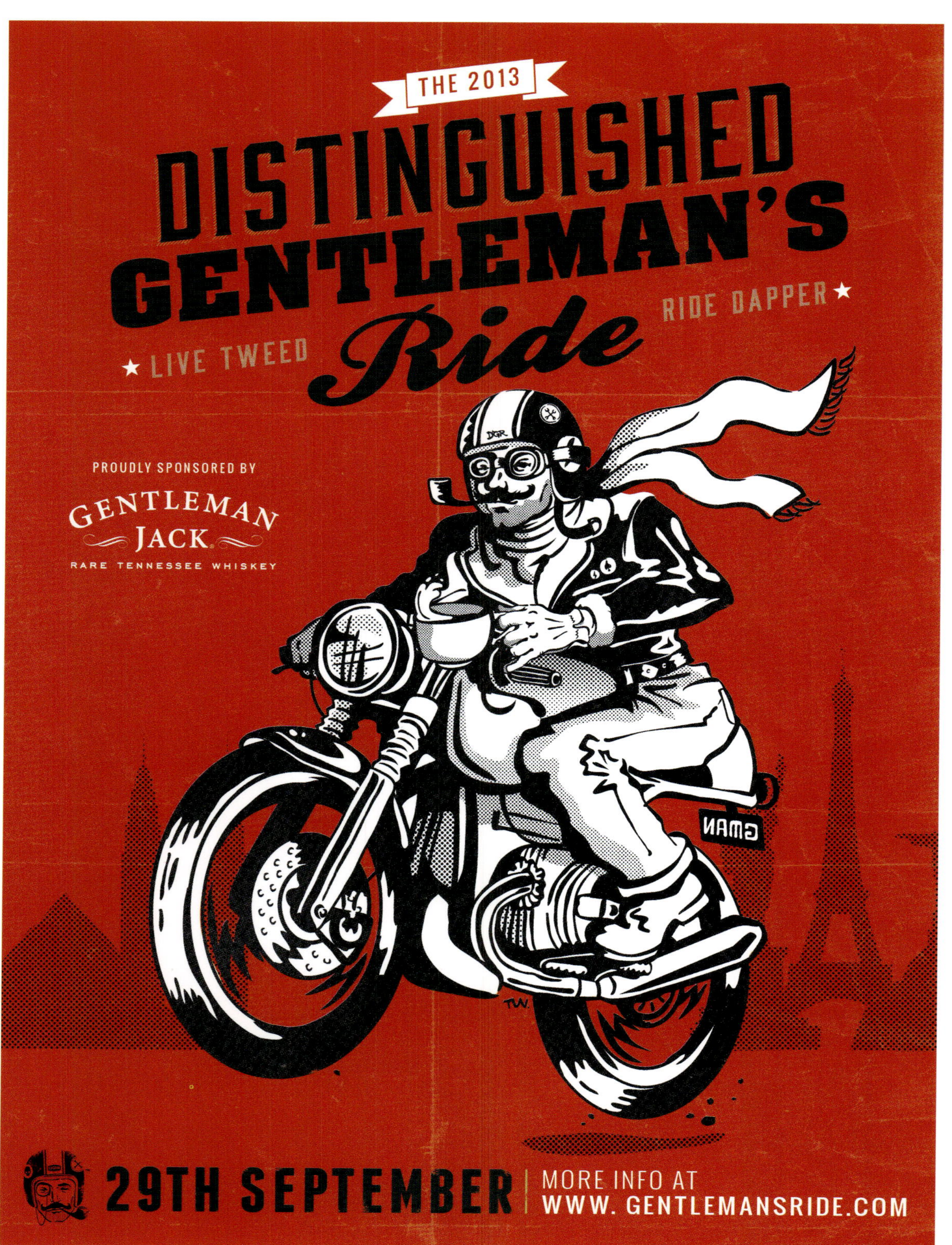

2013 Ride Poster

Designed by Tom Wall
Along with revealing Sir Remington Silversteed astride his classic steed, it was our goal to emphasize the reach of our event through the use of multiple international landmarks in the background. Our first ever sponsor, Gentleman Jack, funded the first ever website built for DGR.

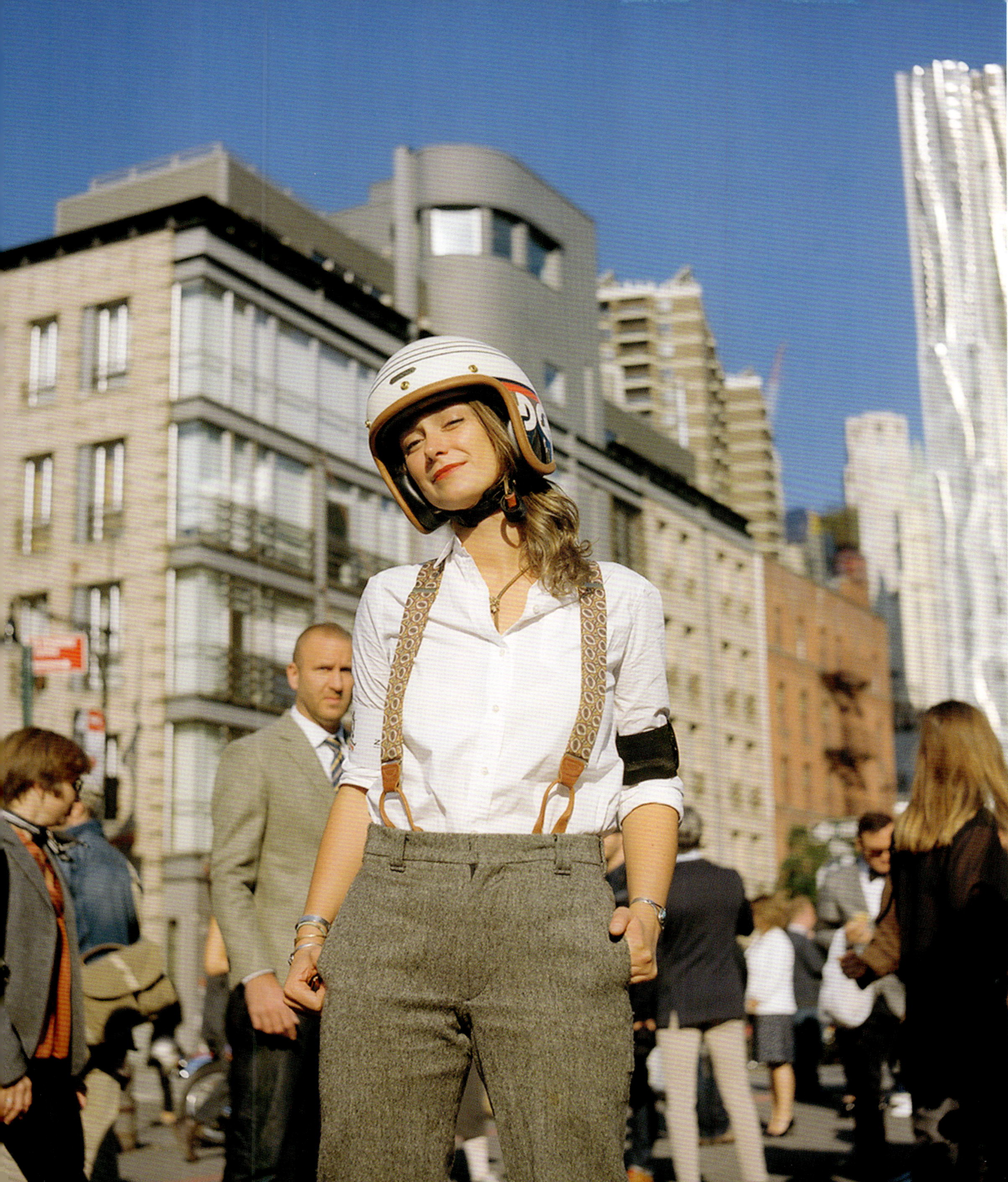

Kirsten Midura

"My first year, I rode with a photographer friend shooting backwards from the back of my bike. For one, it was hilarious to see the faces of men who had never seen a woman ride with a pillion of her own, let alone backwards.

We wanted to get a shot of the whole ride with the city in the background, so I rode to the front. I will never forget the image of riding over a completely empty NYC bridge, save for our ride, with a police escort in the front, and a thousand riders following behind me - including DGR Founder Mark Hawwa - all for an incredibly important cause. At that moment, it resonated for me how special this event really is."

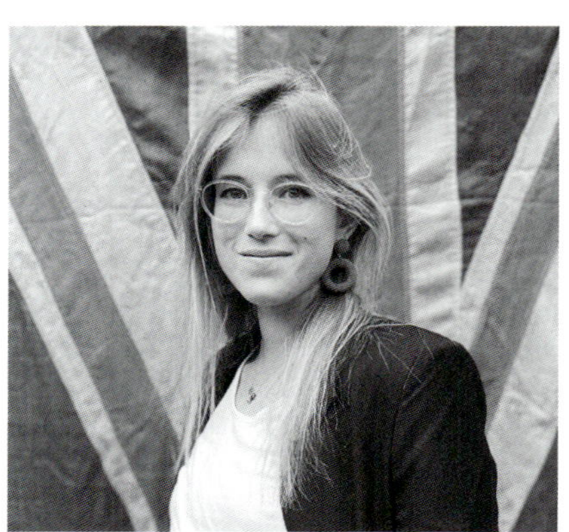

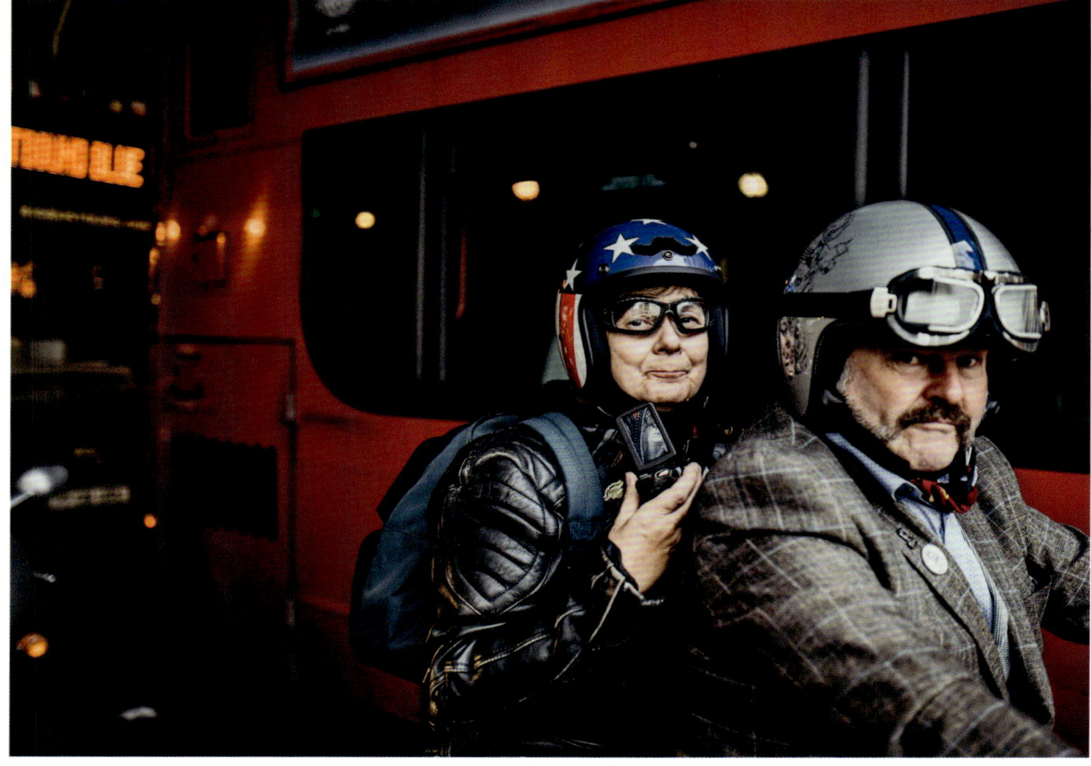

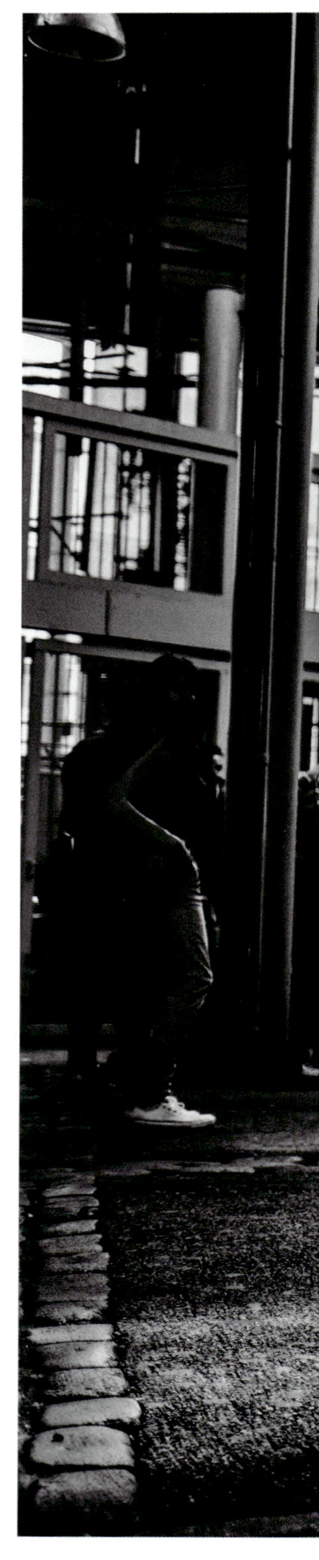

DGR PHOTOGRAPHER:
Amy Shore

The first time I shot the DGR was in London, 2014. At this point, I hadn't really experienced motorcycle life and certainly wasn't a rider myself. But as the sun came pouring through the gaps in the railroad above Borough Market, lighting up exhaust fumes from the 600 bikes that were all shuffling to fit in, I knew I needed to be part of this motorcycle world.

Everyone looked so cool! I mean, that might have been more thanks to the 'Distinguished' part of the ride more than their usual riding attire. The ladies riding came across as confident and full of life, it was inspirational to see so many at the event rather than just feeling like the odd one out stood there in my dress with my cameras hanging around me.

At the 2015 DGR, I sat backwards on a motorbike for the first time, shooting the London ride once again in my new copper colored helmet that I had bought, knowing that I would end up using it a lot more. For the 2016 ride, I was joined by my dad for the first time as my rider, having got my own bike test booked for the following day, this would be my last ride as a non-rider. Since then, I have ridden every DGR and felt fully inside the community that the DGR has created.

For onlookers, it's clearly not a form of showing off, but instead, it's attention-grabbing for all of the right reasons; to promote awareness of men's mental health. The sense of camaraderie between riders, non-riders, families and onlookers is so very apparent and at the heart of this wonderful event.

I feel that I could be on the other side of the world, in a country where I don't speak the language, and still be welcomed to join a DGR. There are very few clubs around the world with that much reach, supporting such a good cause and who can look so damn fine in the process.

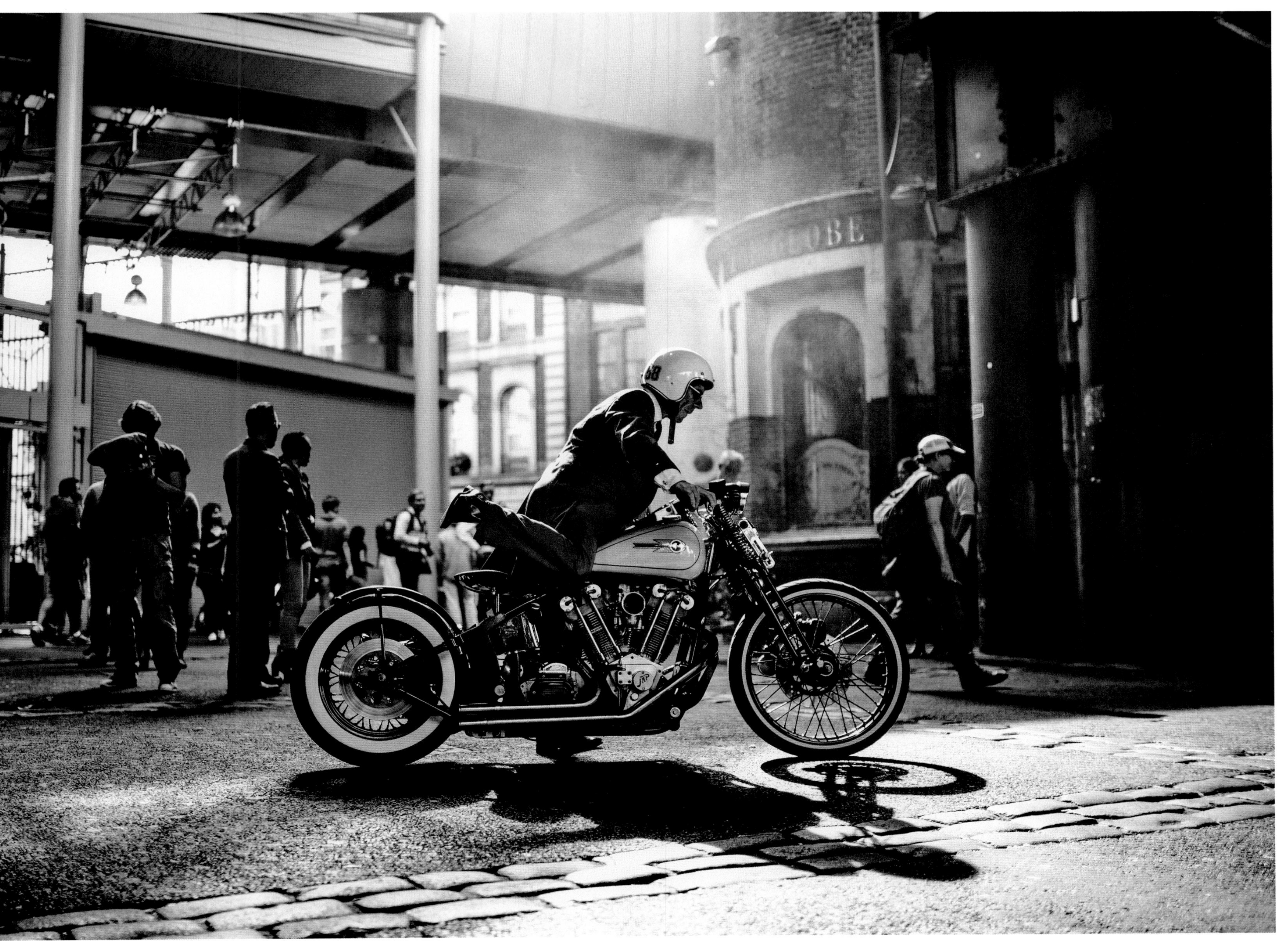

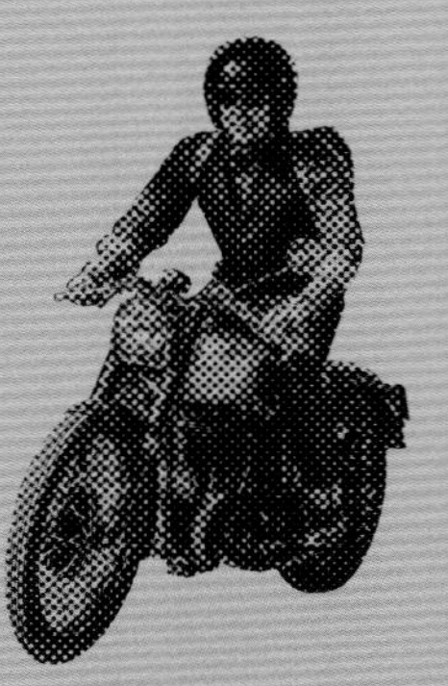

2014

- R I D E   T H R E E -

WITH **257 CITIES** AND **20,000 RIDERS** TAKING PART, THE 2014 RIDE SAW US WORKING WITH PROSTATE CANCER FOUNDATIONS IN AUSTRALIA, USA, UK, CANADA AND NEW ZEALAND. WE ALSO BEGAN OUR GLOBAL PARTNER RELATIONSHIP WITH TRIUMPH MOTORCYCLES.

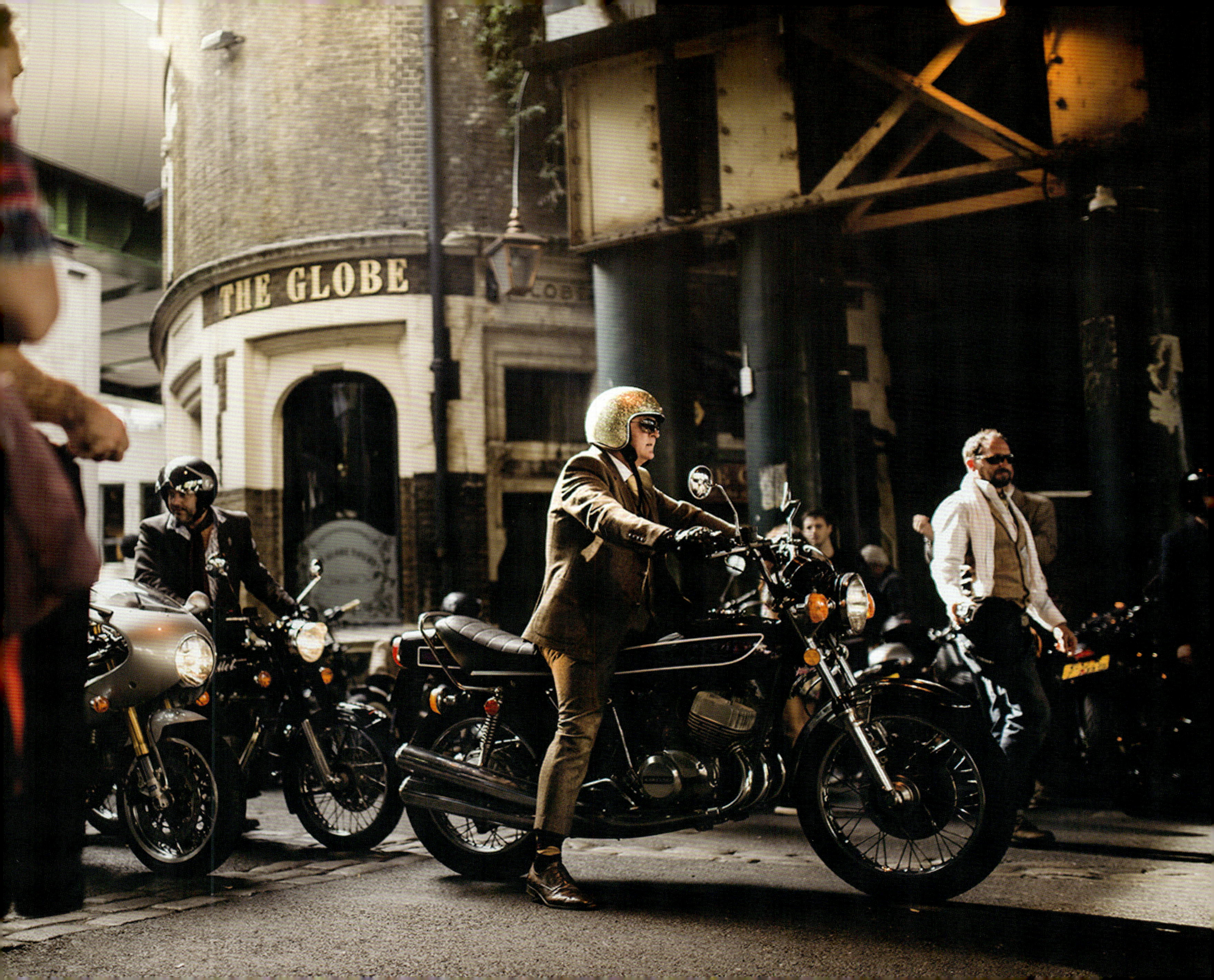
THE GLOBE

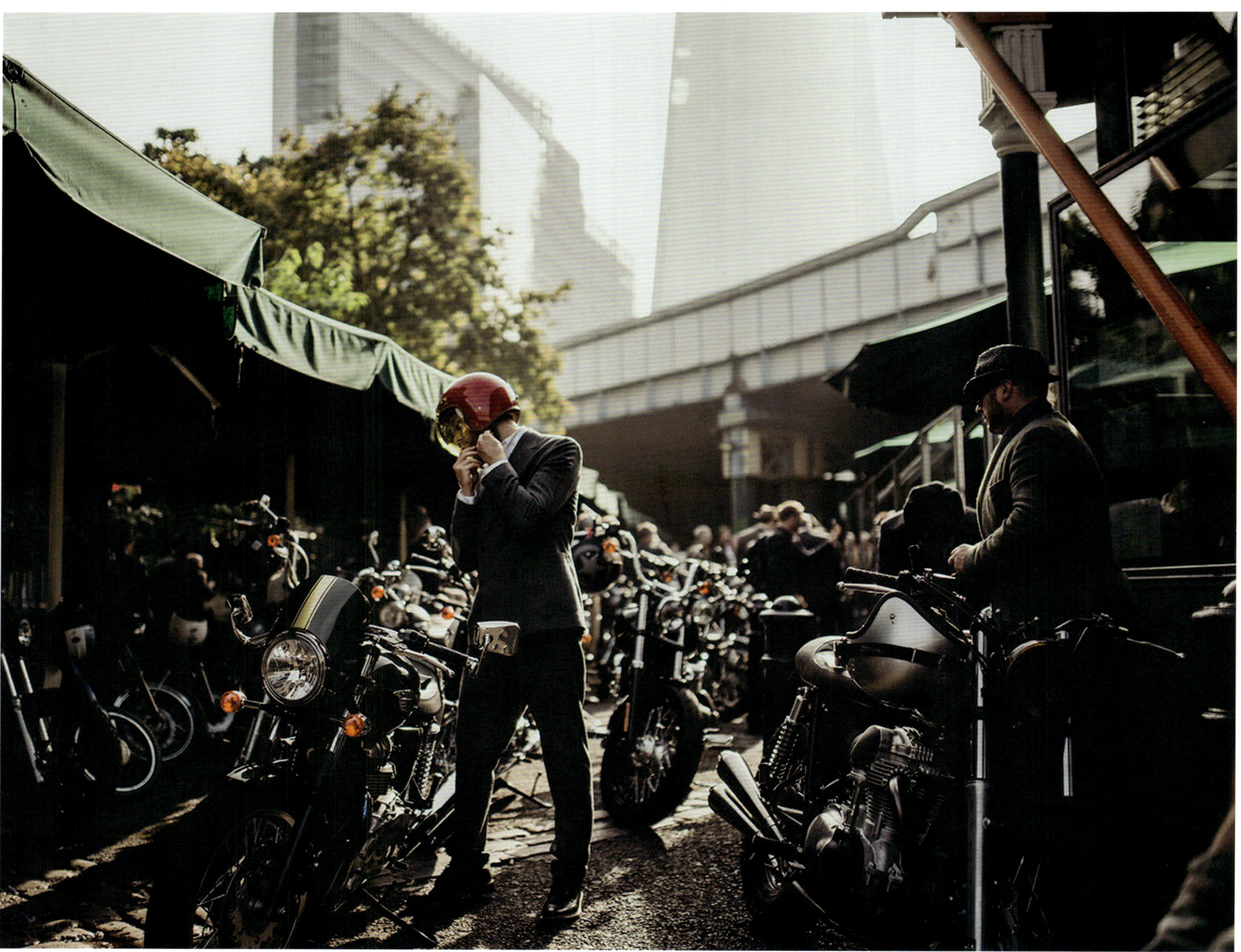

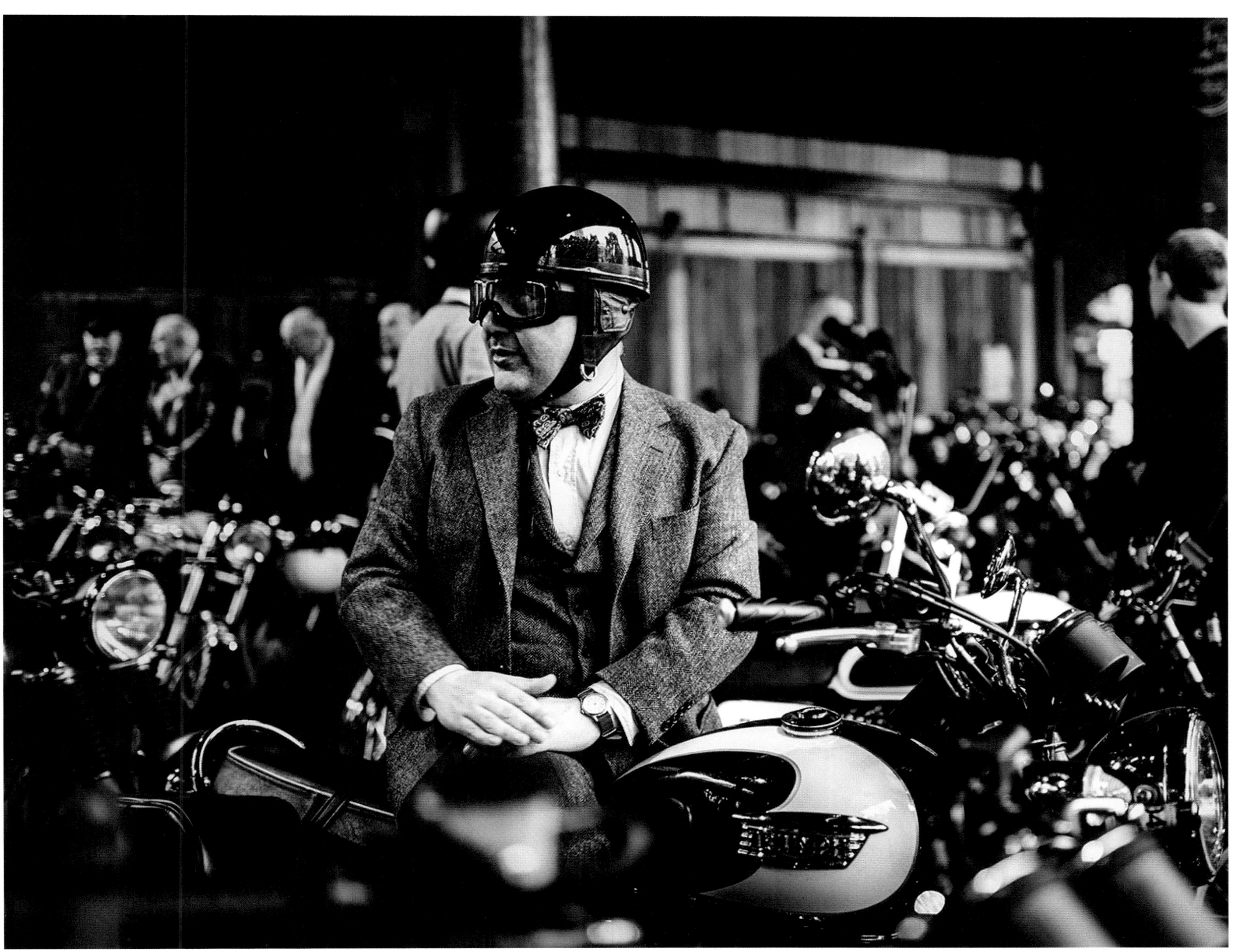

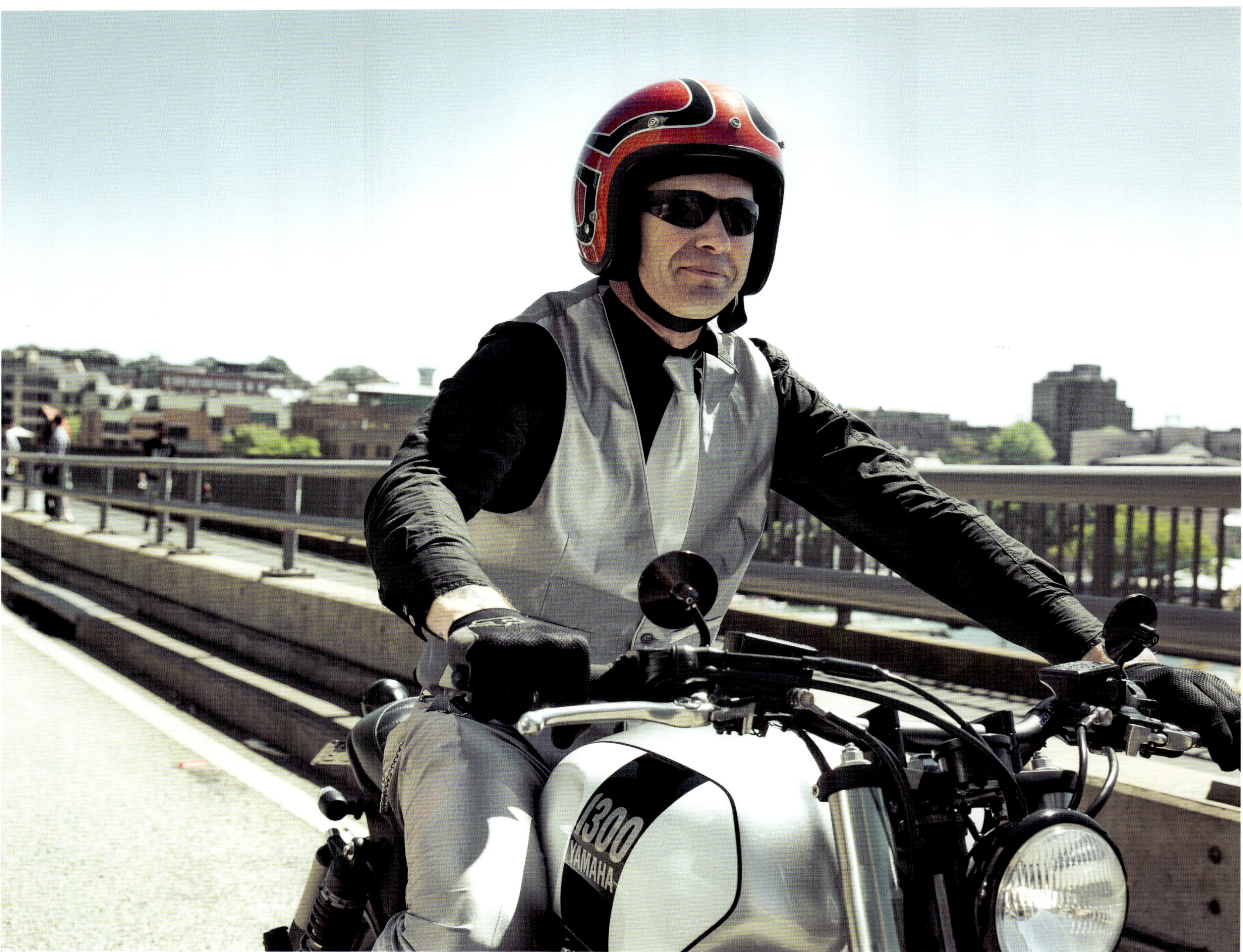
1300
YAMAHA

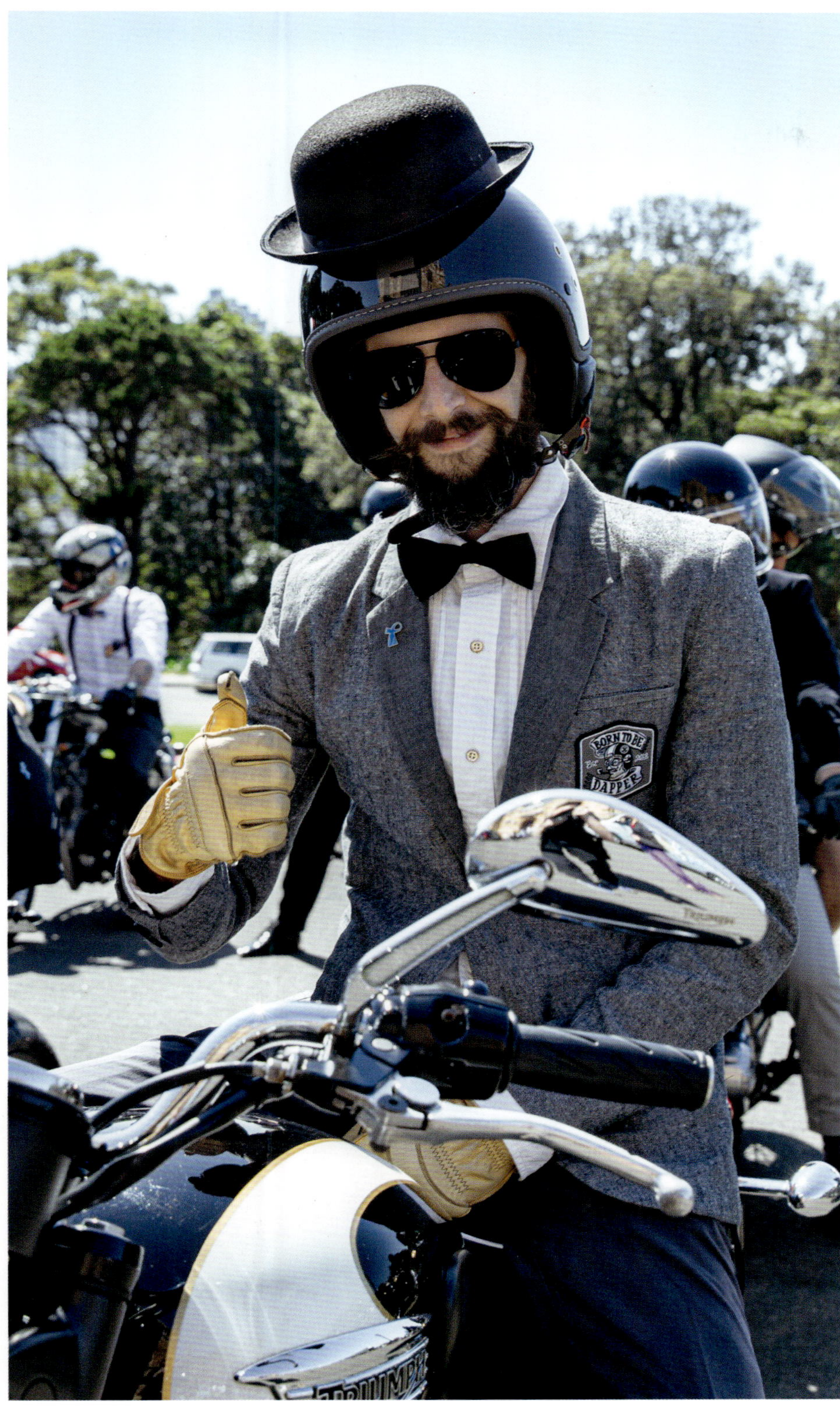

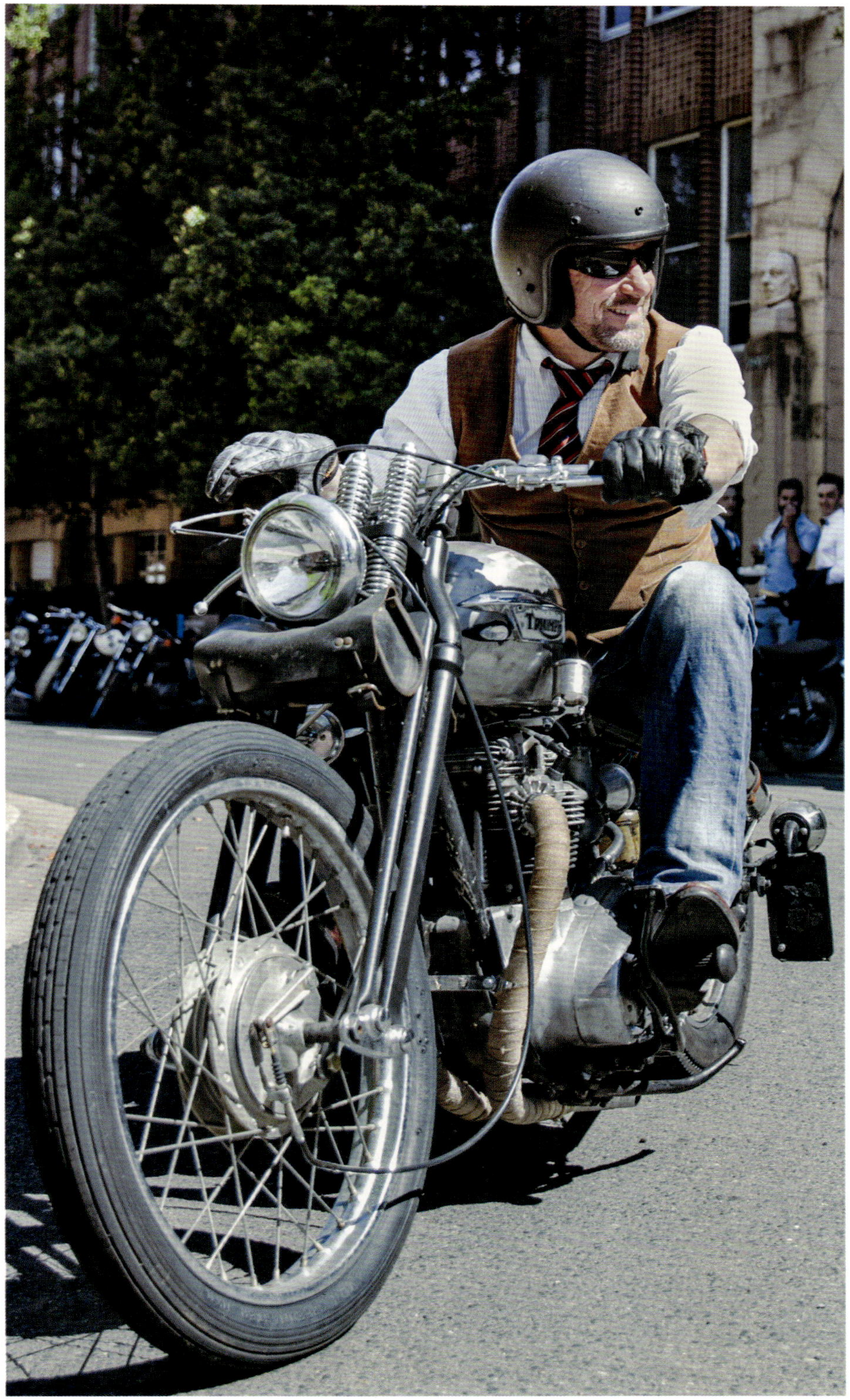

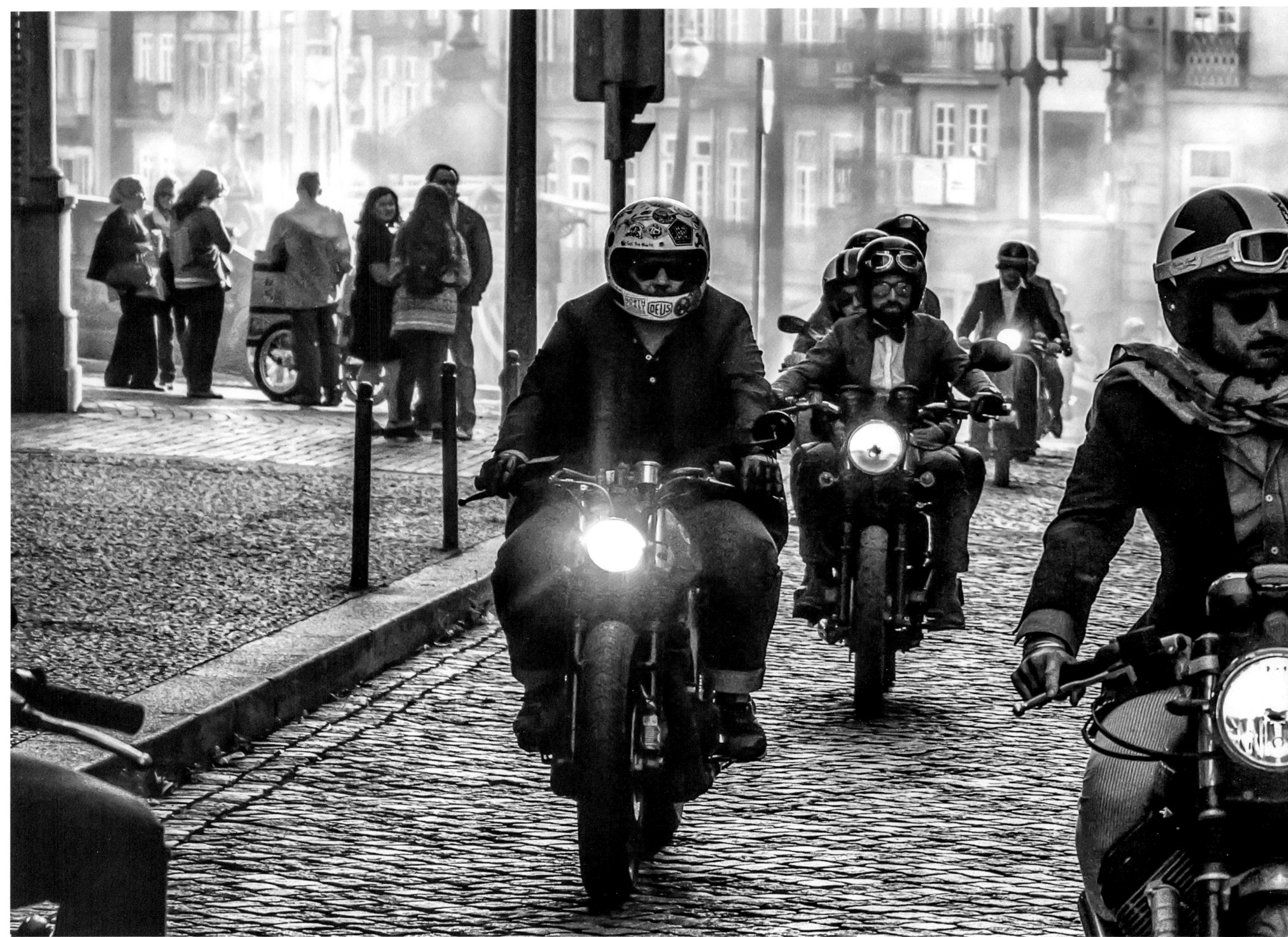

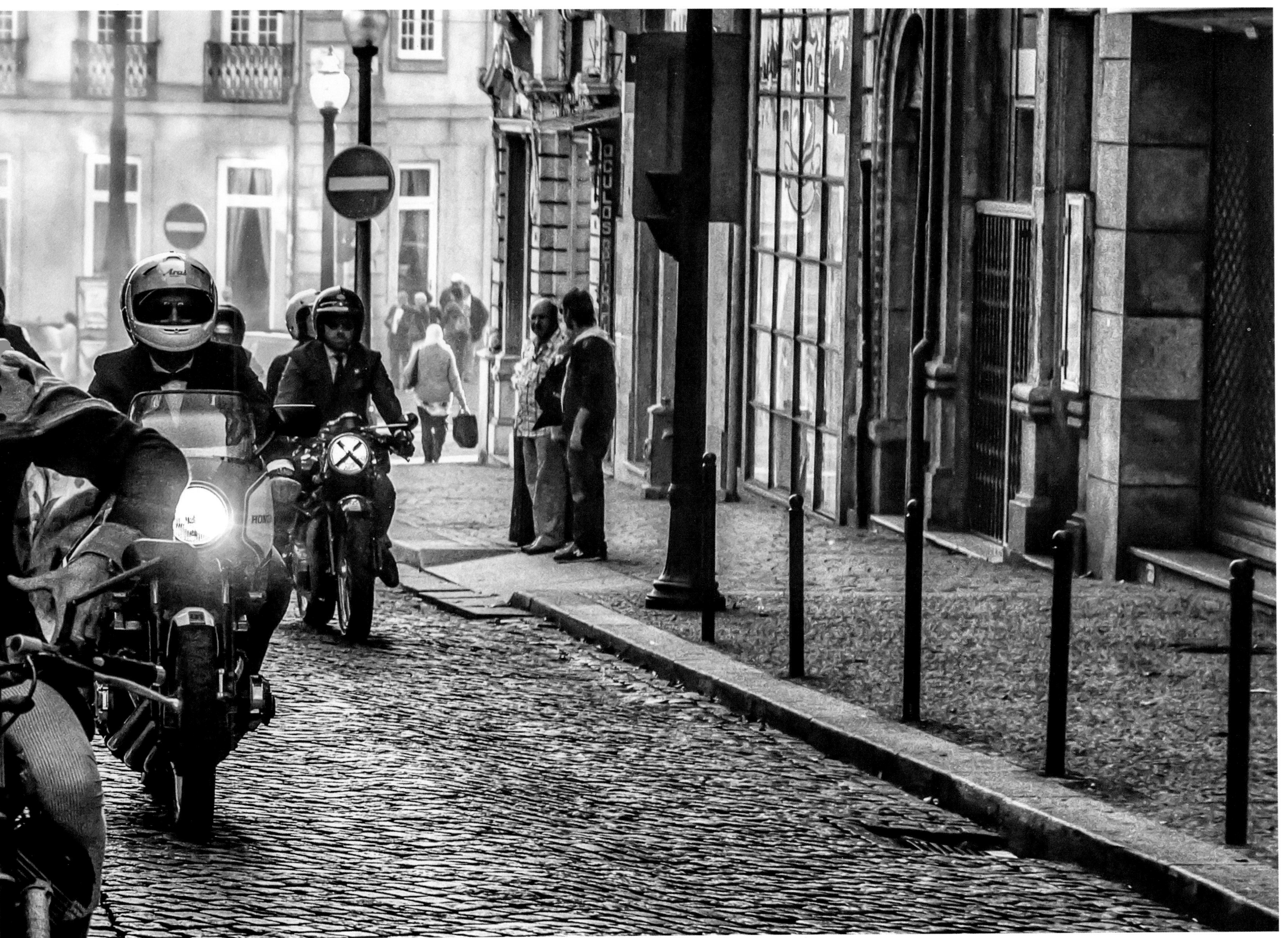

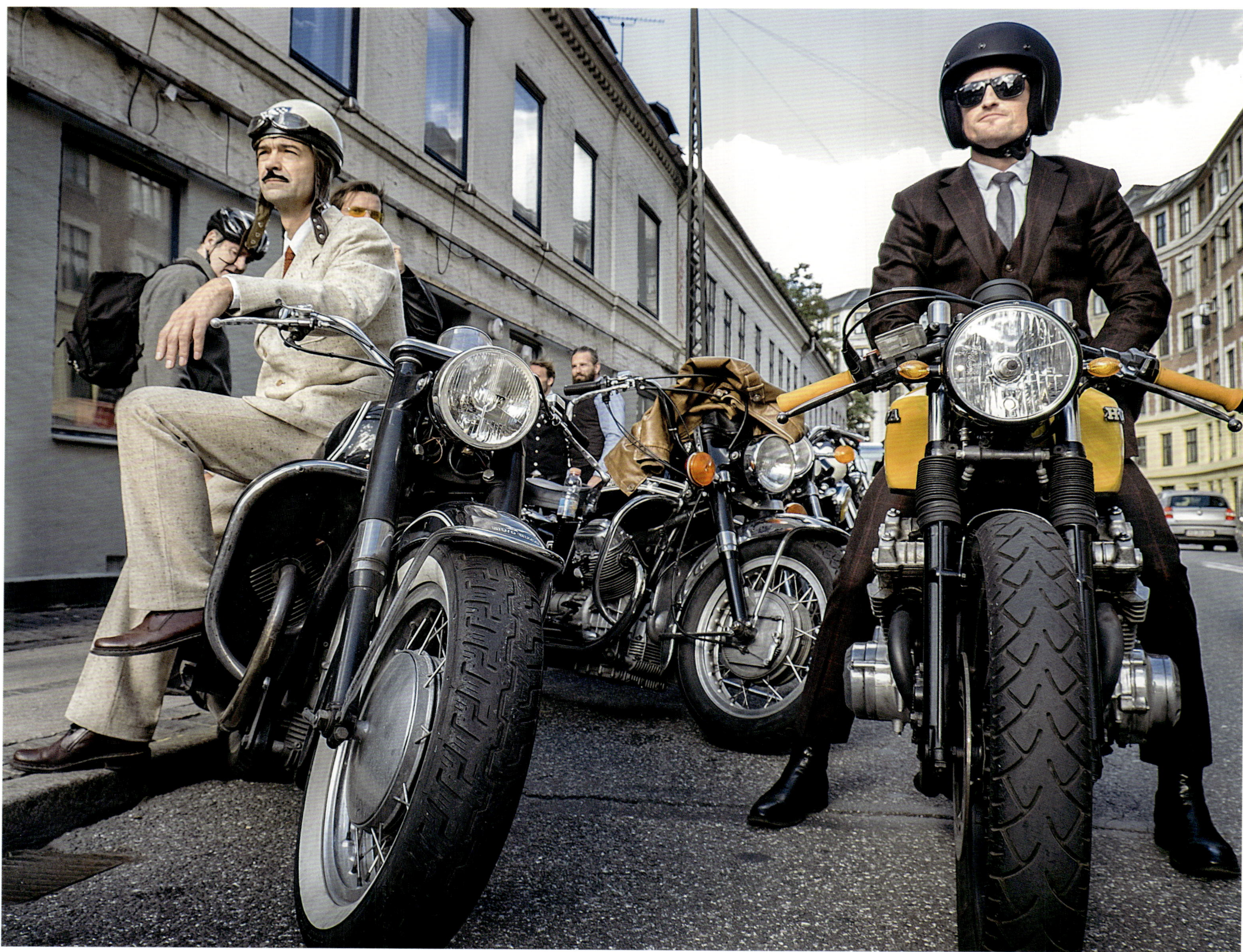

2014 Ride Poster

Designed by Tom Wall

Sir Remington bursts onto the poster, this time accompanied by his female acquaintance while sporting a helmet that showcased the first-ever iteration of the iconic umbrella and spanner design that would go on to be a staple of DGR. This marked the first year with Triumph as a sponsor, who were directly referenced by the use of their scrambler in the poster.

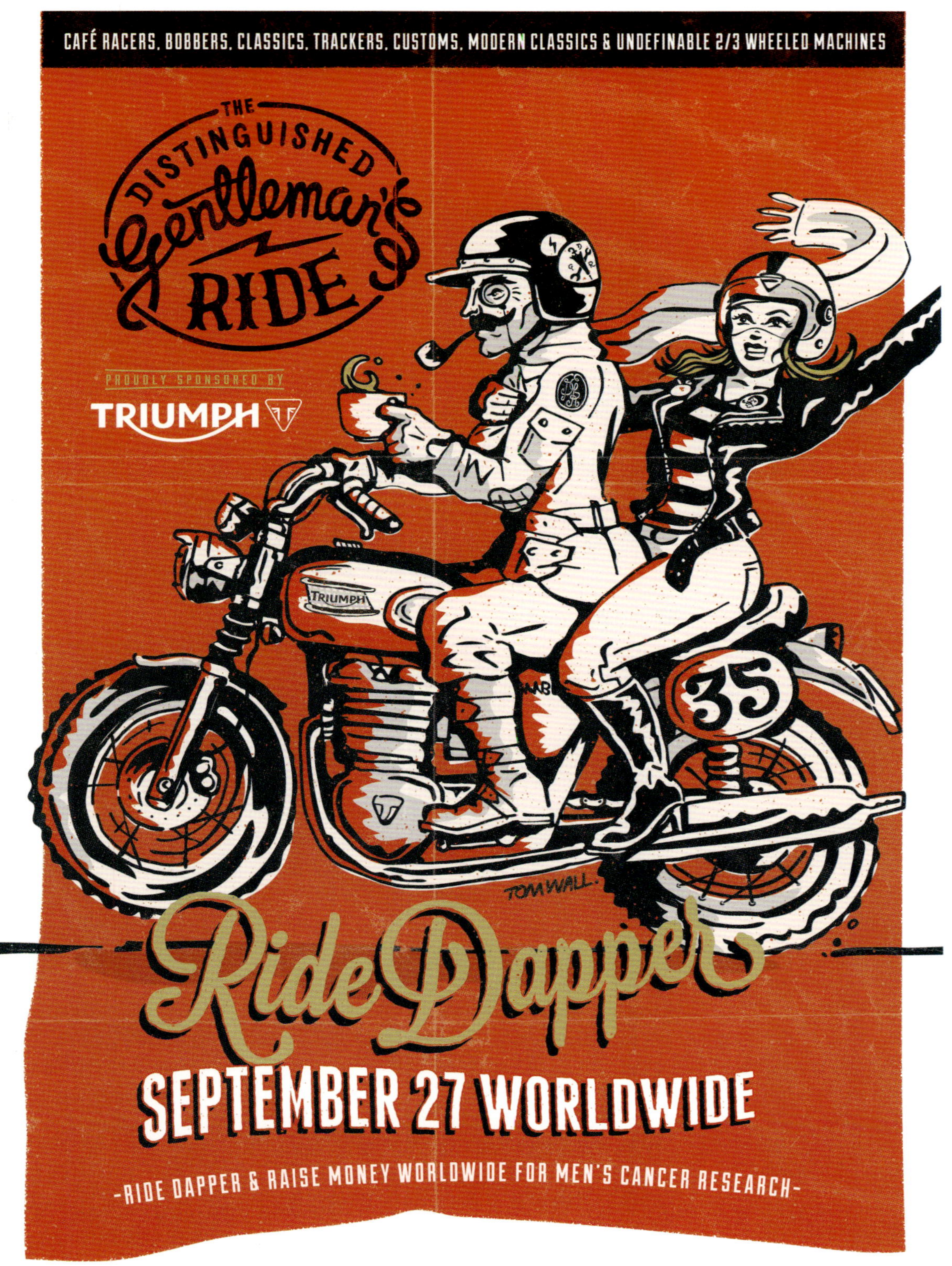

Always humble and wonderful, Phil shared his story of his battle with prostate cancer. His story began with the common symptoms - frequent trips to the bathroom and a bit of pain in his kidneys. A check-up later revealed his prostate cancer diagnosis.

"When you're told that you have cancer, you think the world suddenly stops spinning - but it doesn't... After you get the news, you leave the office and forget almost everything that was said. It's such a shock. I went outside and talked to my wife - we had to go back in again to ask what happened and if I really had cancer.

I remember going for a walk on my own to process it, but at the same time my wife's going through it as well. I didn't have time to be shocked, I've got children to look after, I've still got a job, still got a mortgage and all the bills - and you just try to deal with it.

is everything to me. It's so relaxing, exciting - when I go out on the bike all you think about is the next corner or the next straight. It's that adventure of going places you've never been before. When I'm out on the bike, I don't have cancer. For those hours, I'm just Phil again. I'm 16 again, having a whirl of a time.

I haven't been to The Distinguished Gentleman's Ride before. Luckily this time Triumph have offered me a bike and I'm really looking forward to it. I'm doing this ride to make people aware and to raise awareness. Any chance I get to ride a motorcycle, I'm looking forward to.

We talk about when we do the ride, that we're doing it for our fathers, brothers, our friends - I really want to do this for my son. If we all get together, we can actually beat cancer. And I mean it may not win my battle, but hopefully it'll win the war for the next generation."

to get out there and show London what we're all about," said Phil. Teeming with anticipation for the ride, what Phil didn't know was that the bike wasn't built just for him to ride on the day, it was his to have and take home to enjoy those adventures that he loved so dearly.

Presented on stage by Miles, Phil was introduced to the masses of gentlefolk, along with the Dapper Bonnie. It wasn't until Miles uttered the words "But what Phil doesn't know..." that Phil began to be suspicious. Gifting him the bike in return for his support and bravery in raising such important awareness for these cause areas, Phil's face just lit up. The adventure-seeker now had a new adventure-machine.

Tears of disbelief swelled, but subsided when Phil took his opportunity to do precisely what he came to do - to raise awareness amongst the folks of DGR and to encour-

GONE BUT NOT FORGOTTEN: The Phil Green Story

In 2017, in a video produced by Triumph Motorcycles, The Distinguished Gentleman's Ride introduced Phil Green to the DGR global community. This is his story.

In 7 years, I had 5 operations. I had radiotherapy, chemotherapy, cyberknife - I have cancer and it won't go away.

It's not just about me, it's about my family and my children. If I could have prevented it, or if I can help prevent someone from getting it and going through what I've gone through - it's worth it. It's worth going and getting checked out. I am quite the optimist, always a glass half-full and I try to live like that. Living for now is making the most of what you're doing and not living to exist, you've got to live to enjoy yourself. There are loads of things I've done in between my treatment, but I'm always looking forward to my next chance to go on an adventure with my children, the next chance to have lunch with my wife.

I got into motorcycling when I was 16. I absolutely love it, and I really am passionate about it. Riding motorcycles

At the London ride in 2017, Triumph Head of Brand Management, Miles Perkins, uncovered the Dapper Bonnie; a Triumph T100 custom built with a Harris Tweed seat and burnt orange tank. This bike was built for Phil to ride during The Distinguished Gentleman's Ride, after sharing his story about his battle with prostate cancer with the Triumph and DGR community to bring further awareness to the importance of early detection.

The day was a wonderful one; atypical to the usual London weather, the sun peaked its way through passing clouds, giving the dapper folks warm suns and warmer hearts as they make their way to meet.

Phil met Miles and the team from Triumph and Movember, taking the time to chat to folks and continue his mission to help men take action on their health. "I can't wait

age the men listening to take control of their health and get checked. The weighty message, delivered with humility and hope, culminated in excitement and anticipation to take this wonderful bike on its maiden voyage. On this new adventure, Phil lead hundreds of dapper gentlefolk through the streets of London, with a smile and a wave.

His message is ingrained in DGR history, and Phil will always be an ambassador for Triumph and The Distinguished Gentleman's Ride. Sadly, Phil lost his battle with prostate cancer in January 2021. We were humbled to have been able to share his story and are grateful for all he did to encourage men to get checked.

Thank you to the Green family for allowing us to share Phil's story, and continue his mission of raising awareness and saving lives.

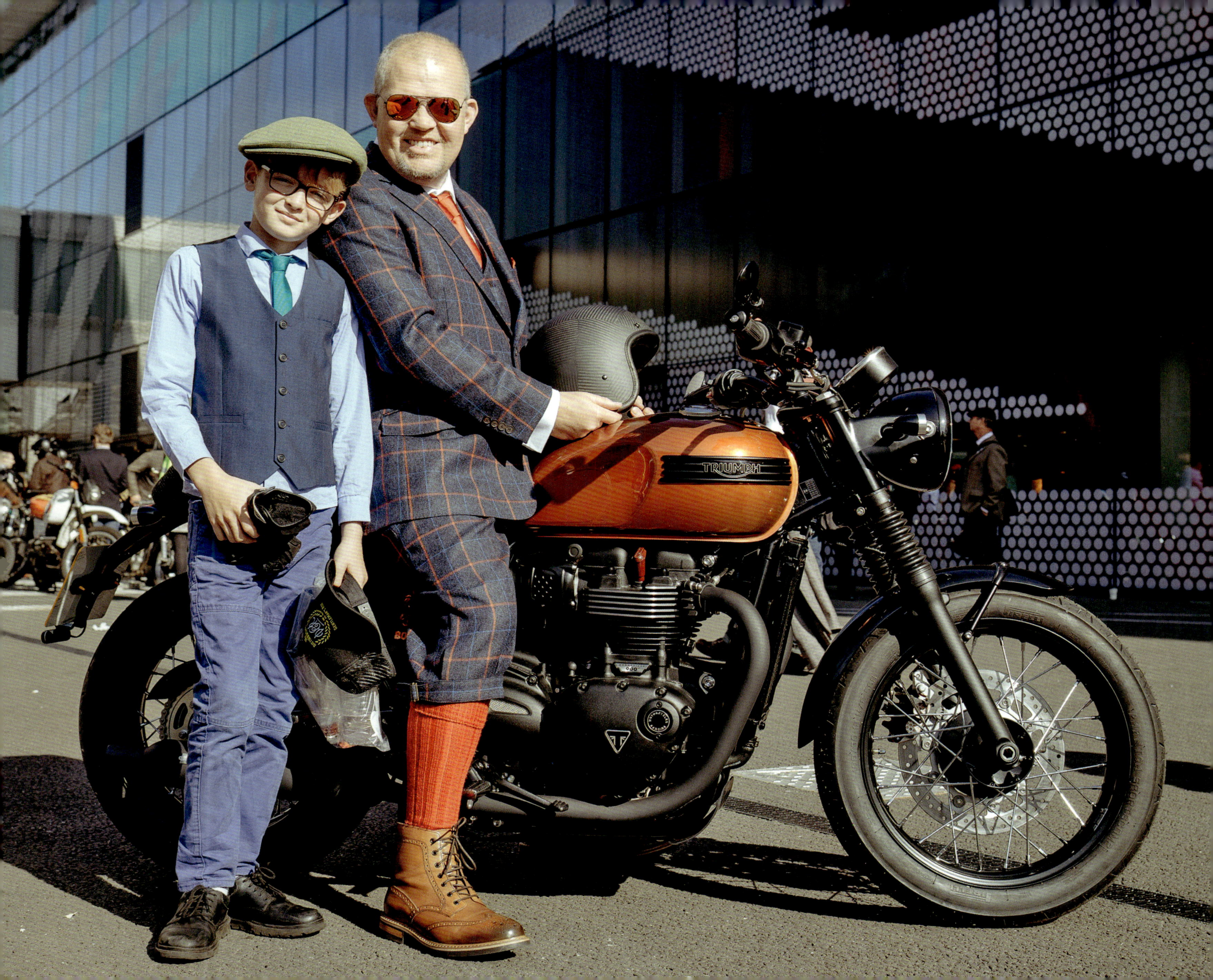

TRACKERS

A genre of off-road classic motorcycles originating from speedway, flat track and grasstrack racing. Built to keep the weight low and the fun high, real trackers are pure race machines that don't have the headlights or indicators required to ride on public roads. Those that do are usually referred to as 'street trackers.'

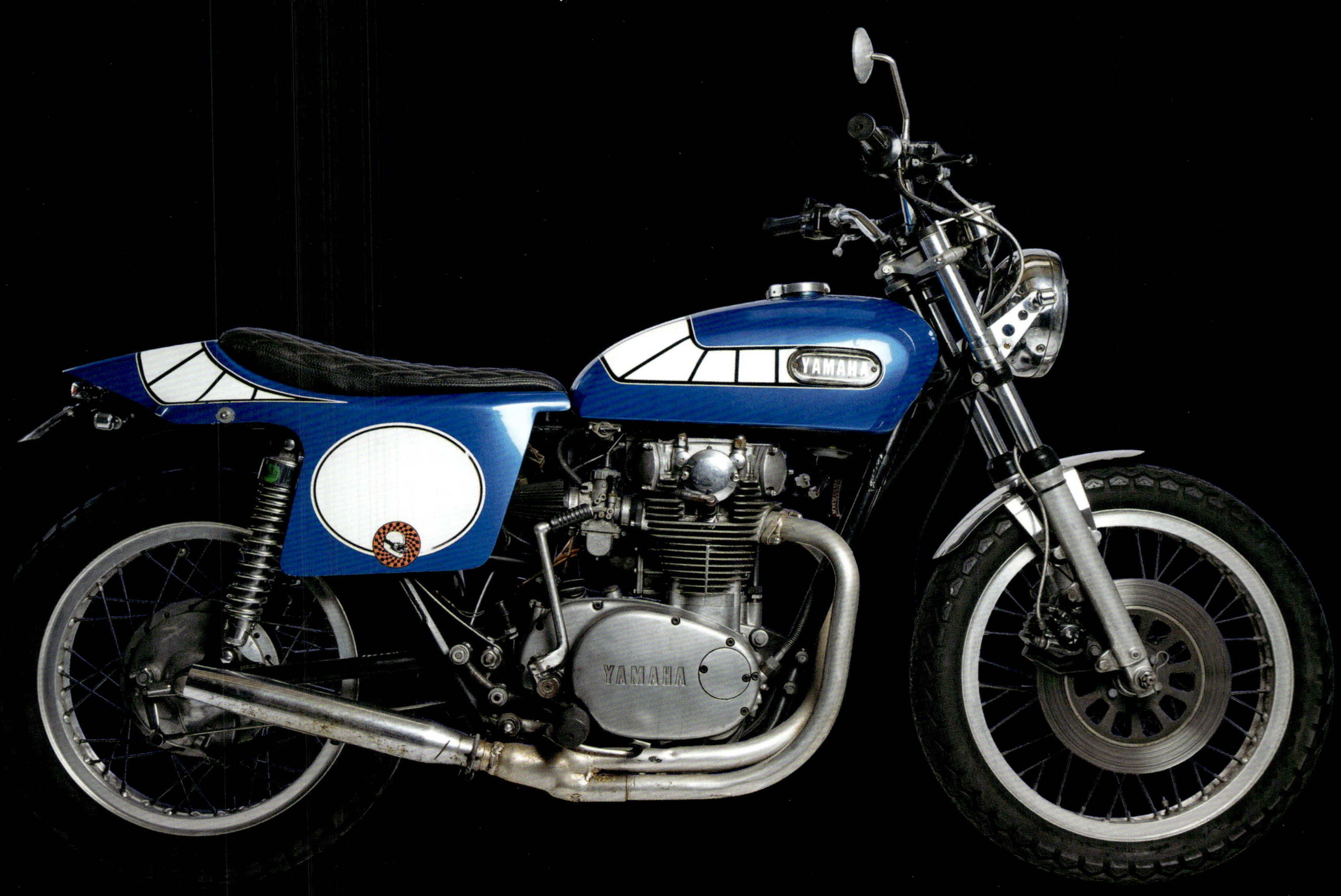

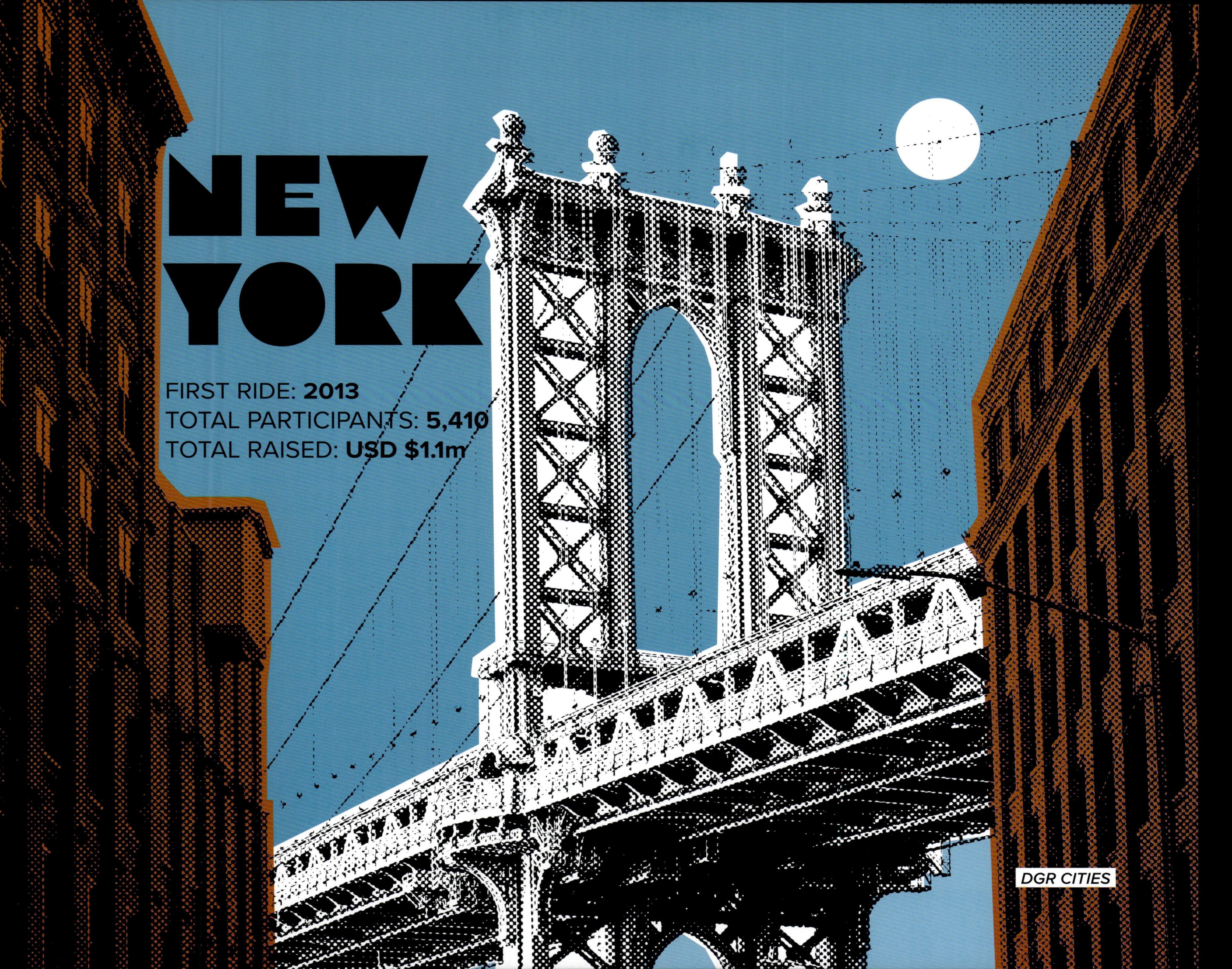

NEW YORK
FIRST RIDE: 2013
TOTAL PARTICIPANTS: 5,410
TOTAL RAISED: USD $1.1m
DGR CITIES

MUSTACHES ON THE MOVE

DGR &
Movember

The world's largest and most stylish charity motorcycling event was growing far beyond what was ever thought. By 2016, The Distinguished Gentleman's Ride was in over 500 cities, and in 90 countries. Riders were joining the gentry by the hundreds, empowered by the charge of their iron horses and a will to use their passions to ride for a cause. It became clear that for these dapper riders, there was a need to do more for them by delivering better health outcomes.

So it's for these people that Movember and The Distinguished Gentleman's Ride united, unified by their joint ambitions of raising funds and awareness for men's health. The world's largest and most stylish charity motorcycling event, and the world's largest men's health organization; riding side-by-side with vintage motorcycles and facial hair to match.

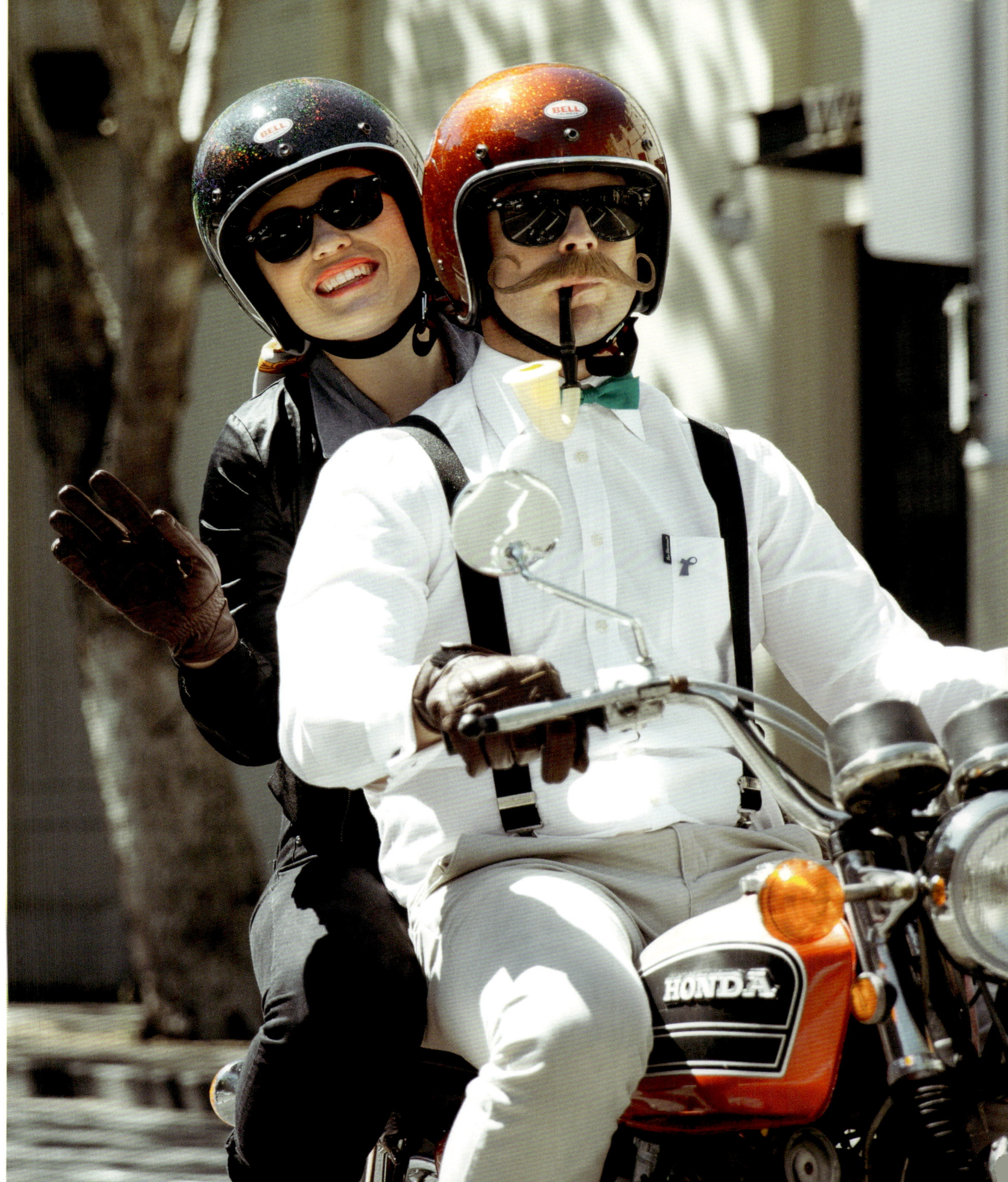

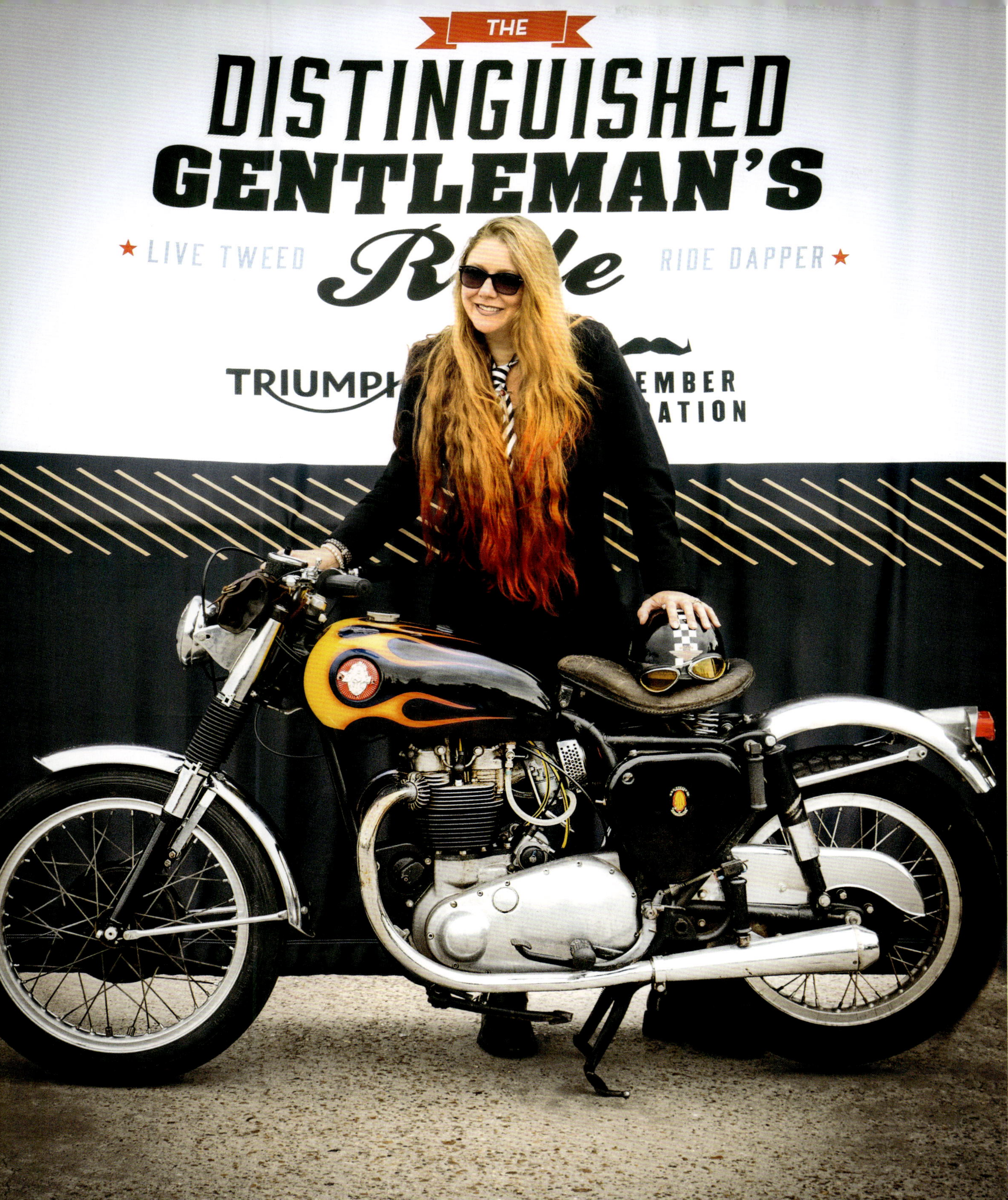

CLOSE TO HER HEART

Jamie Farquhar-Rizzo

"I bought my 1959 BSA Super Rocket when I was 18. By 2011 I was running several motorcycle events and I wanted to do more to improve the image of motorcyclists. Then I found Mark Hawwa and DGR online and brought it to Houston, Texas. We started with 30 riders. Once the photos were online, everyone wanted in for 2013.

This ride is very close to my heart after losing my grandfather to cancer. I have now seen many of my closest riding buddies battle it and win. That's what it is all about.

In 2018 Charlie Morse joined the ride. He had stage 4 cancer; his final wish was to ride in DGR Houston. He rode all day, smiling and handing out ribbons. Charlie passed away peacefully that evening on his terms after having the time of his life.

We love DGR because it connects motorcyclists. I'll make sure there is always a place where riders can meet up, kick tires and talk, because socialization through motorcycles keeps us running strong."

Pipeburn.com

"Has it really been 10 years already? It feels like only yesterday I pulled out the old suit – usually relegated to the likes of court cases, weddings and funerals – and joined a group of Distinguished Gentlefolk in Sydney back in 2012. When I saw 100 sharply dressed people turn up at the first ride, I had a feeling that DGR would become something really special.

It blows my mind to think that this simple idea Mark Hawwa was inspired by after seeing a photo of Don Draper in a suit sitting on a motorcycle has turned into a global event in 804 cities. Seeing all these amazing photos from around the world puts a big grin on my face. Not only does the ride put a smile on everyone's faces, but the fact that the DGR community has raised over $37 million for men's health is staggering.

As DGR has grown over the years, so has the custom motorcycle scene around the world. We've seen so many amazing custom bikes partake in the ride over the years and we've been lucky to feature many of them on Pipeburn.com. Starting out as a nondescript SquareSpace website

in the late-naughties, the site found itself in the right place at the right time. The next thing we knew, we were hosting very small and casual ride days for our Sydney readers as a kind of meet-and-greet.

After a flurry of emails from a guy called Mark, one particular ride in 2011 was attended by a talkative, tall, and very excited custom Yamaha SR500 rider whose last name was 'Hawwa.'

Anxious that the Honda monkey tank on his bike wouldn't last the distance, he brought with him two flasks full of fuel that the bike was wearing like a gunfighter wears their six-shooters. Seven hours and two empty flasks later, we felt like Mark was an old mate.

We feel privileged to have played a small part as media partner of DGR and we look forward to being part of the journey for the next 10 years of riding dapper – I only wish I could still fit into that first suit I wore back in 2012!"

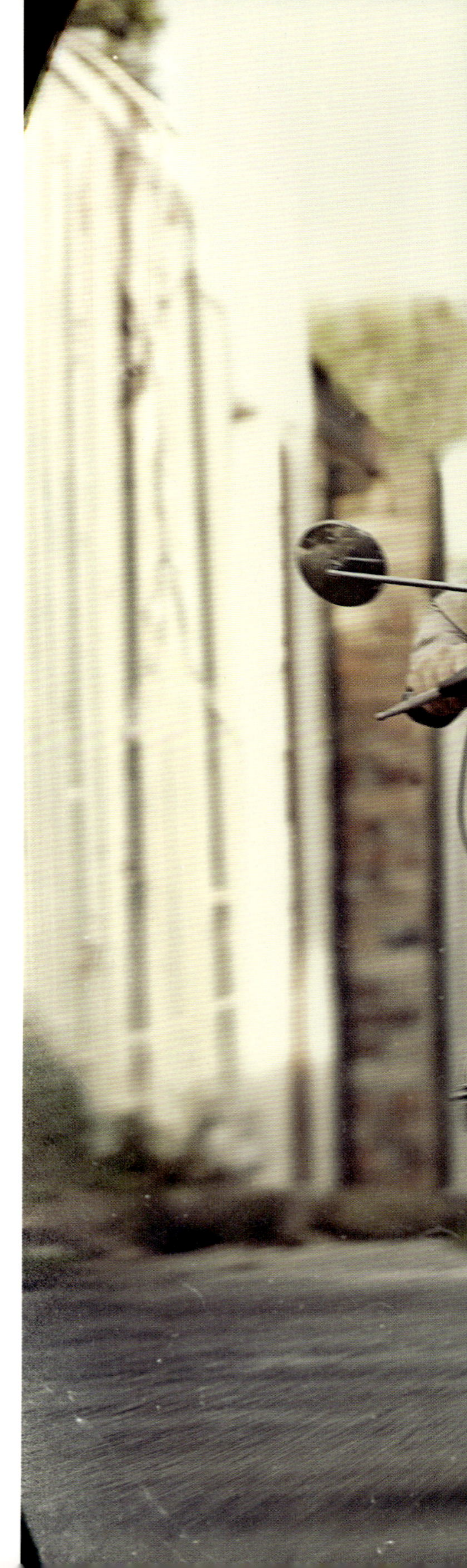

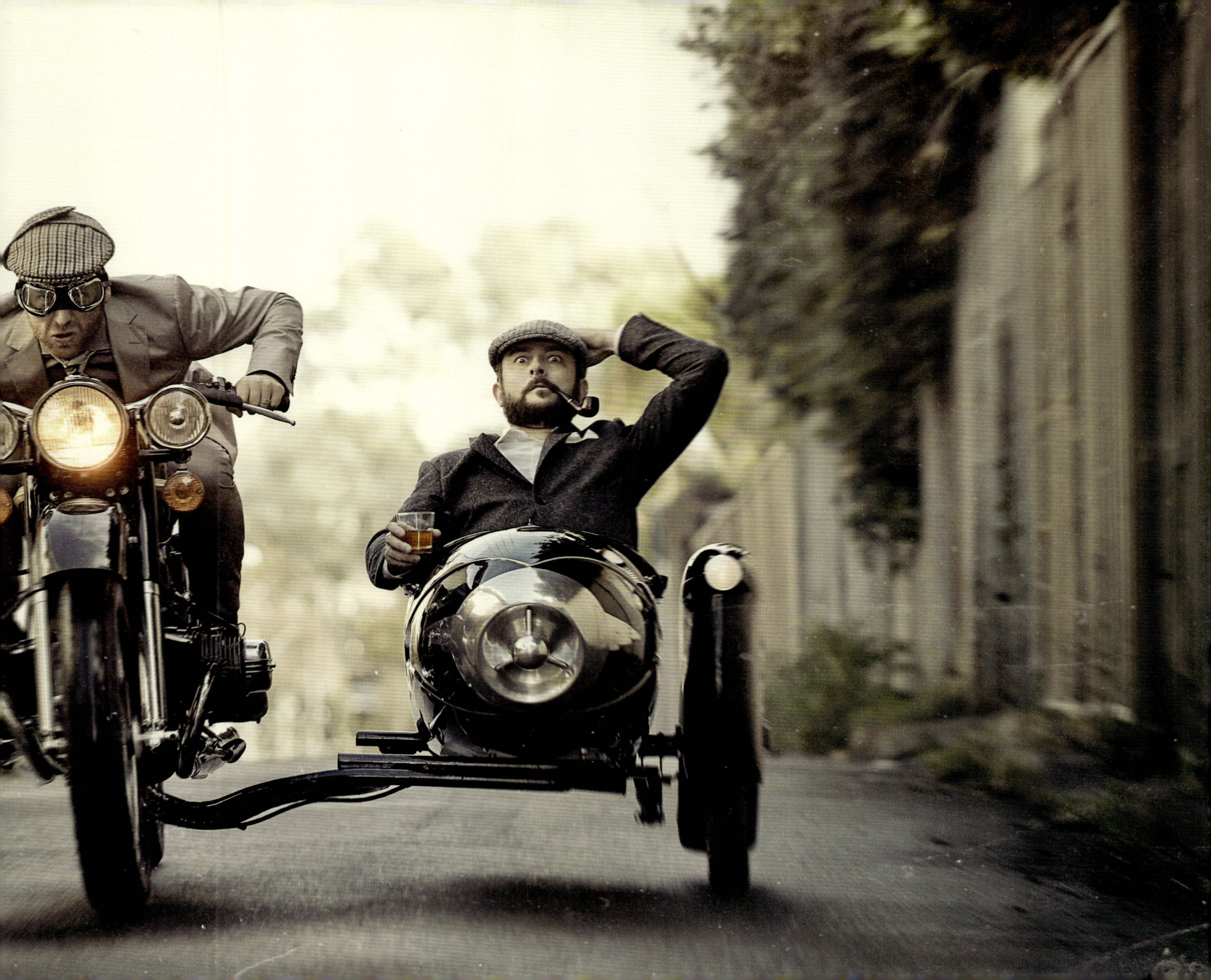

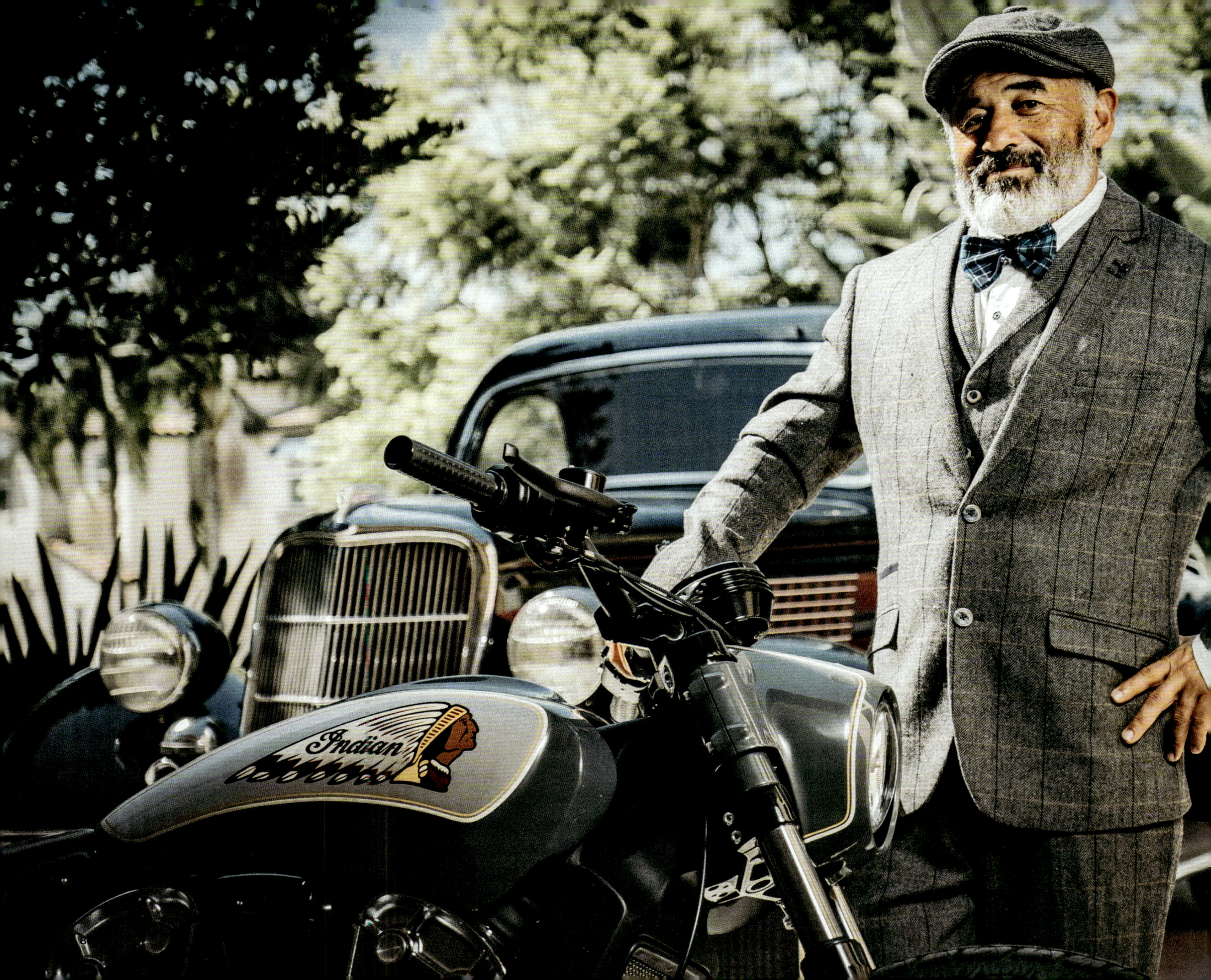
Indian

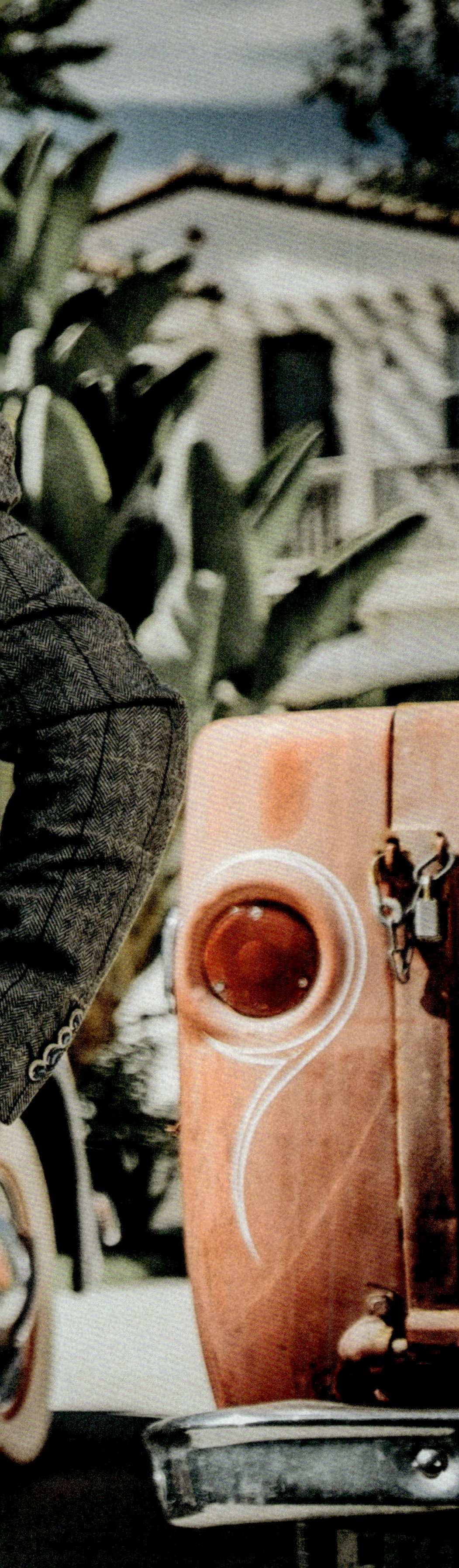

EL CABALLERO

Two wheels aren't the first thing you think of when the name Steve Caballero is mentioned. Known for his exceptional skills as a professional skateboarder, and inventor of the skateboarding trick, the "Caballerial."

He's not quite the man you think of when motorcycling is mentioned, but with a name literally translating to "Gentleman" in Spanish, he truly suited the moniker. Steve Caballero, skating legend and all-round gentleman featured as a DGR Global Ambassador in 2018, and has since continued to be a recurring rider and creative contributor to the DGR community.

Steve picked up his board at the age of 12. Hailing from San Jose, California, he kicked and pushed his way to a career in skateboarding, and those bearings never stopped spinning.

Steve is amongst the original Bones Brigade after being discovered by Stacy Peralta in 1979 and turning pro in 1980; he was voted Rookie of the Year in 1980 and coasted through the Golden Era of skating with his infectious smile and passion to express himself creatively without letting fame or fortune sway his character.

His immense success and being inducted into the Skateboarding Hall of Fame in Simi Valley, California, in 2010 might be enough for any man, but skating isn't the only thing in Steve's wheelhouse. Steve has always been infatuated with riding motorcycles, wanting to be like his childhood hero Evel Knievel. Initially unable to satisfy the insatiable desire to ride, Steve took ownership of his first ever bike once his professional skateboarding career erupted. Much like skateboarding, Steve has pushed his passion to its limits here, too.

Joining The Distinguished Gentleman's Ride as a global ambassador in 2018, Steve paired his Half Cabs with a full Windsor to raise funds and awareness for men's health. No stranger to charity events, Steve proudly rode in his first ever charity on two wheels.

As a creative outlet off the board, Steve uses a brush and a pen to help create and design artwork and graphics for various companies within the skateboarding and motocross industry. Steve also produces original paintings for art shows all over the world.

Steve returned to support The Distinguished Gentleman's Ride in 2021 but this time instead of a throttle, his hands were firmly gripped around a paintbrush. To help celebrate our 10-year anniversary, Steve painted a Hedon helmet in a spectacular fashion, with the auction of the finished item raising an impressive $1,350 USD for Movember.

Steve continues to be a huge part of the DGR community, taking part to experience the bevy of awesome bikes and dapper dudes, and to raise funds for a great cause.

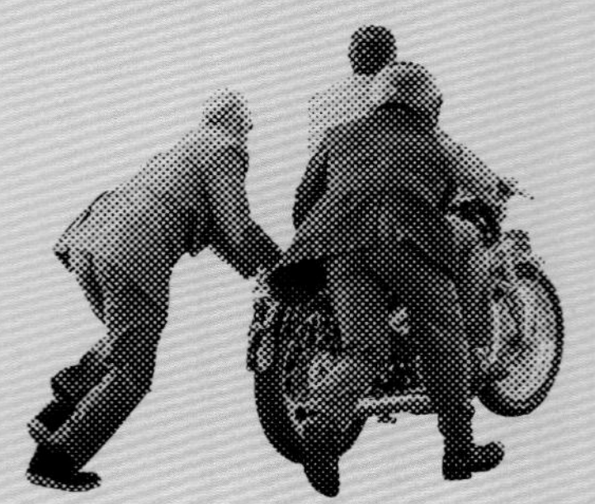

2015

- RIDE FOUR -

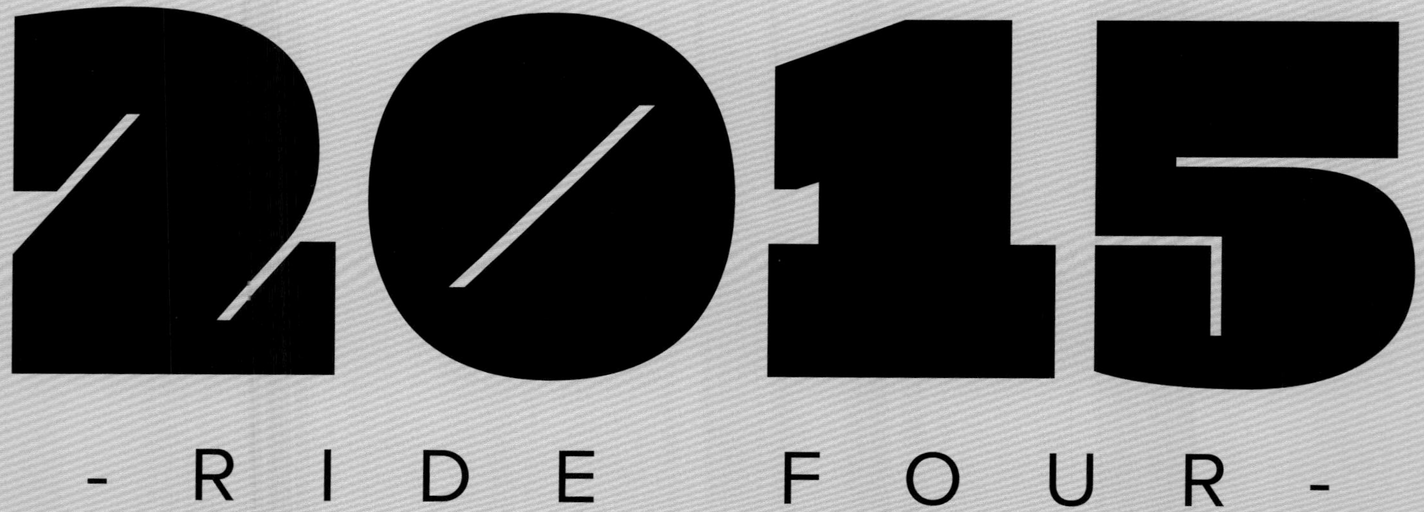

DEFYING EVEN OUR OWN EXPECTATIONS, THE DGR EVENT SHOWED
NO SIGNS OF SLOWING DOWN. WITH **37,000 RIDERS** AND **410 CITIES**
JOINING IN, WE RAISED OVER USD **$2.3M** IN THIS YEAR ALONE.

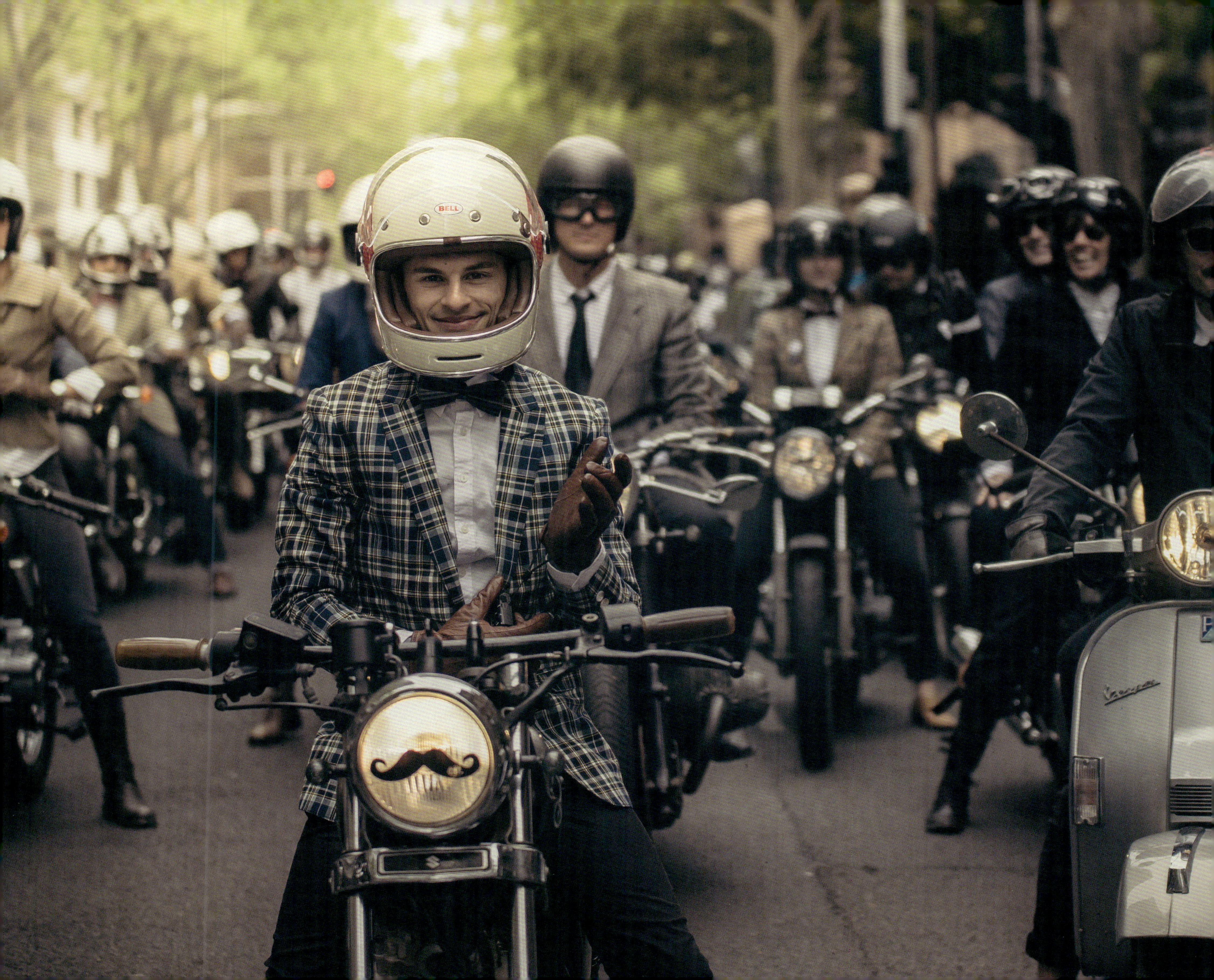

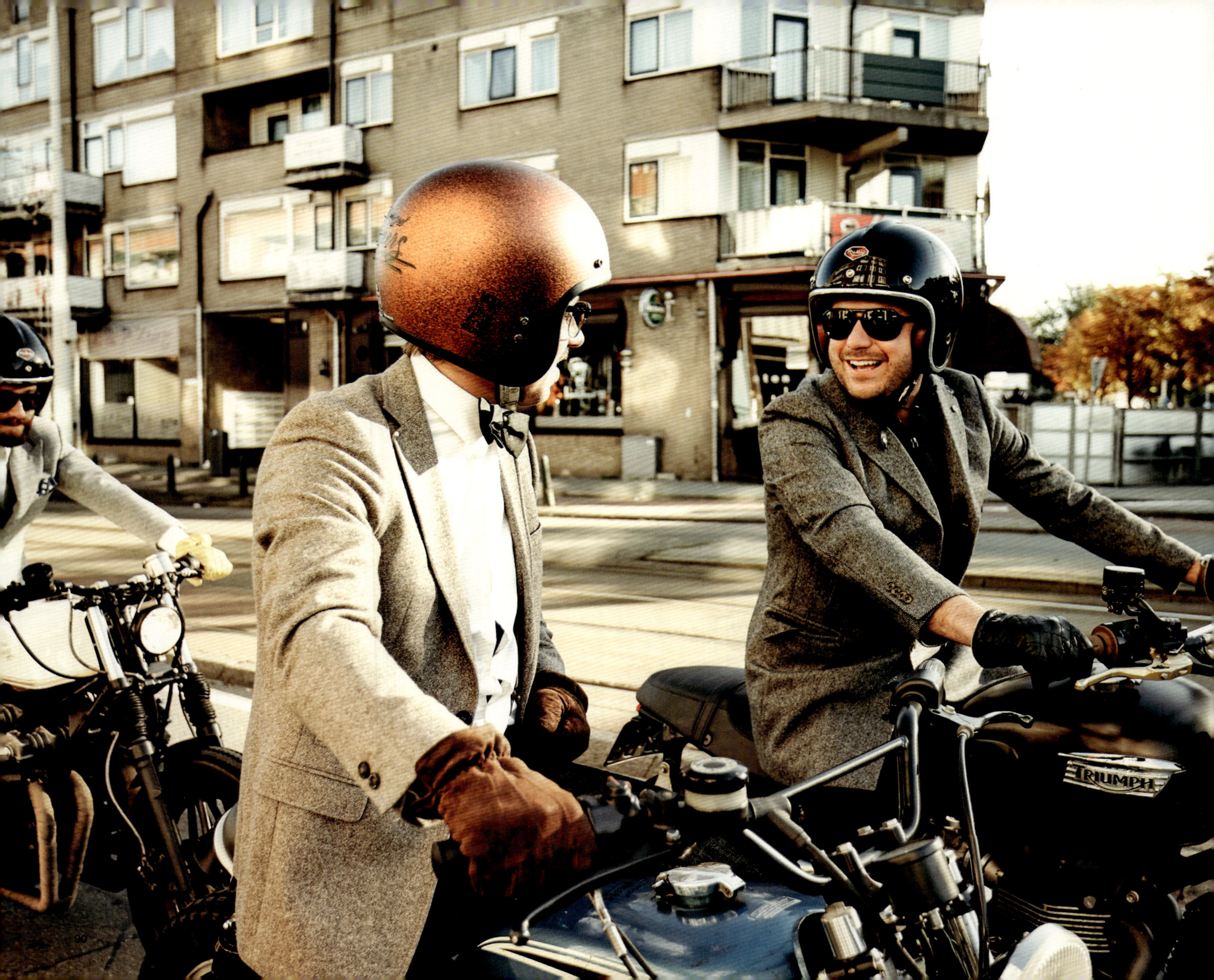

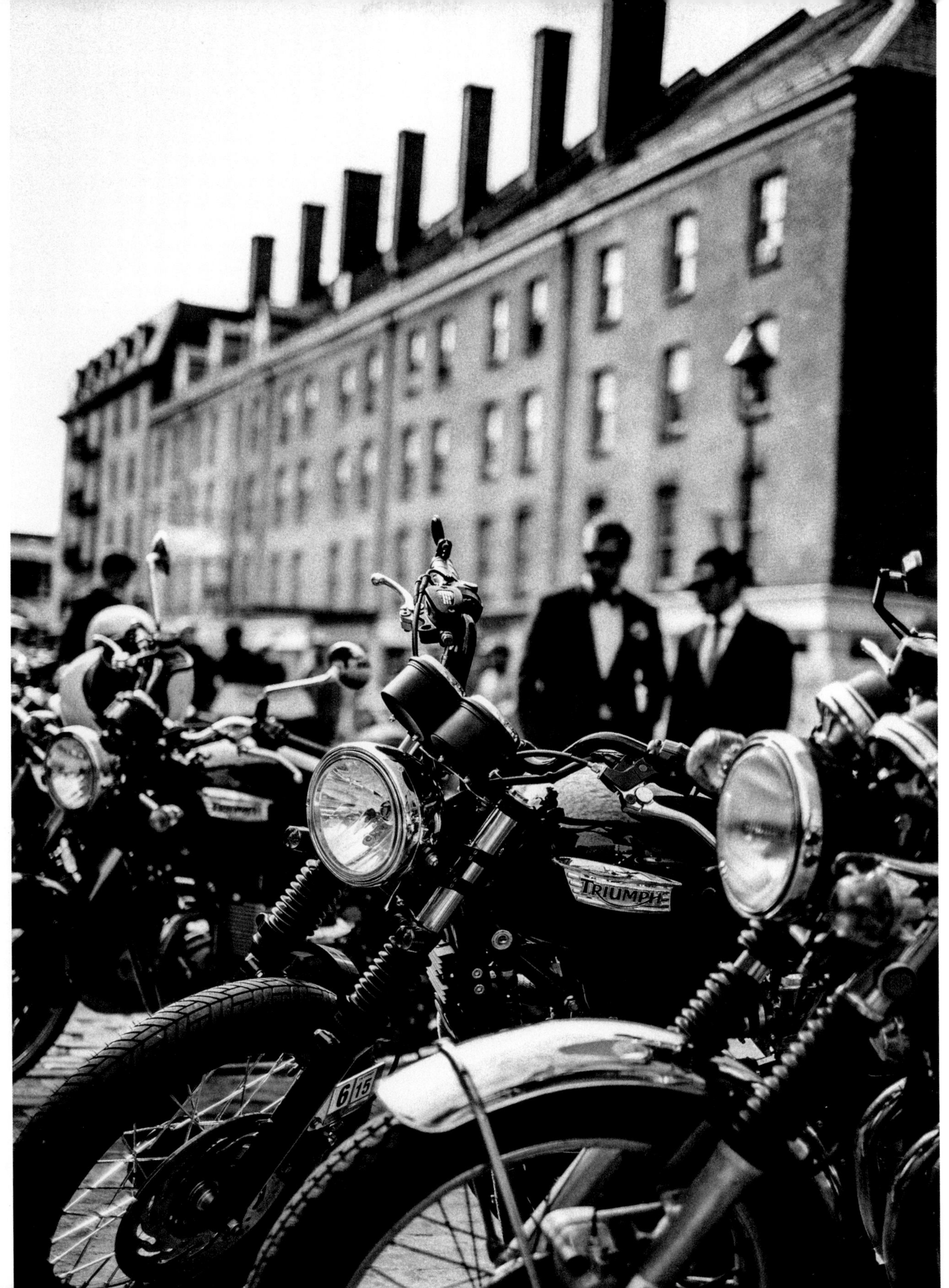

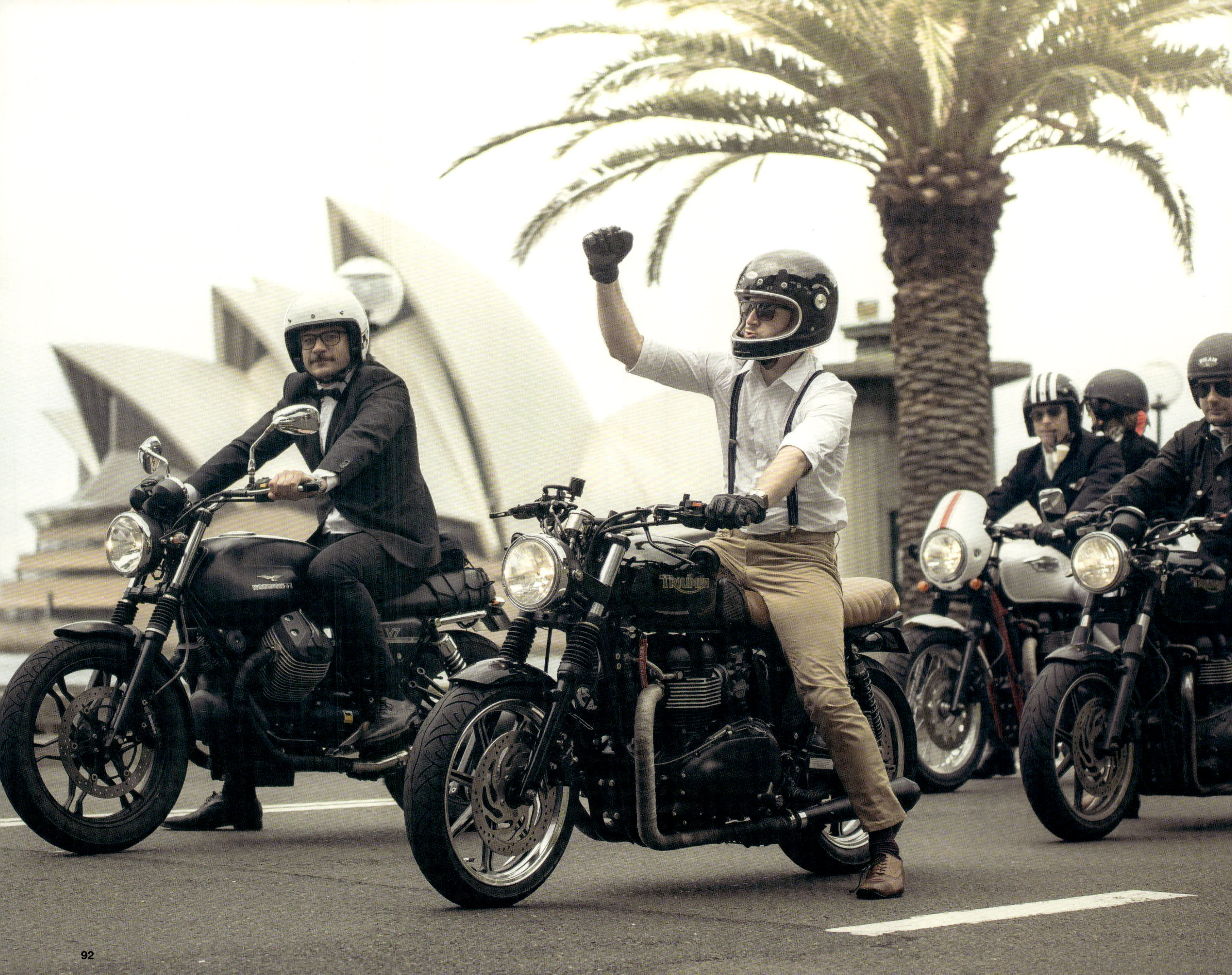

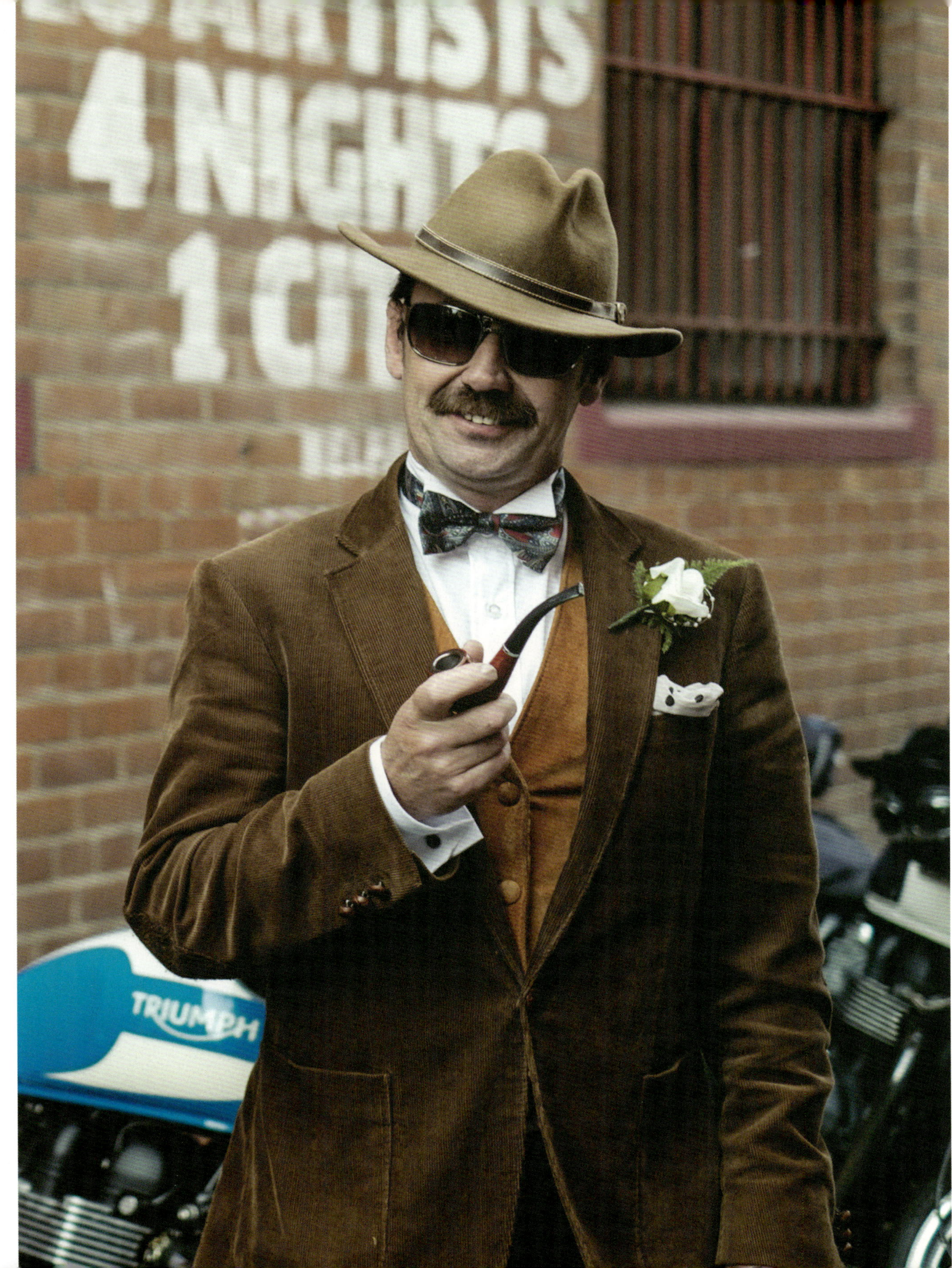

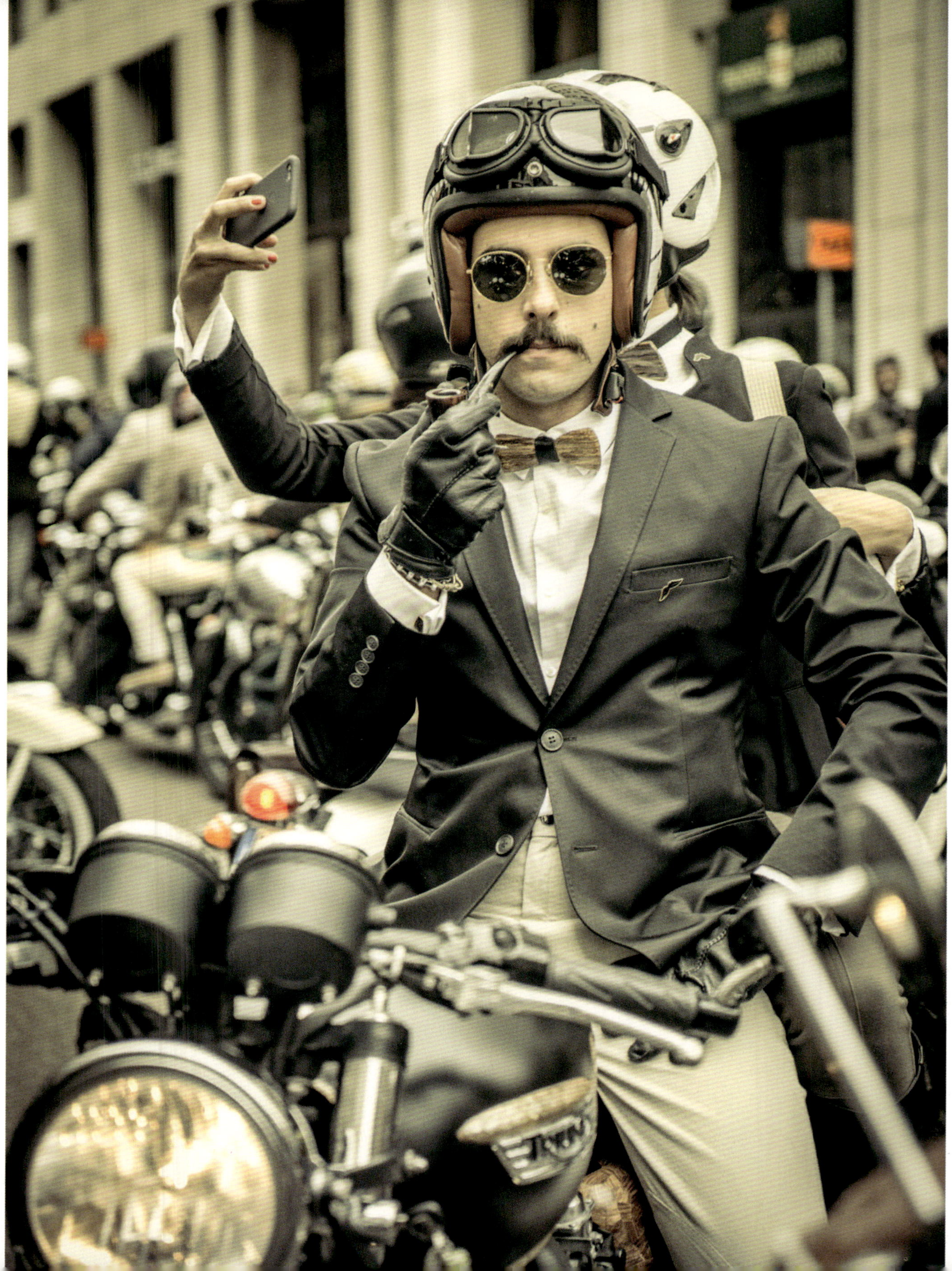

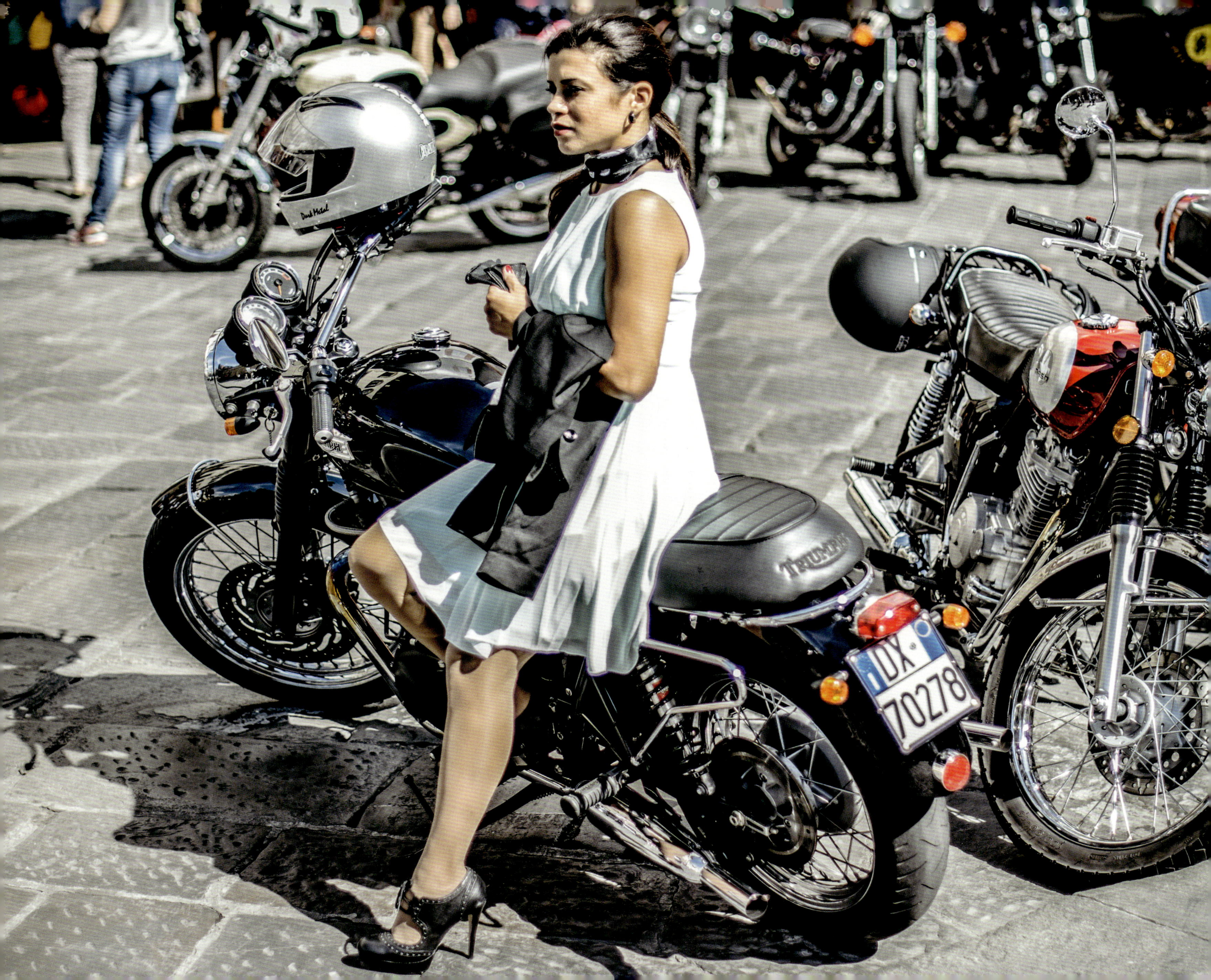

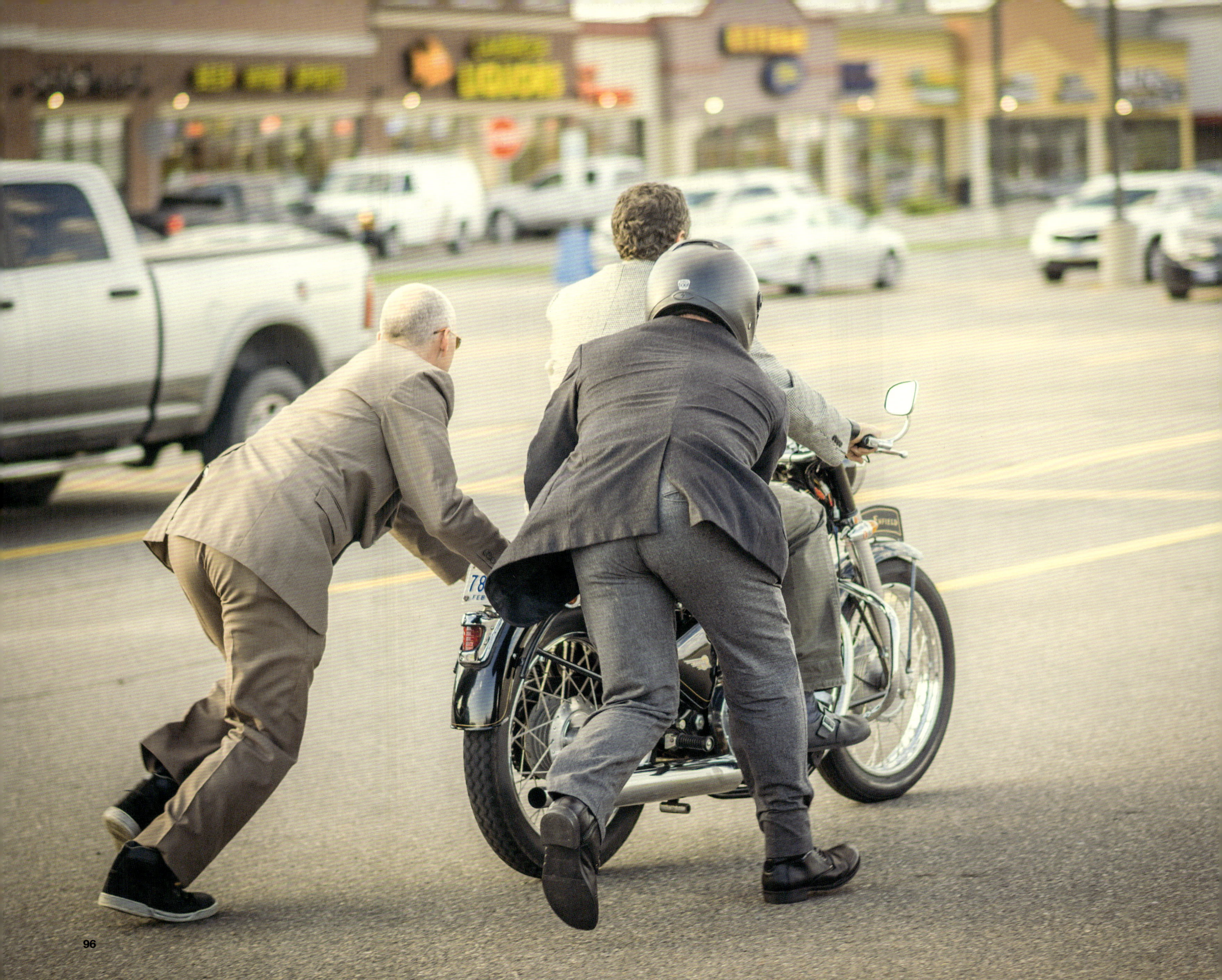

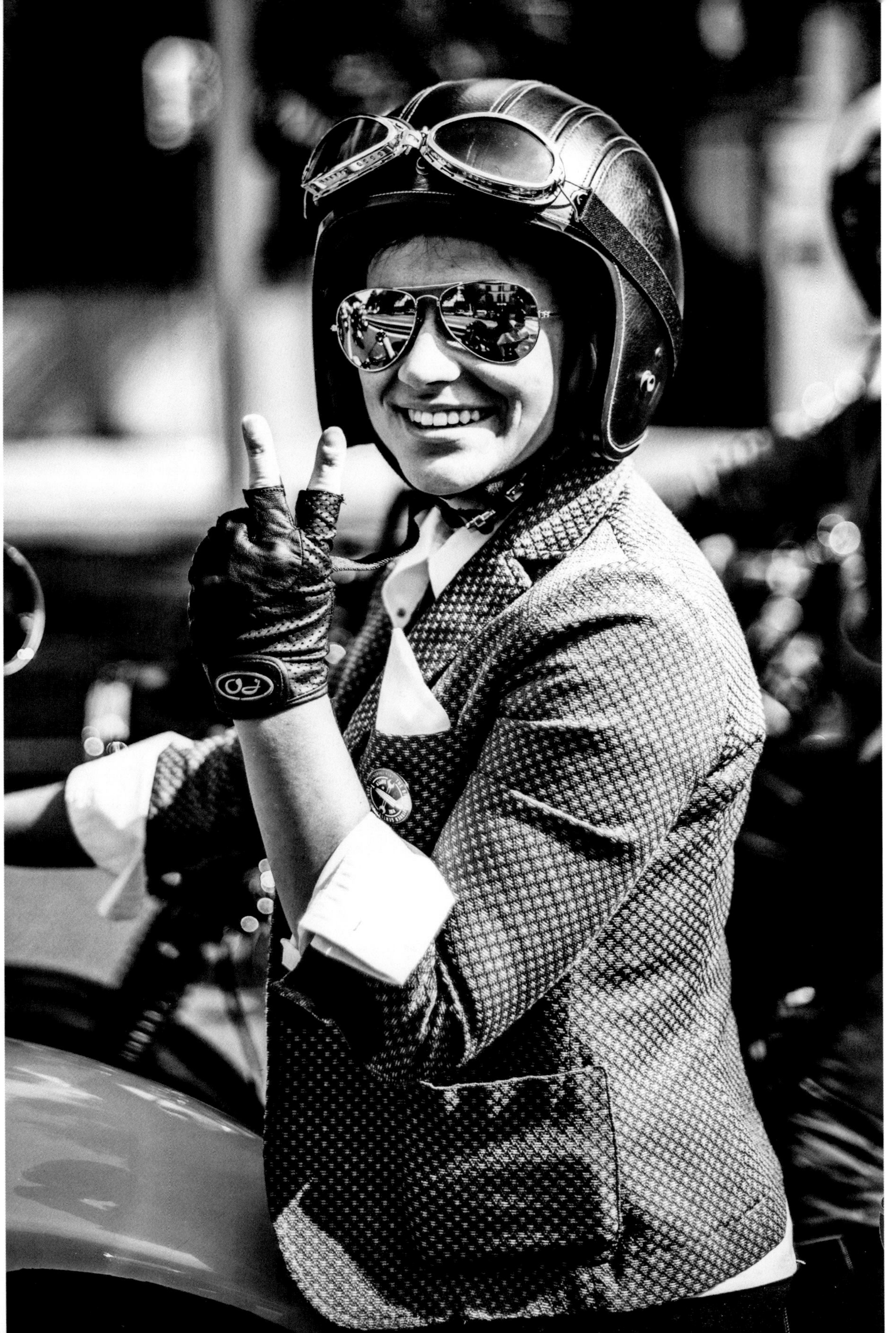

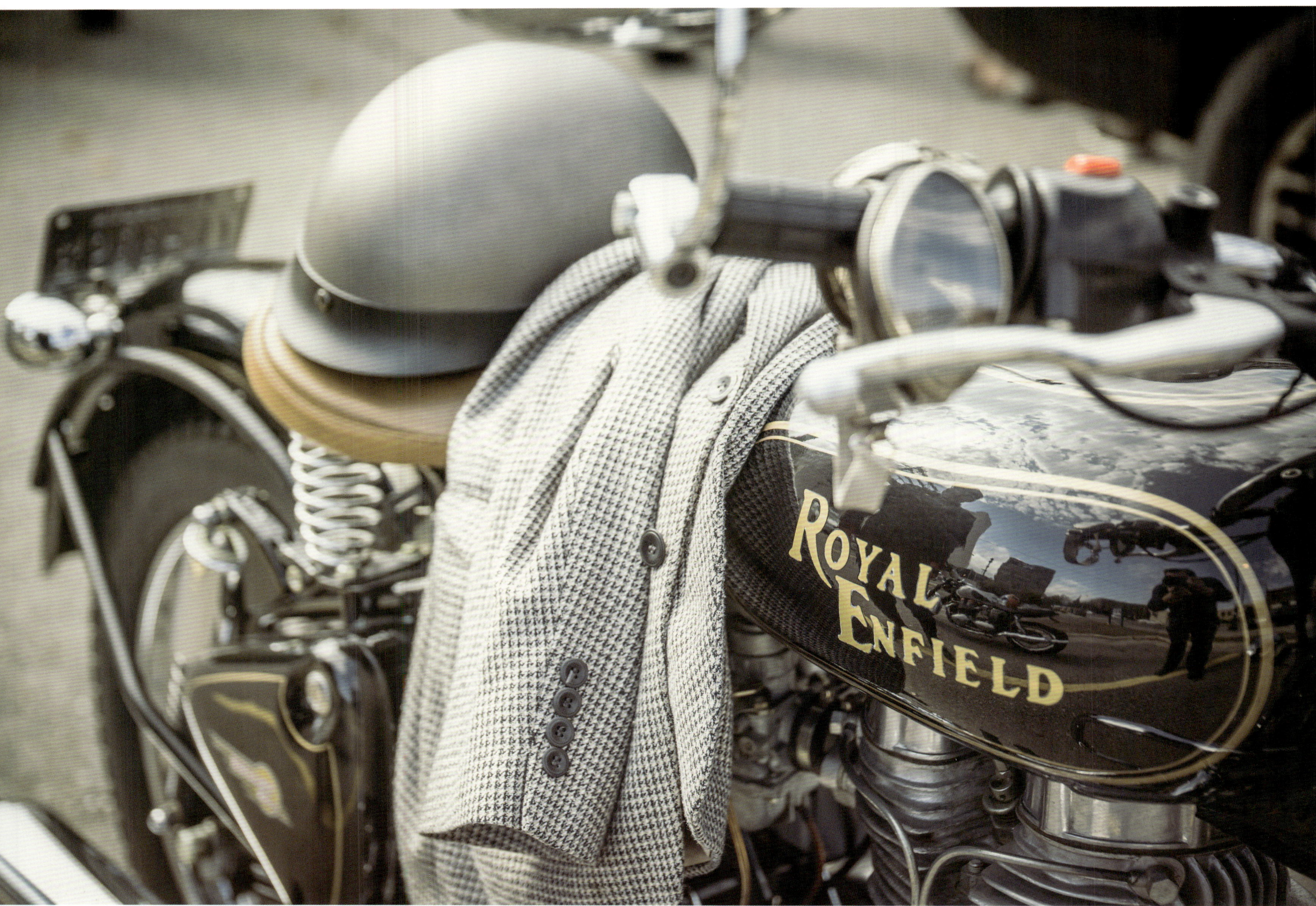
ROYAL
ENFIELD

2015 Ride Poster

Designed by Tom Wall

In this year's poster, we see Remington saluting the participants of DGR while riding a Triumph Scrambler Custom emblazoned with the number 35 as his headlight illuminates the worldwide date. The number had significance not only to his race number, but also the race number of our volunteer ride host, Rodney Champness, who also worked tirelessly to create social media content for previous years' campaigns.

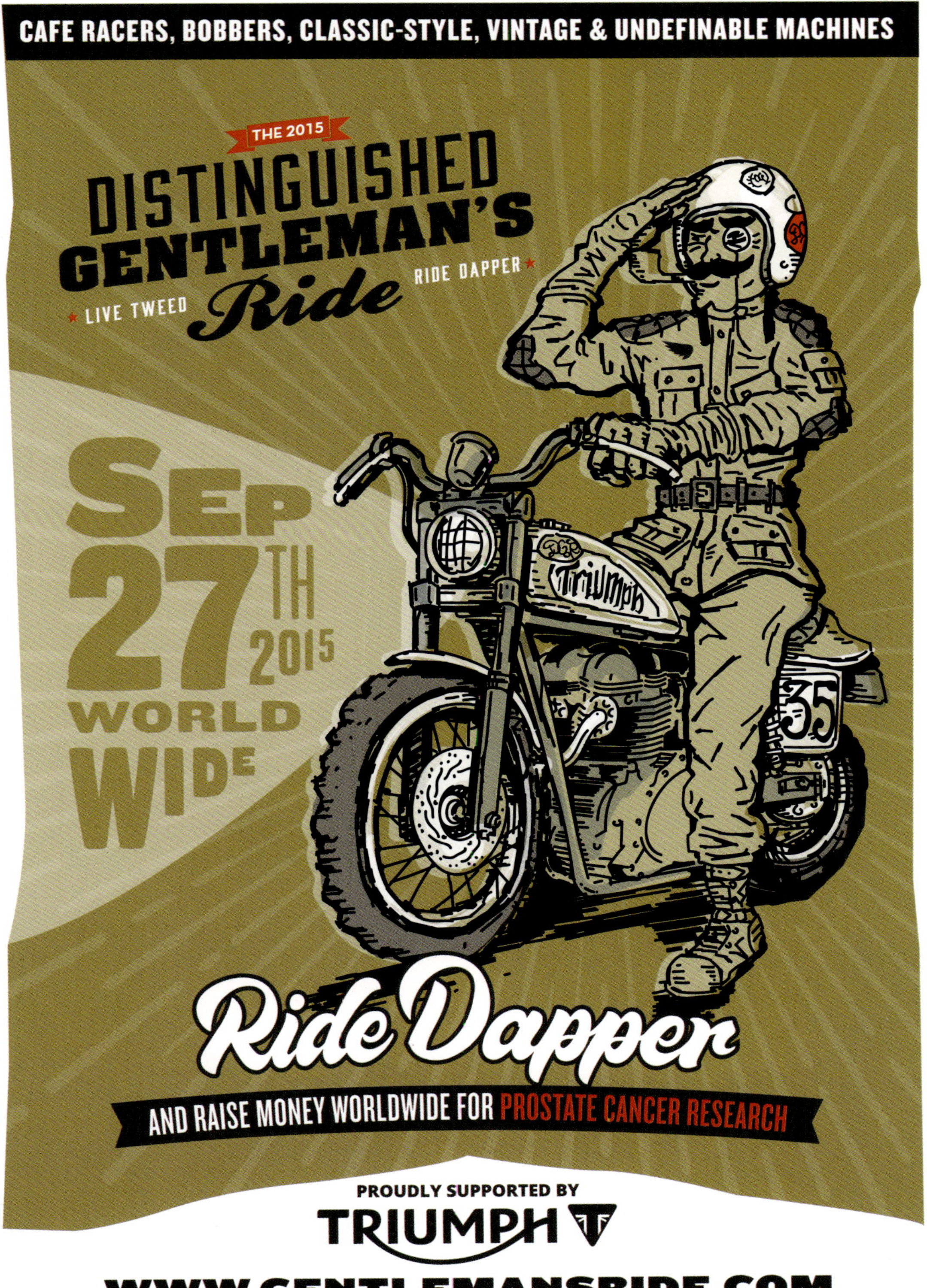

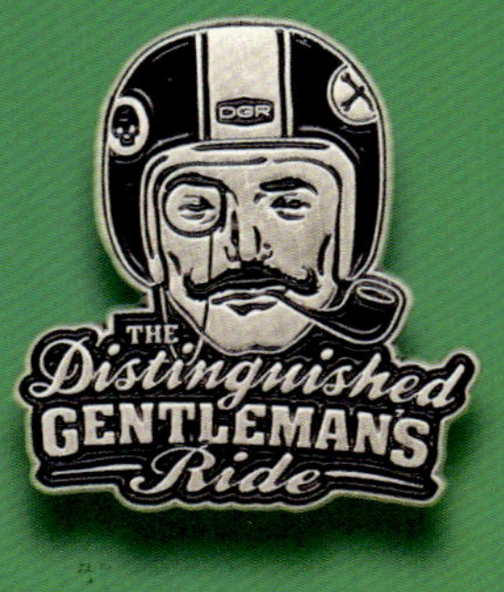

2016

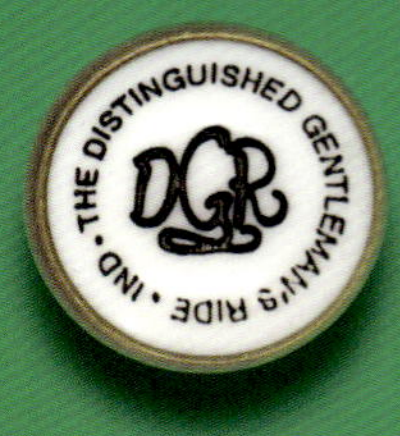

2017

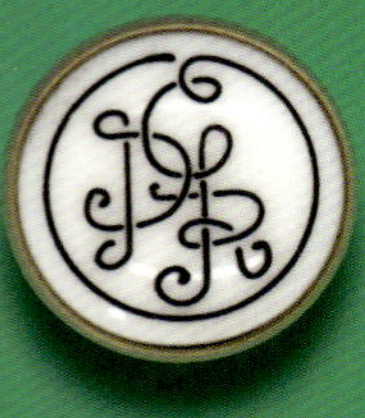

2018

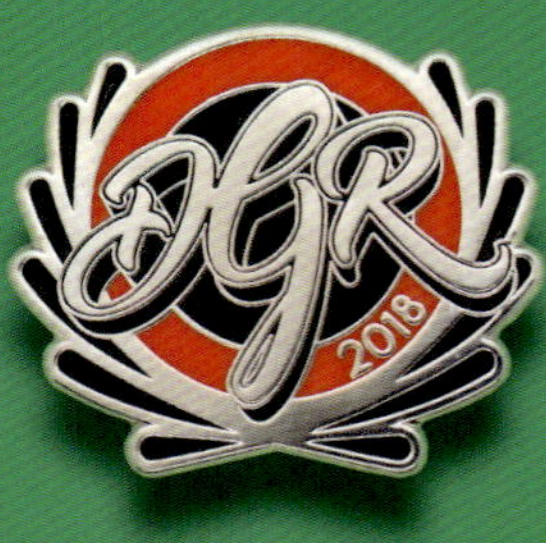

2018

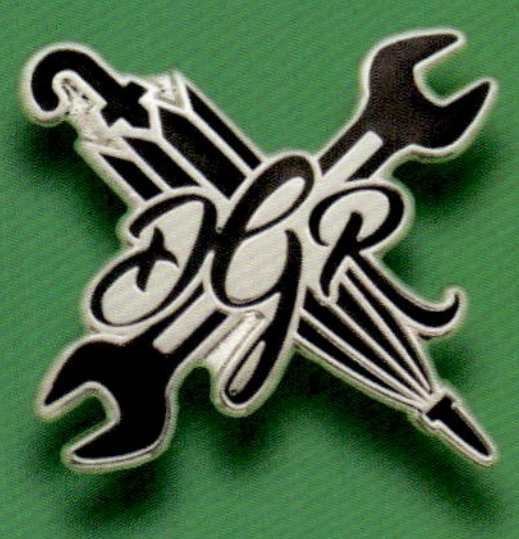

2018

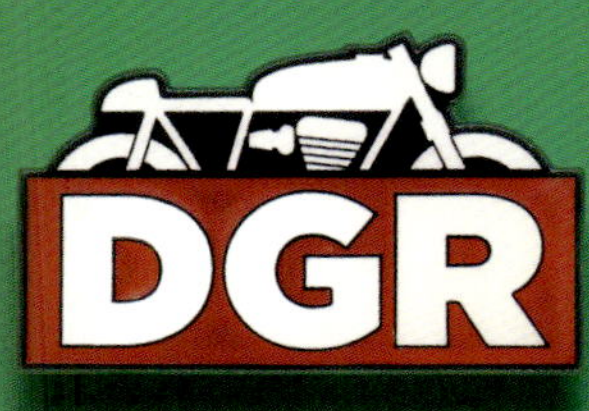

2019

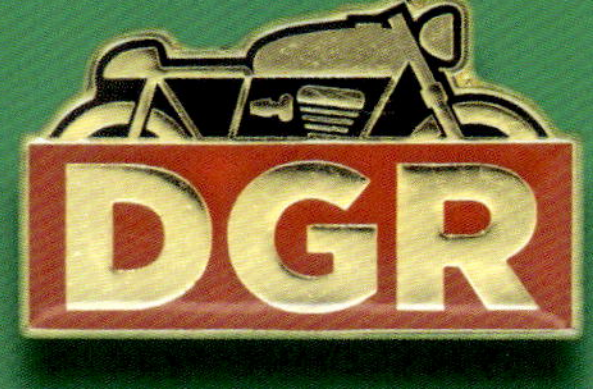

2019

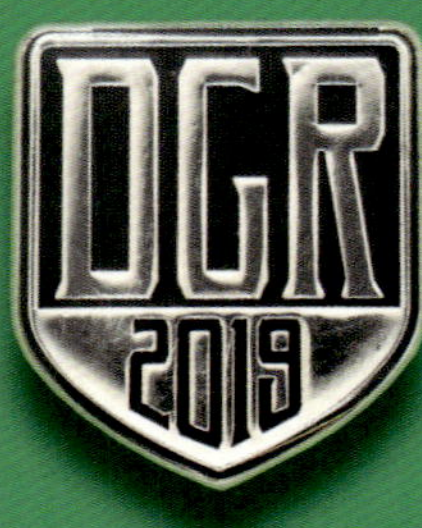

2019

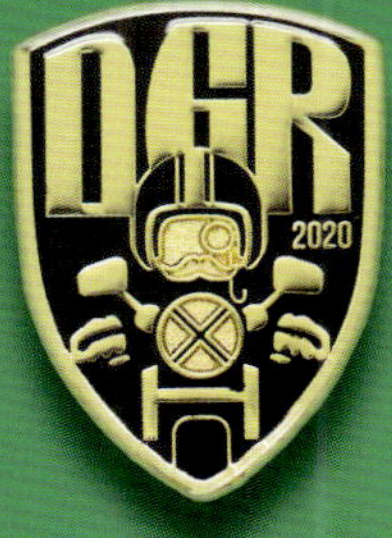

2020

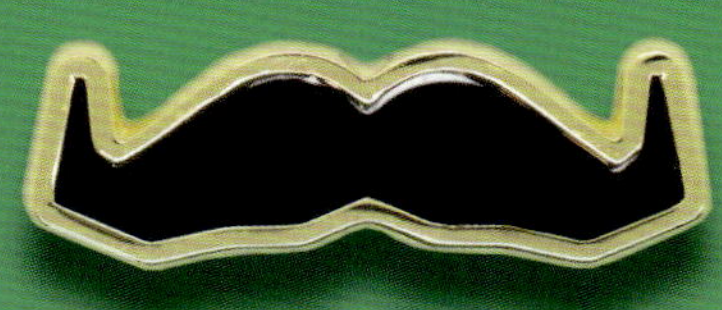

2020

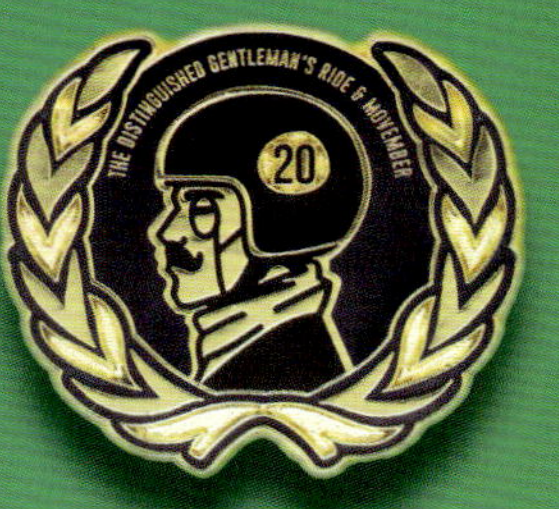

2020

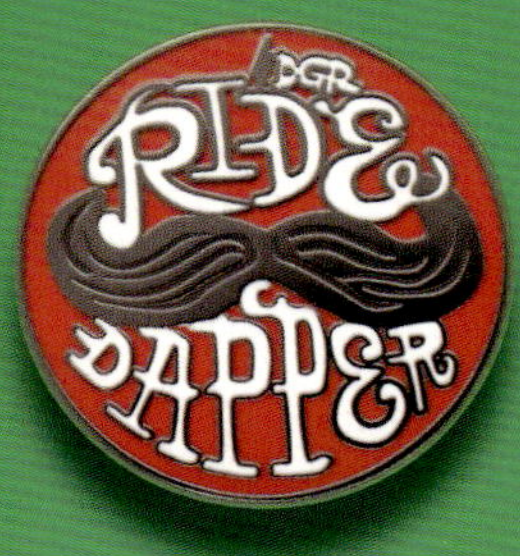

2021

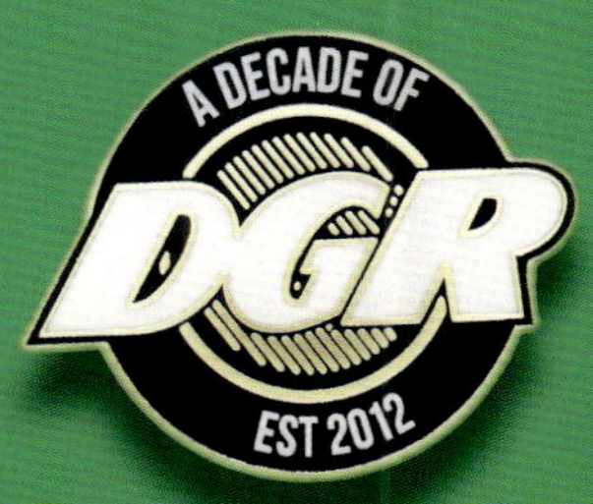

2021

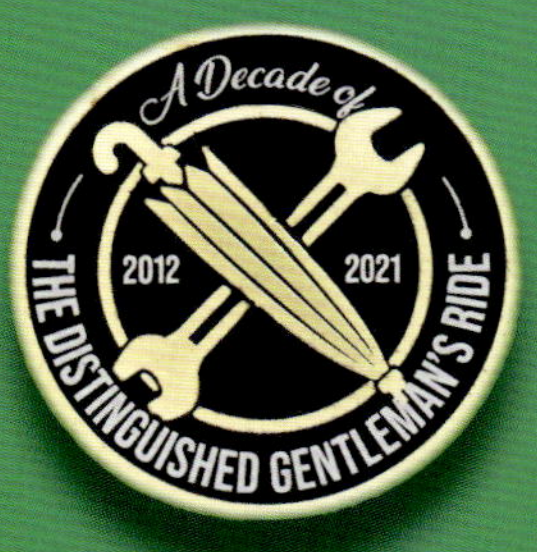

2021

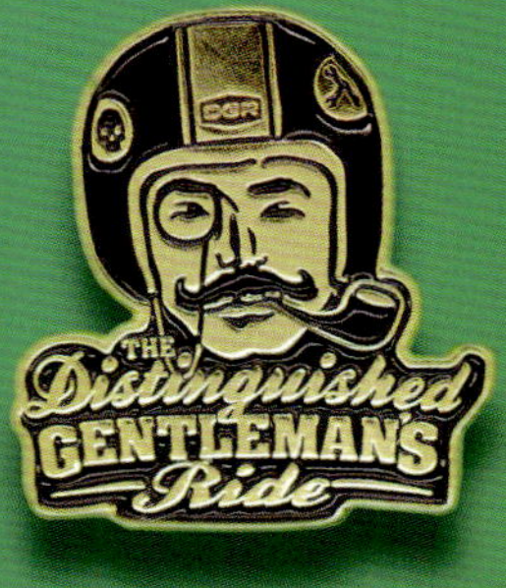

2021

THE OFFICIAL DGR PINS

Badges of honor beginning with the iconic Sir Remington Silversteed, The Distinguished Gentleman's Ride has produced a vast selection of pins for riders to decorate their lapels with pride. Not all pins are made equal, however.

While many are available for sale, some pins can only be earned. Ornaments regaling impressive fundraising efforts and dedication to men's health, many pins were made exclusively for ride hosts and top fundraisers each year to thank them for their commitment to fundraising.

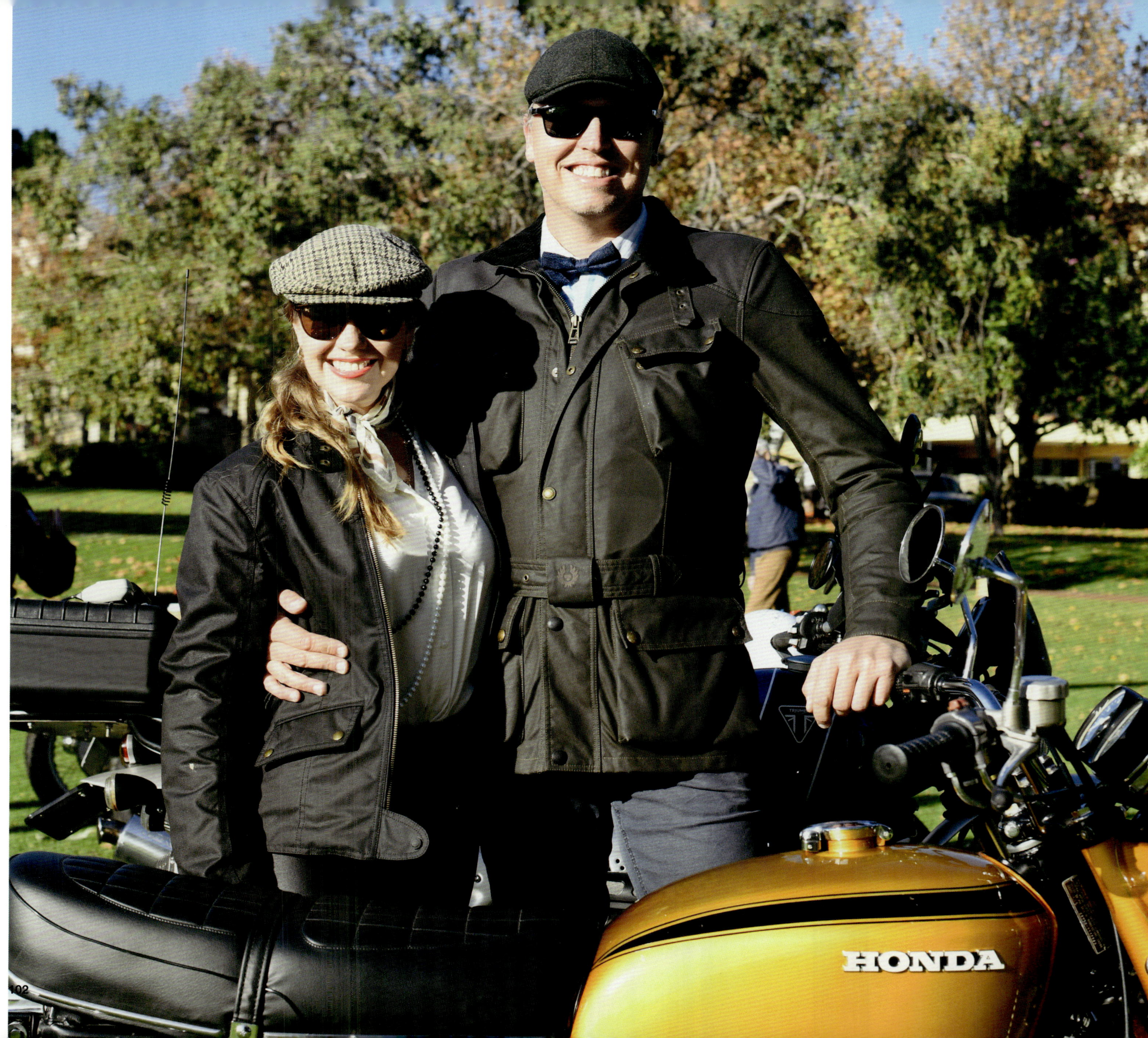
HONDA

Our story started in 2013, my partner Kerry and I were taking a walk and this beautiful bike caught my eye. I had been a Honda lover my whole life, so I took a few minutes to admire this bike.

It was an old Honda K1 CB750, and I just fell in love with it. I bought it a few years later, and it was such a nice return to riding. Kerry and I would take that bike on little coffee dates and go on rides around the foreshore in Mandurah. One day I had said to Kerry that we should take the bike out on a ride with other classic bikes to show it off to people who would appreciate it.

had remembered that couple at DGR the previous year, and told me that I might as well get my PSA levels checked if I'm going in for a blood test anyway.

My blood test results came back, and my PSA levels were through the roof. It was tough, I was 41 at the time, and typically men without a family history of prostate cancer won't get checked until they're at least 50.

The doctor told us that had I not gotten checked when I did, I wouldn't have made it to that first check. Because of the age I was when I was diagnosed, I did wonder whether I had a fam-

SURVIVOR STORIES: Matt Richards

"It's very hard to answer when you're sitting at the dinner table and your 9-year-old son says to you, if granddad's got cancer and you've got cancer, does that mean I'm going to get cancer?"

I Googled to find out the next motorcycle ride in my area, and a week away was something called The Distinguished Gentleman's Ride. It was the exact thing we were looking for.

On the day, we were listening to folks tell their stories of prostate cancer, a husband and wife were sharing their experiences and the impact it had on their family.

That story really sank in for us. In February the following year, I started to get headaches. This was pretty out of the ordinary for me, so I decided to go and get a blood test. Kerry

ily history of it or not. At the time, my dad had never been checked, so I asked him to get a PSA test as well.

His also came back as positive; then it became really clear to me why early detection is so important. It not only saves your life, but it can save your kids as well.

Through all this, that one DGR ride not only saved my life, but it also gave me the knowledge to help prolong my dad's life and to help raise awareness by encouraging other men to get checked.

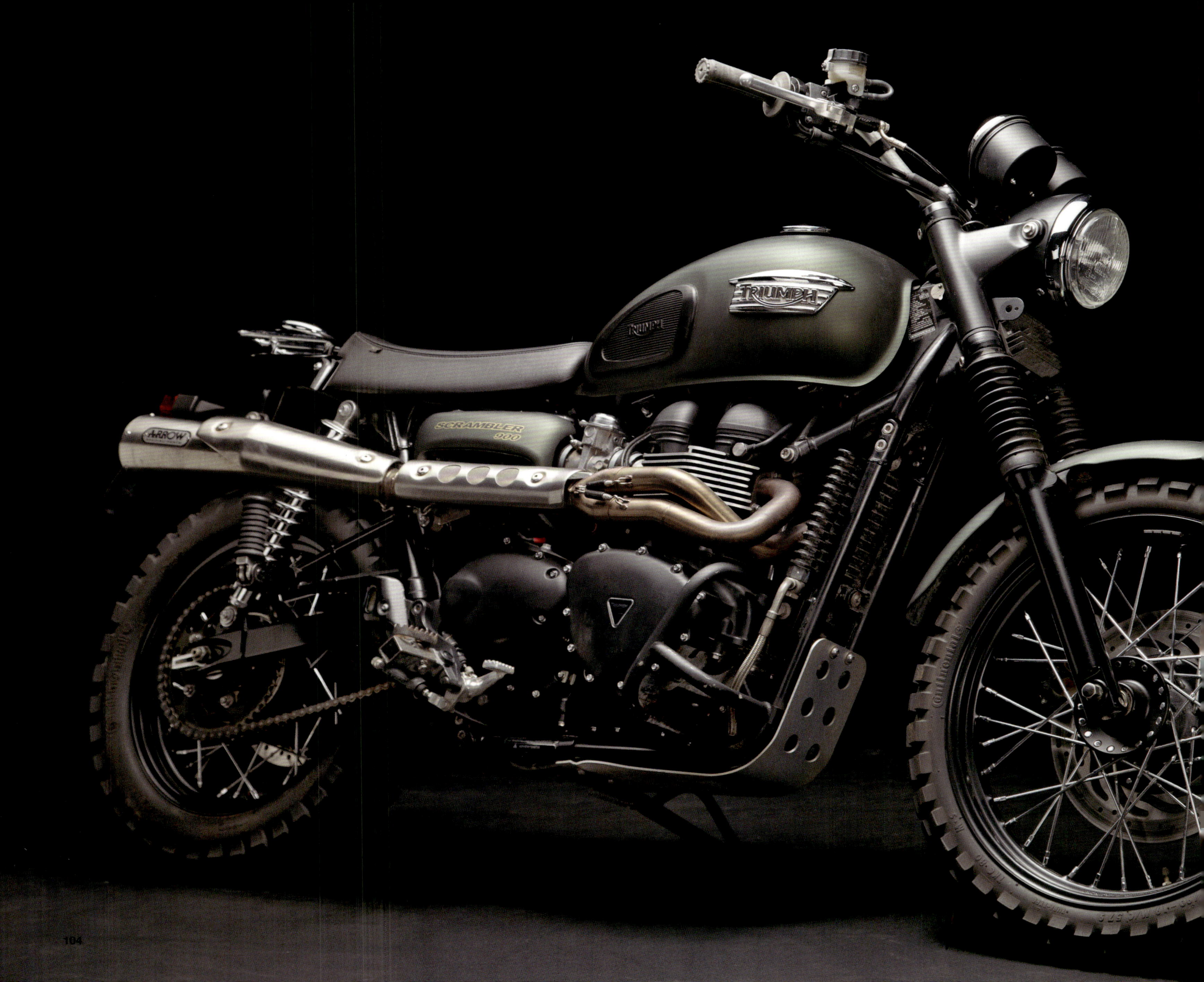

TRIUMPH
SCRAMBLER 900
ARROW

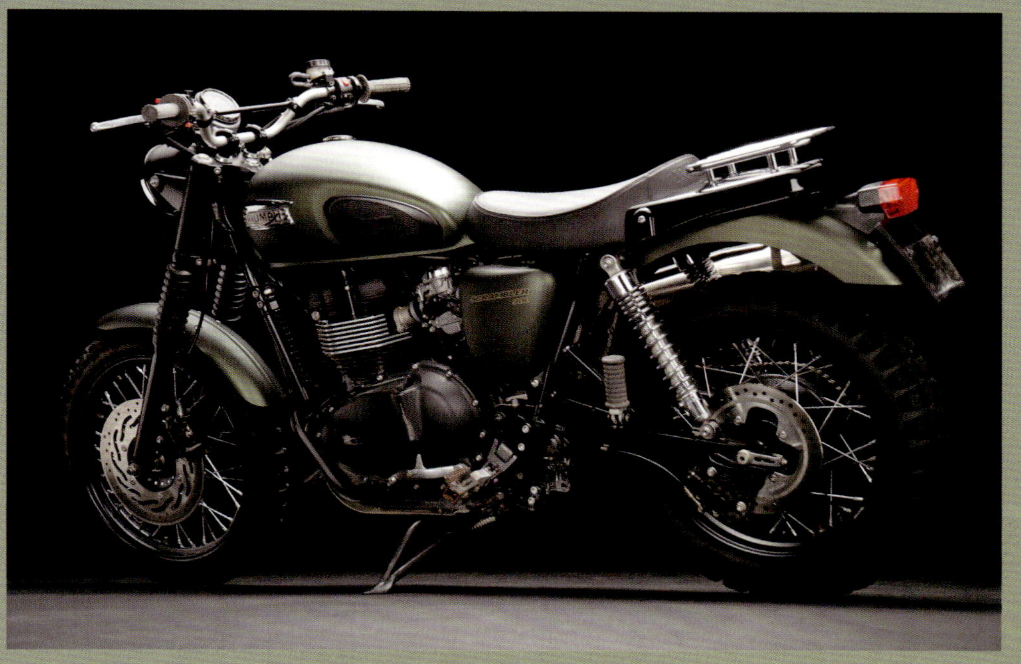

THE JURASSIC PARK TRIUMPH

Presented for auction in 2015 by Triumph Motorcycles was a unique opportunity to bid for a Triumph Scrambler featured in the 2015 Universal Pictures blockbuster "Jurassic World."

On the 23rd of July 2015 Triumph Motorcycles auctioned off the iconic Scrambler ridden by Chris Pratt's character in the film. The bespoke bike, featured racing alongside velociraptors in the film, was sold on eBay to the highest bidder, with the proceeds going to The Distinguished Gentleman's Ride.

Three Triumph Scramblers were customized for the film; one was presented to Jurassic World star Chris Pratt as a gift after filming, the second is displayed at Triumph's headquarters in the UK and this, the third, went up for auction to one lucky bidder.

Modifications to this bike included single seat and rack, Arrow Racing high level exhaust, custom footpegs, and handlebars; with the bike being finished in a beautiful matte green. The bike was sold exactly as it finished duties on the production of the film and was delivered with a certificate of authenticity included in the purchase. The 10 day auction struck 90 bids, and raised a massive $43,900 USD for the 2015 Distinguished Gentleman's Ride.

LONDON CALLING

It was 2012 and the Bike Shed was a small blog with a Facebook page, writing about custom bikes, people and culture. But it wouldn't stay that way for long.

Our first show was in the planning stages, to be held under a couple of railway arches in London's trendy Shoreditch for the first time. Back then, the internet and forums allowed custom motorcycle and cafe racer enthusiasts from all around the world to meet. From faded memory, I remember 'meeting' Mark Hawwa as the founder of the Sydney Cafe Racers motorcycle forum in Australia. In him I quickly discovered a fellow gear-head on a similar mission; to celebrate and elevate moto-culture.

At some point a photo of John Hamm was shared, showing him looking suave, suited and booted on a classic BSA, and something just resonated with us all. There was a timelessness to the image and the gentlemanly vibes the picture emanated was a welcome change to usual Sons of Anarchy imagery associated with motorcyclists. It reminded me that most motorcycle riders are the very best of people, and are more likely to help that old lady across the road than punch-up with a rival gang.

Mark wanted to create a ride that celebrated this difference; with dapper riders on classic style bikes, something just clicked. It felt especially British, despite being inspired by an American and organized by an Aussie. How could we not get involved? I offered to organize a London ride in parallel with the Sydney ride, helping to kick-start the DGR as a truly international event from day one onwards.

Our London ride in September 2012 was held at the carpark behind the Dirty Burger in Kentish Town, just north of Camden. Seventy-seven of us assembled; a fantastic mix of riders from all walks of life, but all dressed in dapper gear and pretty much everyone on appropriate bikes. Vikki and I rode our twin Sport Classic 1000s, which are not the best rides for a 20mph London crawl, but the welcoming smiles from the public on the streets of London, and the warm fuzzy glow we all felt made up for my discomfort and arm-pump from 2 hours of feathering my dry Ducati clutch.

Back then, 77 riders also seemed like such a huge number. It's hard to fathom that a few years later we'd have 1,400 riders assembling near London Bridge or that the DGR would become such an amazing global phenomenon at the heart of the resurgent motorcycle scene.

Vikki and I are grateful and humbled to have been part of this amazing event for a decade, organizing and leading every ride until we found ourselves in Los Angeles last year, joining the pack for another glorious day of smiles and positivity in sunny California.

The Bike Shed members and staff in London will always feel an intimate connection to this event and hope to remain a part of it well into the future, wherever we are.

Anthony "Dutch" van Someren
Founder & CEO, Bike Shed Motorcycle Club
DGR London Ride Host

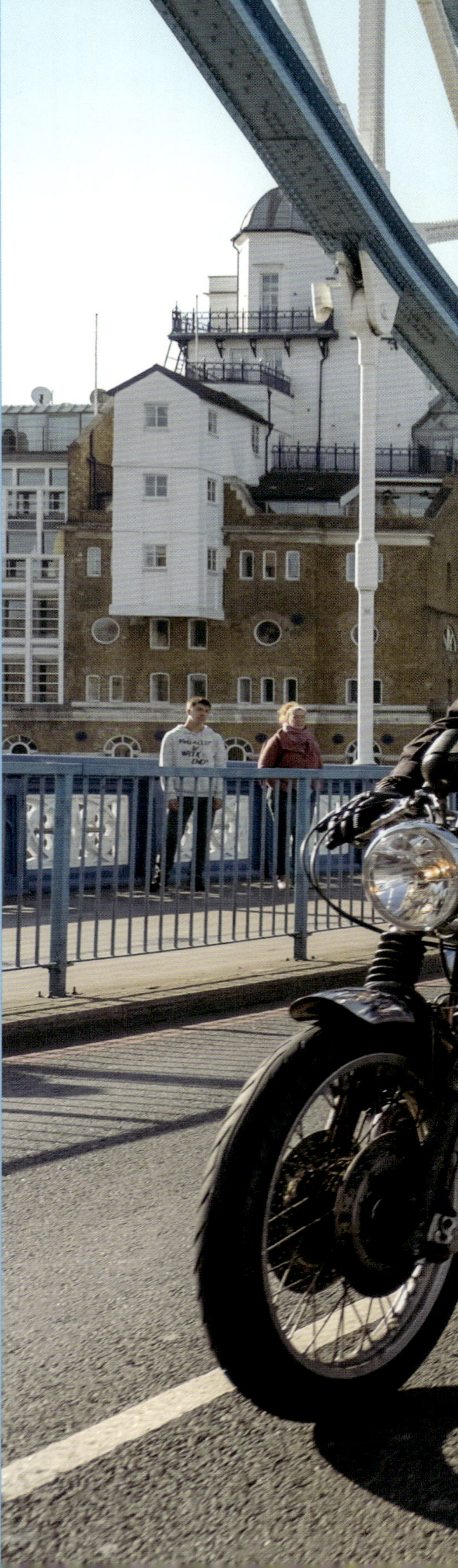

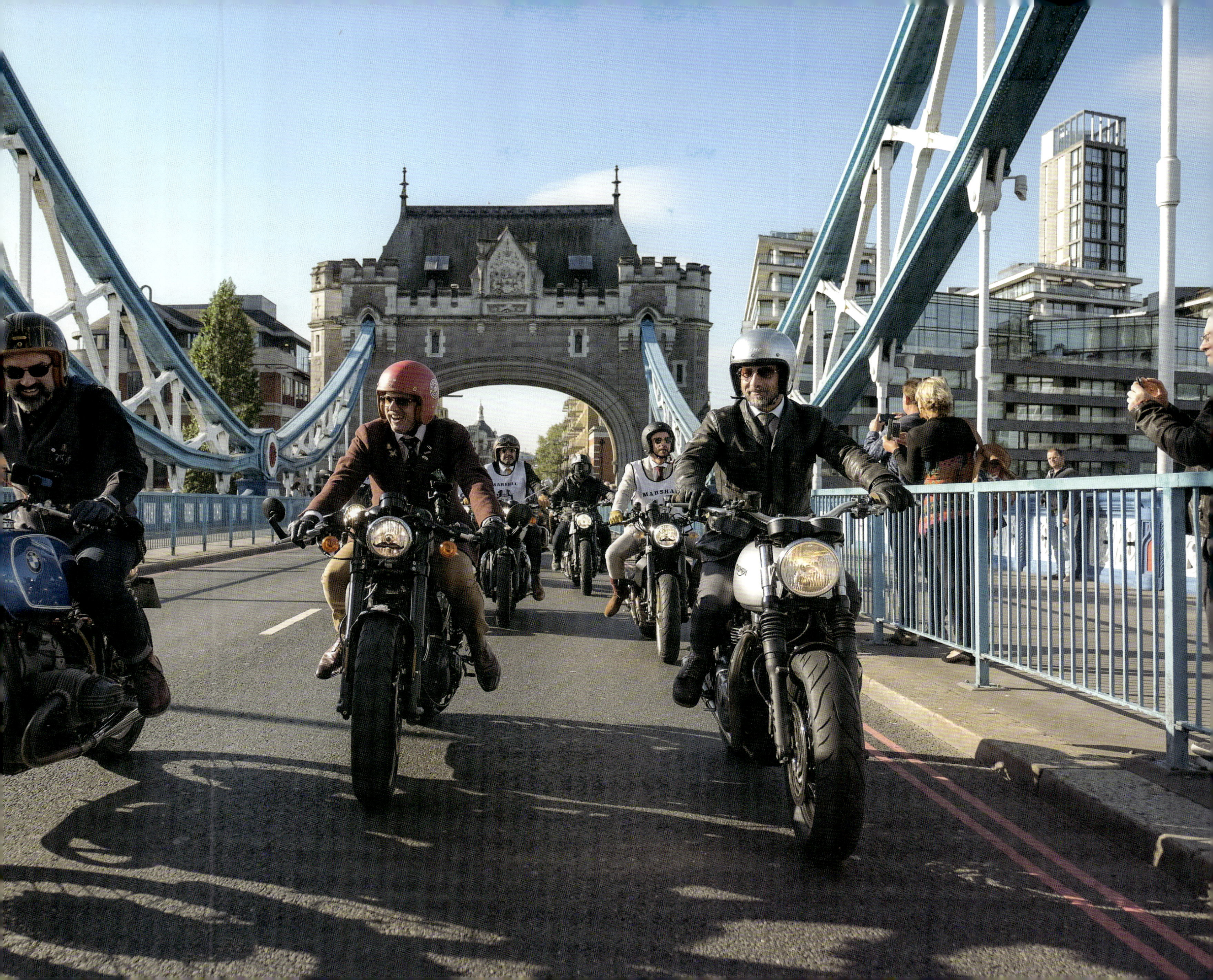

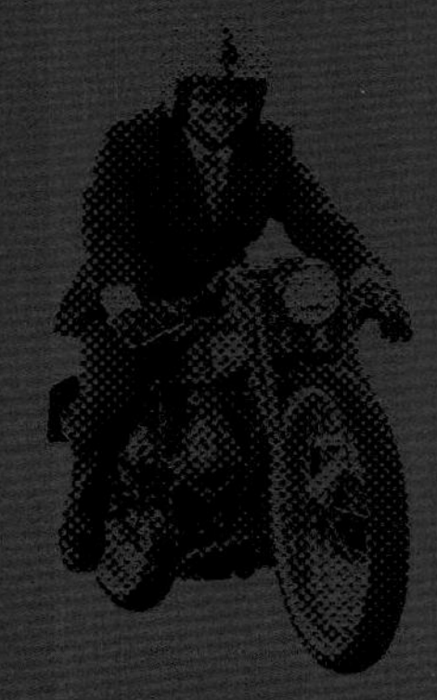

2016

- R I D E   F I V E -

WITH **57,000 RIDERS** AND **505 CITIES**, THIS WAS OUR FIRST YEAR OF
PARTNERING WITH MOVEMBER AS OUR OFFICIAL CHARITY PARTNER. IMPACTED
BY THE LOSS OF ONE OF OUR RIDE HOSTS TO SUICIDE ONLY WEEKS AFTER
THE EVENT, OUR FOCUS ON **MEN'S MENTAL HEALTH** BEGAN TO GROW.

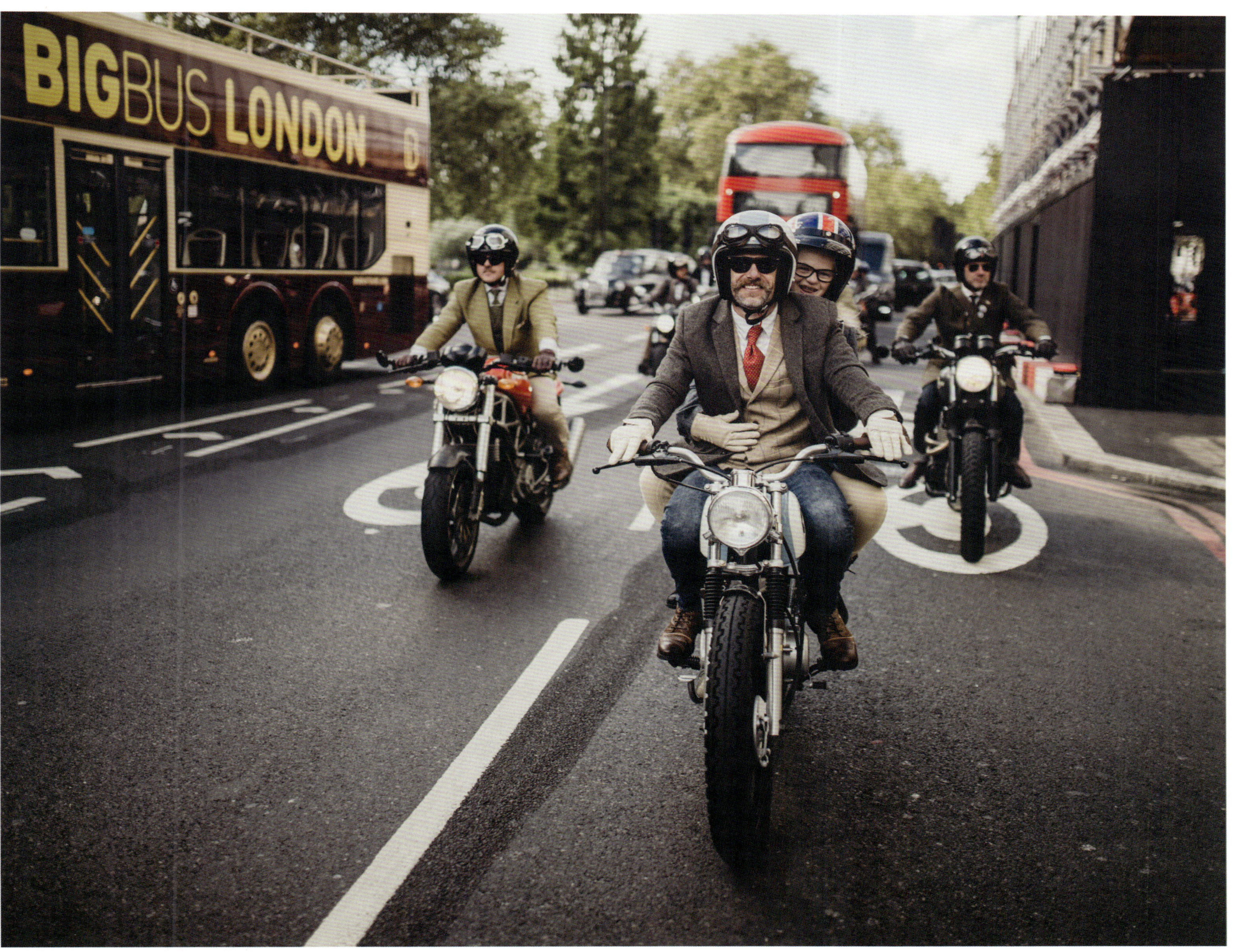

BIGBUS LONDON

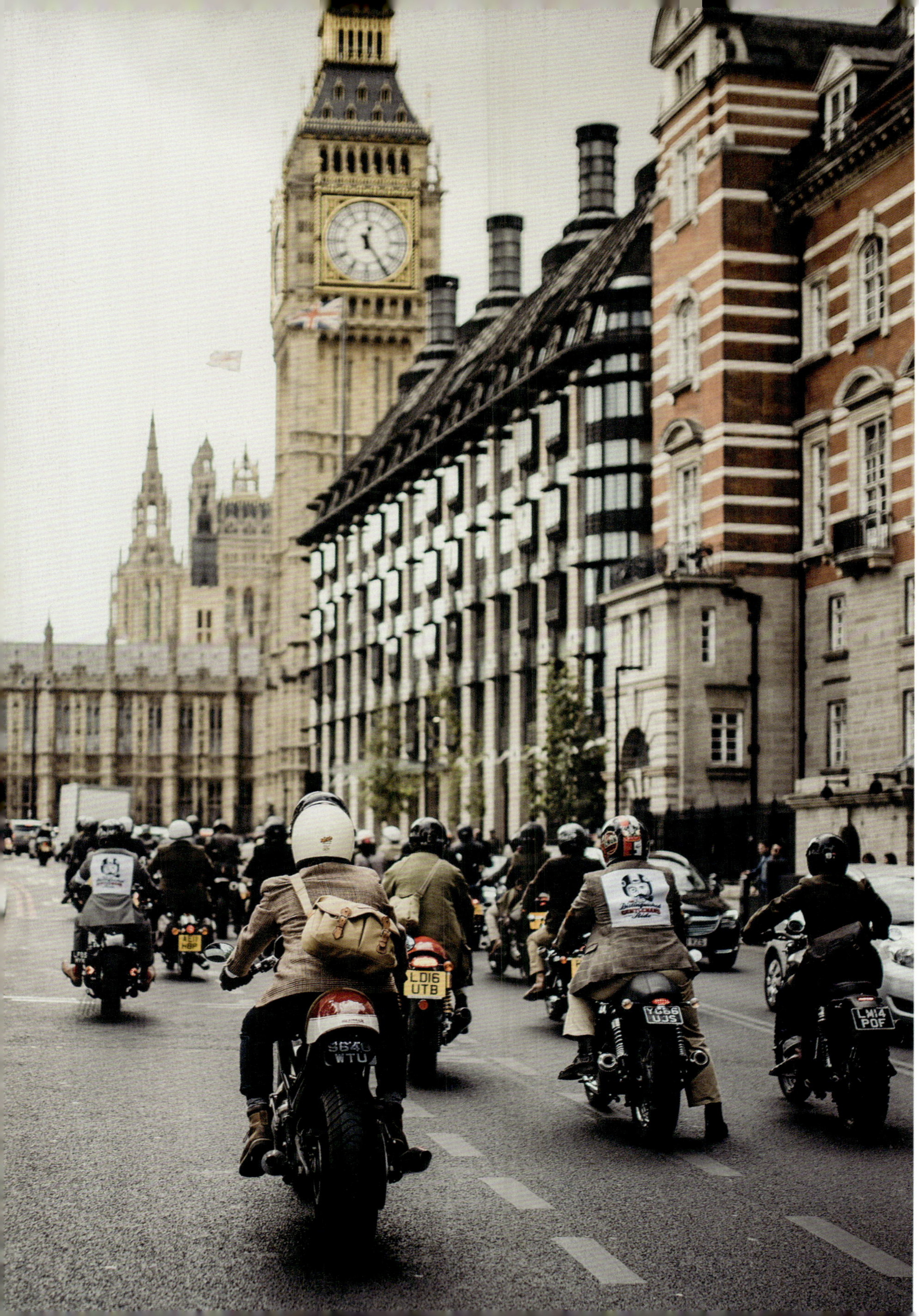
LD16 UTB
YG66 UJS
LW14 POF

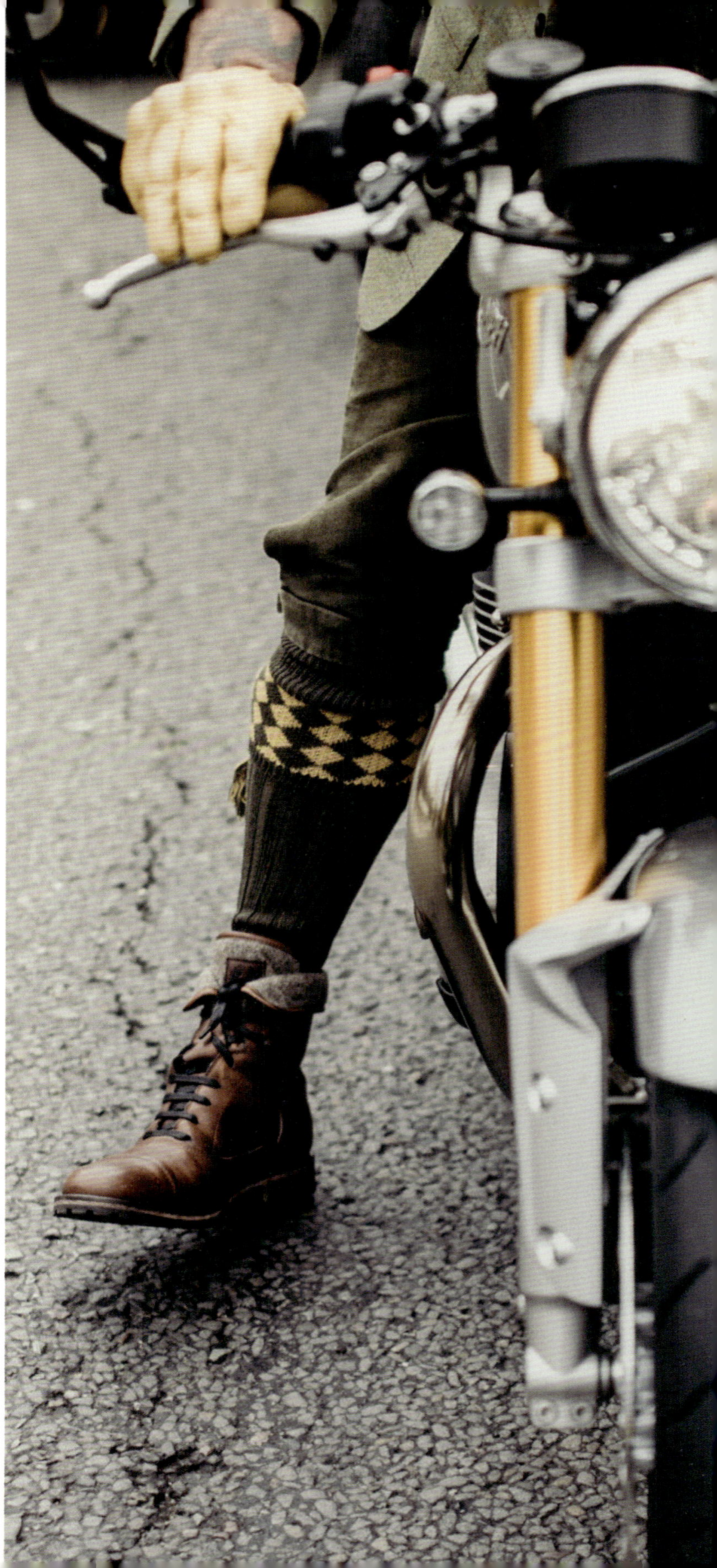

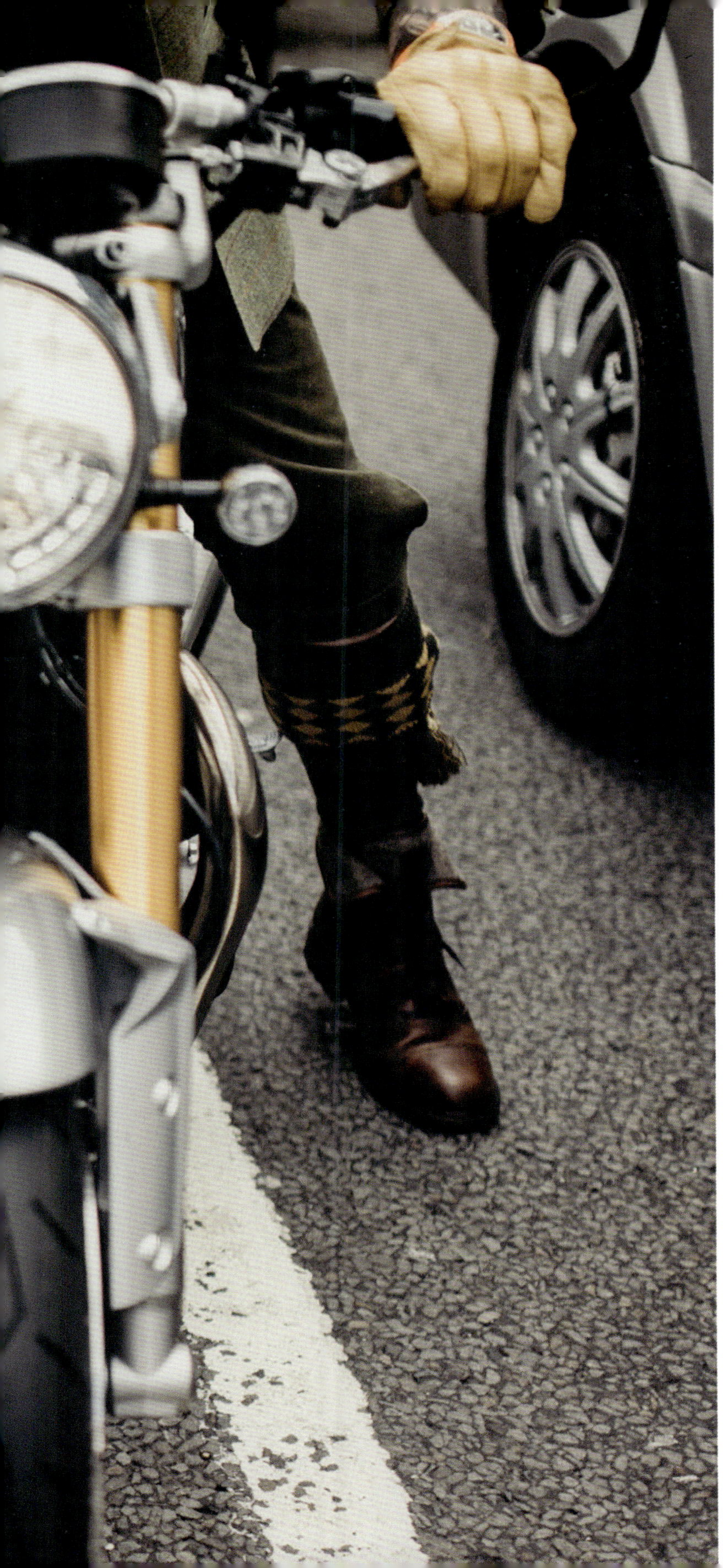

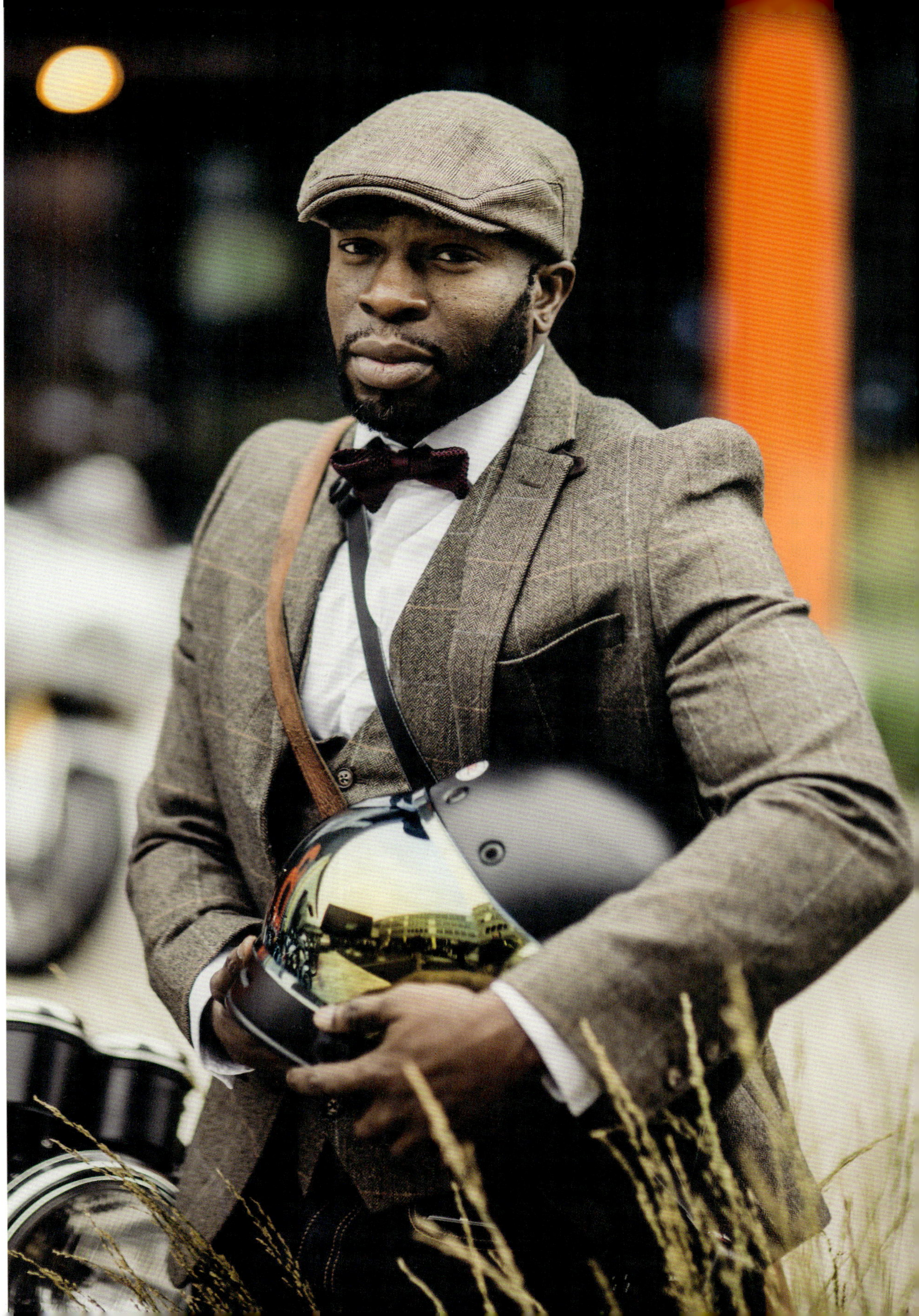

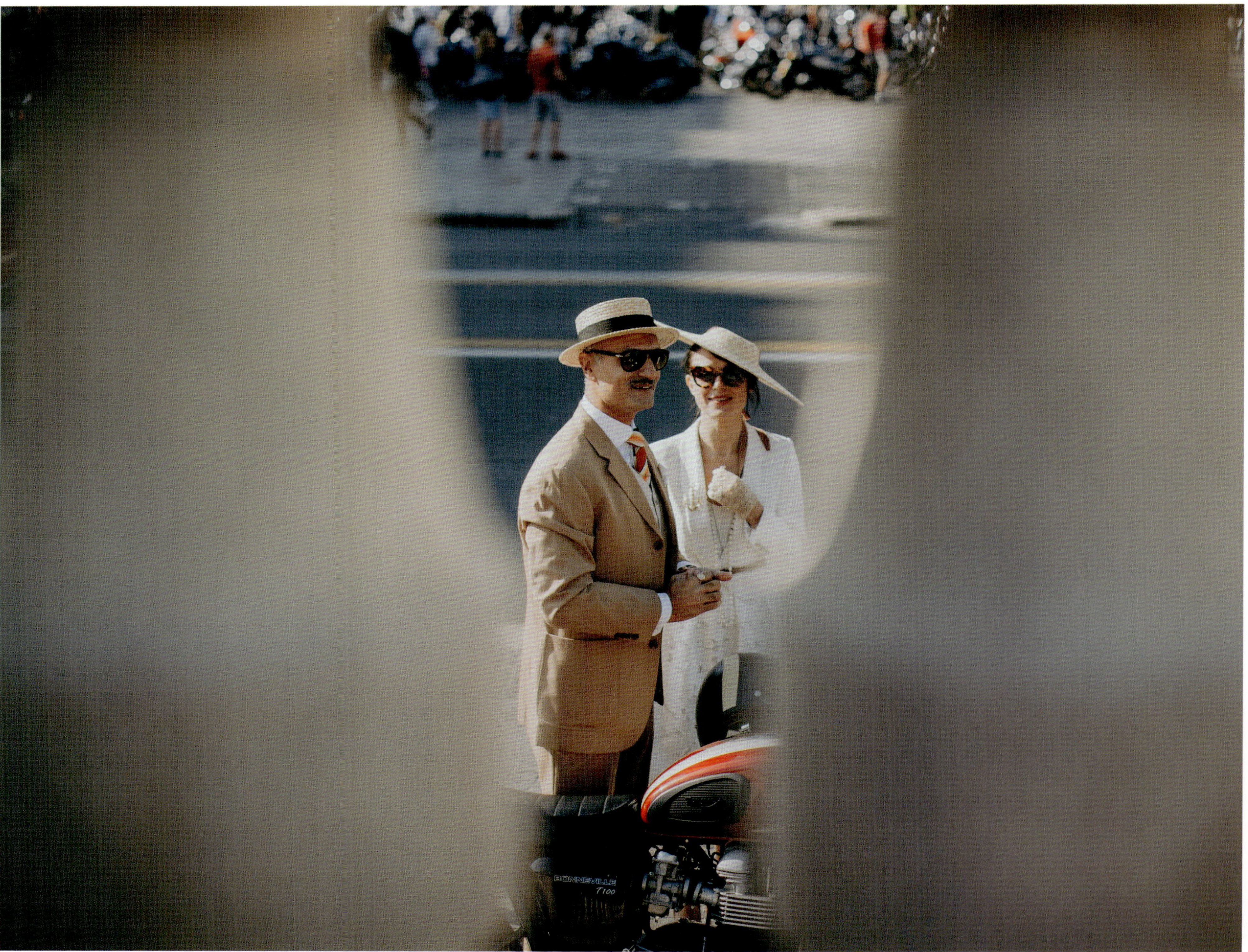

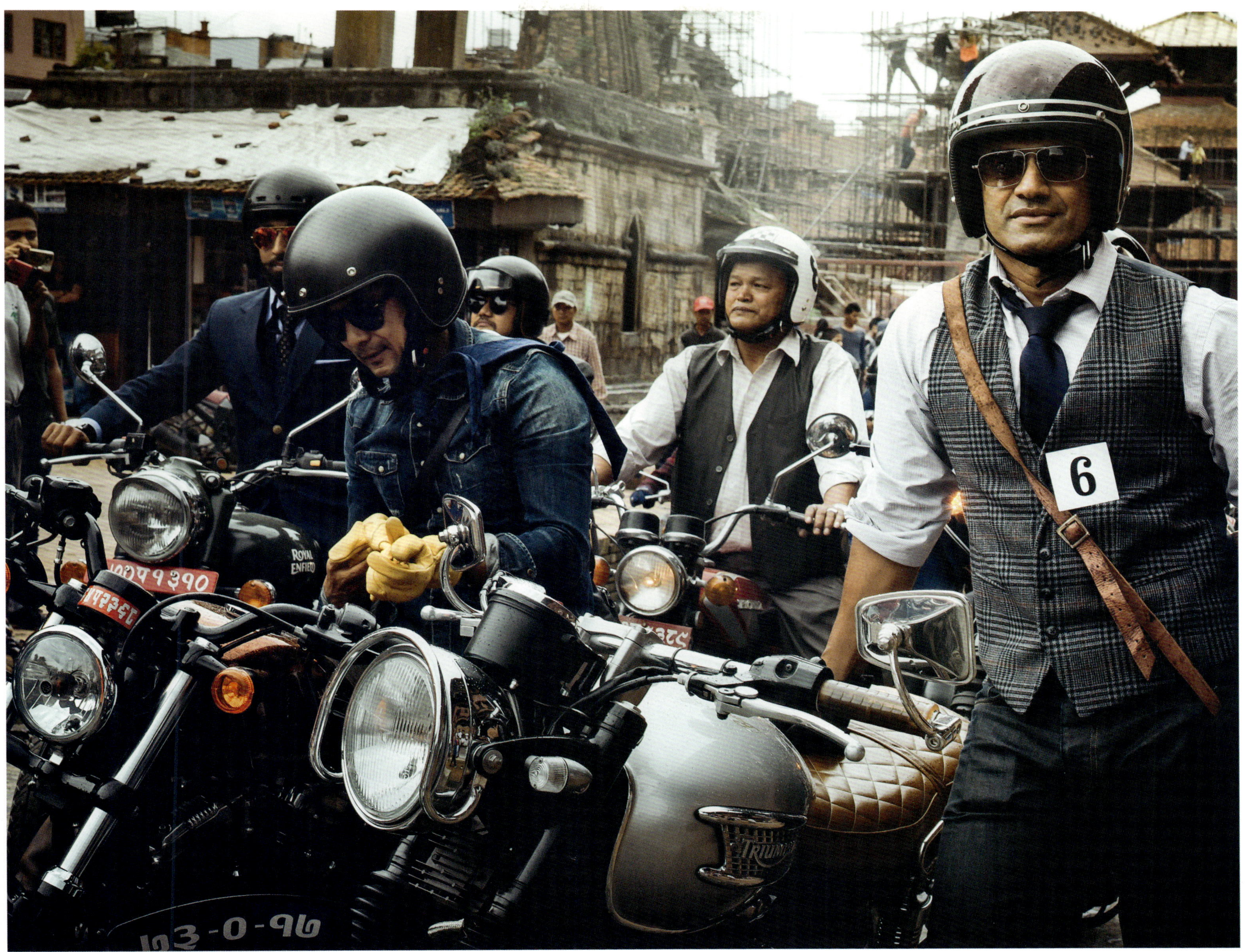

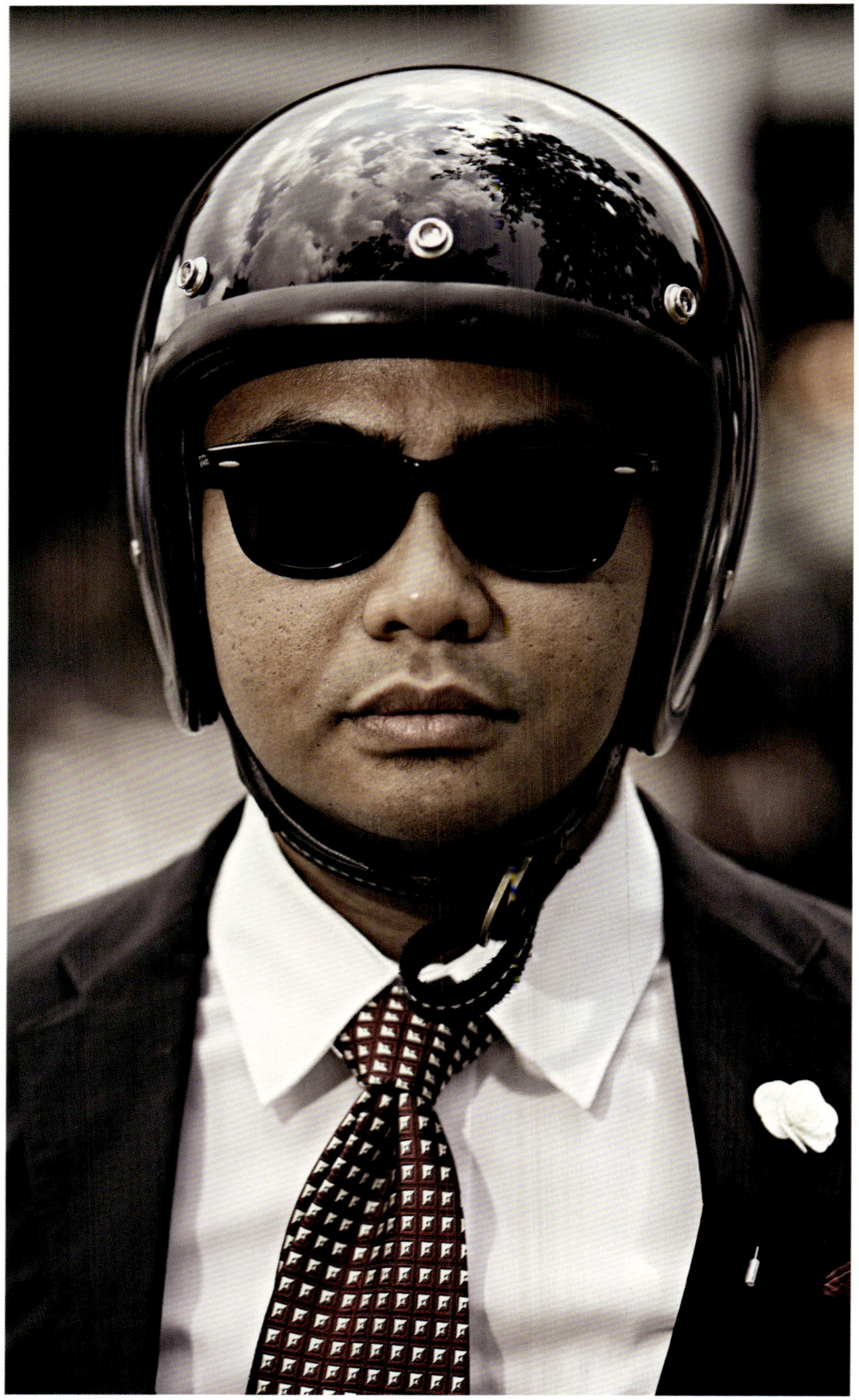

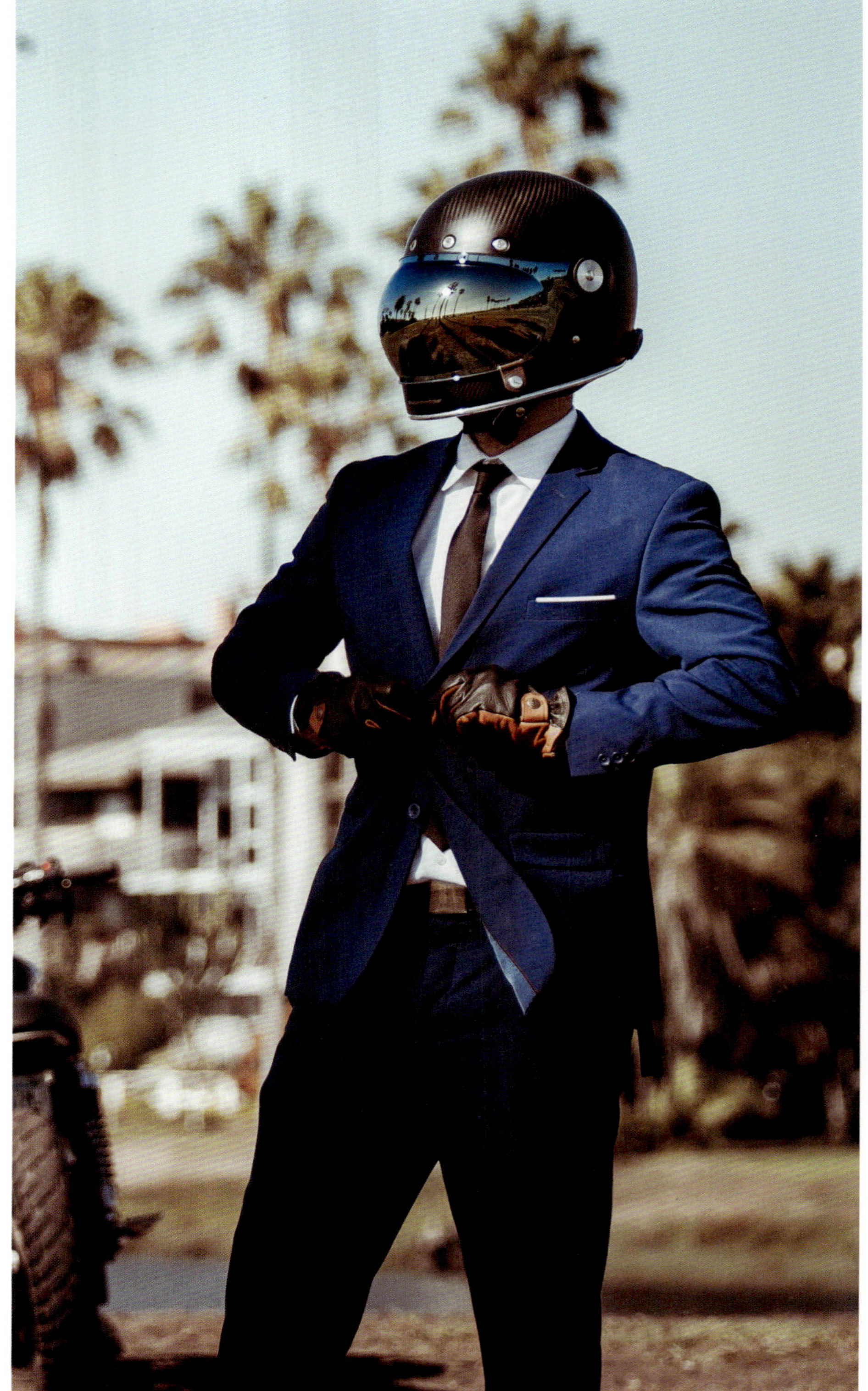

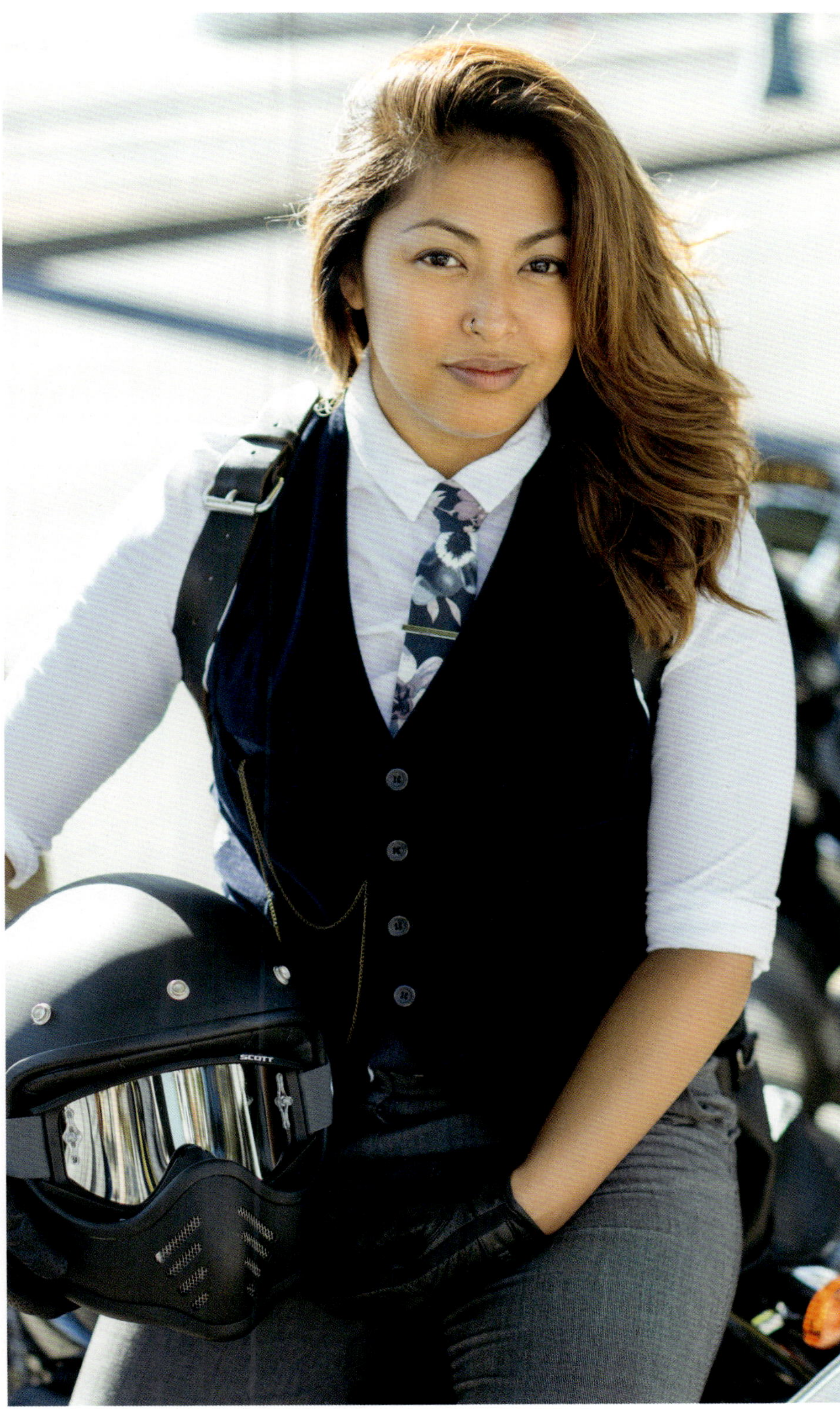

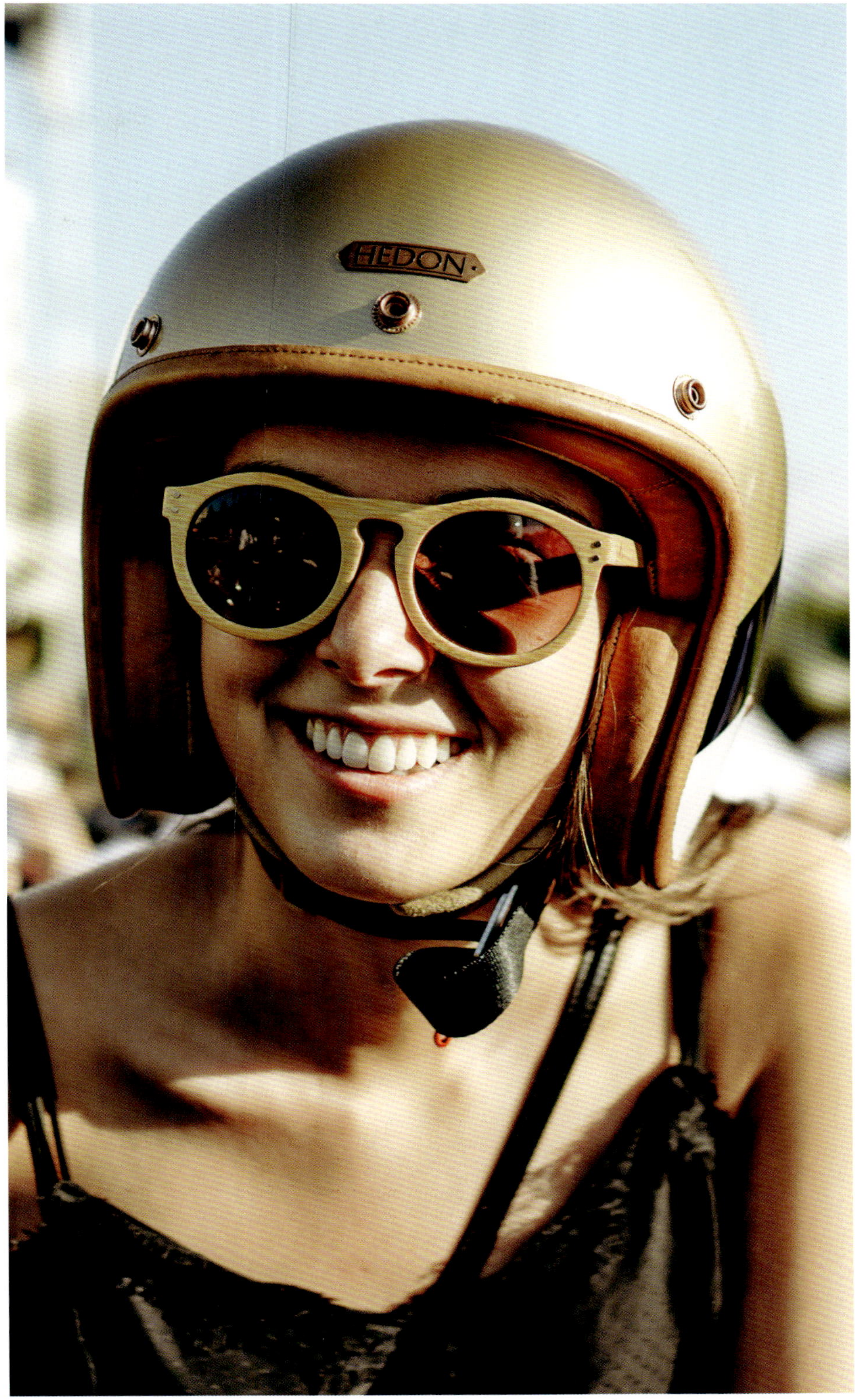

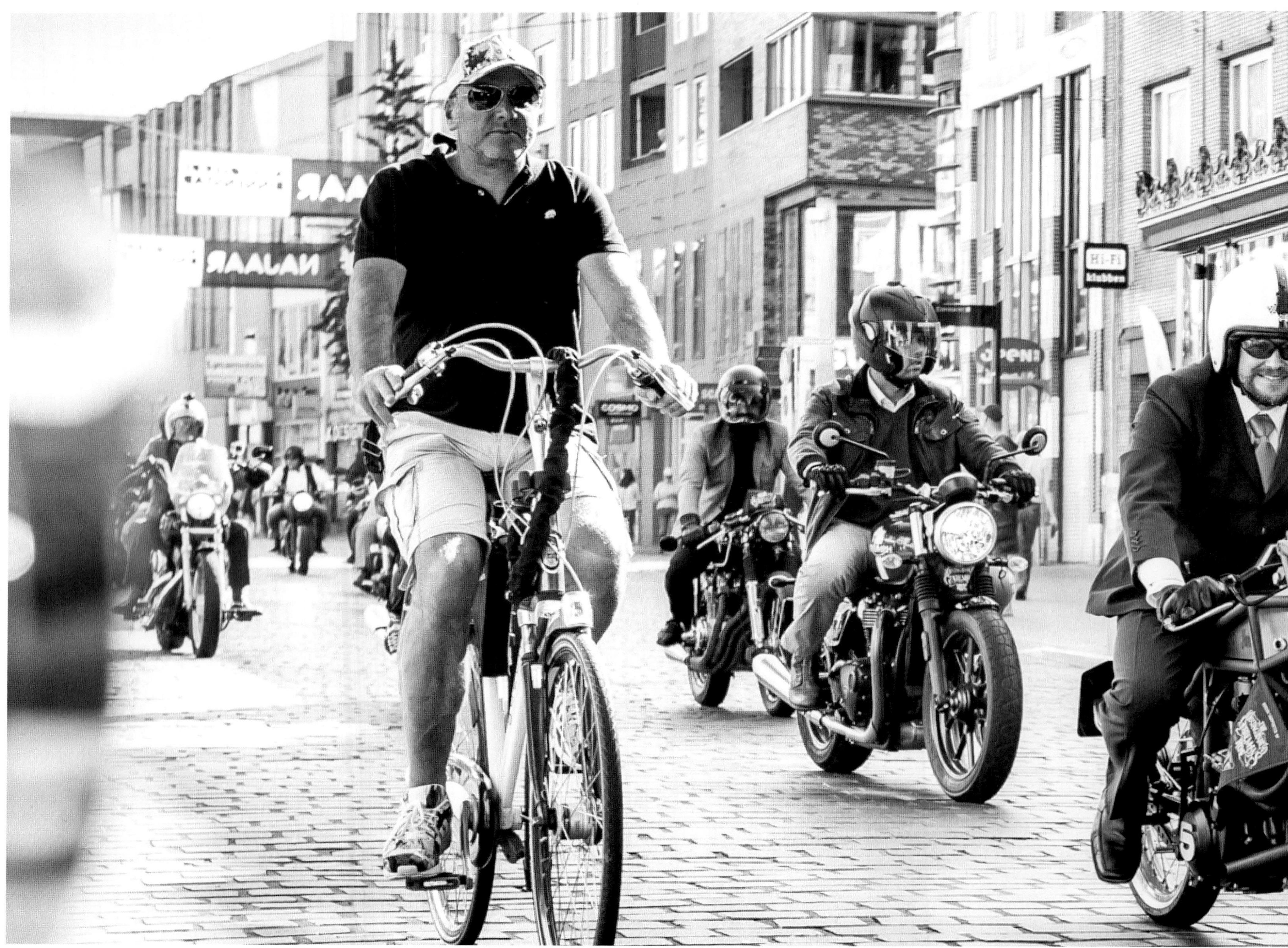

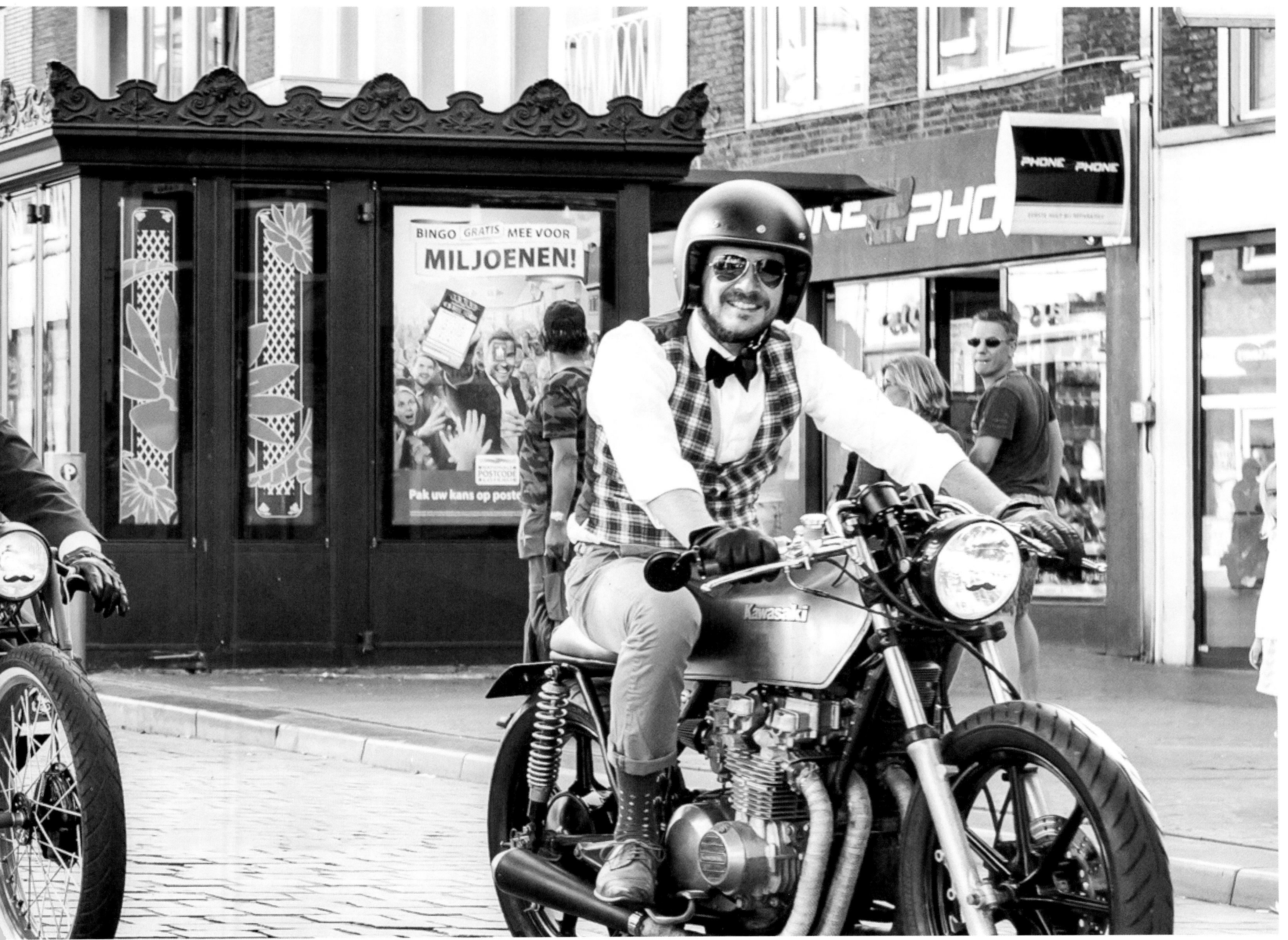

BINGO GRATIS MEE VOOR
MILJOENEN!
POSTCODE
Pak uw kans op post
PHONE
PHONE
Kawasaki

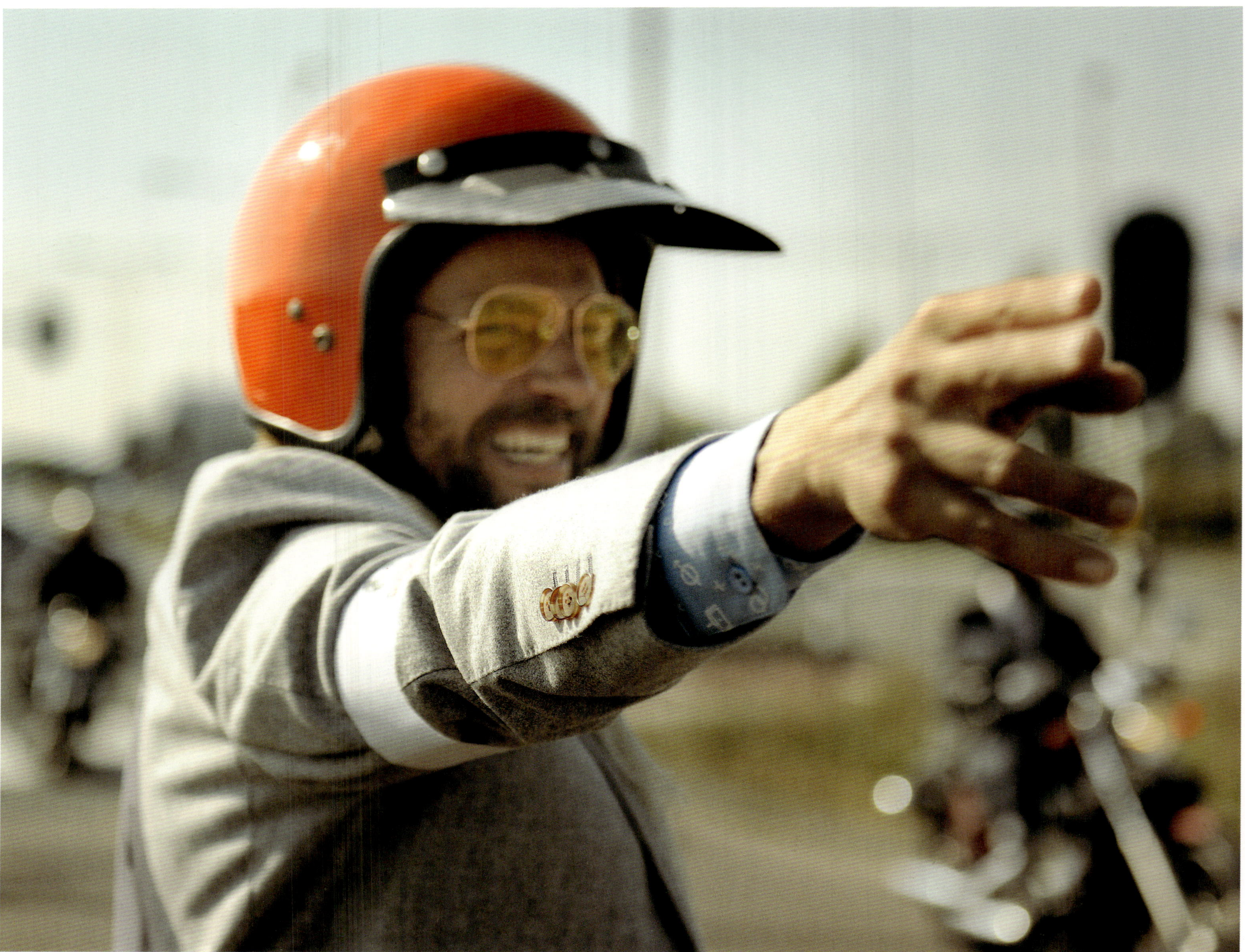

2016 Ride Poster

Designed by Luca Ionescu

This year marked a departure from the previous illustrated style, and a switch to heavily ornate typographic design, backed with up-close photography of a dapper dressed man. The design captured the refined elements of traditional signwriting, tying in with the distinguished craftsmanship of both suits and motorcycles.

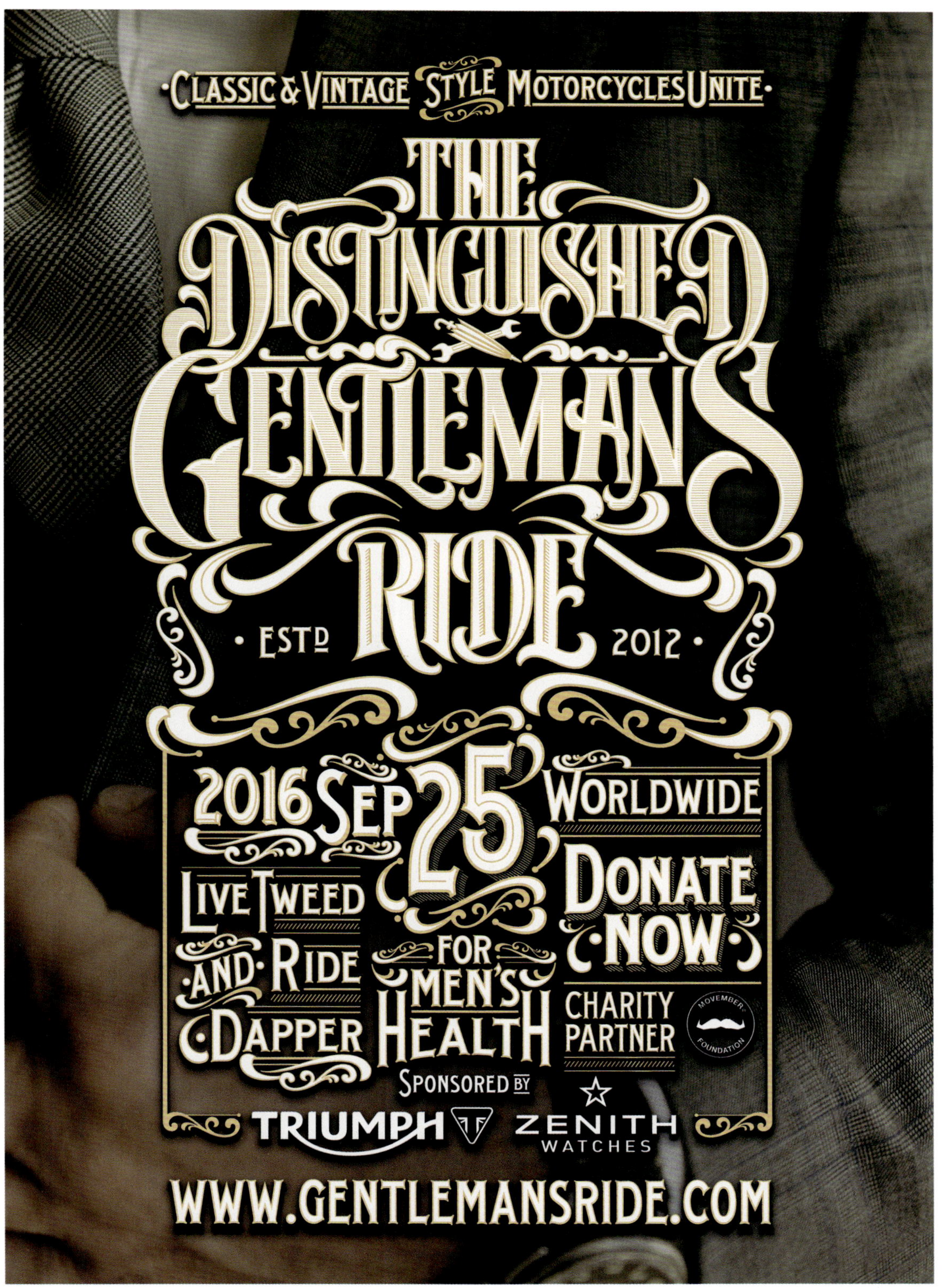

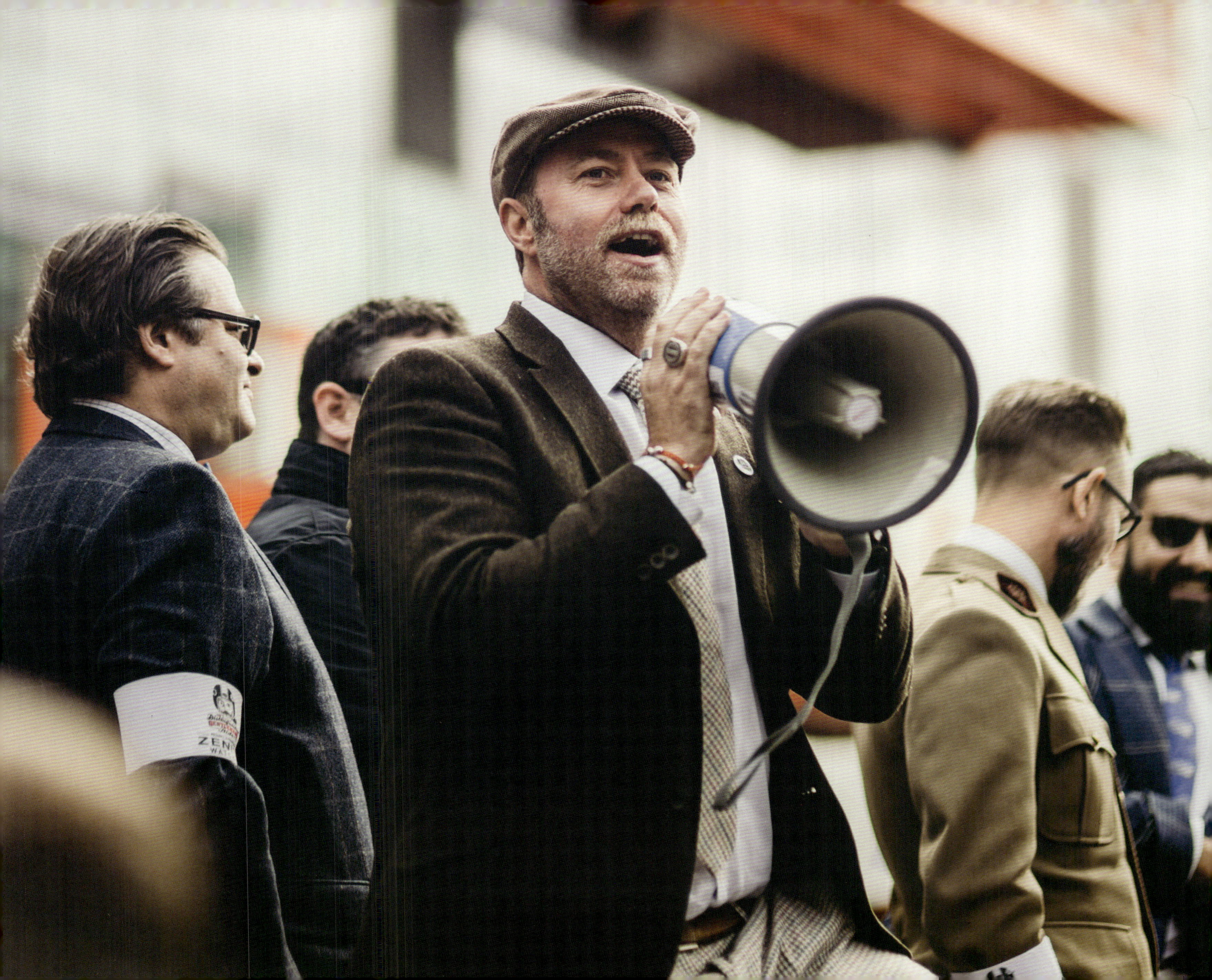

It's hard to believe how fast life is racing past us, especially when you're asked to write a piece for a book designed to close out a decade on one of those life-changing relationships that has so much emotion wrapped up in it. Movember has been and continues to be a life-changing moment for me; and in 2015 I got to be part of another one. In that year, I hatched a new concept at Movember: to build a global innovations team internally.

Its mission was to go where men are outside of our traditional campaigns and to find amazing collaborations that fit the brand, and could deliver scale and impact outside of our campaign month, giving the community we serve more offerings to connect with the causes whilst having fun doing good. DGR for me was a clear stand out by a country-mile on our short list. The teams set up a meet and greet for Mark and me in Sydney, my hometown. The plan was to see if the founders liked each other and if we could hatch a deal.

I clearly remember meeting Mark for our first official meet. As soon as we started conversations, I knew it was a fit. From a

spots, which randomly happened to be some of the old Surry Hills haunts from my media days.

A lot has happened since our first meeting, looking back and seeing how aligned we have been with our communities and the scale DGR has provided, growing globally across hundreds of countries. For me, this is super emotional. When I think about it, what a collective we have created, reaching more people than we could have ever without joining forces, people who care so much for men's health.

Seeing first-hand this community of incredible humans together, who are socially connected whilst wearing their very best outfits, bringing out their personalities to the amazing bikes is something you have to see to believe. One of my best moments was the New York City ride with thousands of bikes and a volunteer team complete with police escort on their bikes, directing us through all the amazing parts of the city. A day I will never forget from the experience to the lifelong friends I met.

We can't thank you all enough for the impact you have and will continue to have on our joint mission to support and change the face of men's health globally.

Launching to 2021 we have taken on the world together with our incredible teams and communities, we've been agile with the challenges we've faced along the way. Great recent examples of how to stay connected with our community through a pandemic that closed the world down, creating Ride Solo and staying connected.

The stories are endless, the life moments we will have forever, the impact we have delivered, to the many lives we have saved. But most importantly the lifelong bond we have created in having fun and doing good together. This has been personally an absolutely humbling experience, I mean who gets to help build a second global movement in their lifetime with incredible humans?

The future is a bright one for having the DGR team in it. We

BEARDS OF A FEATHER: DGR & MOVEMBER

It seems like a match made in heaven now, but just how did two
of the world's biggest men's health charity events come to work together?

chance meeting on stage many, many years before at a Movember Sydney Luna Park Gala party in our early days of launching Movember, there was even a photo of Mark rocking an incredible MO with me on stage congratulating him. To our mirrored journeys and challenges in so many ways, our early days of growth in building a movement starting with Prostate Cancer and then after establishing ourselves expanding into Mental Health and Suicide Prevention, a result of shared experience in losses through suicide we have each had to face.

Even the overall brand fit was synchronized, from our brand pieces around what it is to be a gentleman, styles, culture, and language. We spent an incredible amount of time together with the team hatching out plans on what the future together could look like and the impact we could have collaboratively. I also remember enjoying more than a few good beers together in local

The impact has been enormous, the social connections made to the shoulder-to-shoulder conversations over the many seasons of events. The atmosphere this event creates, which has led to so many conversations personally, with now lifelong friends who aren't afraid to talk about the hard stuff and getting into the habit of looking after themselves with as much love and care as they do with their incredible bikes.

DGR and Movember, through the extraordinary fundraising that has taken place, is fueling world-class programs for Prostate Cancer with biomedical research, precision medicine, clinical trials, real-world evidence networks, survivorship, True North, specialist nurses, mental health with veterans and first responders (an incredible piece of content that shows real-time lives saved), social innovation challenges, men building better relationships, Movember Speakeasy, events just to name a few.

have become true family and brothers in arms through all the challenges and opportunities that have been thrown at us and tackling them together has only made us stronger. Mark has one of the biggest hearts, with incredible passion and drive to change the world, with Mikey as his wingman, an absolute rock star and rock for all of us, to Ramsey with his magical herbs and spices, and just being Ramsey, in completing the core team.

I salute you all, what a privilege and honor it has been to be part of the first decade. So, so many life moments for me across the world to meeting lifelong friends. I'm excited for the next decade of having fun, saving lives and putting so much good into the world with you through our next evolution together. Big love.

Justin Coghlan (JC)
Co-founder, Movember

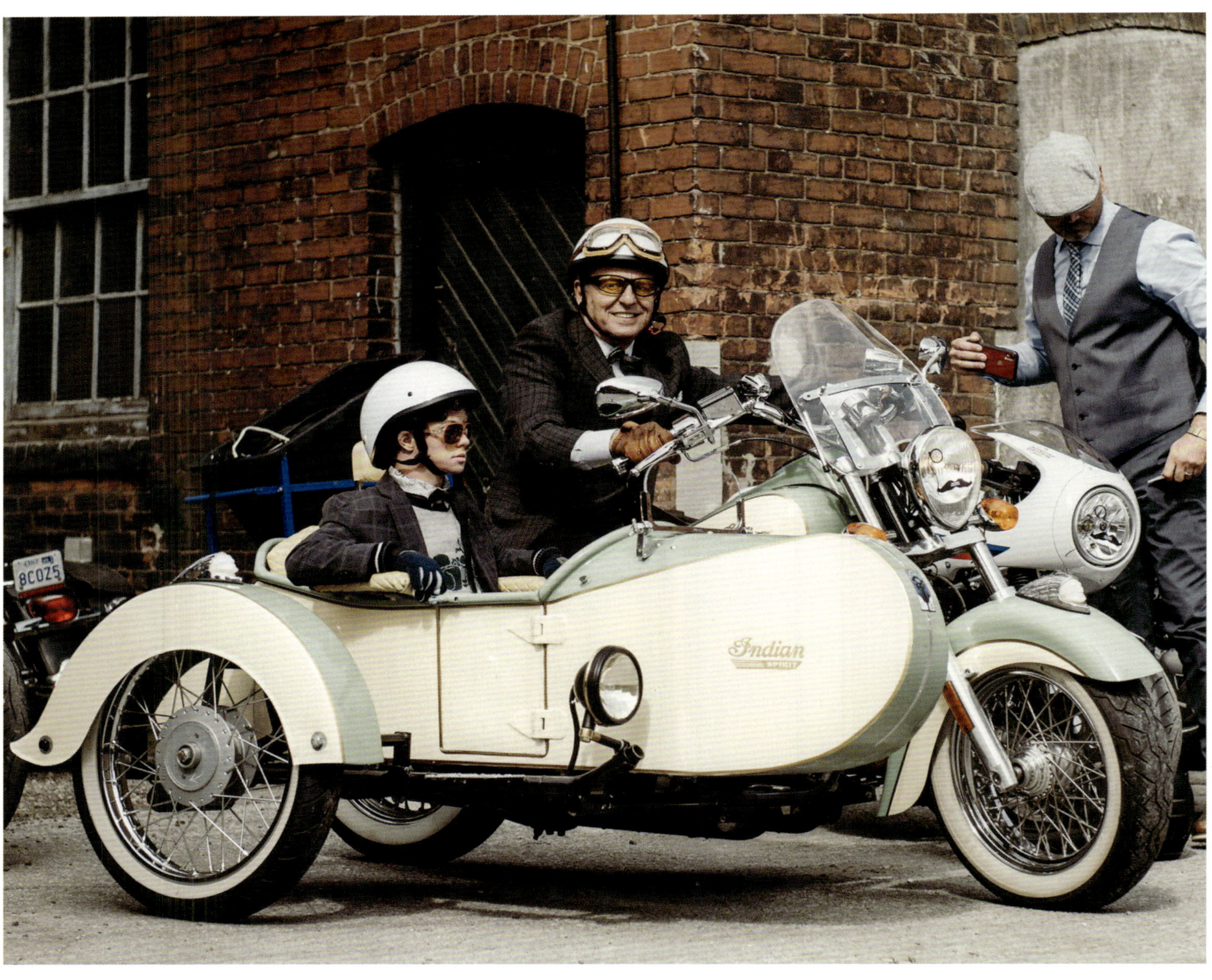

Ride Location
HAMILTON, CANADA

I have been a motorcyclist for several years. I have also been an advocate for men's mental health and prostate cancer, and numerous other fundraising initiatives. I ran into Jeff Campagna, the local Hamilton CA host, several years ago at Steeltown Garage. He told me about The Distinguished Gentleman's Ride coming up, and I thought to myself, "What a perfect way to raise funds for a worthy cause!"

DGR is an important event for me since I can enjoy a day with fellow motorcyclists around the world. I have been an active advocate for men's health all of my working life. I have been working for the Laborers International Union of North America for 44 years in different positions, and presently as the International Vice President. LUINA represents approximately 600,000 American construction workers who are primarily men, and therefore has shaped my advocacy for men's health.

Mental health is an important issue since men do not communicate well regarding mental health, and in many cases only when it's too late. My father also had prostate cancer, so through this experience it was obvious to me that men do not take care of themselves, and that early intervention on prostate issues can save lives. My son, Enrico, who was born with Down Syndrome, rides as a passenger on my bike at DGR every year. He loves being on the bike

with me. My other son, Michael, has his own bike and my son in-law, Alex, has also joined us on the day as well. It's special that my family members participate and understand the importance of why we are raising funds together. The most important success of DGR, and of course Movember, is the raising of awareness for men's health issues that are typically ignored.

The Hamilton event has been great, Jeff is committed and has done a great job in preparing and promoting the ride. We have a large group of riders who come out rain or shine. This last ride we had brutal rainy cold weather. However, regardless of the weather, we have great participation. I love the fact that we leave from Liuna Station, a restored Canadian National rail station that I was responsible for saving from demolition. We have since restored it into a conference center that is now designated a National Historic Site.

For the past several rides, I was pleased that I raised the most funds worldwide. Whether 1st, 2nd or 3rd, a motorcycle prize is awarded by Triumph. I did not accept the bikes and had Triumph sell them and forward the proceeds to DGR. My involvement is twofold, first and foremost to raise as much funds to create awareness for men's mental health and prostate cancer, and second to have some fun riding with like-minded people around the world!

BIKES OF DGR:

SCOOTERS

Effortlessly stylish and with a strong Italian heritage, these are motorized bikes with an 'under bone' or step-through frame and a platform for the rider's feet. They are often powered by a two-stroke engine. Emphasizing comfort and fuel economy, they have come to be known as metal-bodied classics that were built the old-fashioned way.

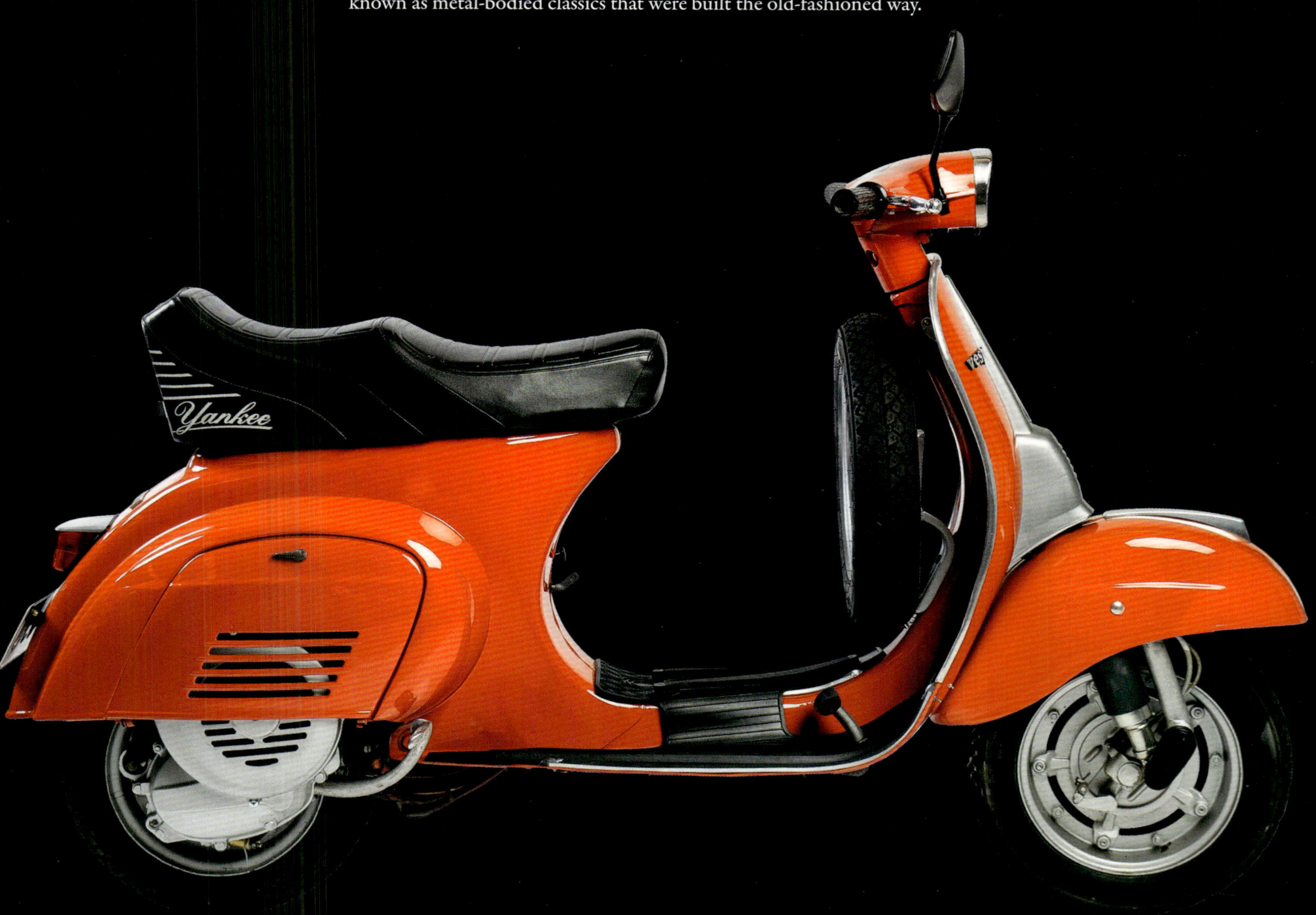

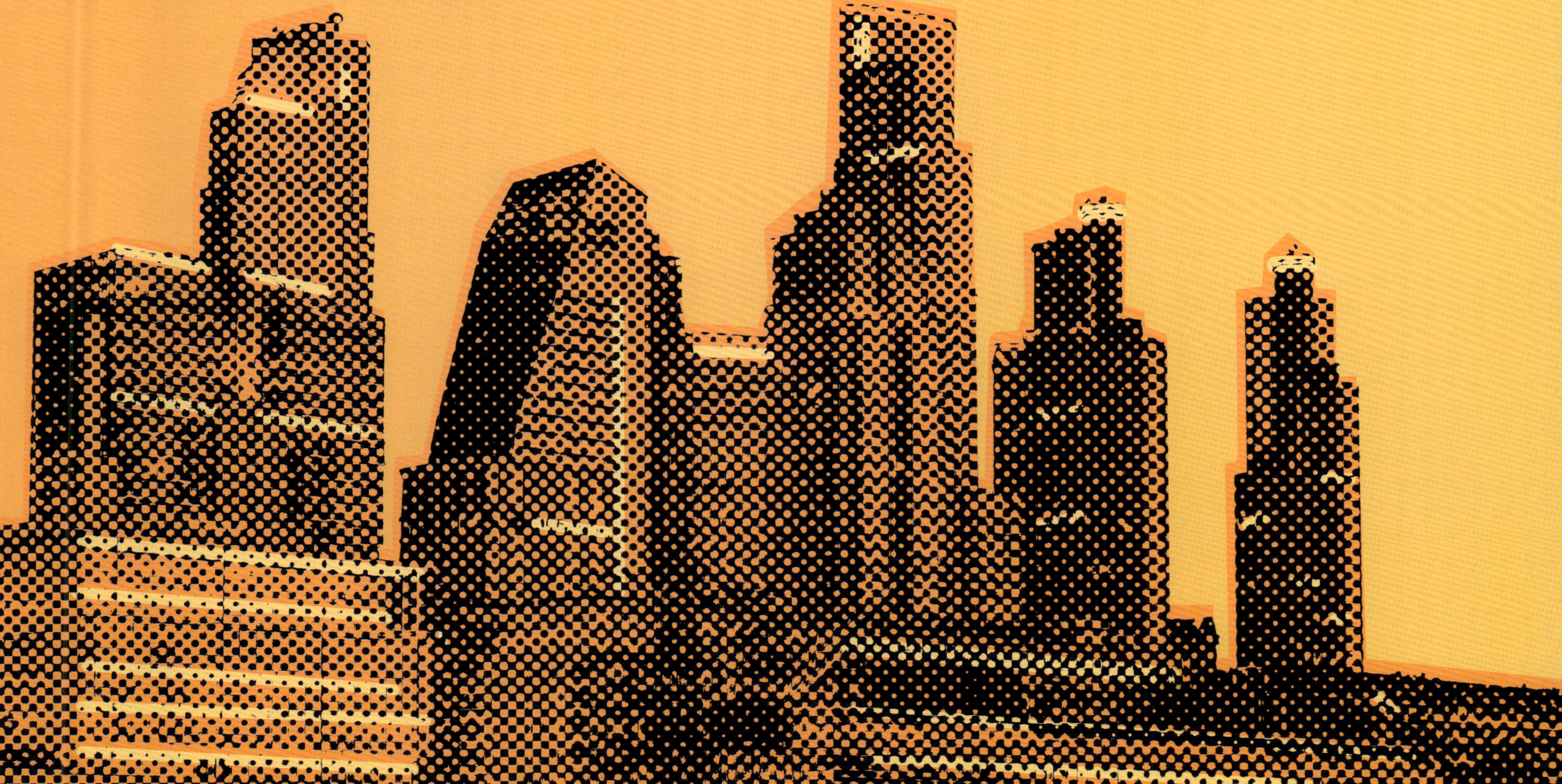

BUENOS AIRES
FIRST RIDE: 2014
TOTAL PARTICIPANTS: 9,080
TOTAL RAISED: USD $60k
DGR CITIES

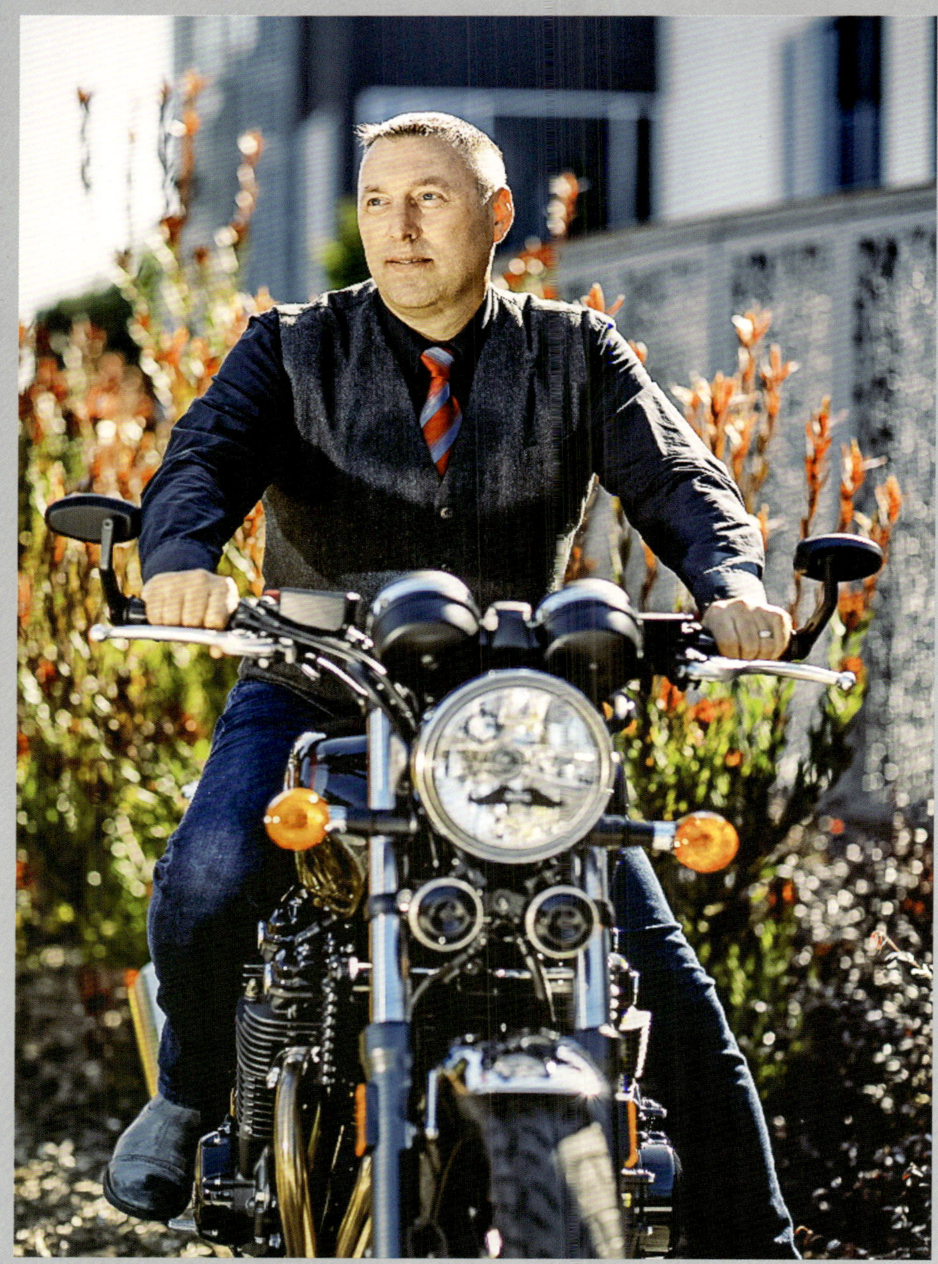

Fundraiser: **RON KRIETMEYER**
Location: **SAN FRANCISCO, UNITED STATES**
Total Raised: **USD $226,344**

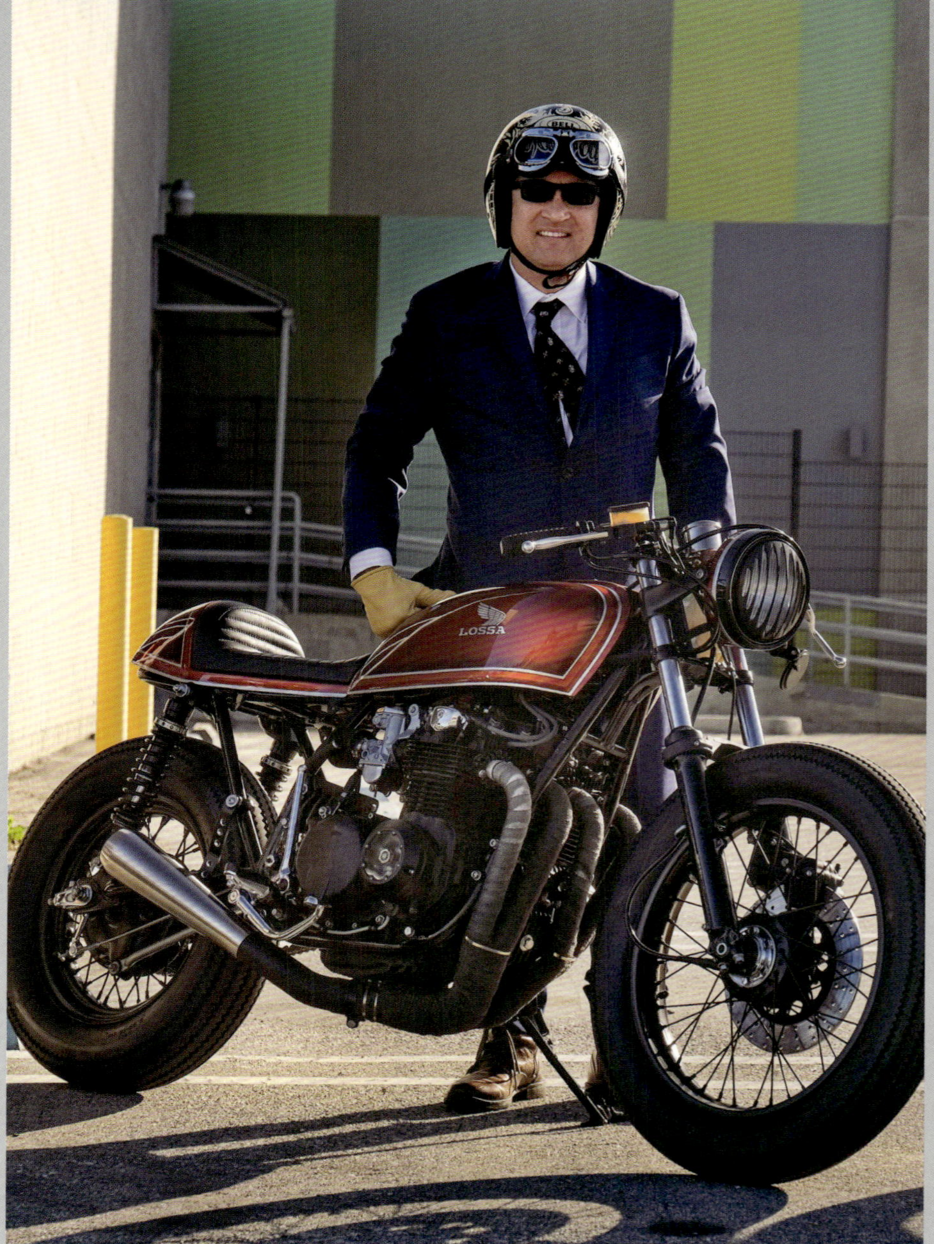

Fundraiser: **DONALD LEONHARDT**
Location: **LOS ANGELES, UNITED STATES**
Total Raised: **USD $70,860**

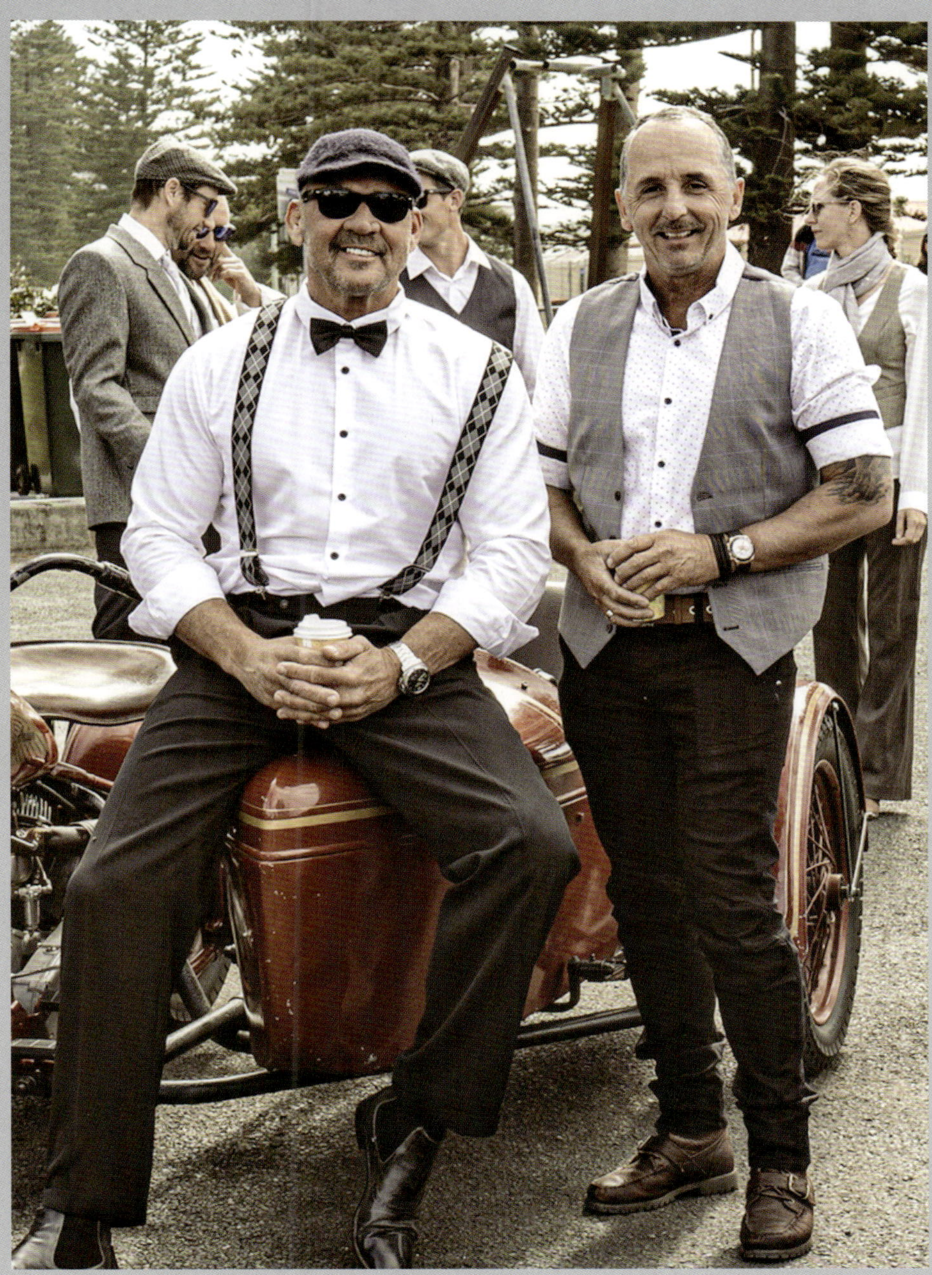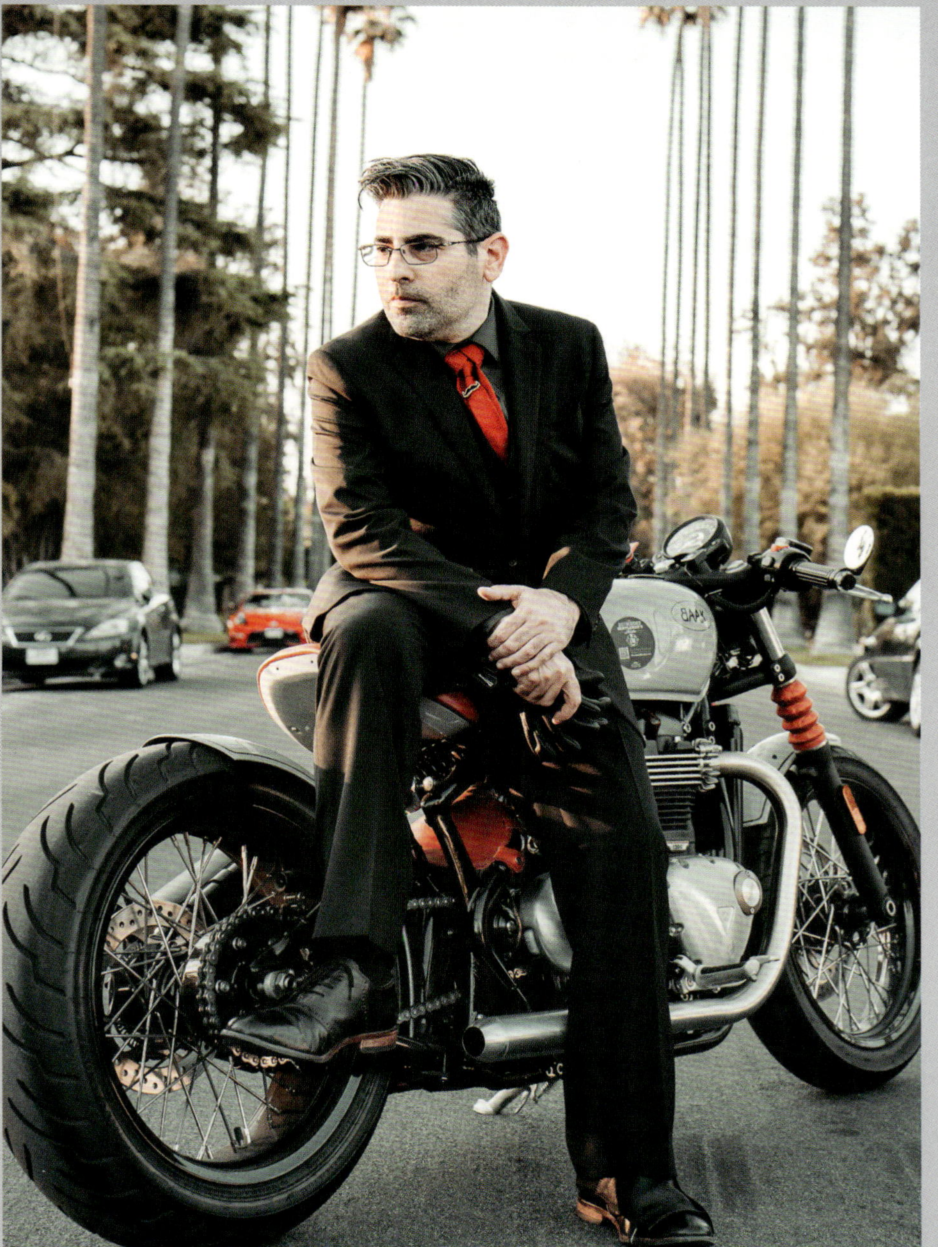

Fundraisers: **PHILL CRITCHER & ERMOND MORELLI**
Location: **WOLLONGONG, AUSTRALIA**
Total Raised: **USD $86,771 & $66,837**

Fundraiser: **ANTHONY BROWER**
Location: **LOS ANGELES, UNITED STATES**
Total Raised: **USD $61,303**

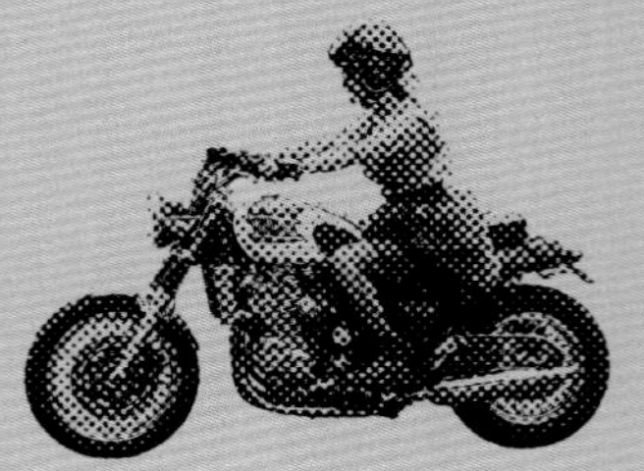

2017

- RIDE SIX -

SPURRED ON BY OUR NEW MEN'S MENTAL HEALTH FOCUS, DGR
REACHED NEW HEIGHTS IN 2017 WITH **581 CITIES** AND **94,000 RIDERS**
DRESSING DAPPER FOR A POSITIVE CHANGE GLOBALLY.

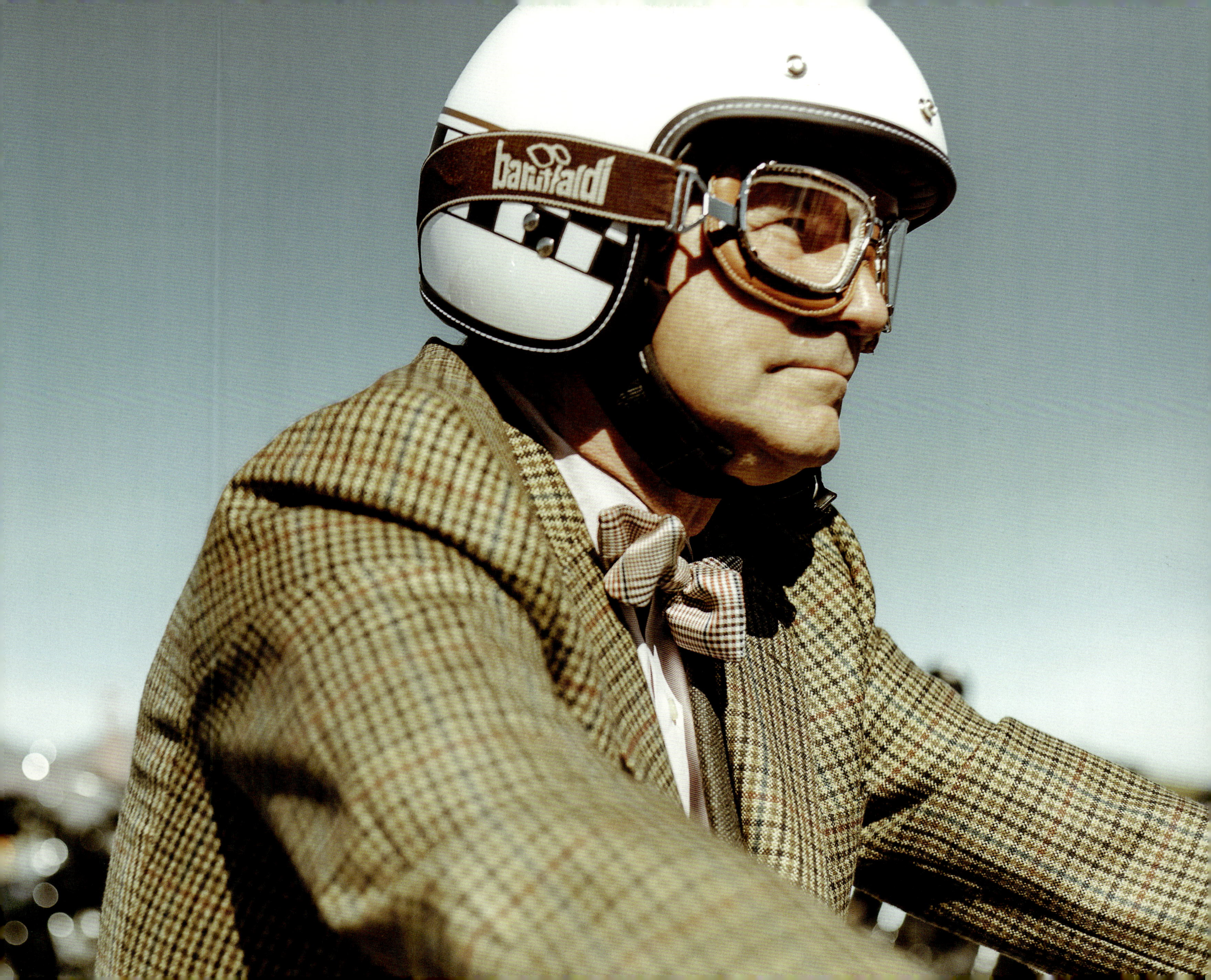
baruffaldi

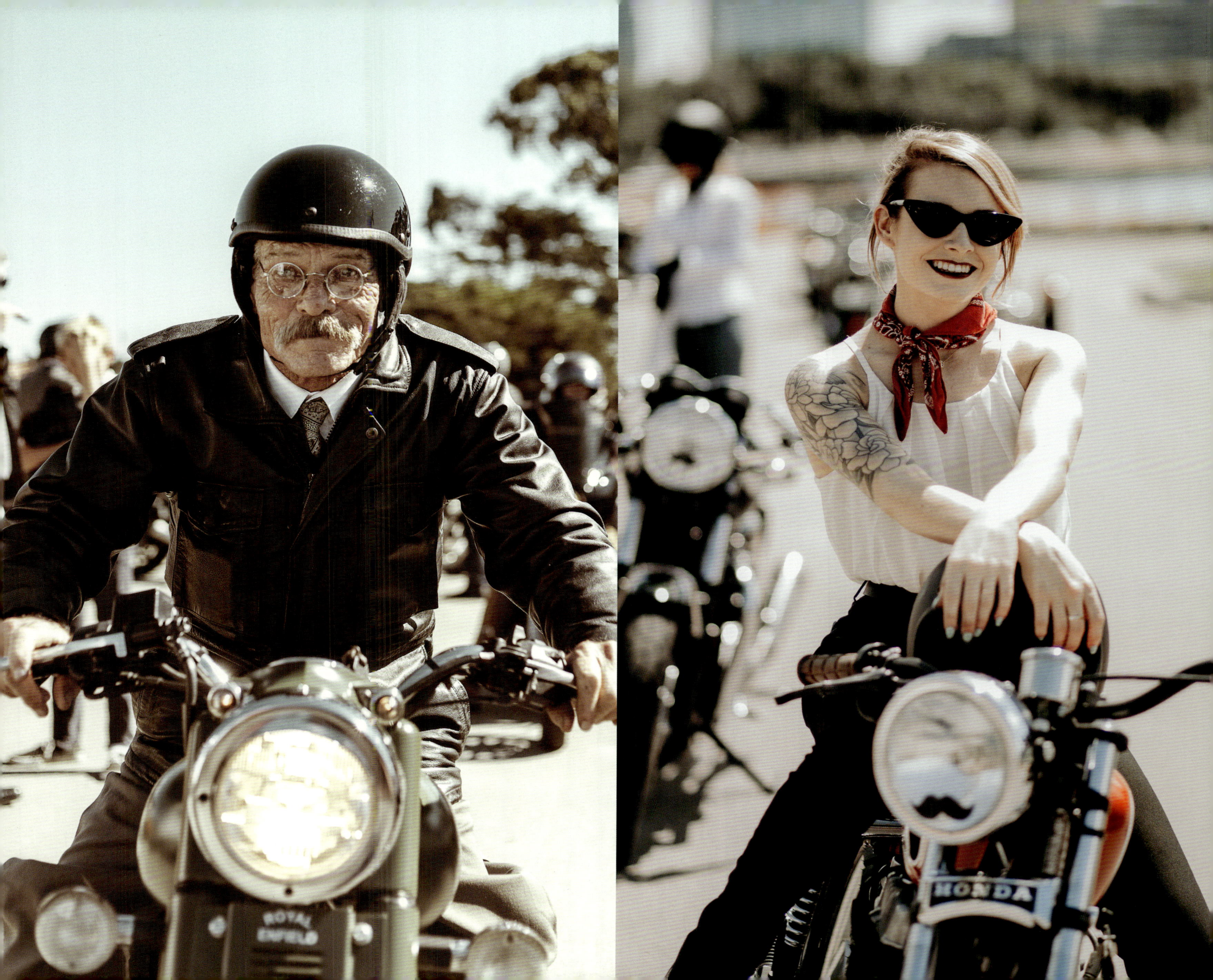

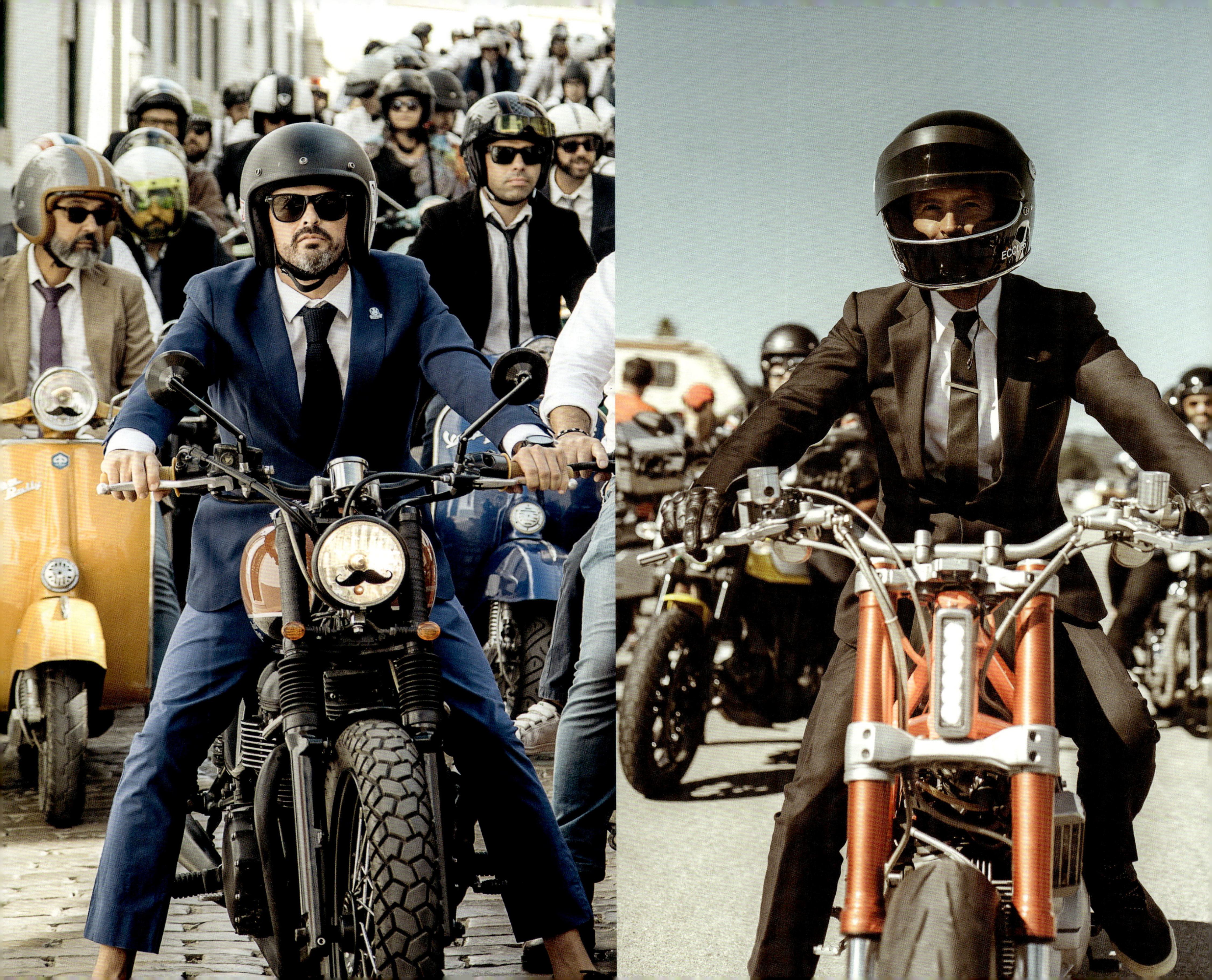

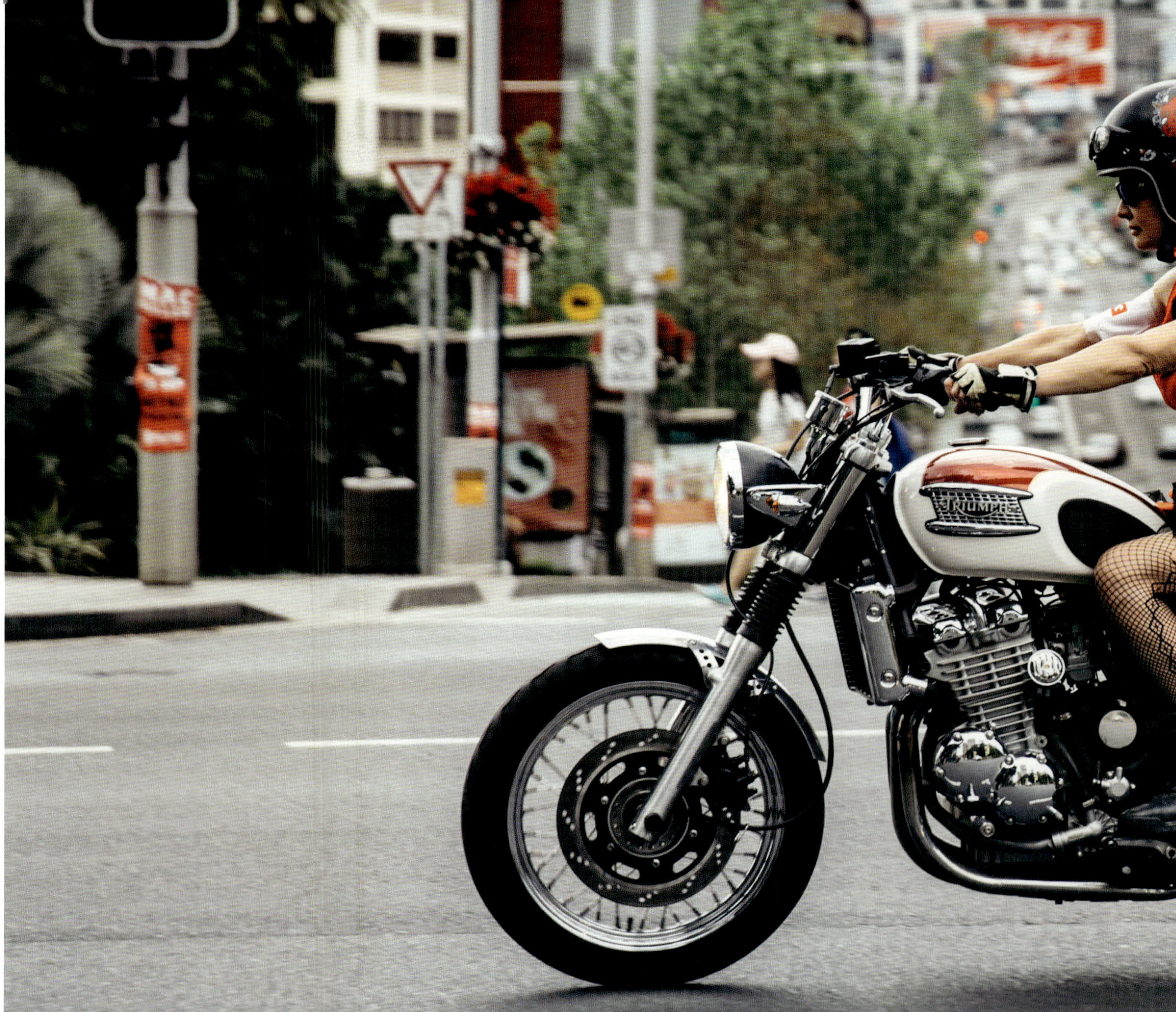

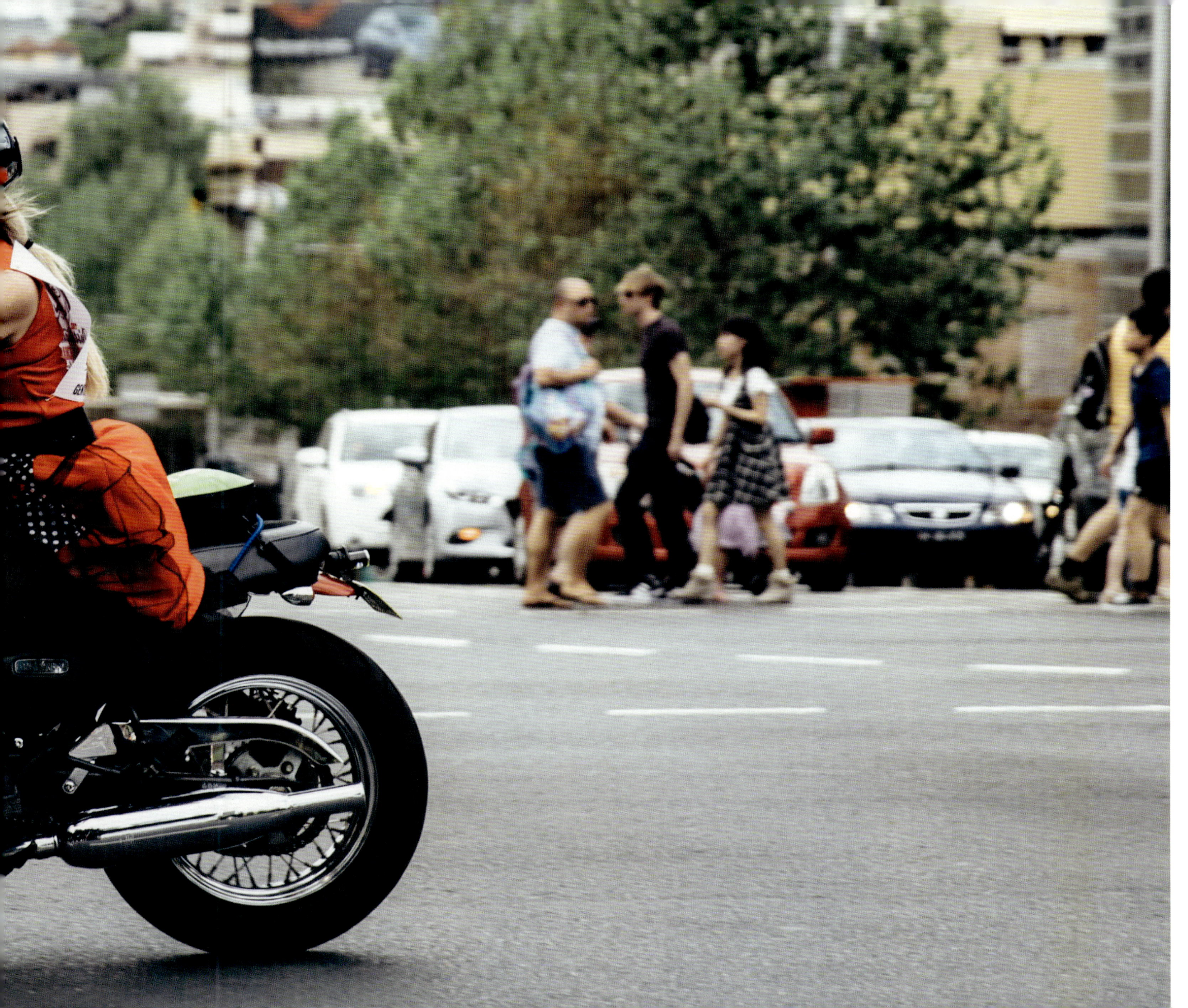

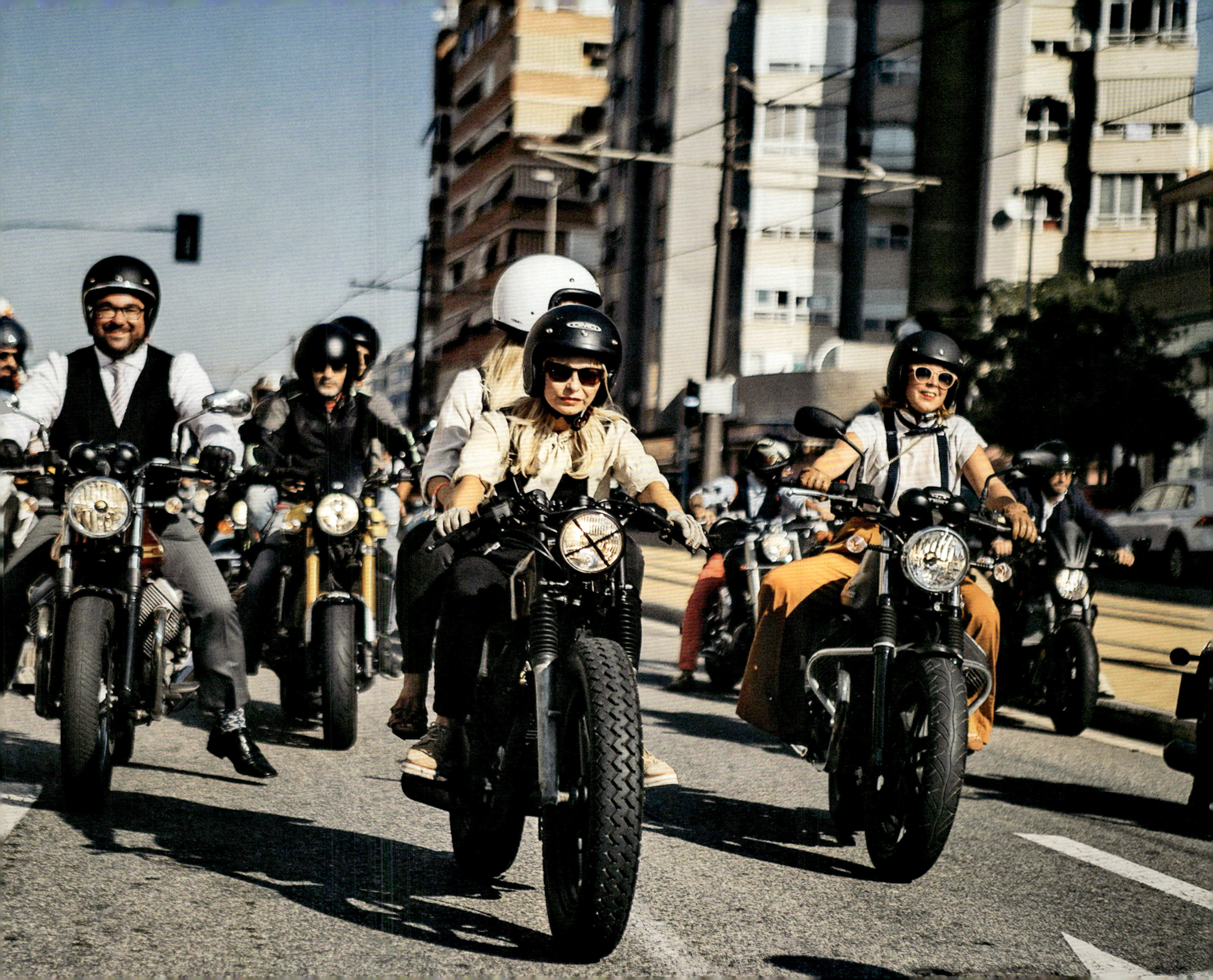

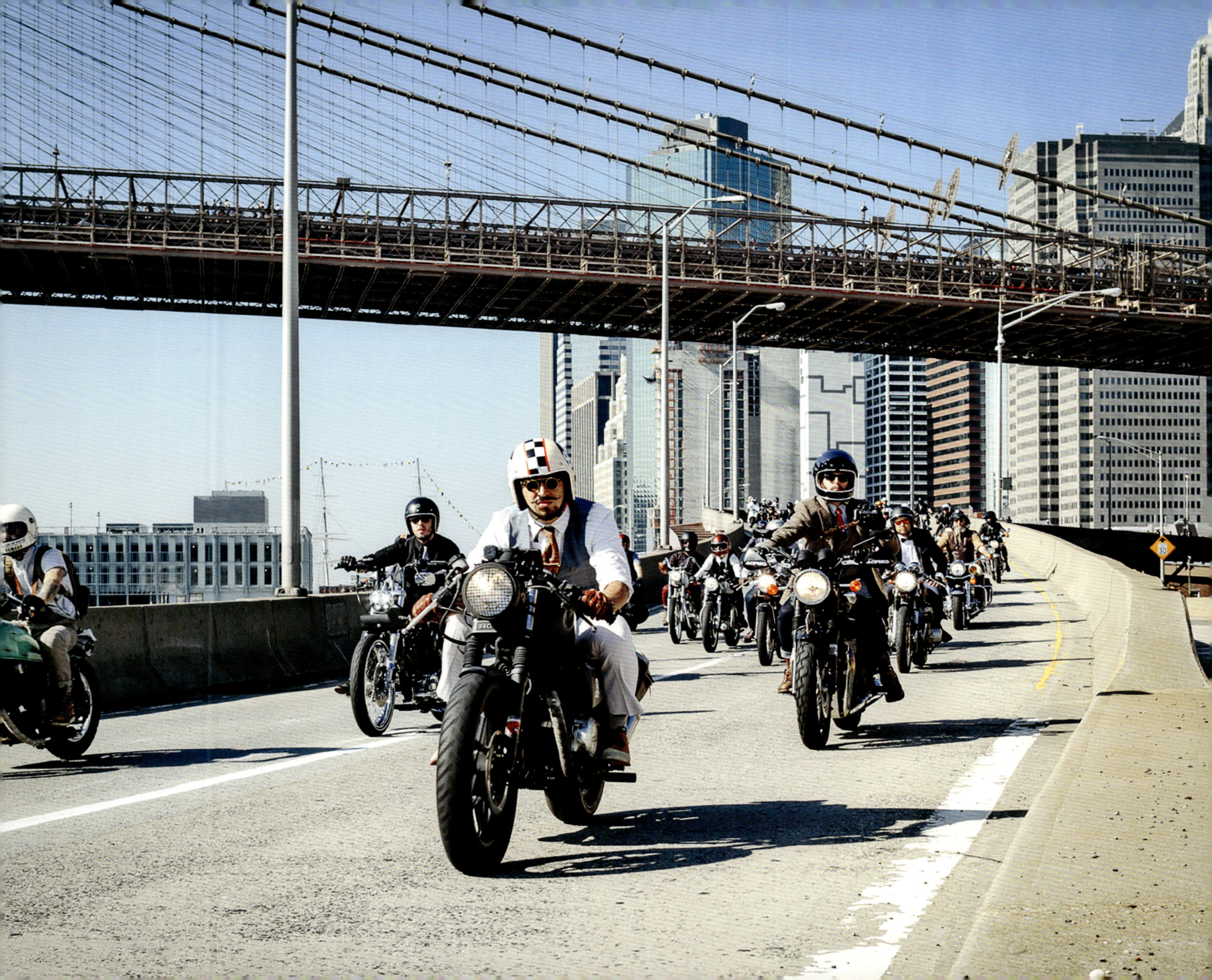

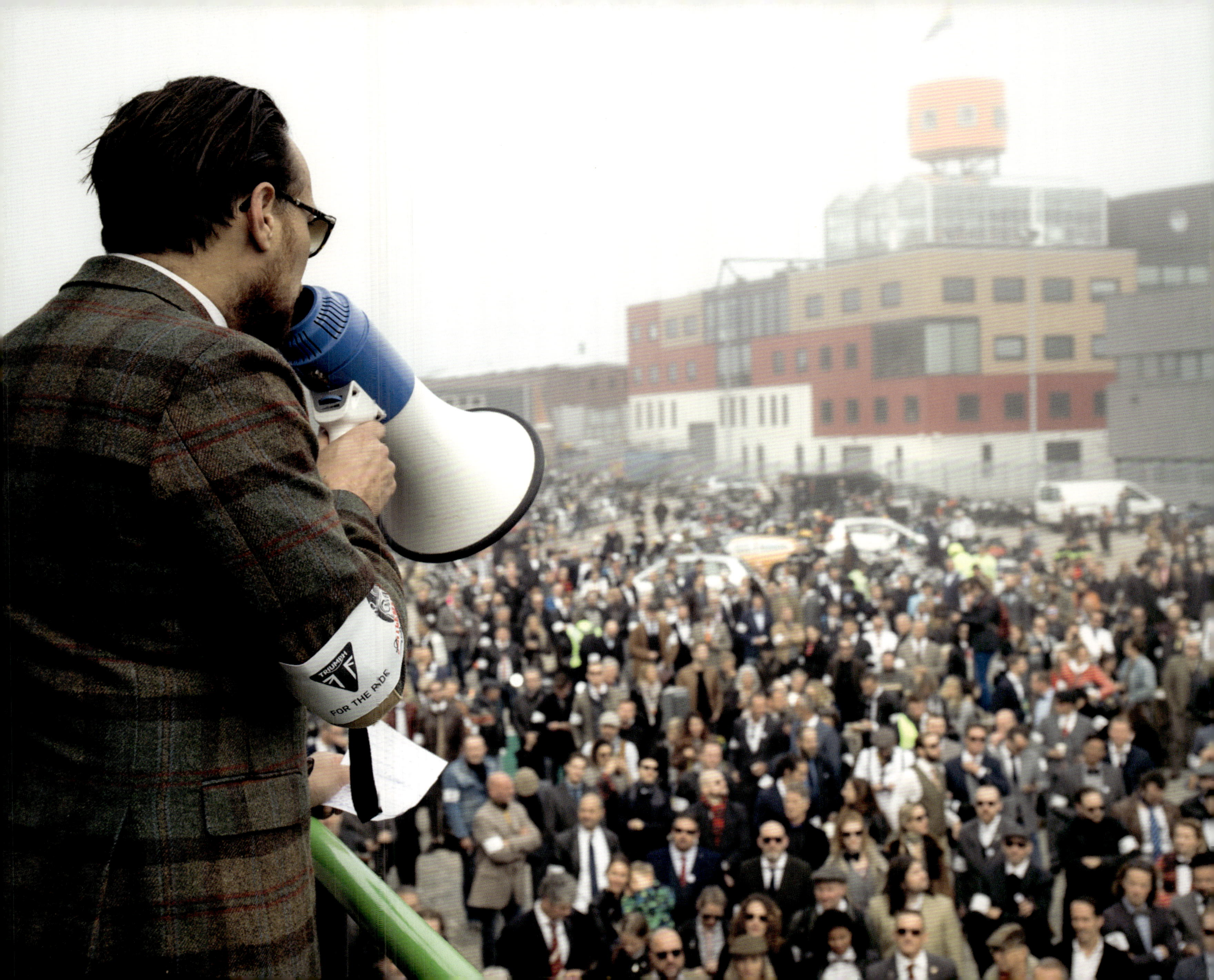

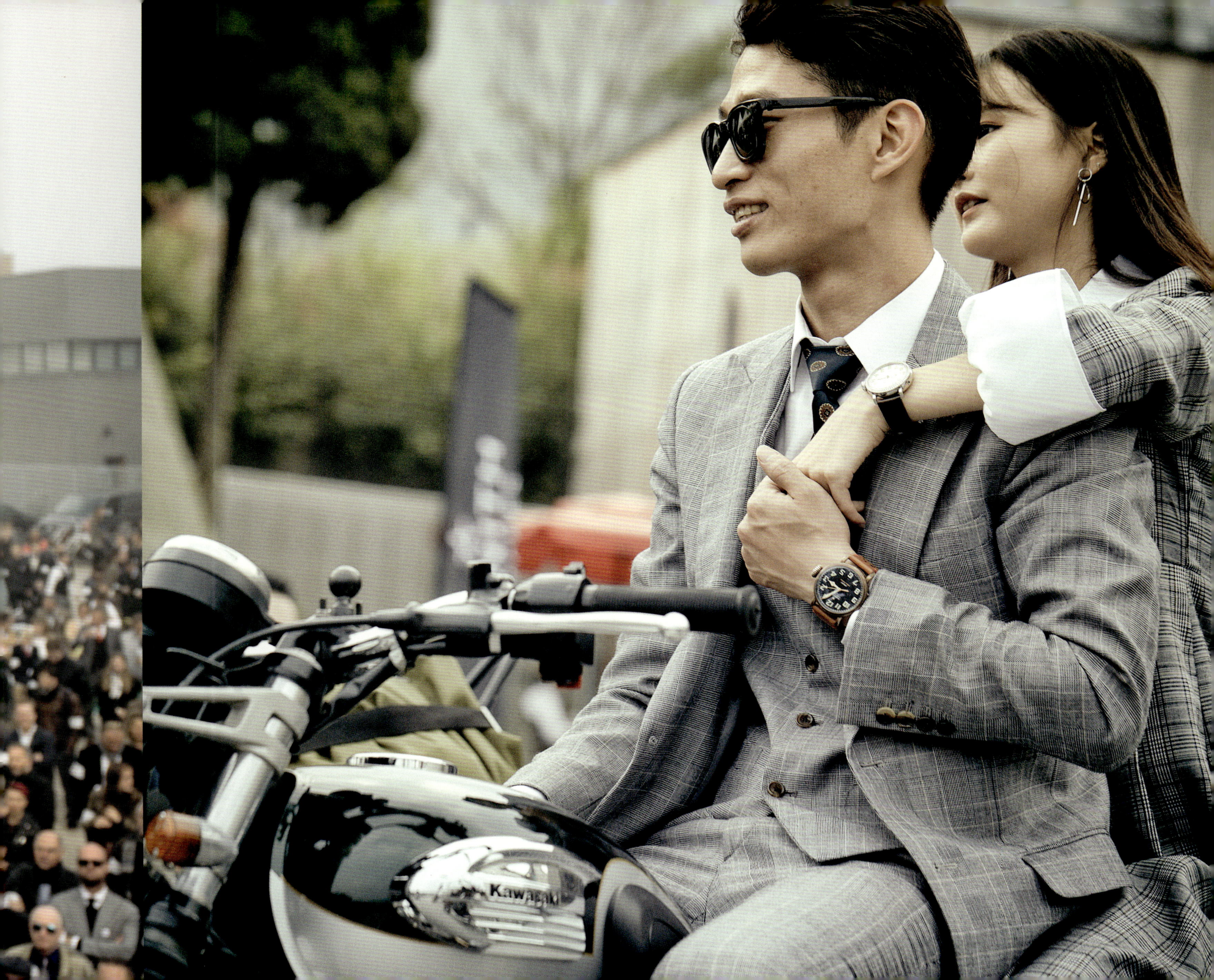

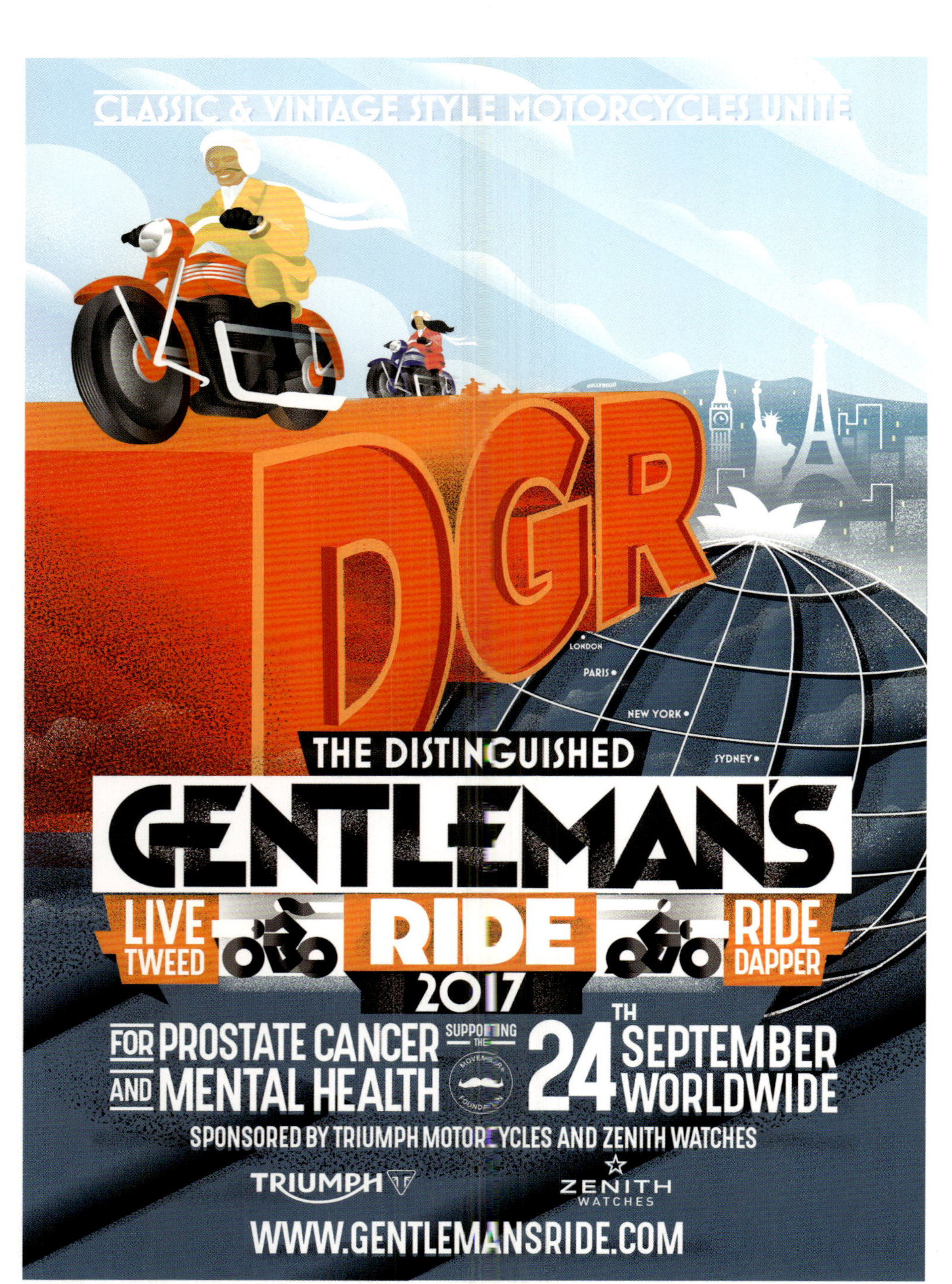

2017 Ride Poster

Designed by Luca Ionescu
Like Minded Studio
Classic Art Deco style posters from the 1940s were the main inspiration for this year's poster, which showed multiple iconic international landmarks along with major cities pin-pointed across a spinning globe, while a group of riders of different genders pass across the blockbuster DGR text.

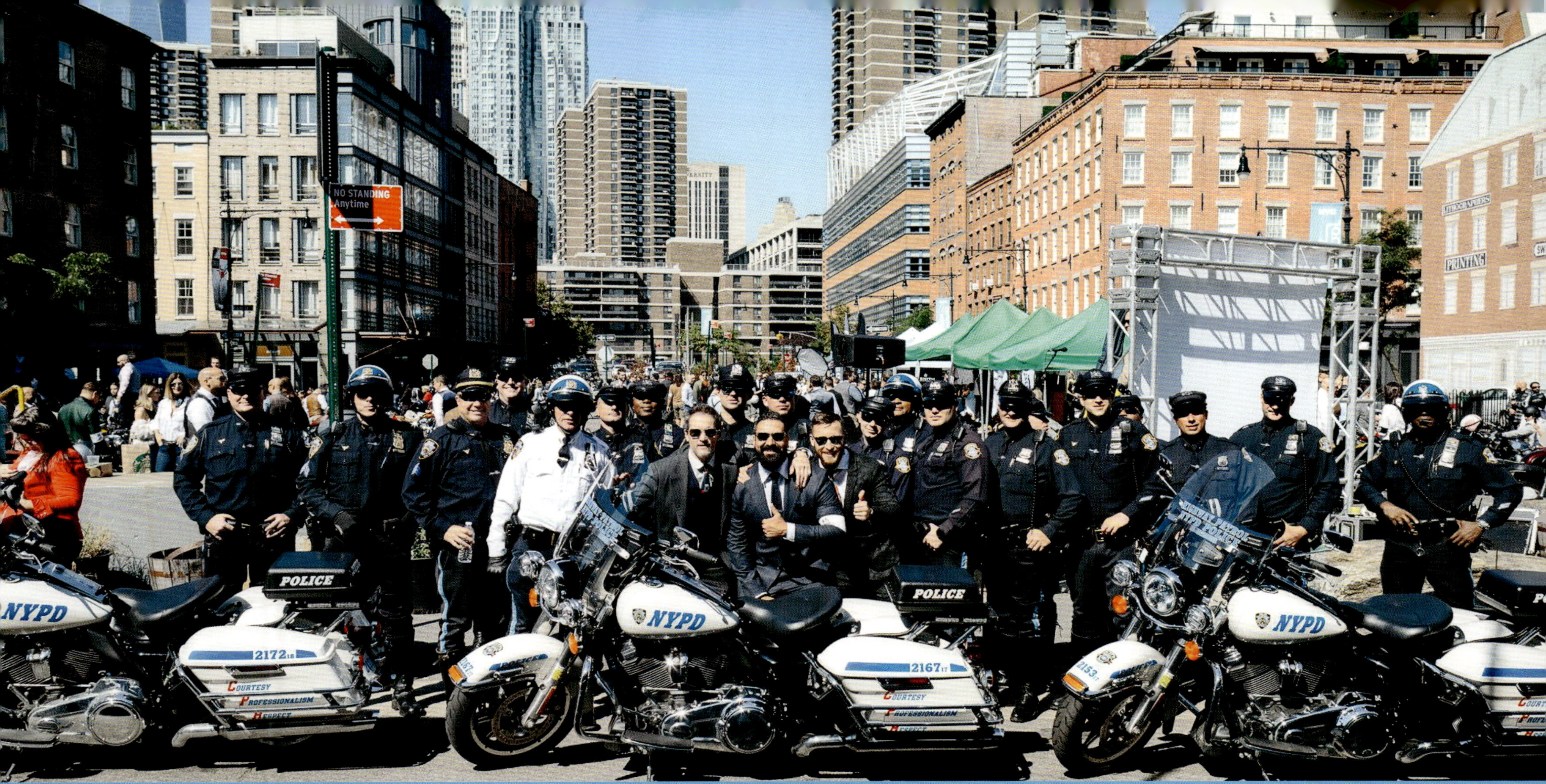

Veterans & First Responders
A DGR-FUNDED PROJECT

They show up on the front line every day, often putting themselves in harm's way to keep our communities safe and well. Firefighters, paramedics, emergency medical responders and police officers are amongst our first responders providing essential services around the clock, and military veterans are some of our most honored, having served and sacrificed for their countries, building the foundations for many of our community freedoms.

Yet, the world over, this group experiences higher rates of mental ill-health and suicide compared with the general population. There are many programs in play that aim to support these groups, but a multi-country review commissioned by Movember and conducted by Dr Donald McCreary has revealed a lack of publicly available evidence of the effectiveness of these programs. To help address this, in partnership with Movember, The Distinguished Gentleman's Ride proudly funds this mental health grants funding program in support of Veterans and First Responders, as well as their families across a number of countries.

An initial investment of USD $5.74M over two years was earmarked to support First Responder Initiatives in New Zealand, Germany, Ireland, the UK and the US as well as Veteran and First Responder Initiatives in Australia and Canada. A total of 14 programs have been selected for funding through this initiative. The programs displayed a focus that had already shown promise in improving mental health or suicide prevention outcomes for these vital groups and building the evidence for effective interventions.

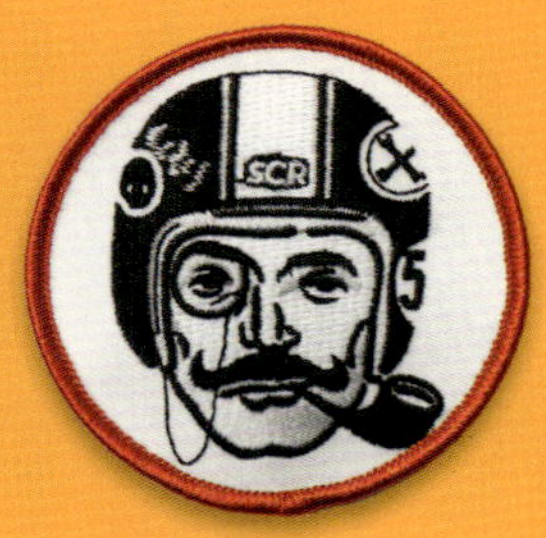

2012

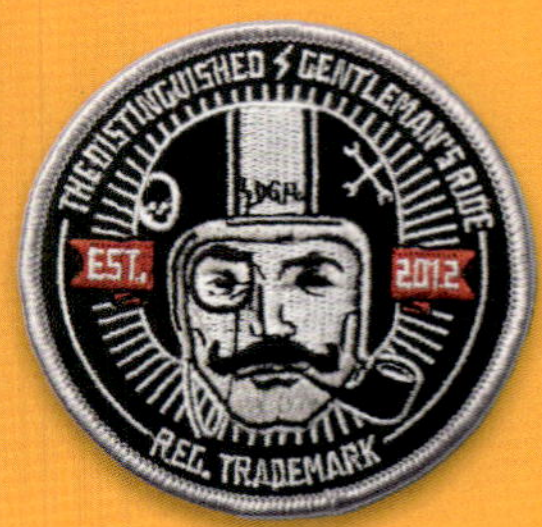

2013

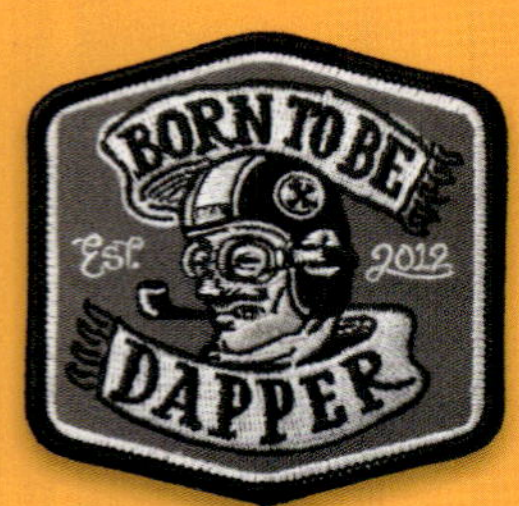

2013

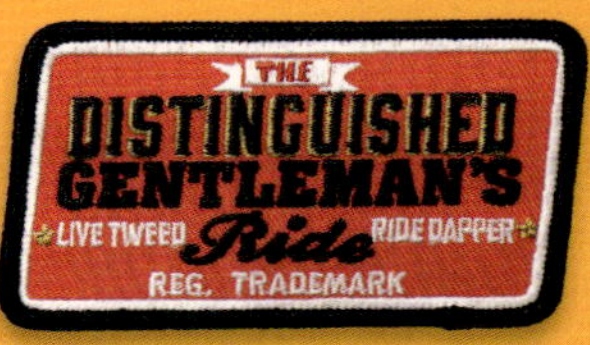

2013

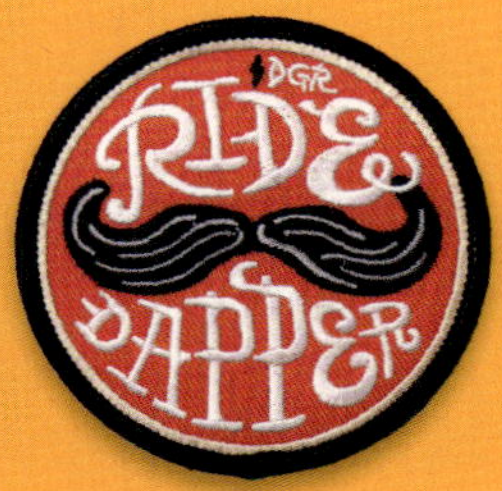

2013

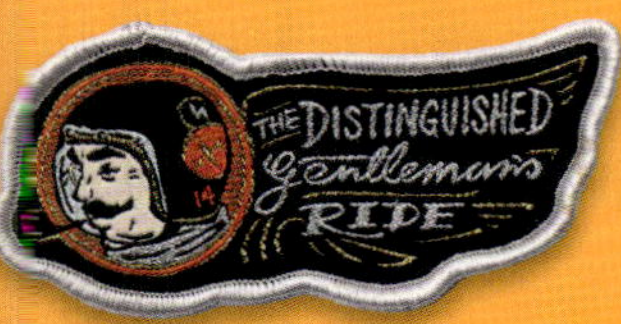

2014

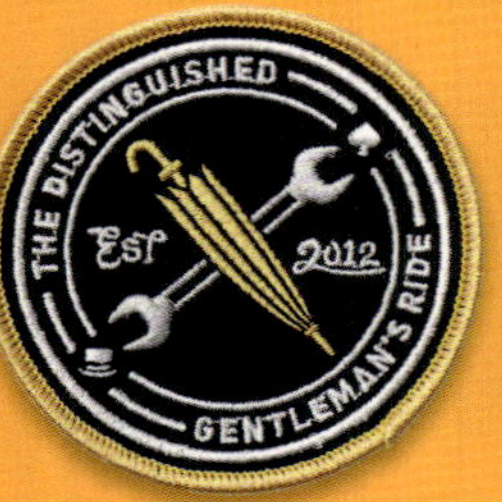

2015

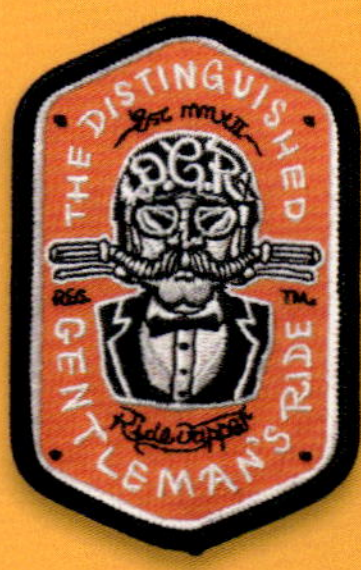

2015

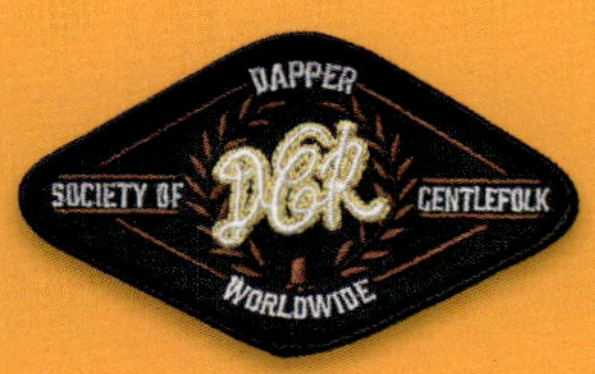

2015

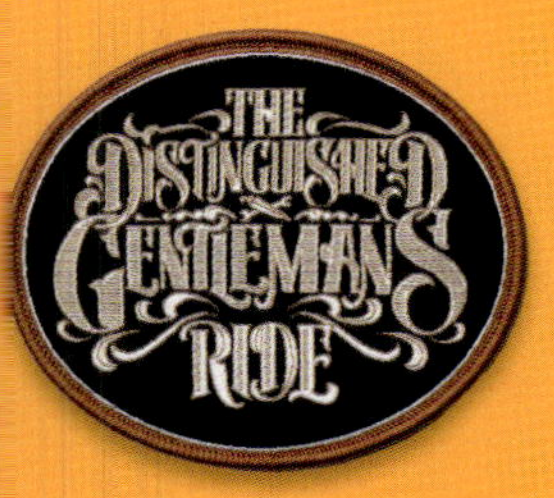

2016

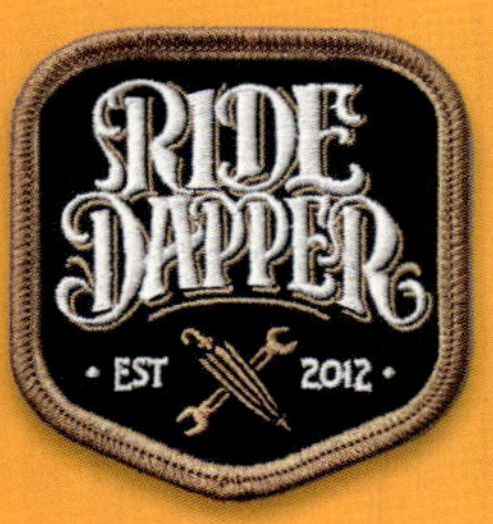

2016

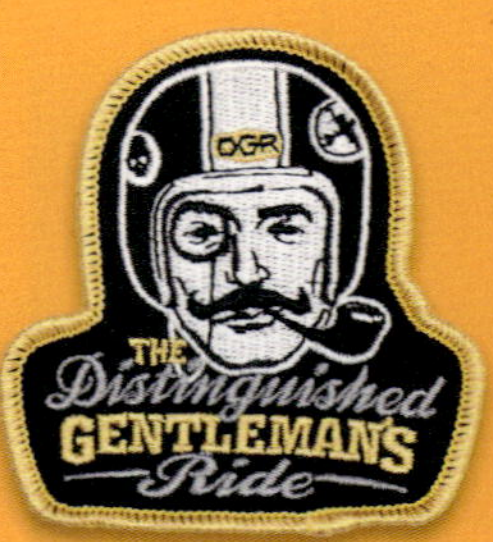

2016

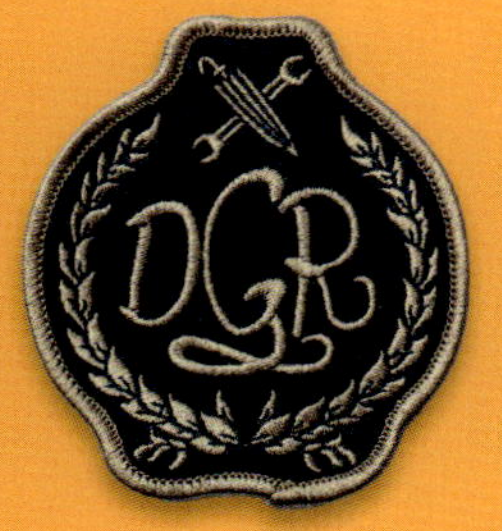

2017

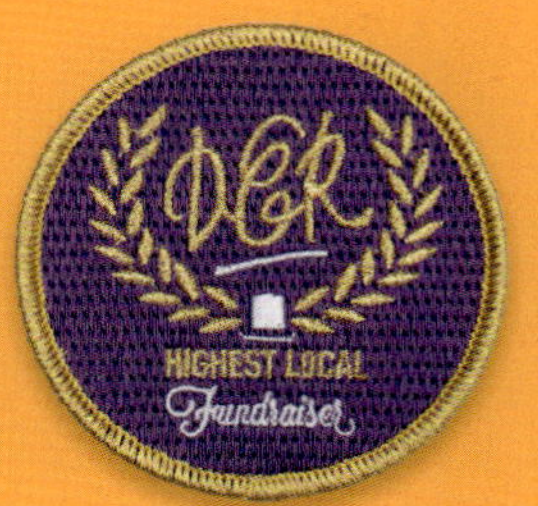

2017

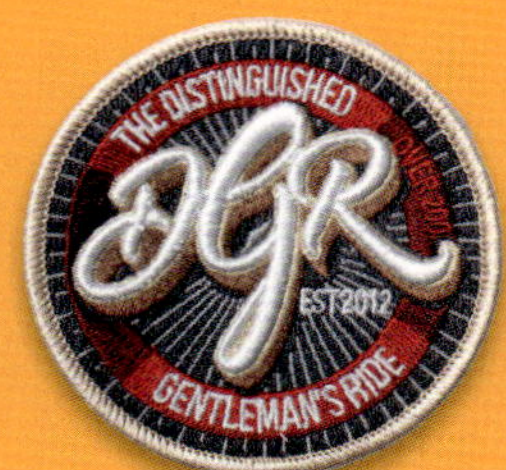

2018

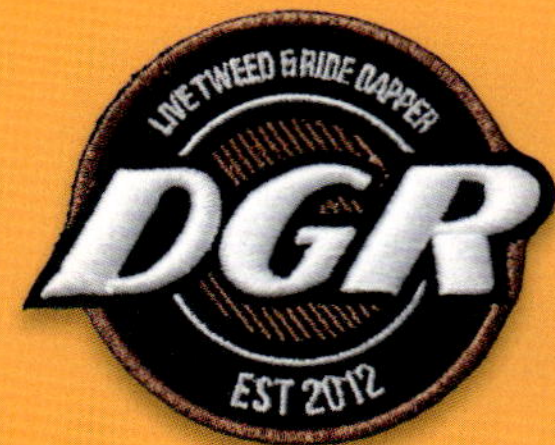

2019

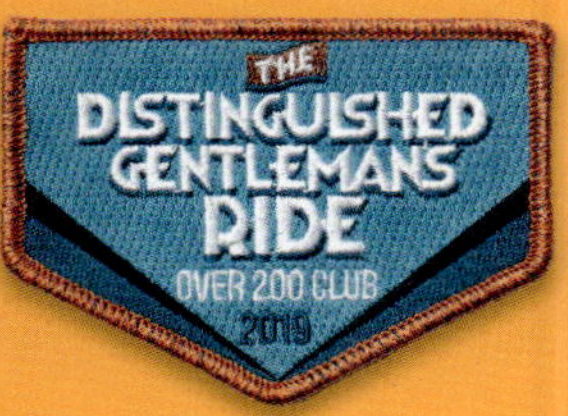

2019

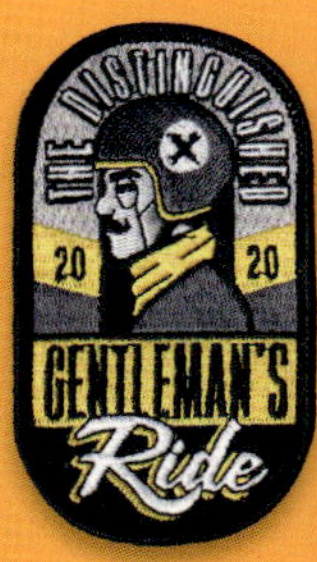

2020

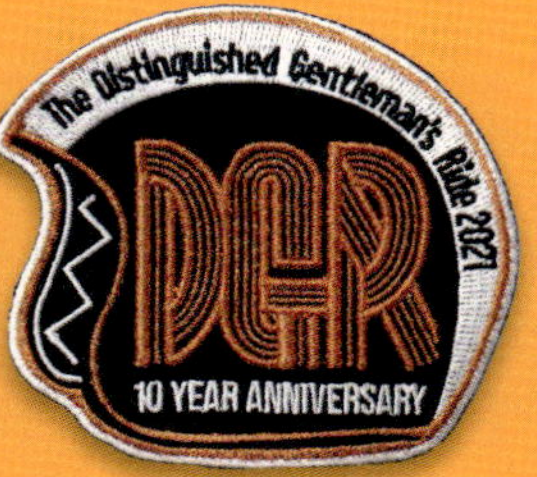

2021

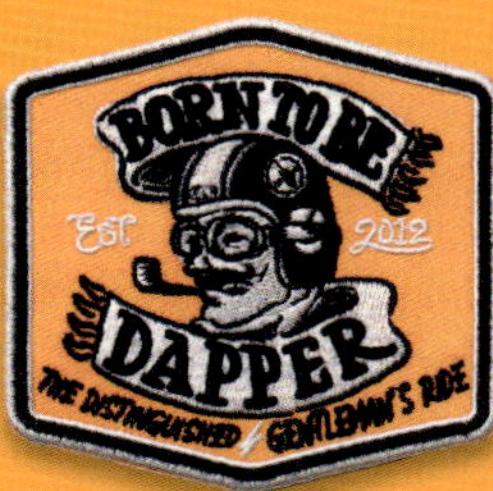

2021

THE OFFICIAL DGR
RIDE PATCHES

Iconic additions to any motorcyclist's vest, patches have always told stories of rides past. Paying homage to the motorcycling tradition, The Distinguished Gentleman's Ride has produced patches to commemorate each year of events. A special selection of patches has always been produced to represent entry into the Gentlefolk's Club, a celebratory stitching to be emblazoned on the breast of all fundraisers whose contributions gain them entry into the illustrious league.

Many patches have been sewn to spread awareness and celebration of the ride each year; whether adoring a tweed blazer or a rider's vest, they tell the same story of commitment to fundraising and men's health.

One of my riding buddies, Andrew, introduced me to the event in 2014. I believe it might have been the first or second one for New York City as it was a fairly small riding group. The following year, with fond memories of the last event and the perfect motorcycle for it, I decided to actively start participating and fundraising for The Distinguished Gentleman's Ride.

I spent the first half of my life in France, where motorcycles were a huge part of my independence and freedom. The second half I spent in the United States, where I happily gave away my independence to a cute New Yorker, and together we gave up our freedom in a heartbeat to have our son. Motorcycles still represent an important link between those two stages of my life as well as a great way to keep my hands filthy, and escape from time to time just to clear my mind.

The DGR causes are hugely important to me. When it comes to prostate cancer and men's mental health, I see silence as our worst enemy. They both rely heavily on uncomfortable stereotypes that were unchallenged. The DGR, in addition to research and program funding, is changing this deadly status quo. We are making it look good to talk about the prostate check. We are making it easier to open up to friends as well as learning how to reach out and recognize when a friend is in need. The DGR's positive effect on people has changed the perception that men have of their health by giving them a platform to help fight those stereotypes.

The DGR in NYC is incredibly special to me. Watching a thousand riders assembling on a sunny morning by the water in an historic neighborhood like downtown Manhattan is something to remember. It is an incredible feeling to be surrounded by so many people smiling, who are so excited to be there. Everyone in their best outfits, freshly cleaned and polished beautiful motorcycles shining like gems everywhere, surrounded by your riding buddies and friends you might not have seen since last year's event. To finish the perfect picture we have our local police motorcycles escorting us through lights and all of the city intersections. Cruising throughout Manhattan without traffic is a modern-day miracle.

My favorite DGR moment is the one pictured. This was at the event's after party a couple of years ago. We were just four friends from all over the place reunited once again for the event. We chatted and caught up, asking how our lives had been since the previous year. This was about seven months after my fire accident and talking about it would trigger tears in my eyes. After sharing that moment and a hug with my buddies, Chris stepped back and snapped that photo. It will always be a special one to me.

I use fundraising in the DGR to reach out to as many people as possible, as I believe that the mentality around men's health has to change—and that begins with communication. It does not take long before encountering many people affected directly or indirectly with a loved one. With this in mind I reached out to everyone I knew. I also contacted my workplace and asked to post about it on the daily bulletin, this generated a tremendous amount of support at all levels and I now have people reaching out earlier and earlier every year to support.

The same way I've reached out to people for donations, I also get in touch afterward. I make sure to email them with this year's campaign final numbers and accomplishments, as well as sharing pictures I took of the day. Despite the generosity of my donors, my biggest pride comes from the number of people donating to me every year. There are about 200-300. Having more and more people donating what they can every year means so much to me as it allows DGR to fund research and programs while increasing our reach and support to more and more people.

Every year, the weekend before the ride, my 10-year-old son and I organize a BBQ Bike Wash Fundraiser at our house. My son and his school buddies wash all the bikes for tips to donate to the DGR. Those little tiny hands can get the dirt out of places we rarely get access to, and the event has become quite popular as riders get to catch up with friends and enjoy a nice burger and a cold one while their bikes get pampered.

Standout Fundraiser
VINCENT NICOLAI

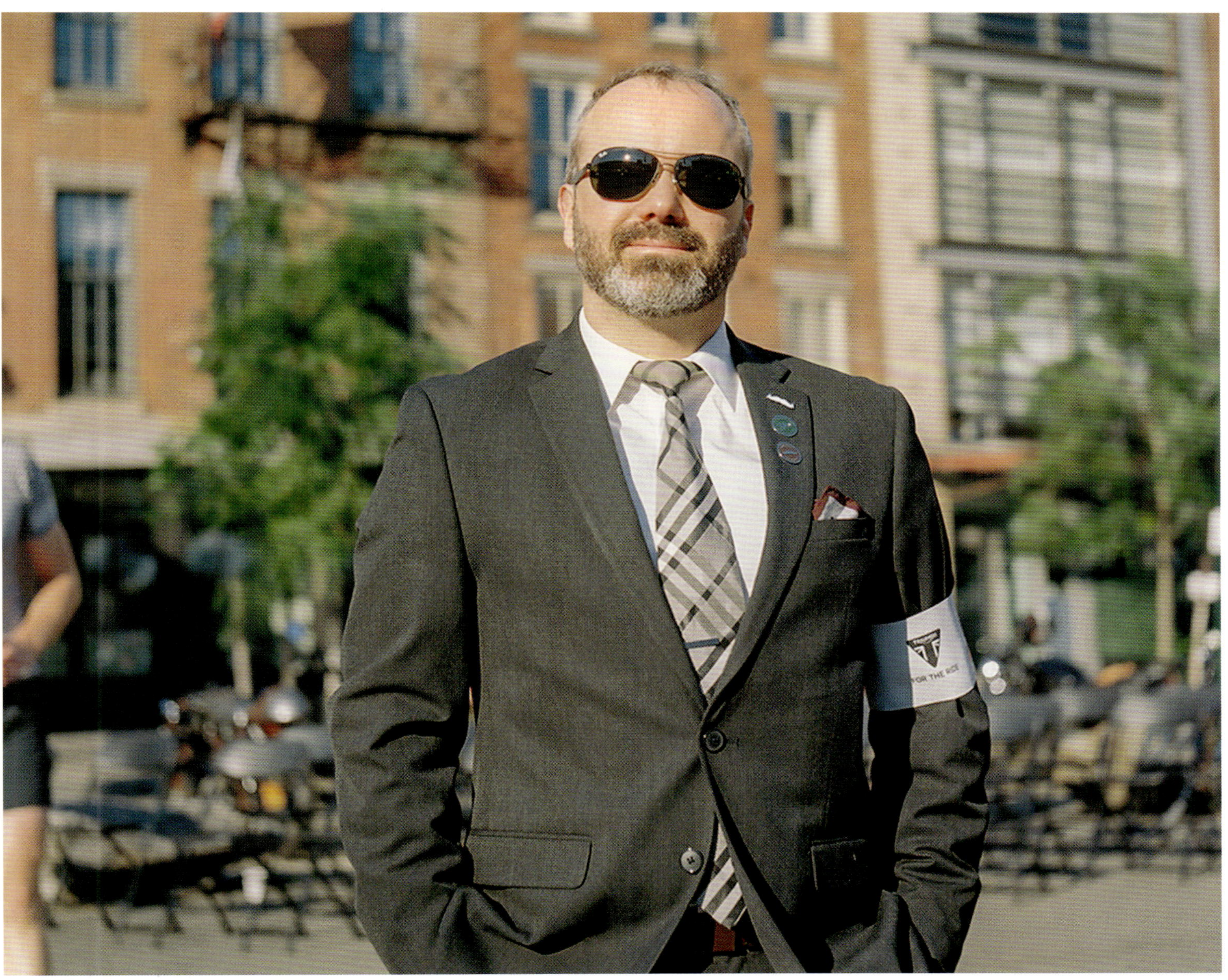

Ride Location
NEW YORK CITY, UNITED STATES

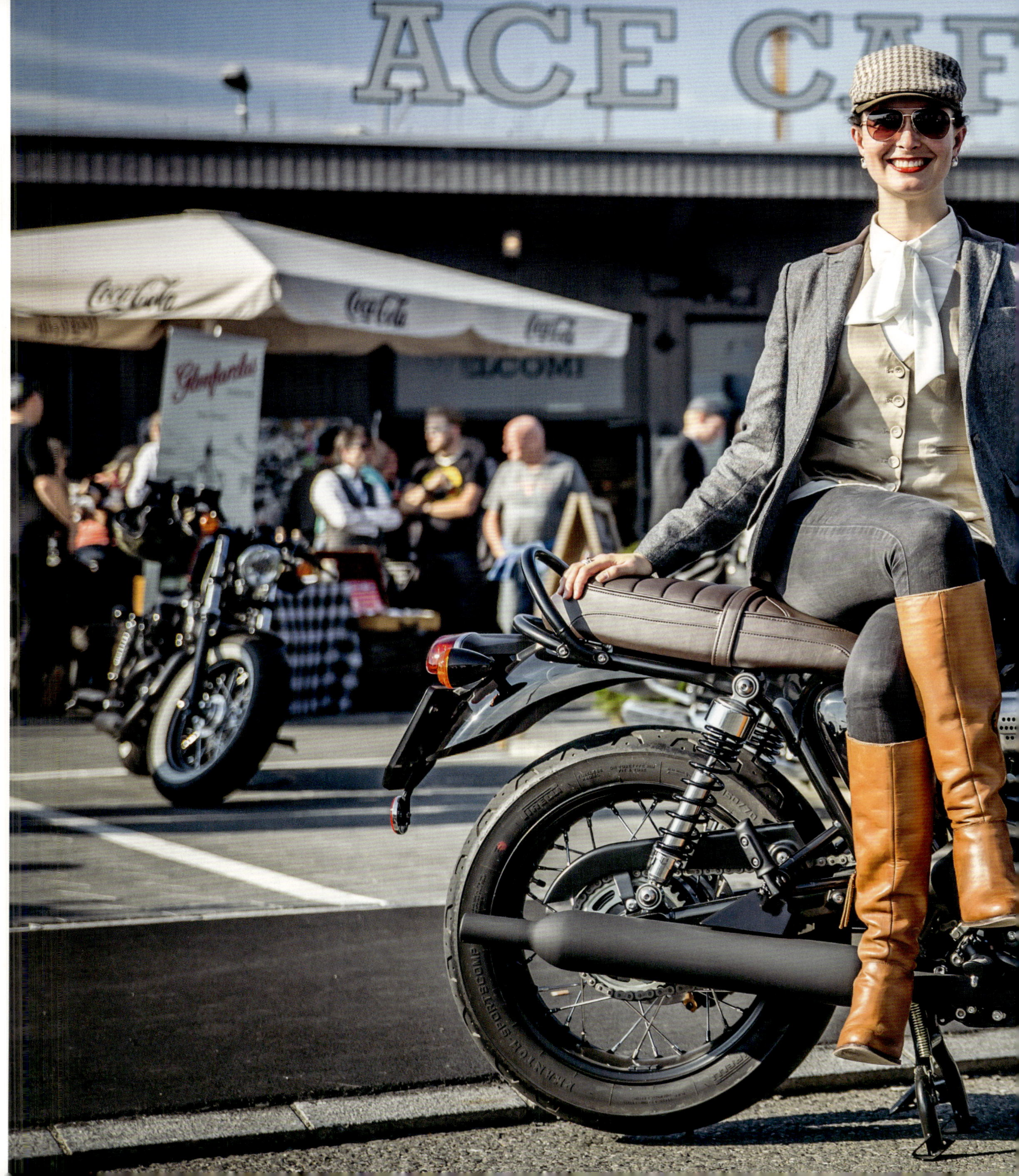
ACE CAFE
Coca-Cola
Coca-Cola
Coca-Cola
Glenfarclas

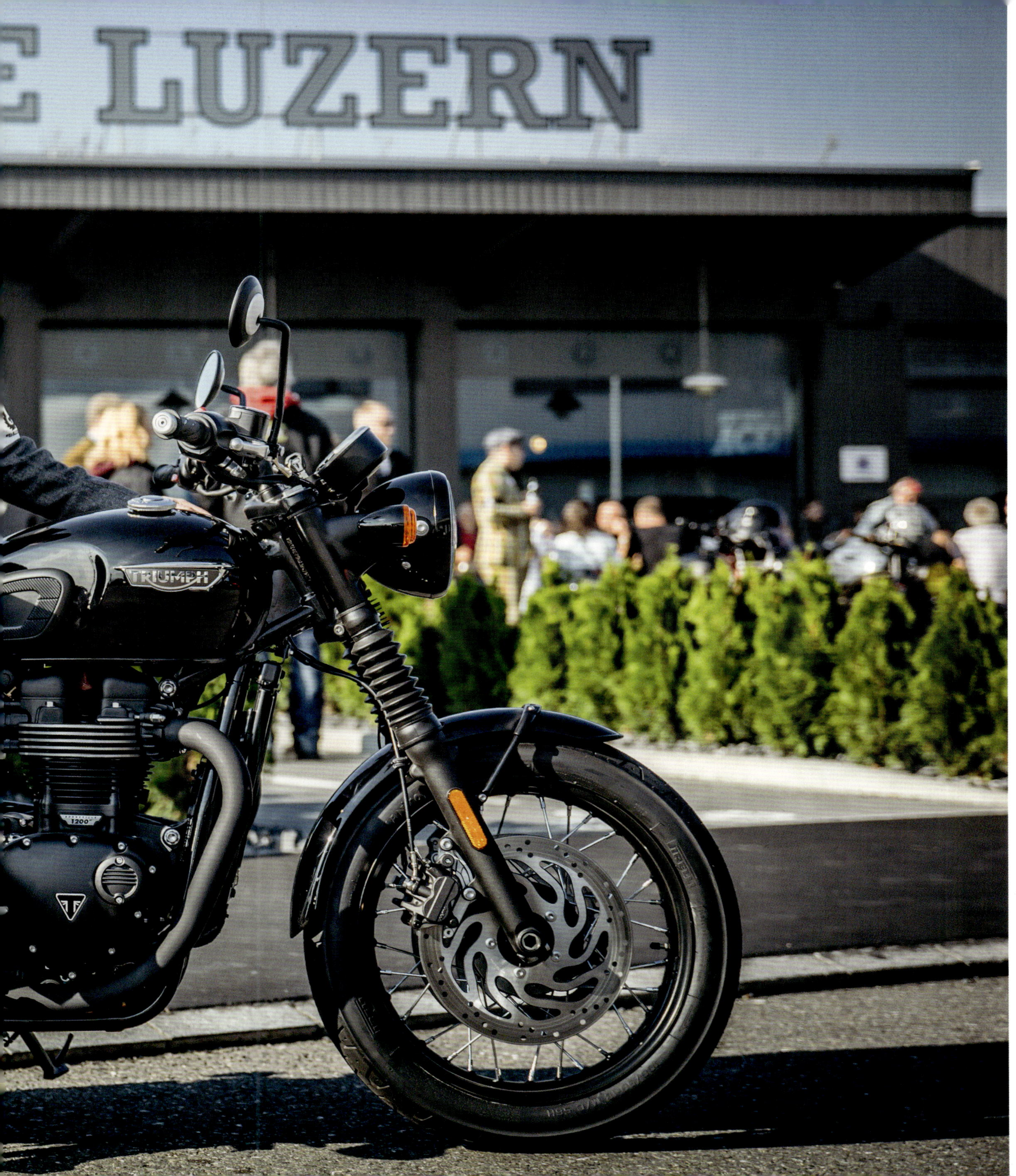

LUZERN
TRIUMPH
1200

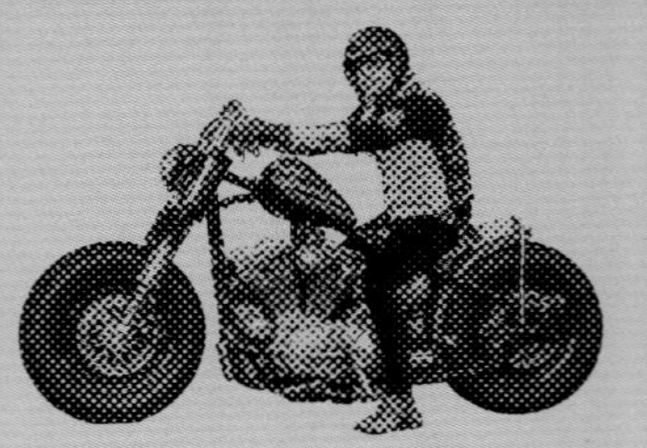

2018

- R I D E   S E V E N -

REACHING A NEW HIGH, DGR RAISED OVER USD $6M IN 2018, WITH **648 CITIES** AND **114,000 RIDERS** RIDING DAPPER FOR THE CAUSE. THESE RECORDS CONTINUE TO PROVE HOW COMMITTED OUR GLOBAL MOTO COMMUNITY IS.

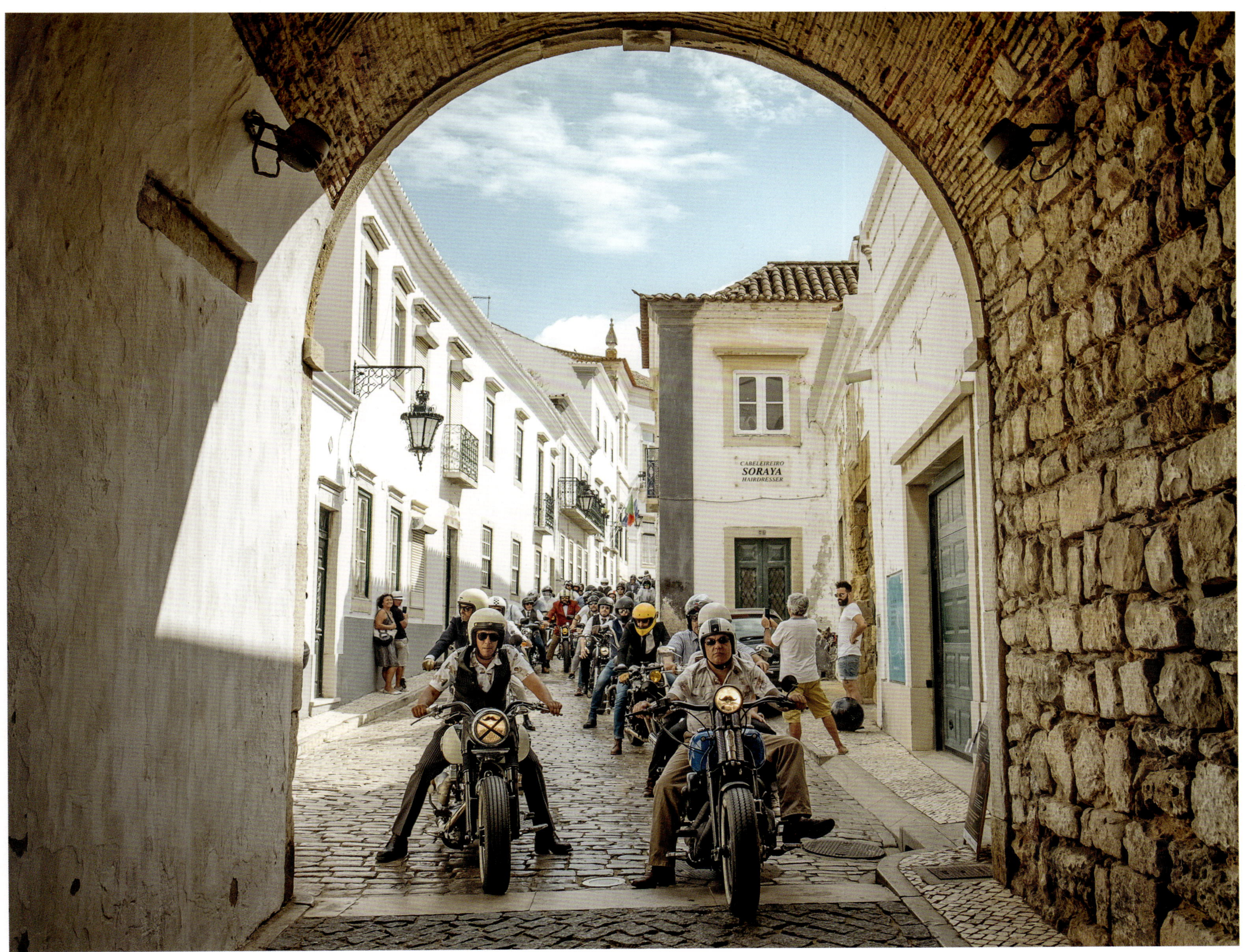
CABELEIREIRO
SORAYA
HAIRDRESSER

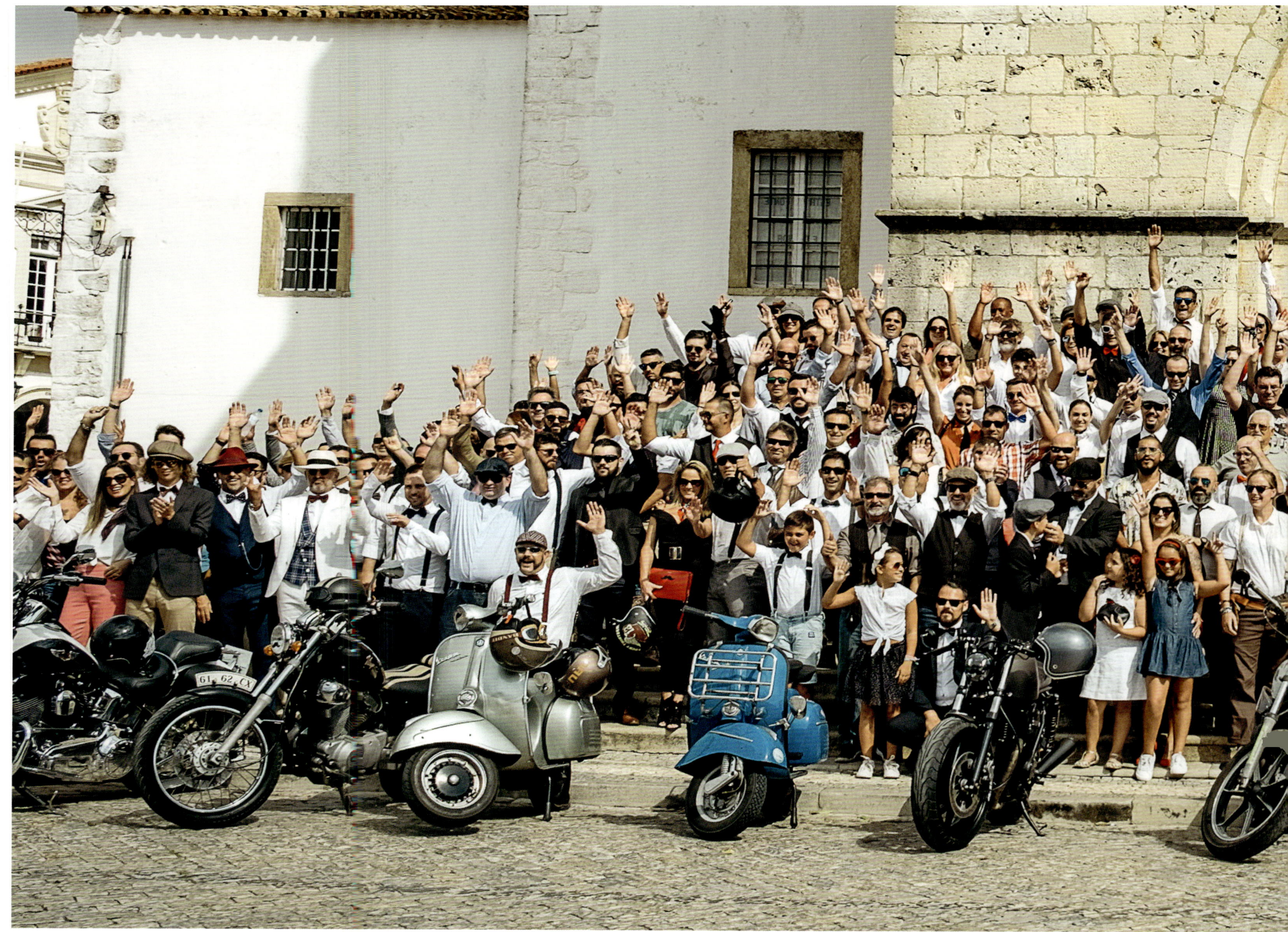

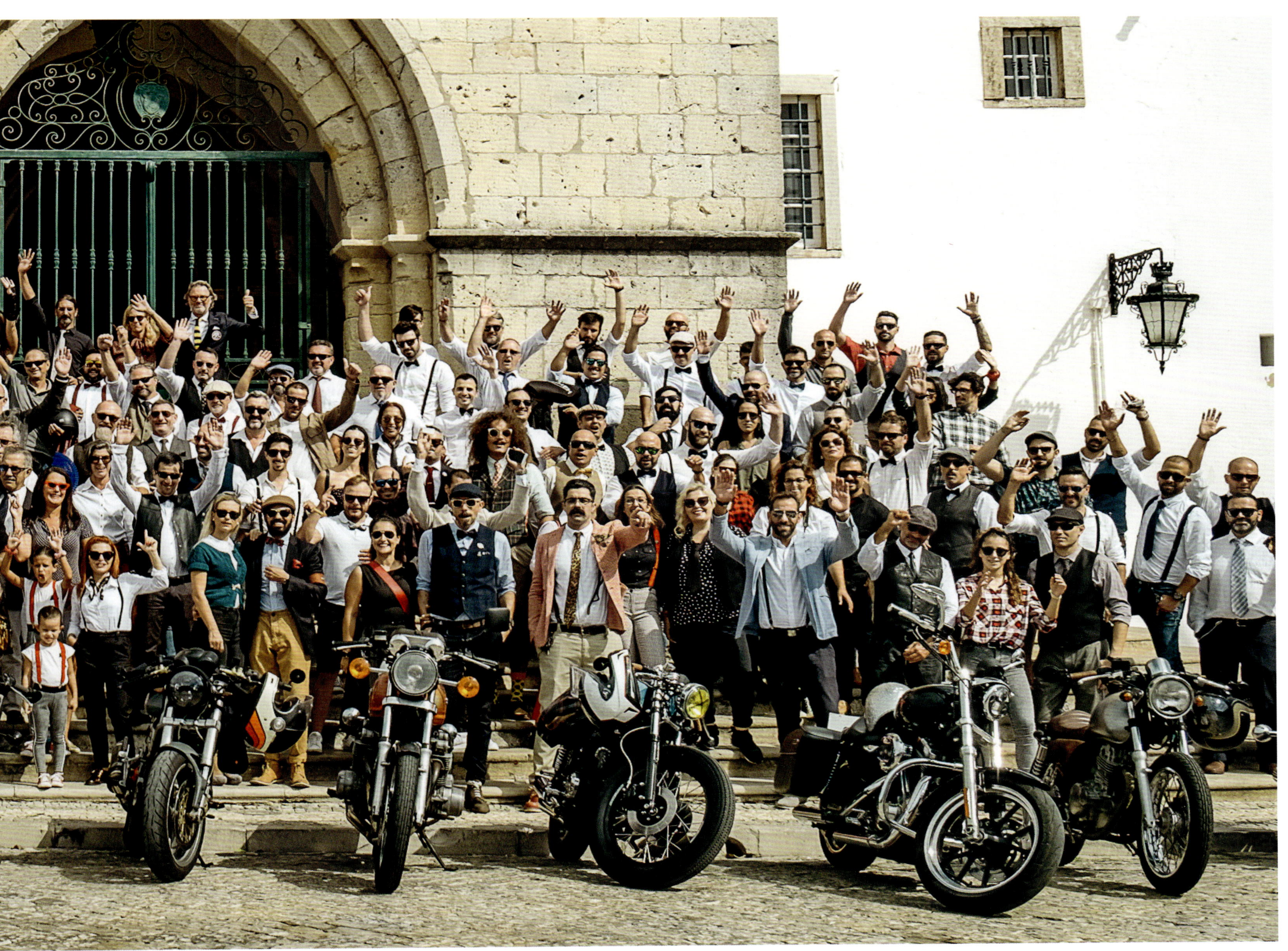

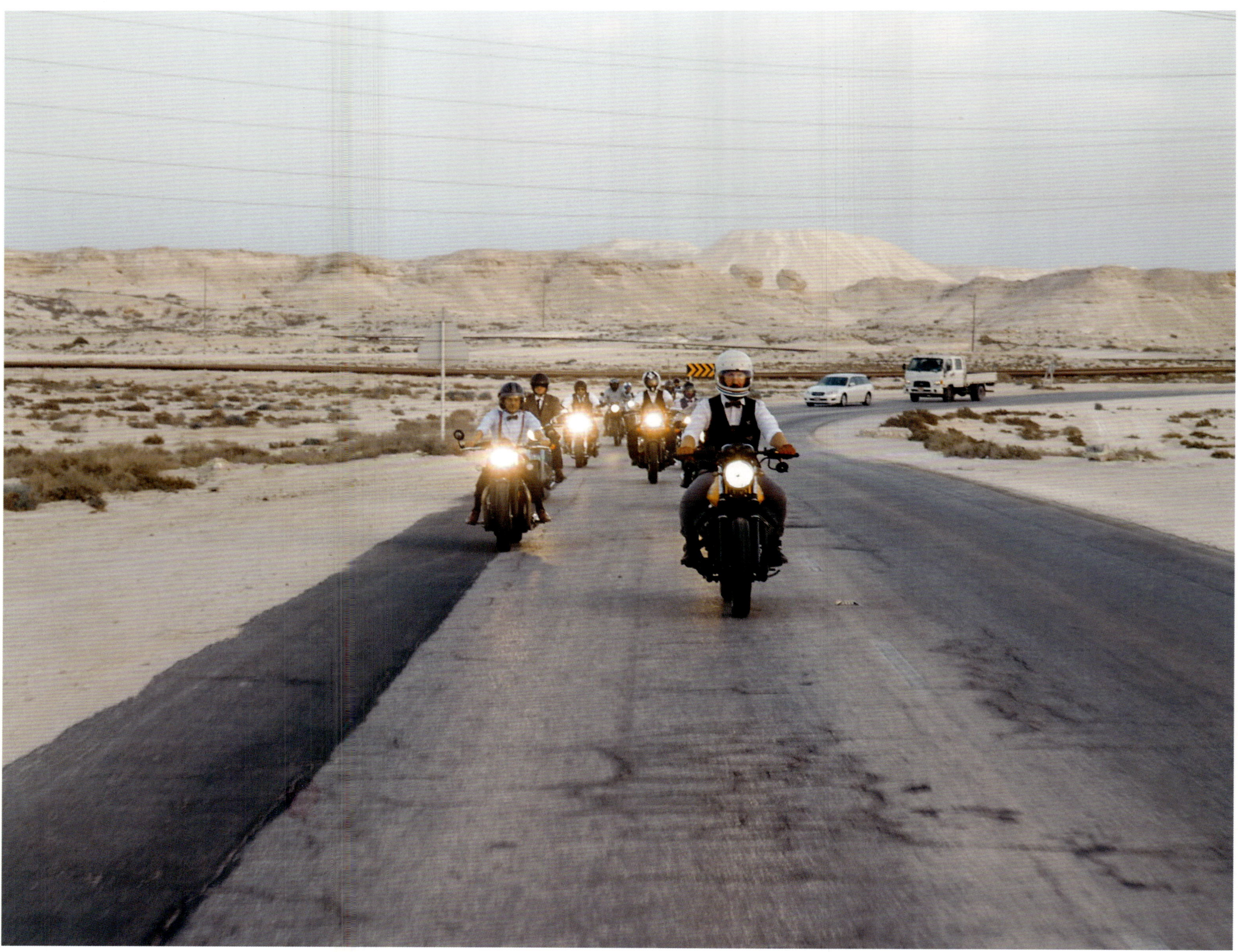

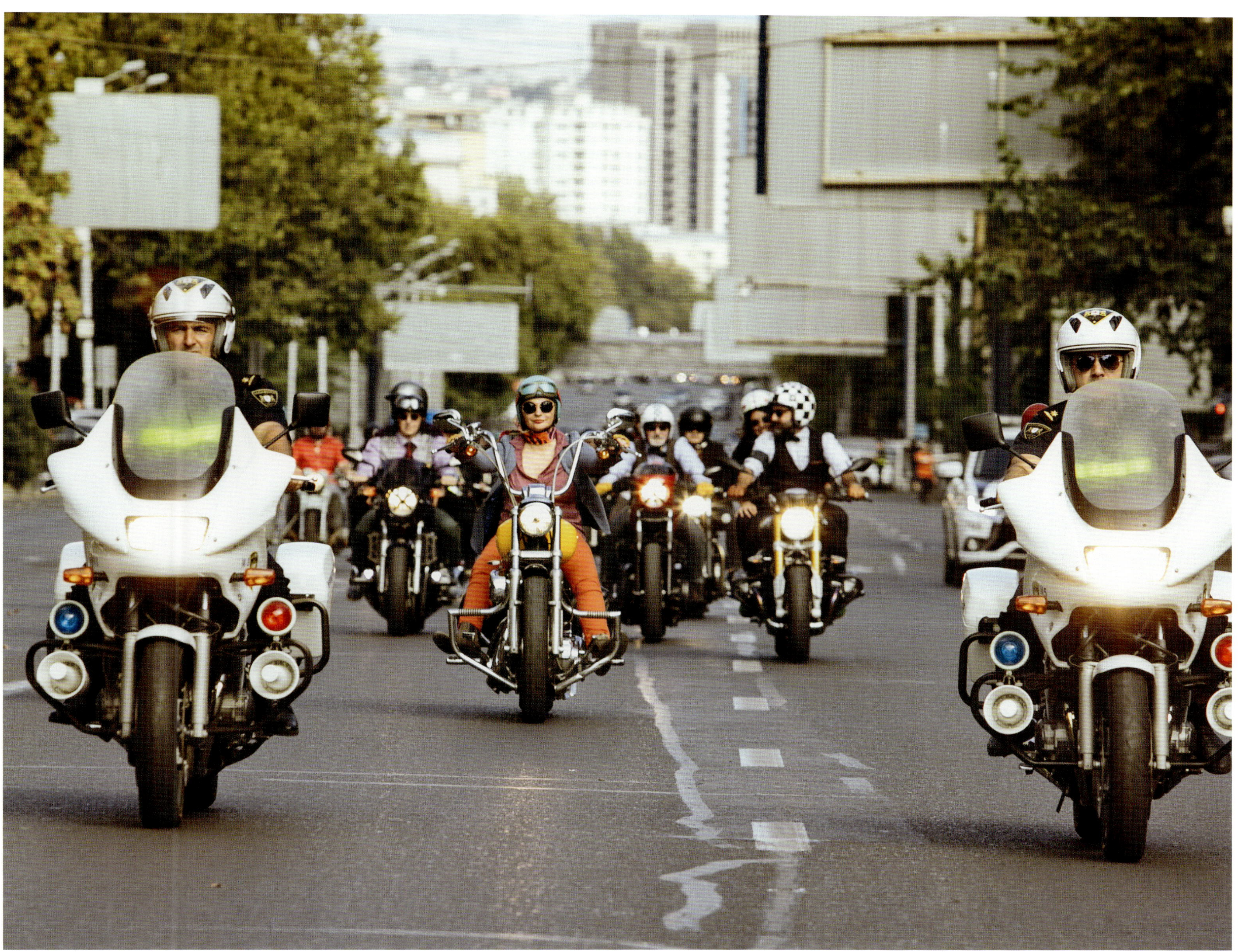

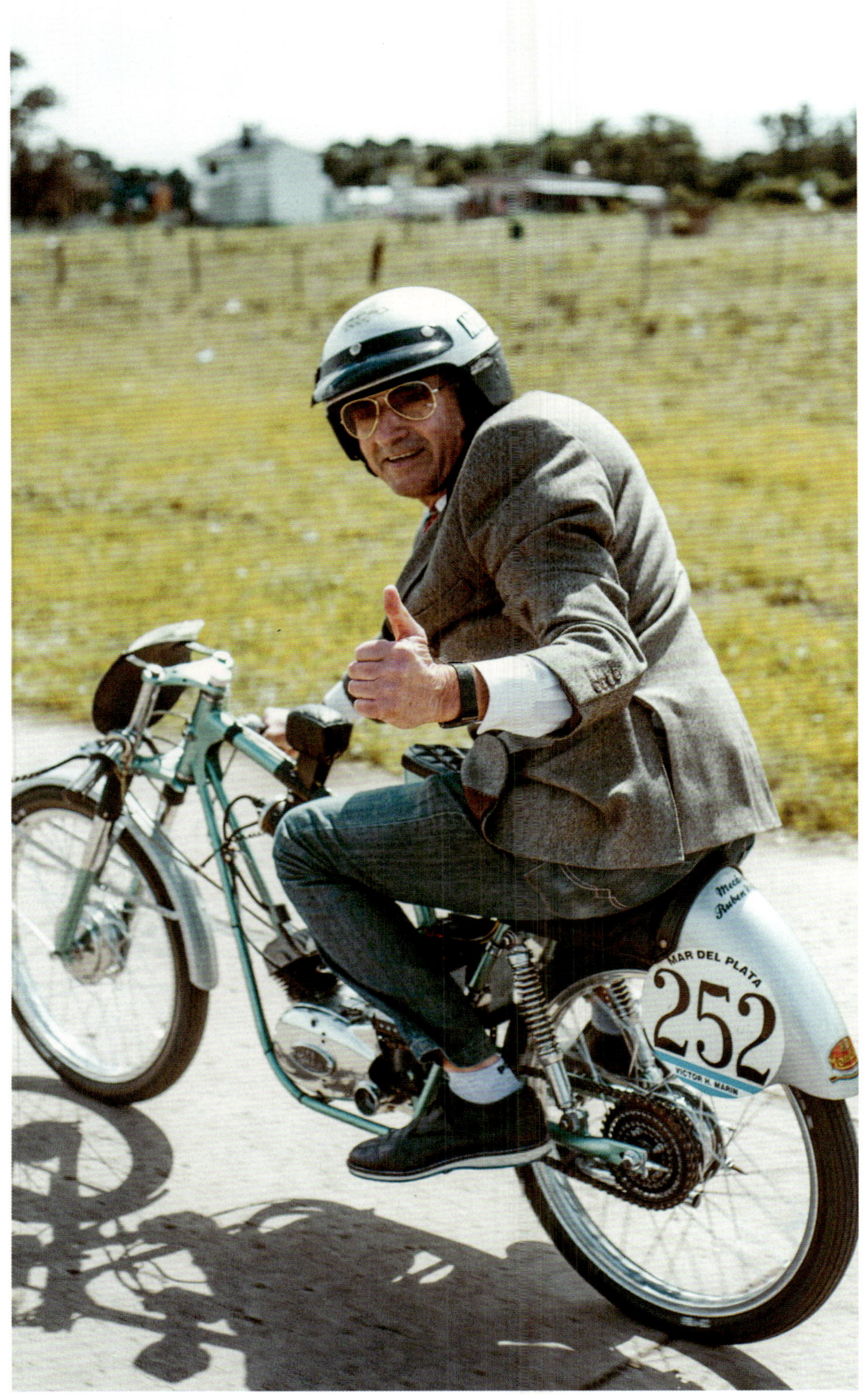
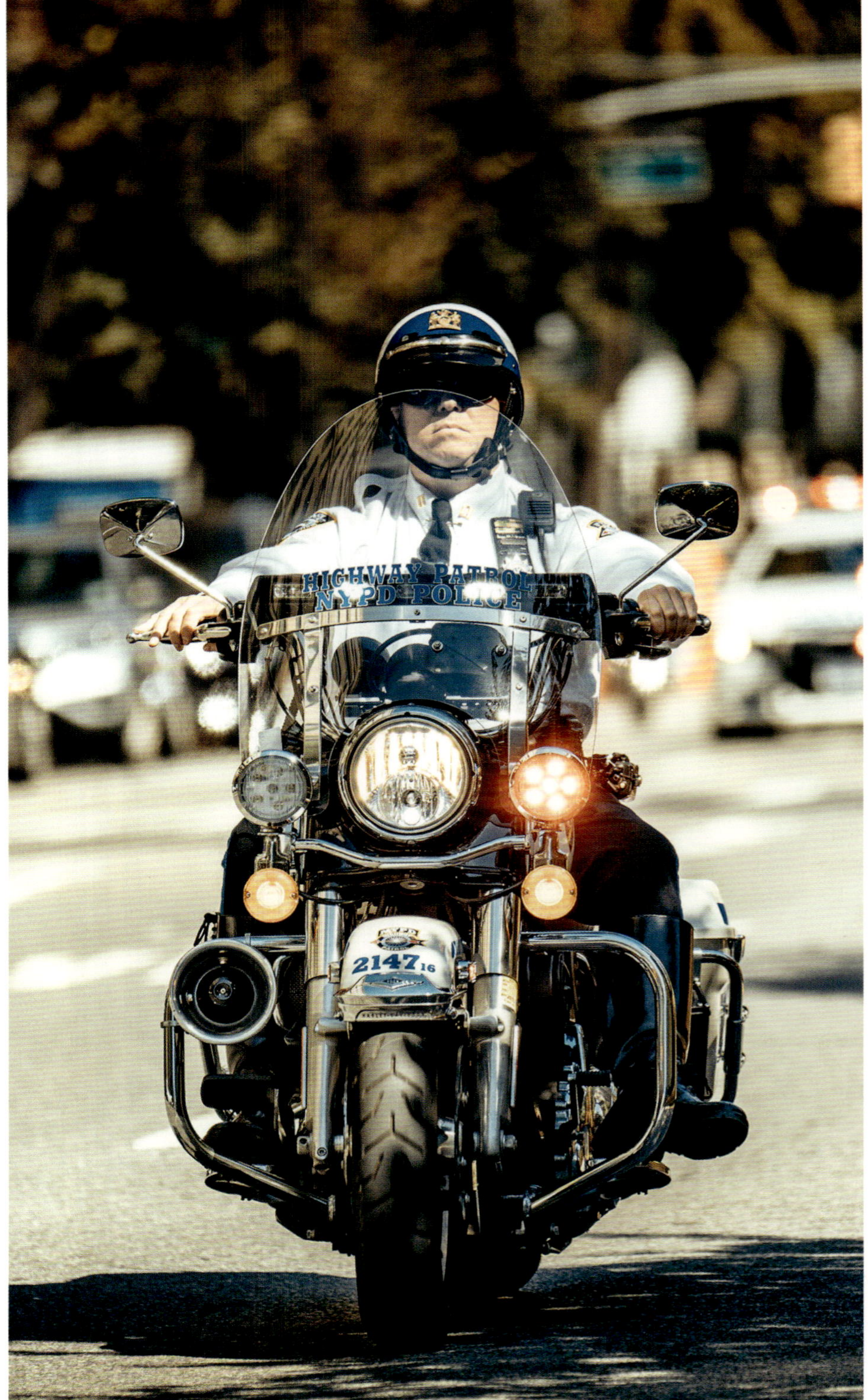

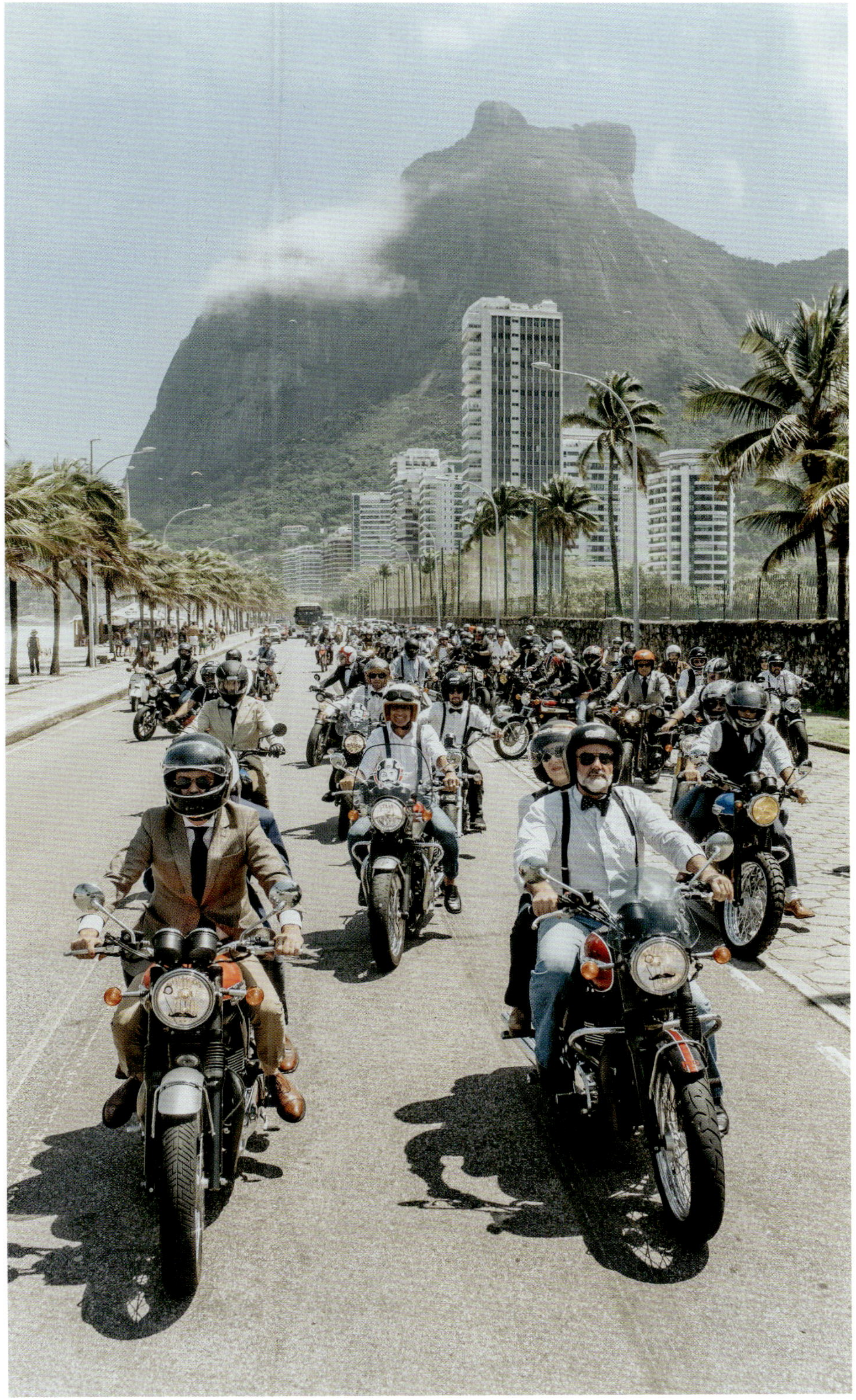

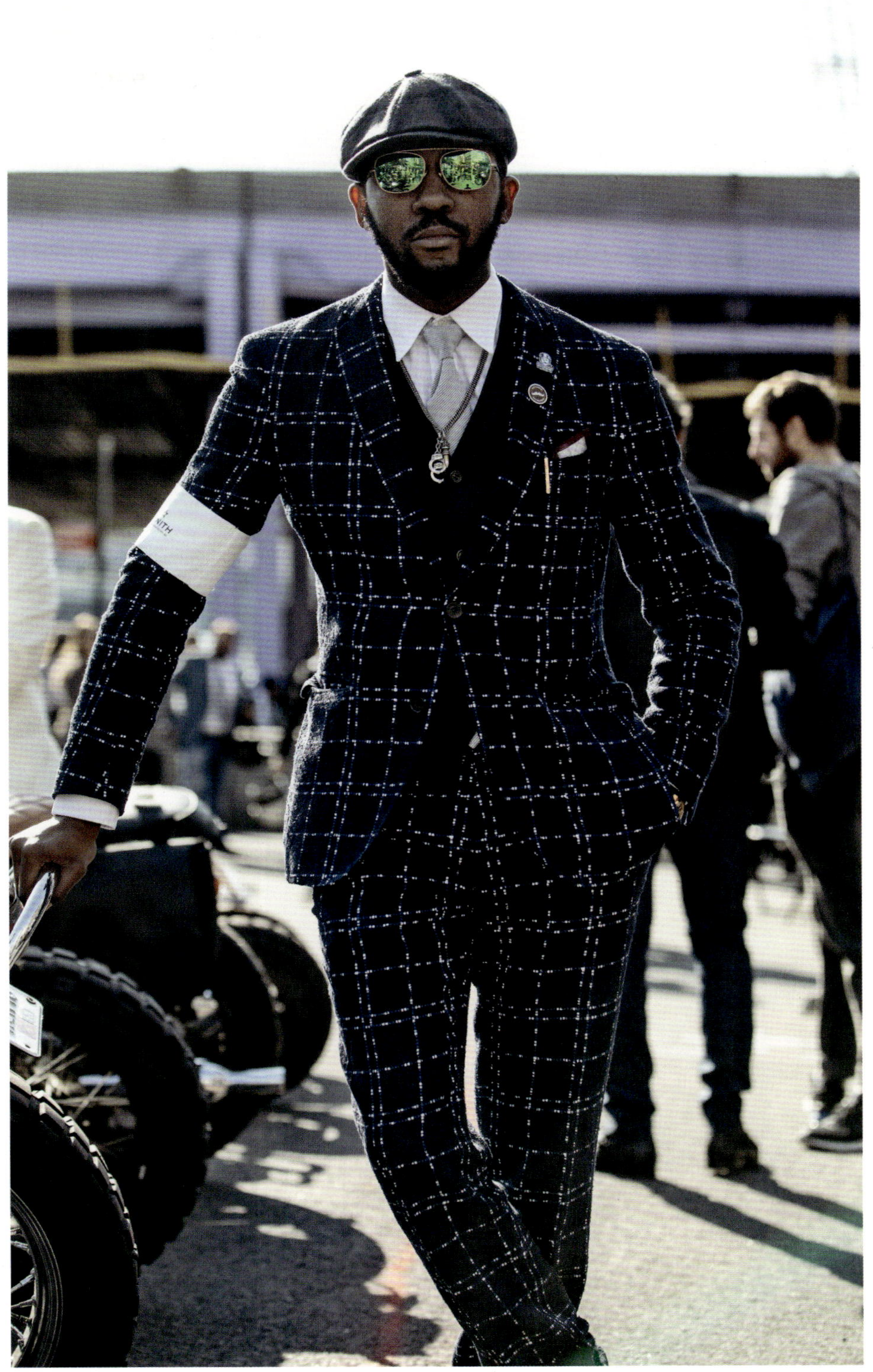

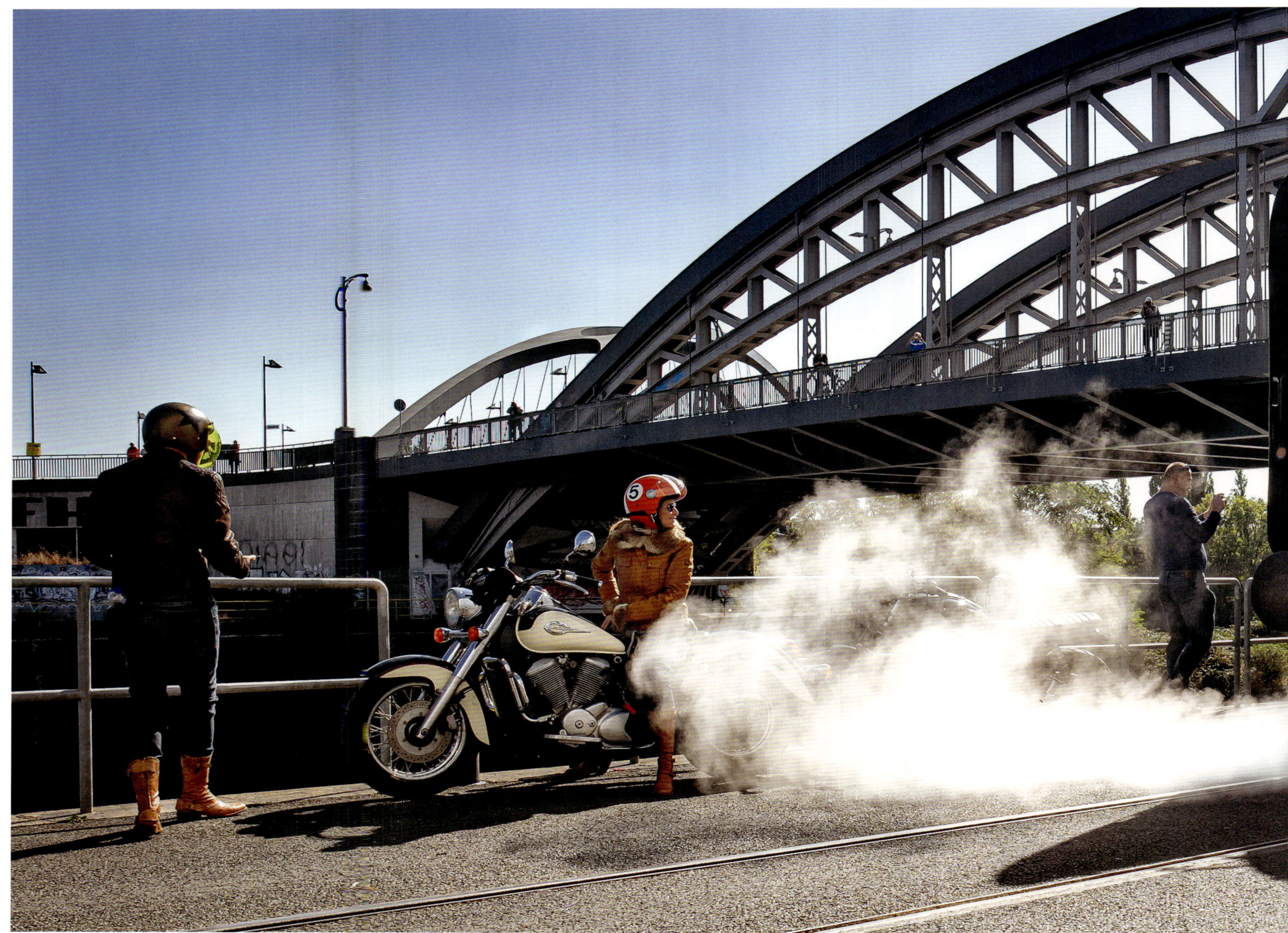

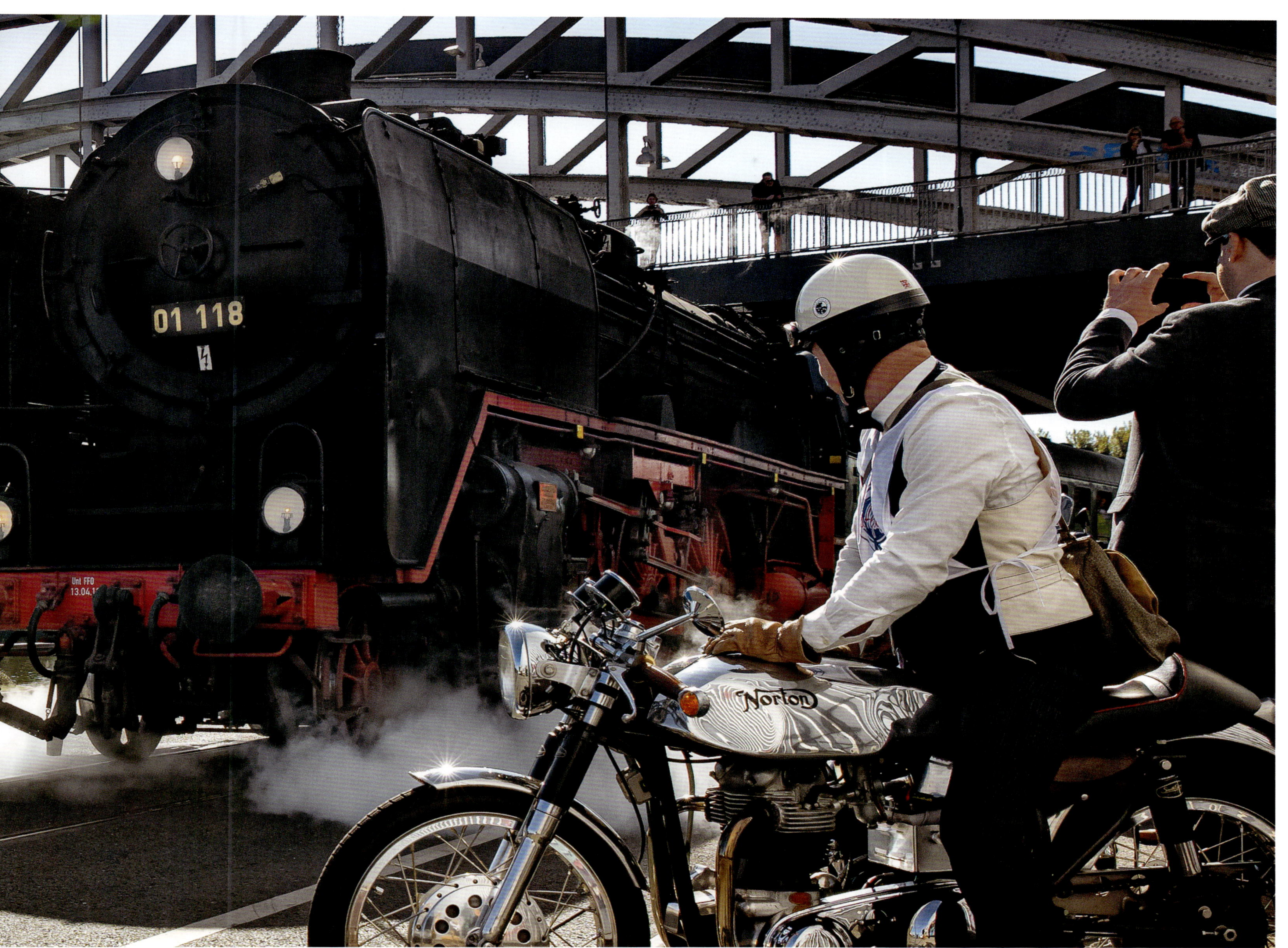

01 118
Unt FFO
13.04.1
Norton

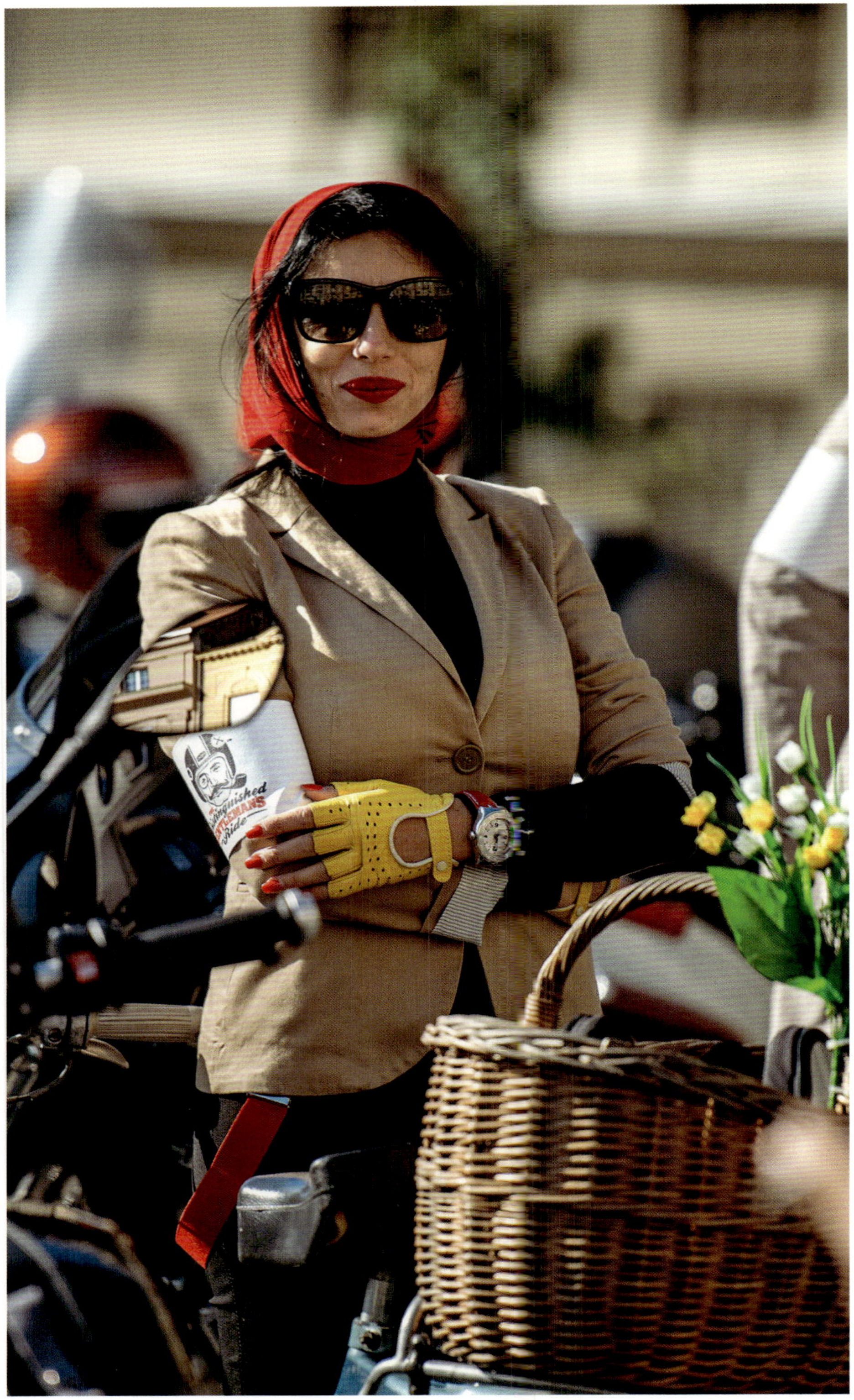

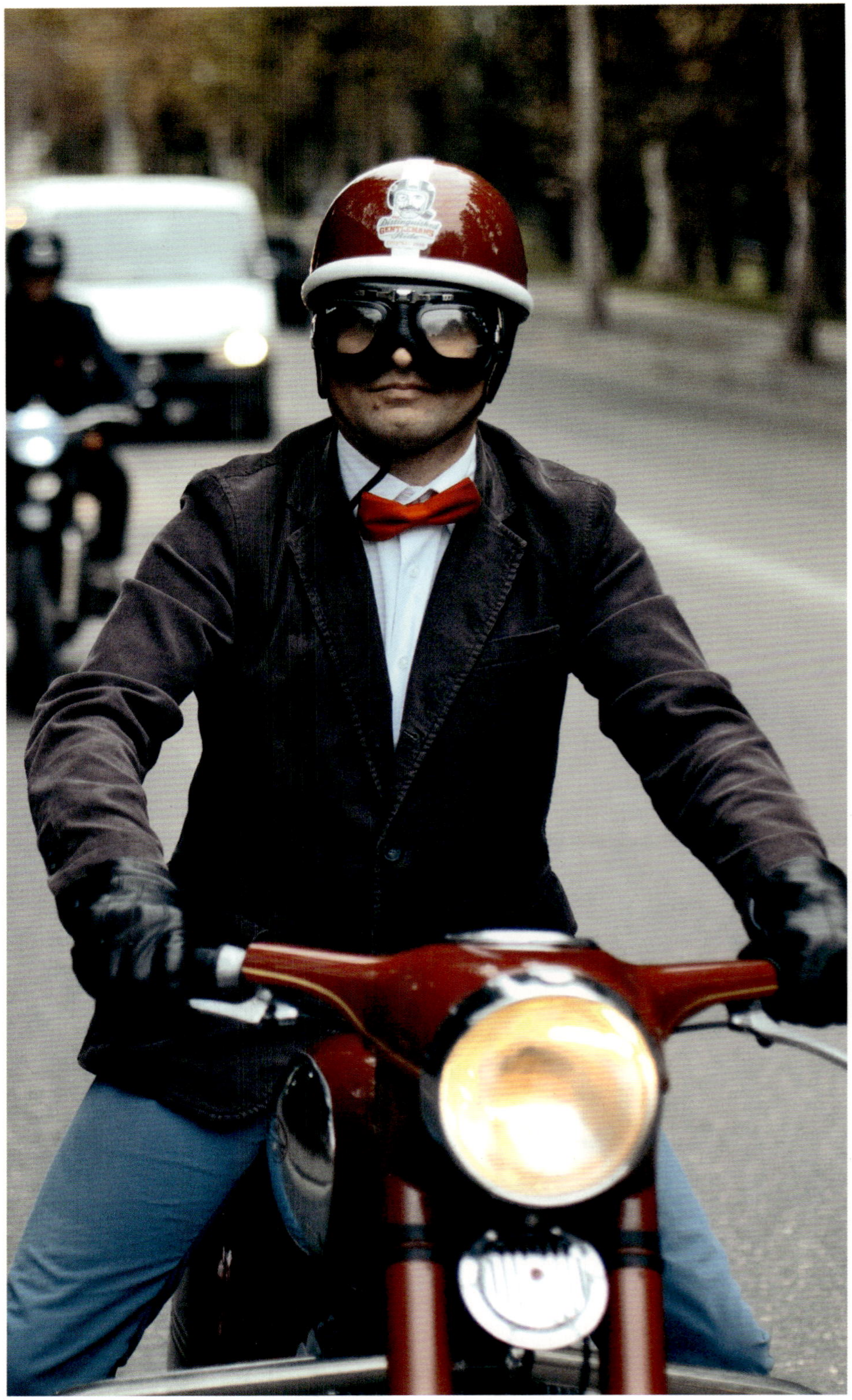

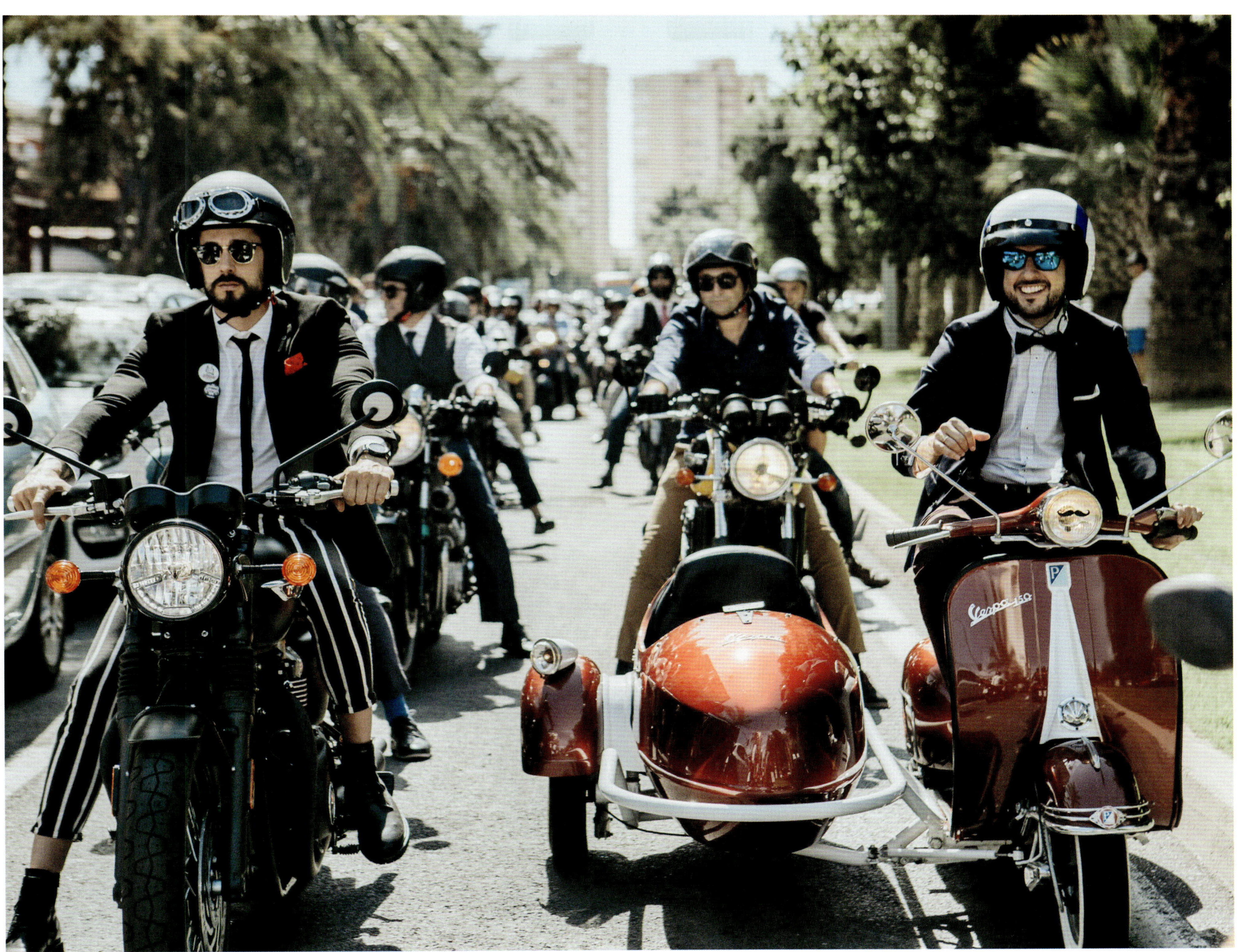

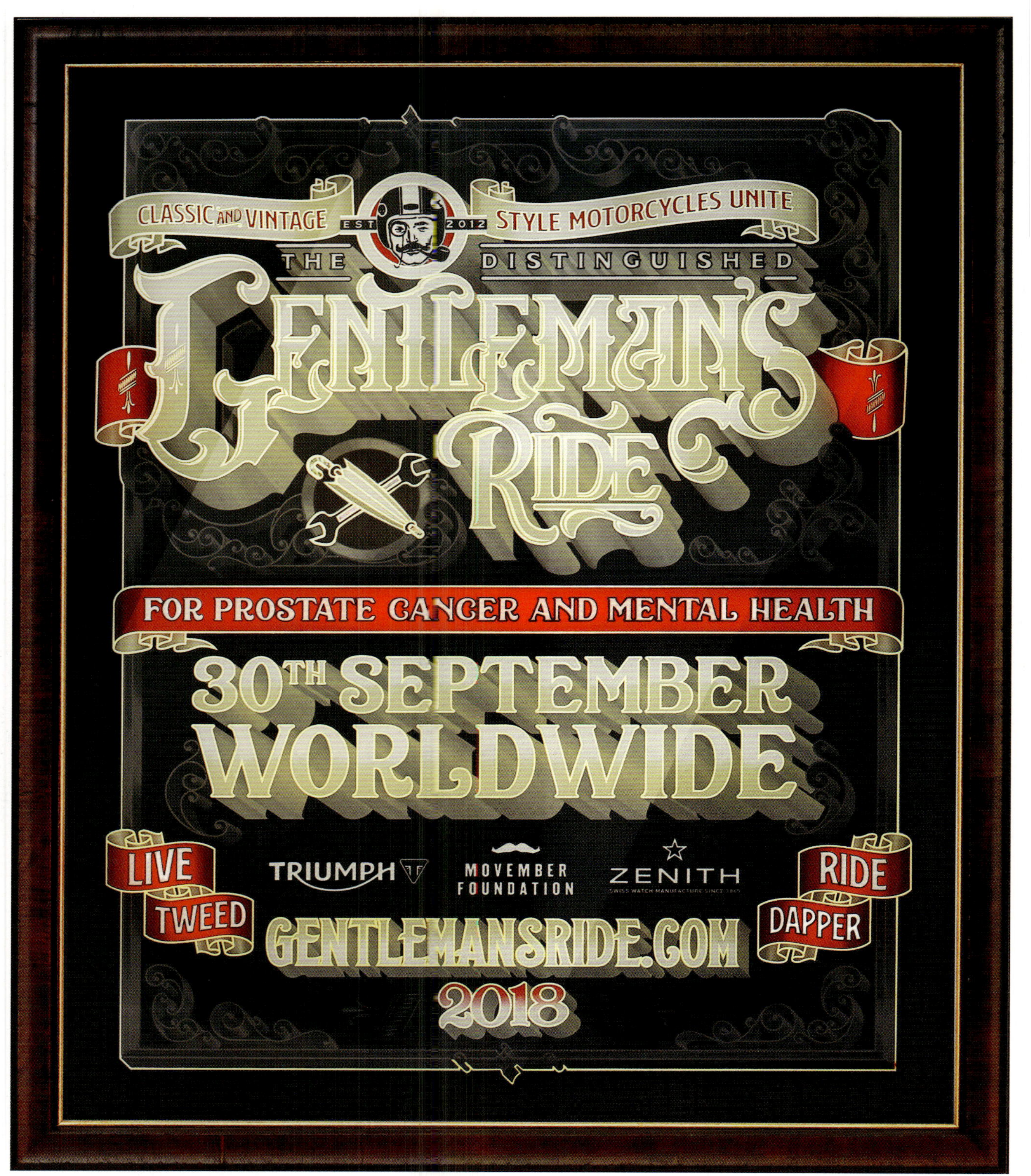

2018 Ride Poster

Designed by Luca Ionescu
Signwriting by Lance Corlett
The combination of Luca's meticulous design skills and Lance's steady hand culminated in a poster that references traditional intricate, gold leaf signage. It was hand painted directly onto glass with ornate gold pinstriping and opal stone inlays.

SCRAMBLERS

A style of classic off-road motorcycles derived from point-to-point races in England in the early 20th Century. Usually powered by big twins or single cylinder engines, they are fashioned into highly capable off-road machines by ditching excess weight, increasing ride height and making sure that exhausts are kept high to avoid obstacles.

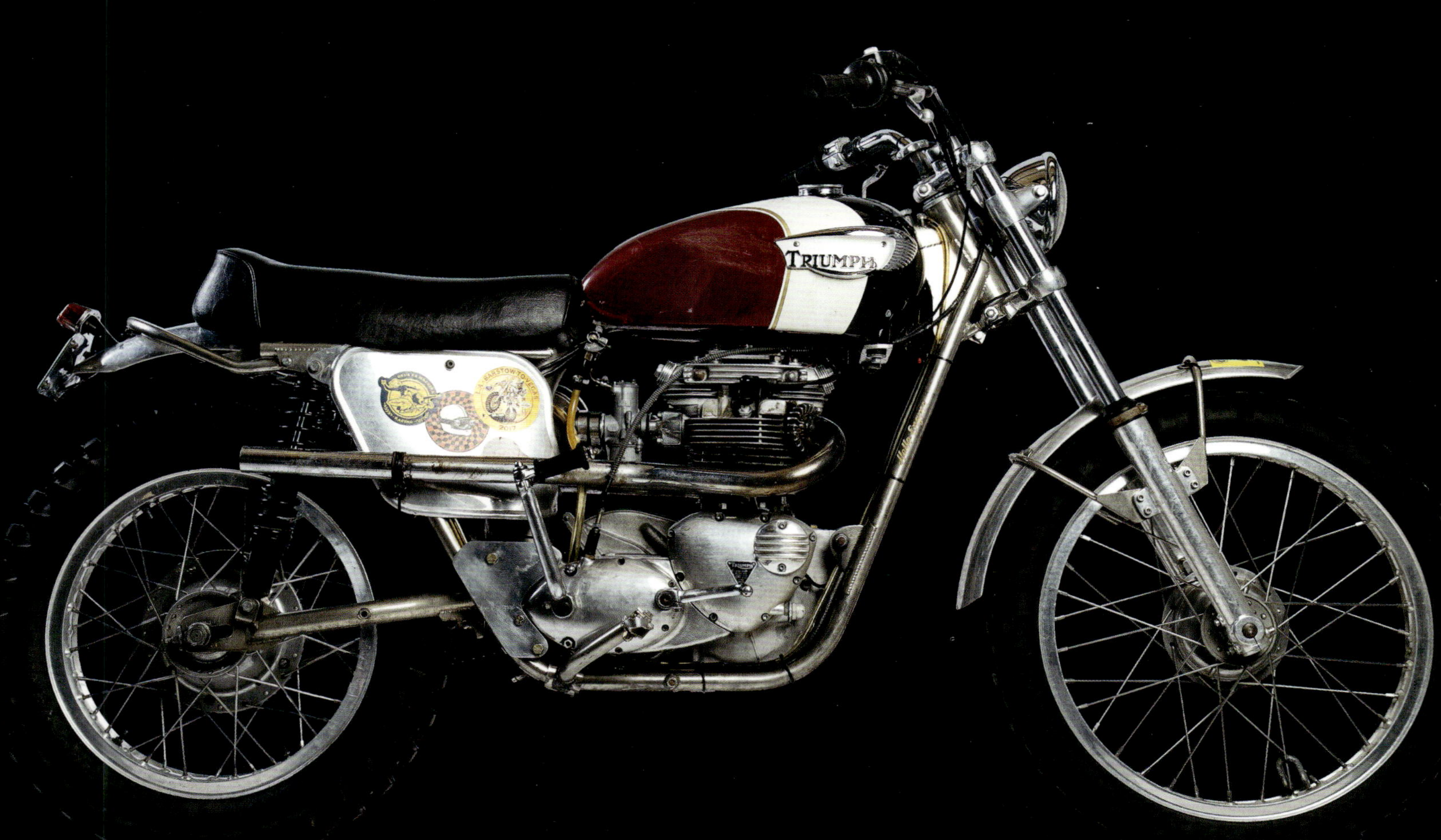

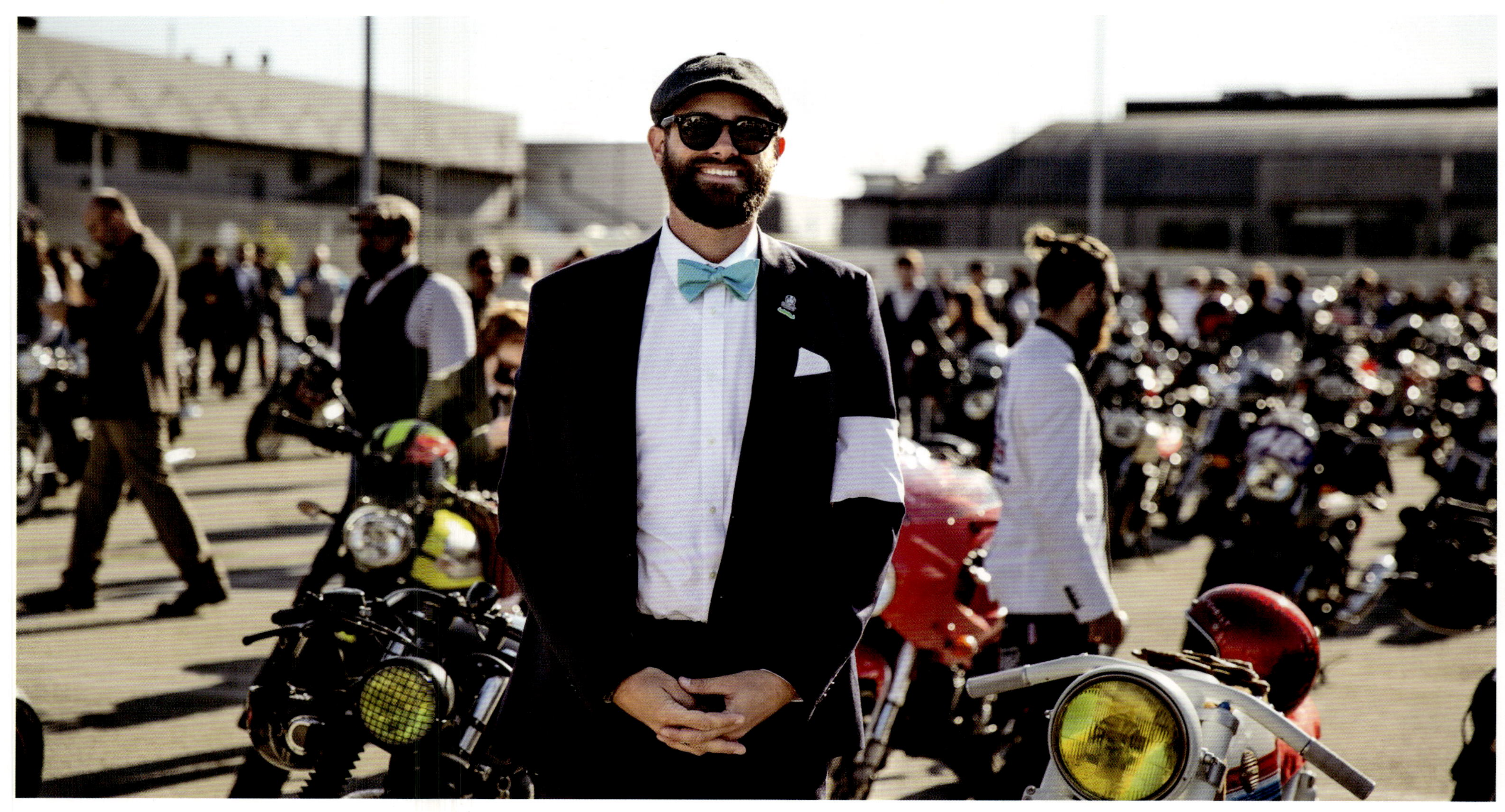

THE FIRST TO ARRIVE
& THE LAST TO LEAVE

Ride Host: **SAM BENDALL**
Location: **LOS ANGELES, UNITED STATES**

It was 2014 and I was working for Triumph Motorcycles America at the time as their Public Relations Manager. I had caught wind that we were a global sponsor for the DGR, and thought the entire concept of the DGR was really great from a corporate social responsibility perspective. I channeled that excitement and put together a plan to have our executive team, marketing, and PR departments make a showing of support for the US-based rides. I directed our CEO at the time to Minneapolis (his hometown), our Lead Product Director showed up for the Atlanta event, and I went to Los Angeles (my hometown) to represent our interests in a few major cities.

Aside from the corporate connection, the event meant something deeper to me as well because my father had just beaten prostate cancer a couple of years earlier, so it felt somewhat serendipitous to get involved. Somewhere along the line I met and spoke deeply with Mark Hawwa and became friends with him. After leaving Triumph in 2015 I was conscripted to take over running and organizing the Los Angeles ride.

Motorcycling plays a huge part of my life. I have been working in the motorcycle industry for almost the last decade, so the lines have become blurred. My stoke for motorcycles along with my professional background got me to where I am today, but a divergence is occurring and I feel myself going back to a more pure form of what I feel it means to be a motorcyclist.

As for the motorcycle itself and what it means to me, I would have to say it allows me to tie back to those moments in childhood where the world opens itself up by the sheer fact that now you have an amazing way to move through it on this incredibly well-engineered machine. Motorcycles give me a sense of awe and wonder. It ties me to a landscape and provides me time for

self-reflection, and most recently they have served as a means to challenge myself by becoming a better rider. I don't care much for the scene or looking cool anymore; I am more enamored with the personal and athletic growth of becoming a better rider and helping others do the same.

The DGR has brought people together within the Los Angeles Riding community, unlike any other event. Most motorcycle rides and events are notoriously cliquish, but the DGR has been a staple event each year around the

"HAVING THE CHANCE TO LOOSEN OUR TIES, TAKE OFF OUR JACKETS AND RELISHING ANOTHER SUCCESSFUL YEAR; NOW THAT'S A GREAT FEELING."

country. I think it resonates with a lot of people especially since we partnered with Movember to highlight mental health issues alongside prostate cancer.

Running the ride isn't easy. In fact, it's a lot of fucking work; but it's also very rewarding. I also don't help myself much by wanting and trying to one-up the previous year ride with a bigger and better event. There are always these little things that come up each year during the planning phase which need to be attended to but I have always had the good fortune of being assisted by the home office in Sydney and a cadre of dedicated co-hosts and volunteers here in LA. I do love watching it all come

together on the day of the ride, seeing a ton of familiar faces, and building up everyone's stoke for the event. As the ride host for the past eight years, I am often the first to arrive and last to leave. I do get great prolonged excitement from the moment I give our announcement speech and safety briefing to the ride, until its conclusion when I see that final tail rider dismounting their bike.

The DGR in itself is a special one to me but having my dad there at my first DGR as City Host is an unbeatable memory. Having him see what I was responsible for and having him tell me how proud he was of me for putting on a hell of a show—that meant a lot. Overall though, the post-ride party and getting together with my volunteer team and local friend is always the best. Having the chance to loosen our ties and take off our jackets and relish in another successful year; now that's a great feeling.

I also look forward to the day when I get to enjoy the DGR as a participant and not as a host. That will be a weird but memorable and interesting experience.

Fundraising in the event is massively important. I've learned to tap my network of industry colleagues to provide some rad products which I in turn raffle off based on donations. I also call previous supporters and ask them kindly to continue supporting this cause which I've been embedded in for the past eight years of my life.

I am not a terribly high-level fundraiser nor do I have access to labor unions or big corporate clients, but I make a concerted effort to set and meet a goal each year. I'm proud to say I achieved that, but I am most proud of what I am able to achieve through my hosting duties. Dedicating time and energy into putting together this amazing event helps give every single rider in LA a celebration to mark their incredible fundraising successes each and every year.

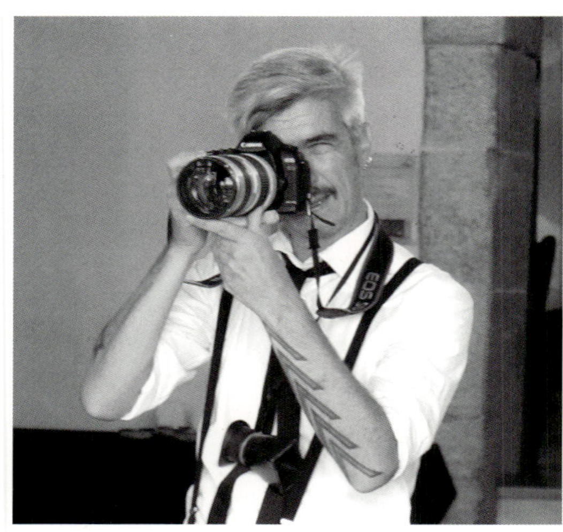

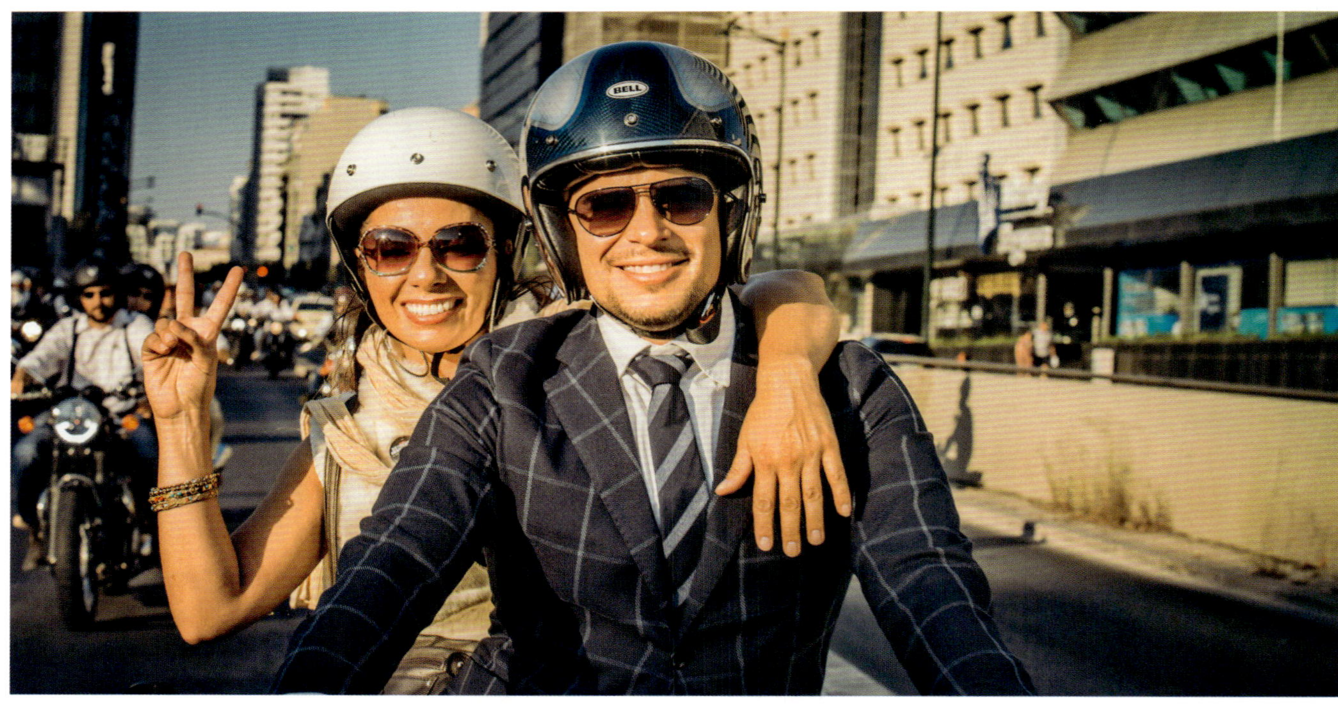

DGR PHOTOGRAPHER:
Manuel Portugal

"I started shooting the DGR in 2015. I was asked by the Triumph Motorcycle dealer in Portugal if I could do the job and from then on I didn't miss any rides. It seems people are always happy and the overall environment is one of amazing solidarity, partnership and help.

That vibe shows in the photos. It's like a mission people are on and their faces show their commitment and the joy of helping. For me it is also a mission; the better the job I do, the more the word is spread about the DGR. It's really hard to choose the best photo of DGR I've shot so far. There are thousands of them, but I like to focus on details and things that usually people don't notice.

I'd like to mention that I was involved as a member of the Lisbon Motorcycle Filmfest. For DGR Lisbon in 2018 and 2019, all the ticket sale profits from the festival went to DGR. These were the years that the relationship between DGR and Lisbon really blossomed, too."

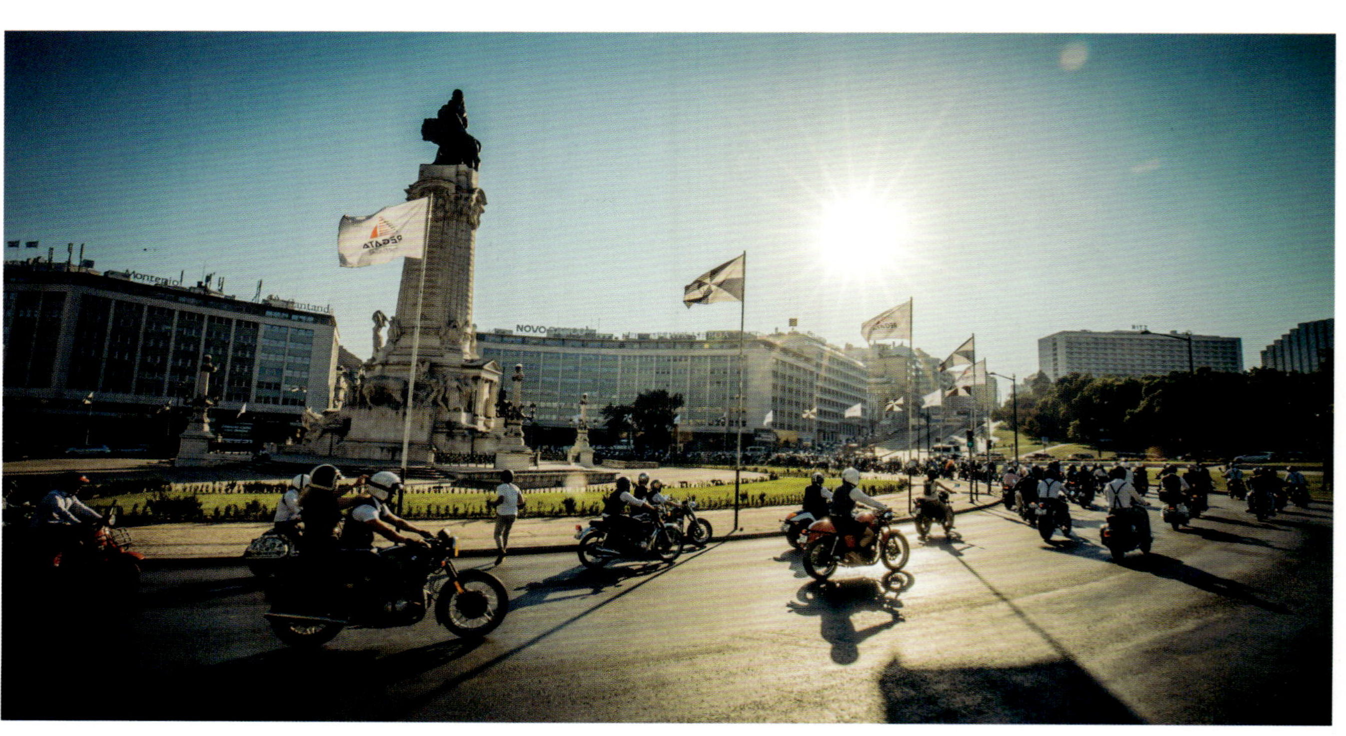

SIDECARS

Sidecars are classic vintage motorcycles with room for three. Specifically, it is a one-wheeled device attached to the side of a motorcycle or scooter, making the whole a three-wheeled vehicle. Developed by the French Army in 1893, its main purpose was to increase the carrying capacity of two-wheeled vehicles.

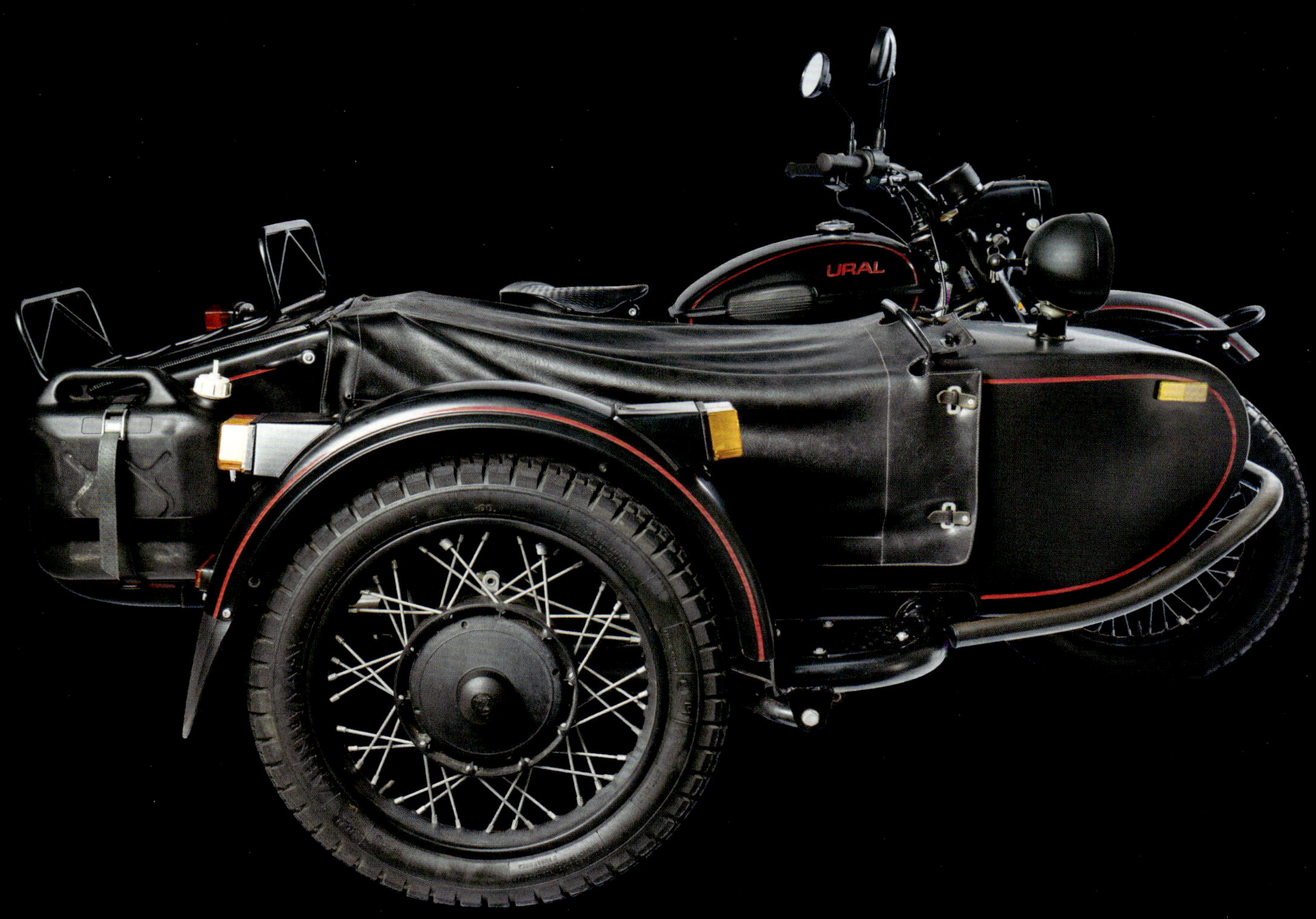

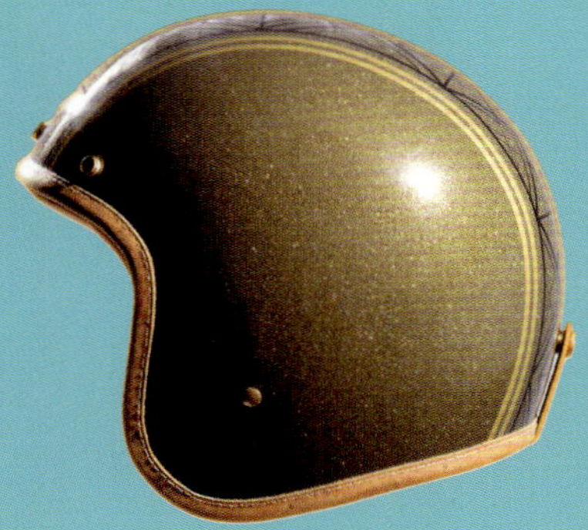

2016

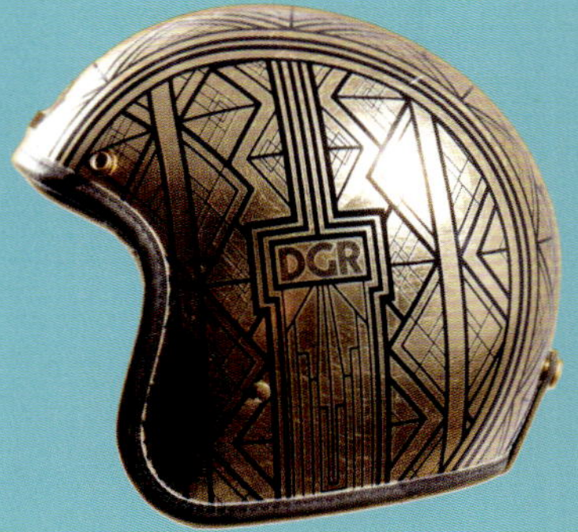

2016
KINGPIN

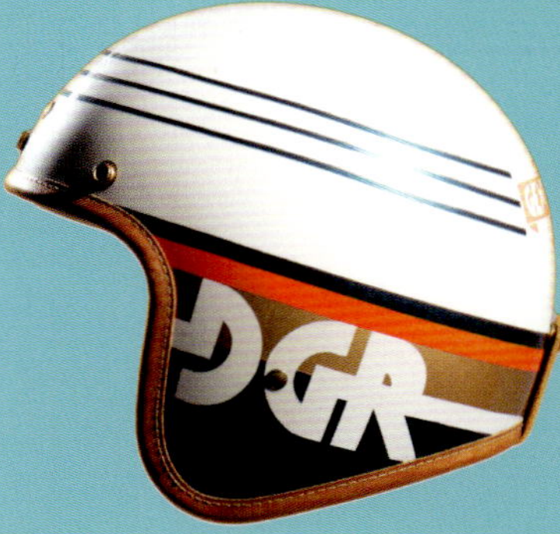

2017

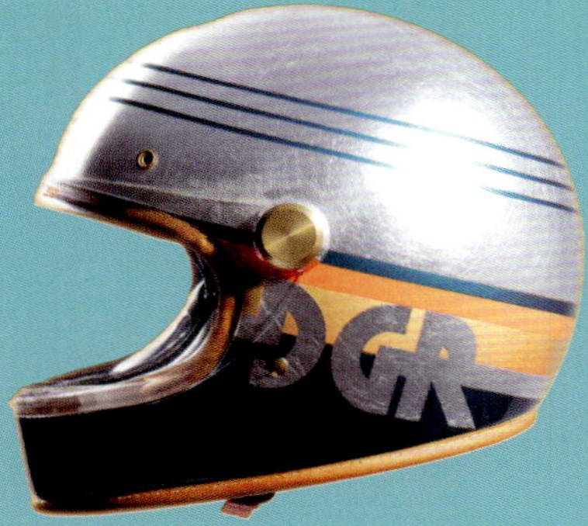

2017
KINGPIN

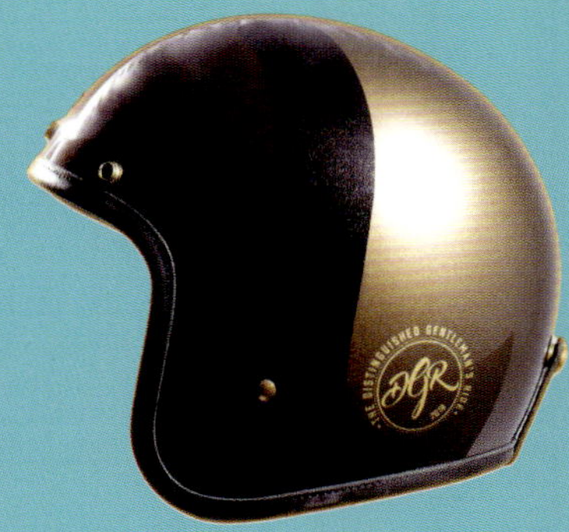

2018

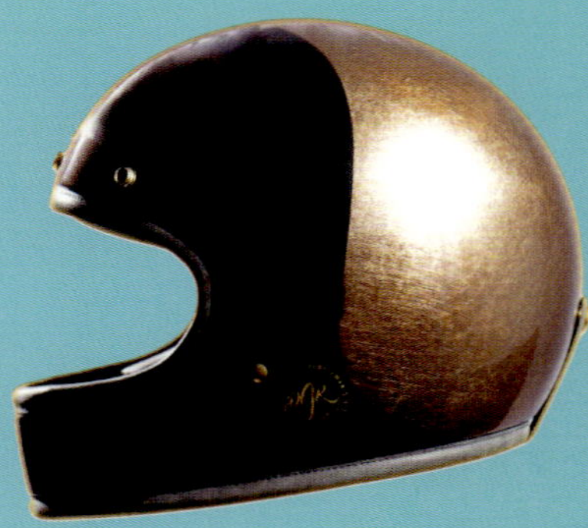

2018
KINGPIN

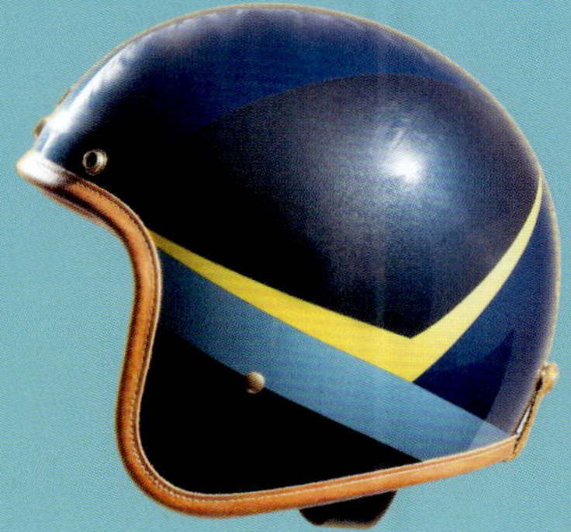

2019

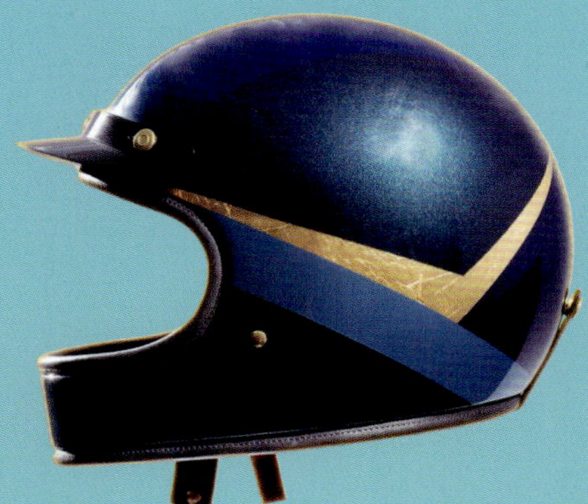

2019
KINGPIN

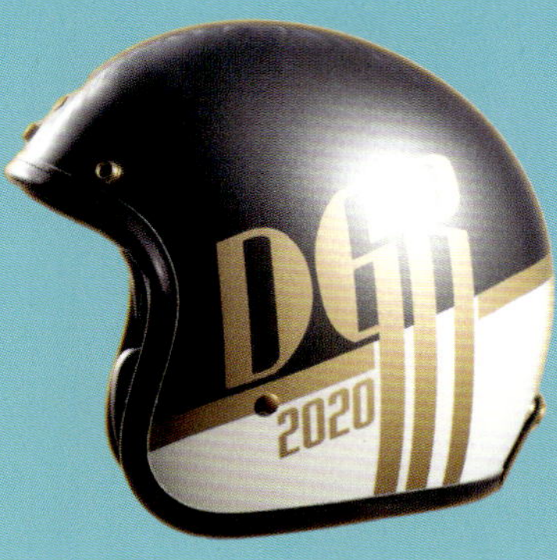

2020

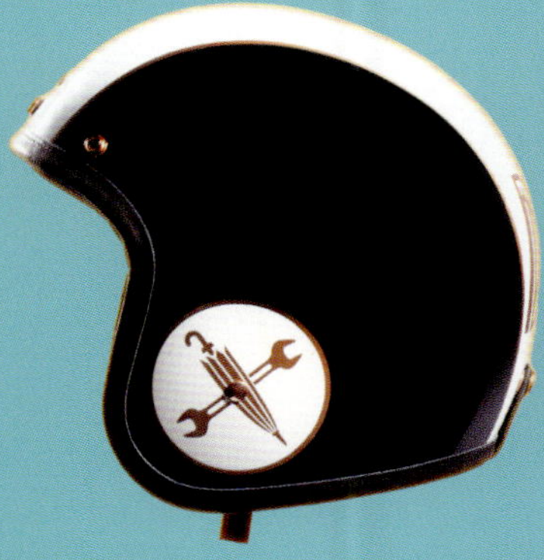

2021

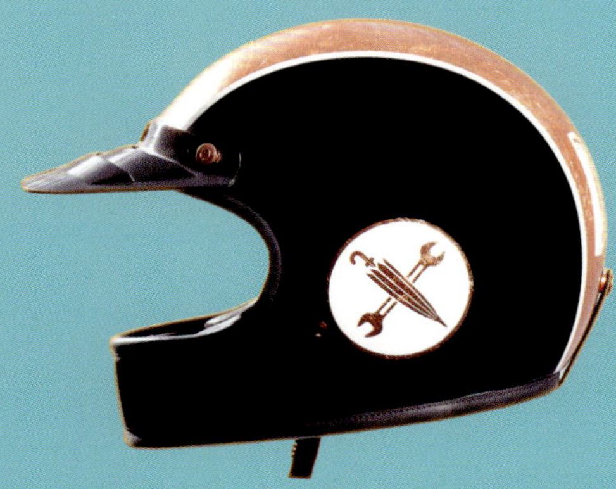

2021
KINGPIN

DGR & HEDON HELMETS

One of the most illustrious and desirable prizes known to fundraisers in The Distinguished Gentleman's Ride are the annual Hedon x DGR custom helmets, uniquely designed and produced every year. Since 2016, Hedon and The Distinguished Gentleman's Ride have partnered to reward fundraisers and offer something special for the DGR community.

With new designs revealed within each year's campaign, The Kingpin stands above them all as the rarest helmet produced as a single one-off variation to be gifted to the highest fundraiser. Often including gold, silver, or bronze foil to add a sense of grandeur to the piece, alternate versions are also made to be gifted to the top fundraisers of each year. For those who miss out, however, Hedon also create a limited edition run of each design with slight variations available for sale.

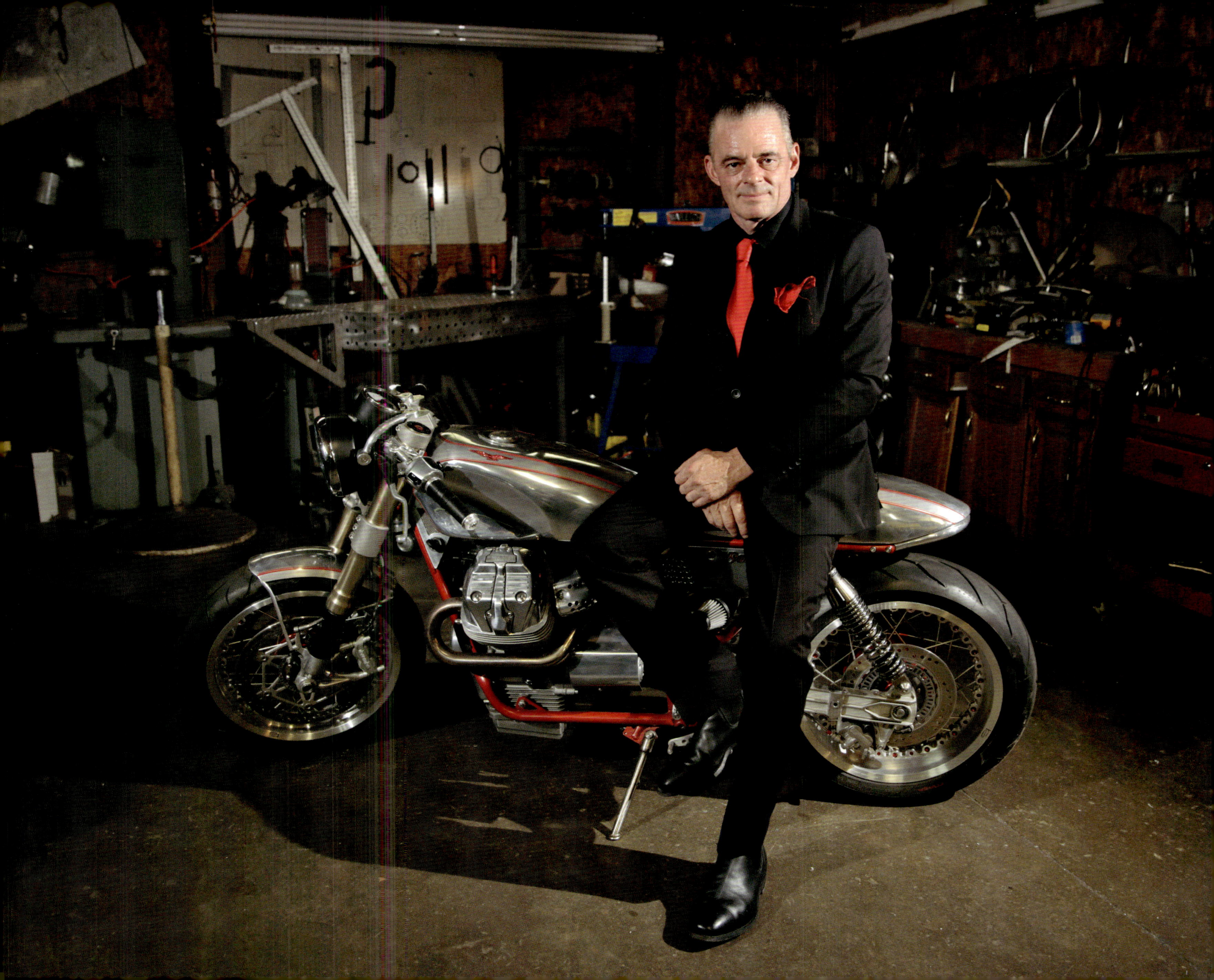

KARMA CHAMELEON

Before Mark asked me to be an ambassador for The Distinguished Gentle-man's Ride, I thought it was a bunch of horseshit, I thought, "This is just a bunch of fucking doofuses that are looking for an excuse to put suits on to try and look cool." And then ironically, Mark asked me to be an ambassador, and pretty much at the same time I was diagnosed with cancer.

This gave me a whole new perspective; it couldn't have been planned better. "I think you guys are a bunch of dickheads." "Do you want to be an ambassador on our ride?" "No. Hang on. I've got cancer. Yes, I will." I'm a dick. Talk about karma chameleon.

I didn't have health insurance. I was struggling emotionally. I'm living in a foreign country. The only family I have here are my children. I just felt very lonely, so the timing was good. Mark said, "Tell me what I can do to help you. I'm coming to New York to do the ride." So I decided fuck this, I'll drive from Chicago to New York and do the ride with him.

You know what the last person said to me when I had a suit on? "Would the defendant please rise." Honestly, I'm not a suit guy. I go to funerals in a black tee, black jeans and Chuck Taylors. The fact that Mark asked me to be an am-bassador was flattering. In fact, maybe that's why I got cancer? Maybe it was divine intervention? "Oh, you think this is horseshit asshole? Fuck you! You've got cancer."

But in all seriousness, everyone wants to be a tough guy who's unbeatable. But life's short and you have to open up and tell people how you are feeling and that you love them before it's too late. What have you got to prove that's more important than living?

Craig Rodsmith
DGR Ambassador &
Custom Motorcycle Machinist

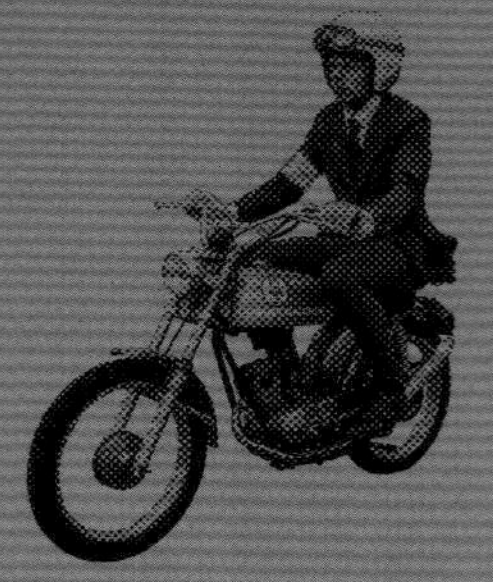

2019

- R I D E   E I G H T -

WITHOUT KNOWING IT, THIS WOULD BE OUR LAST RIDE BEFORE COVID-19 STRUCK. DGR CONTINUES TO BREAK ALL PREVIOUS RECORDS, WITH 2019 SEEING **116,000 RIDERS** IN **678 CITIES** TAKING PART GLOBALLY; OUR BIGGEST YET.

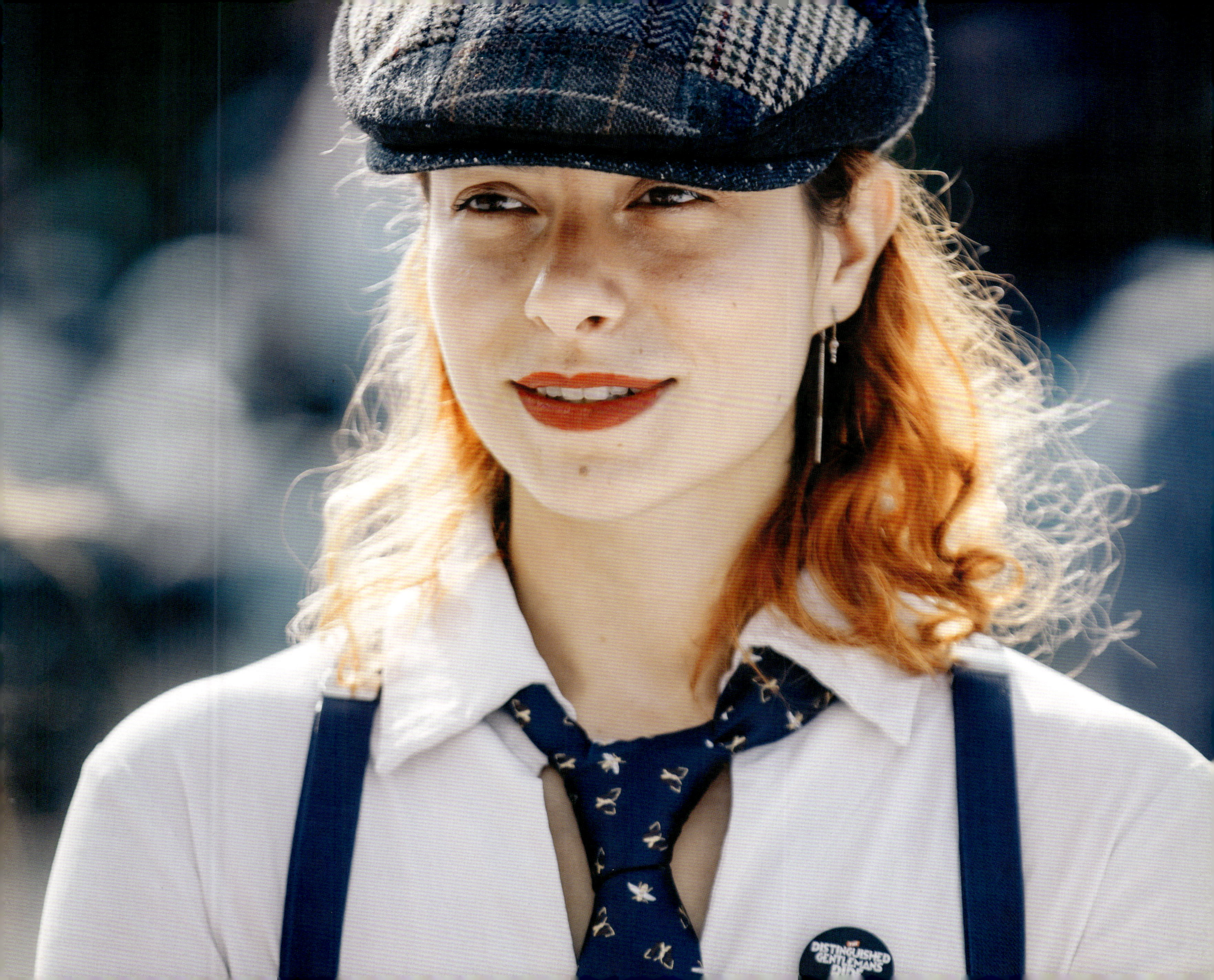

DISTINGUISHED
GENTLEMAN'S
RIDE

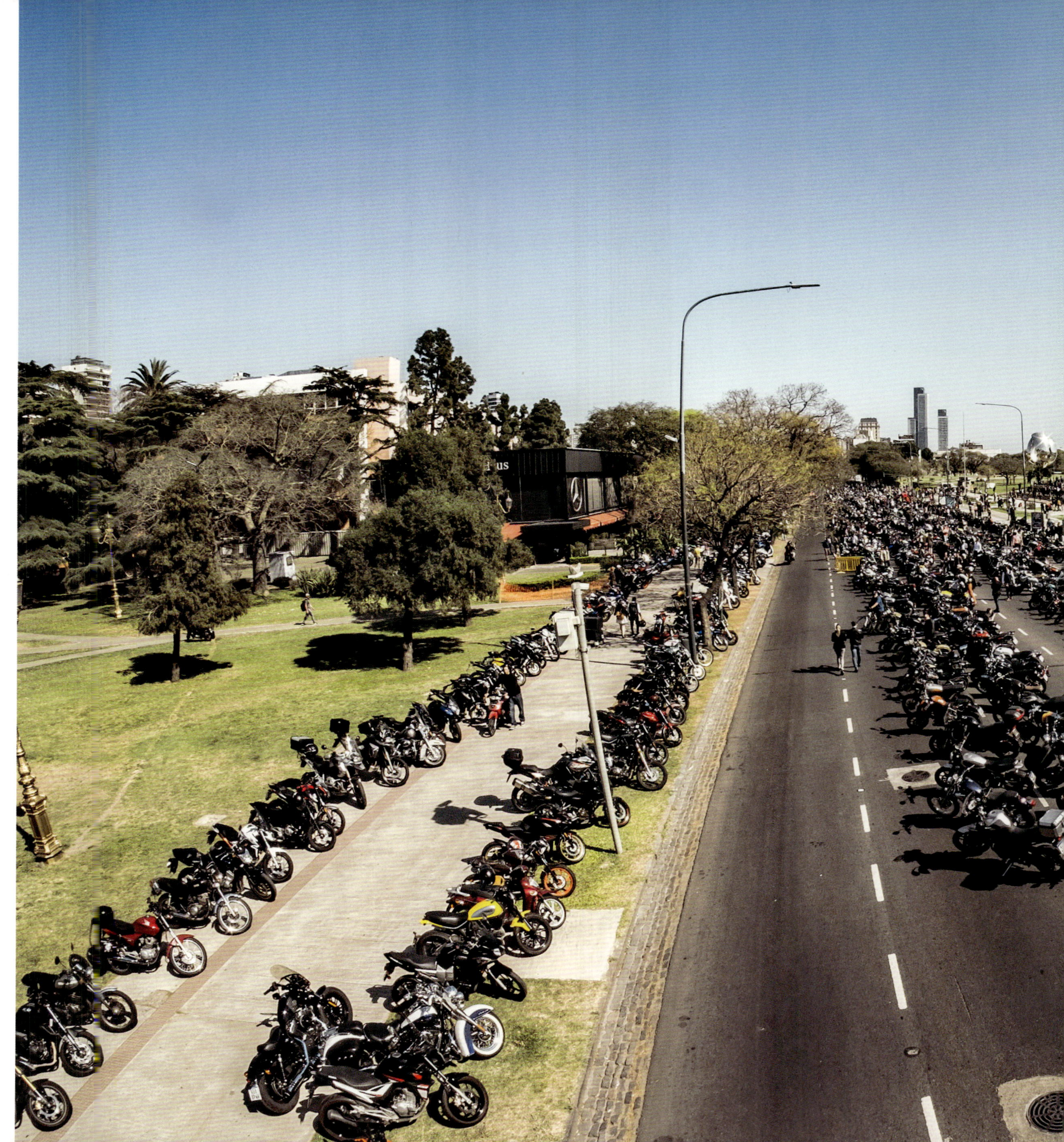

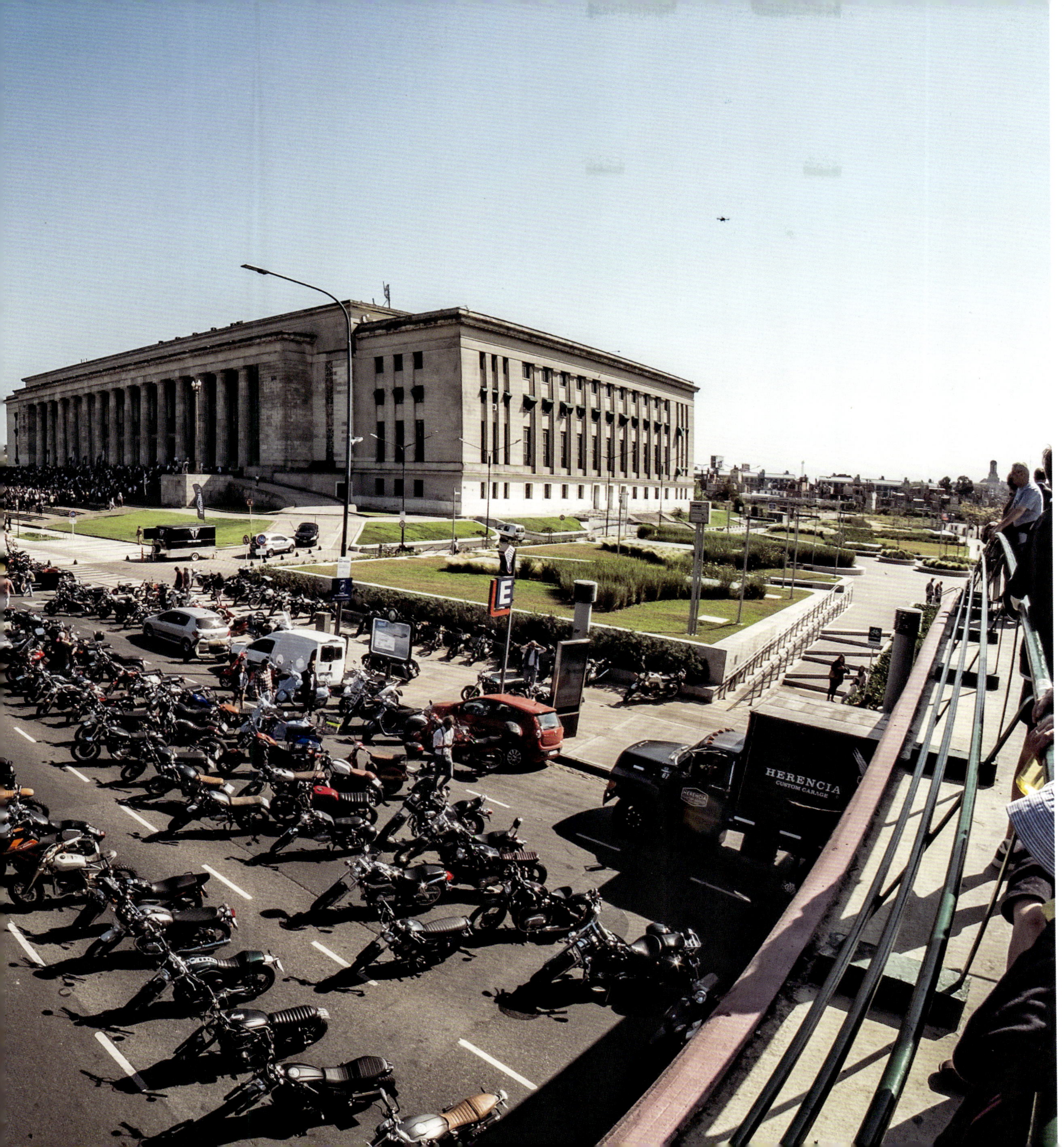
HERENCIA
CUSTOM GARAGE

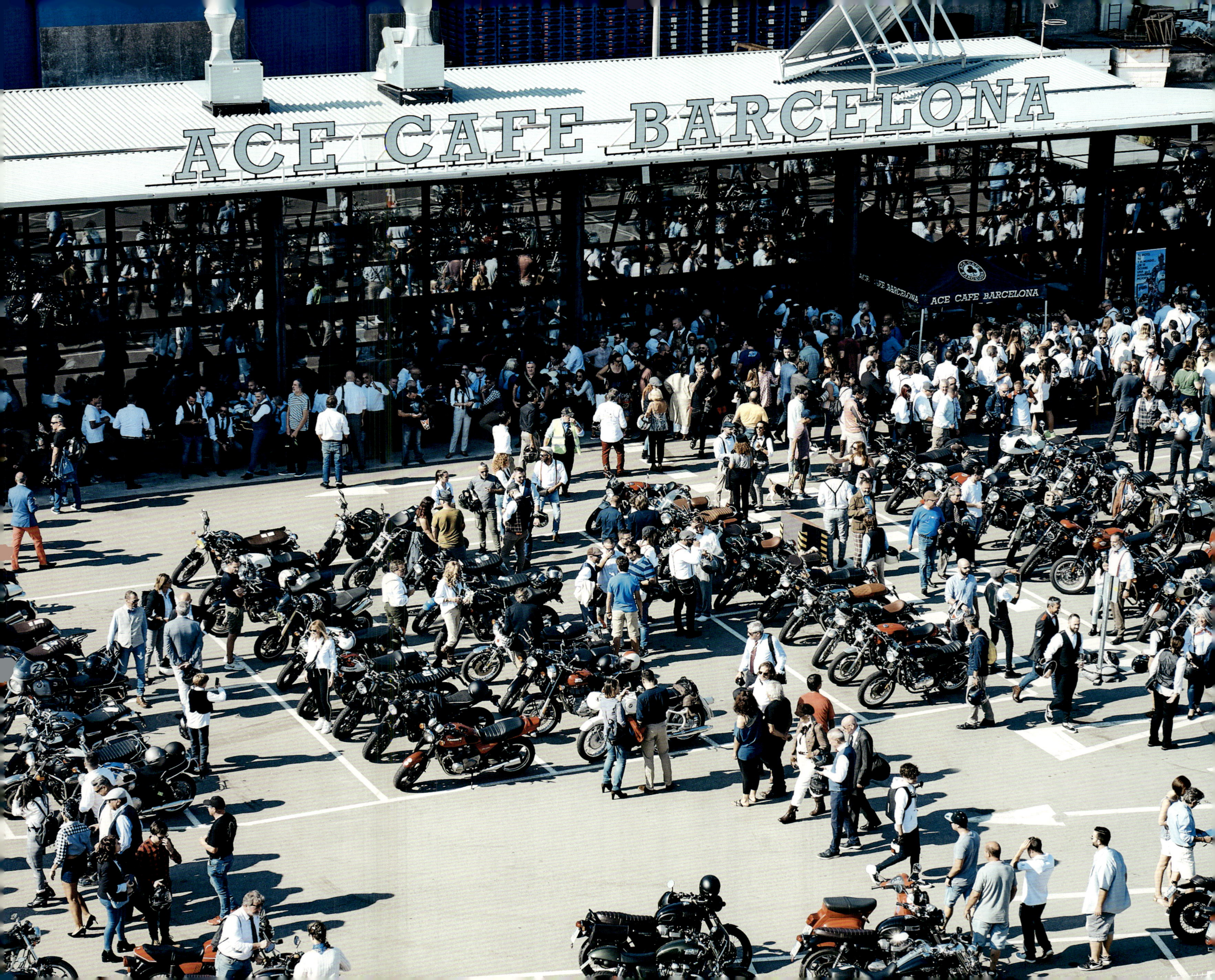

ACE CAFE BARCELONA
ACE CAFE BARCELONA
ACE CAFE BARCELONA

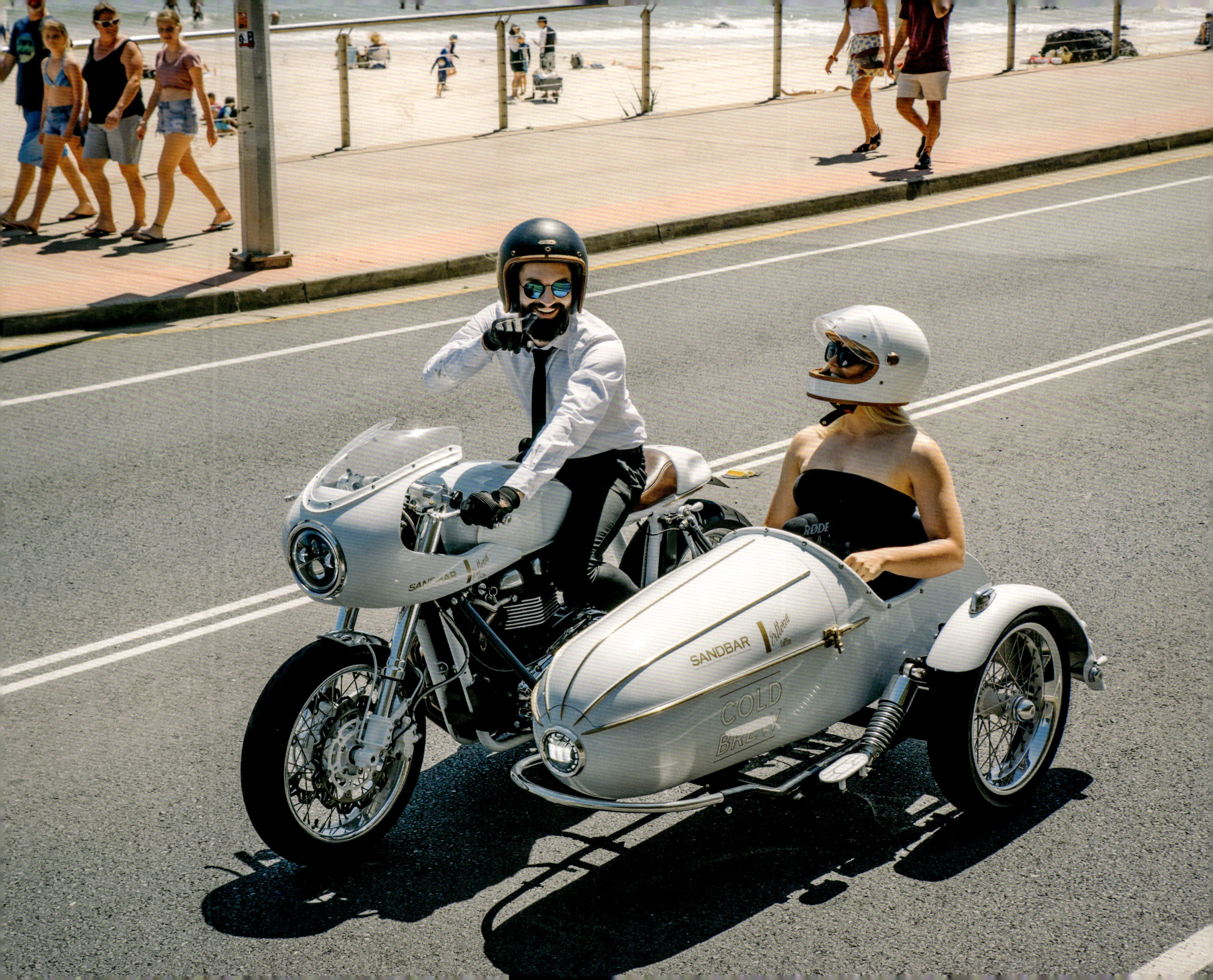

SANDBAR
SANDBAR Valleria
COLD BREW
RØDE

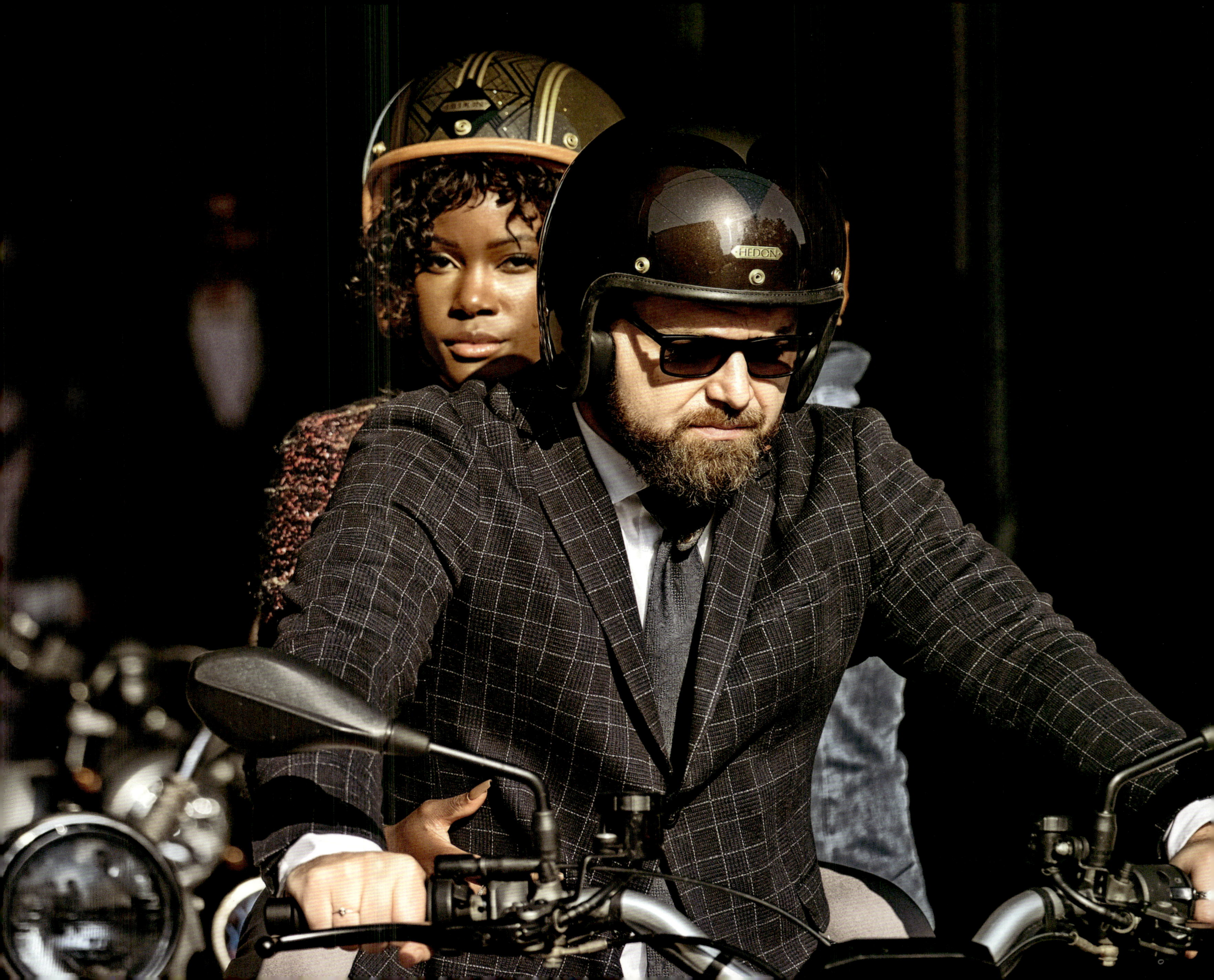

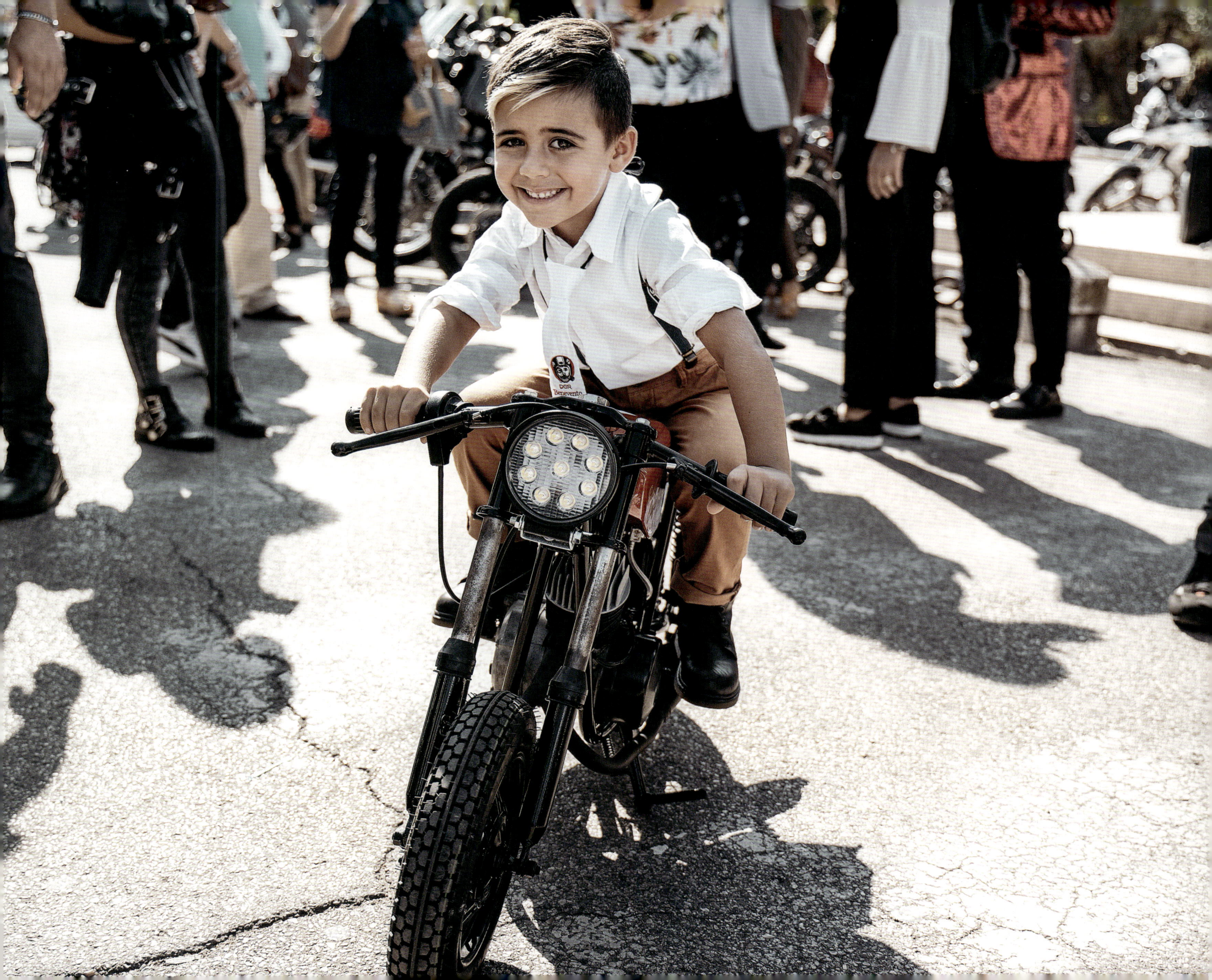

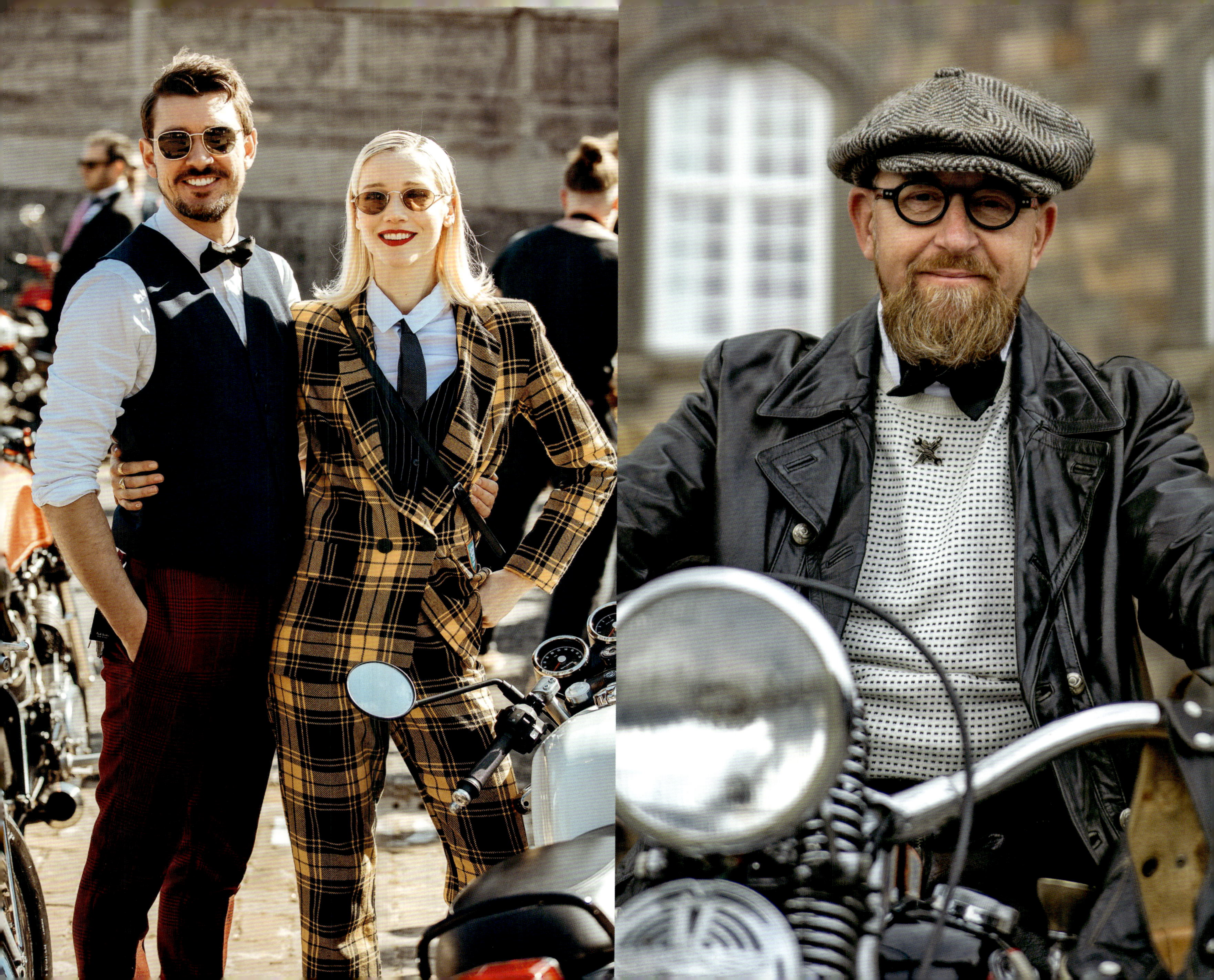

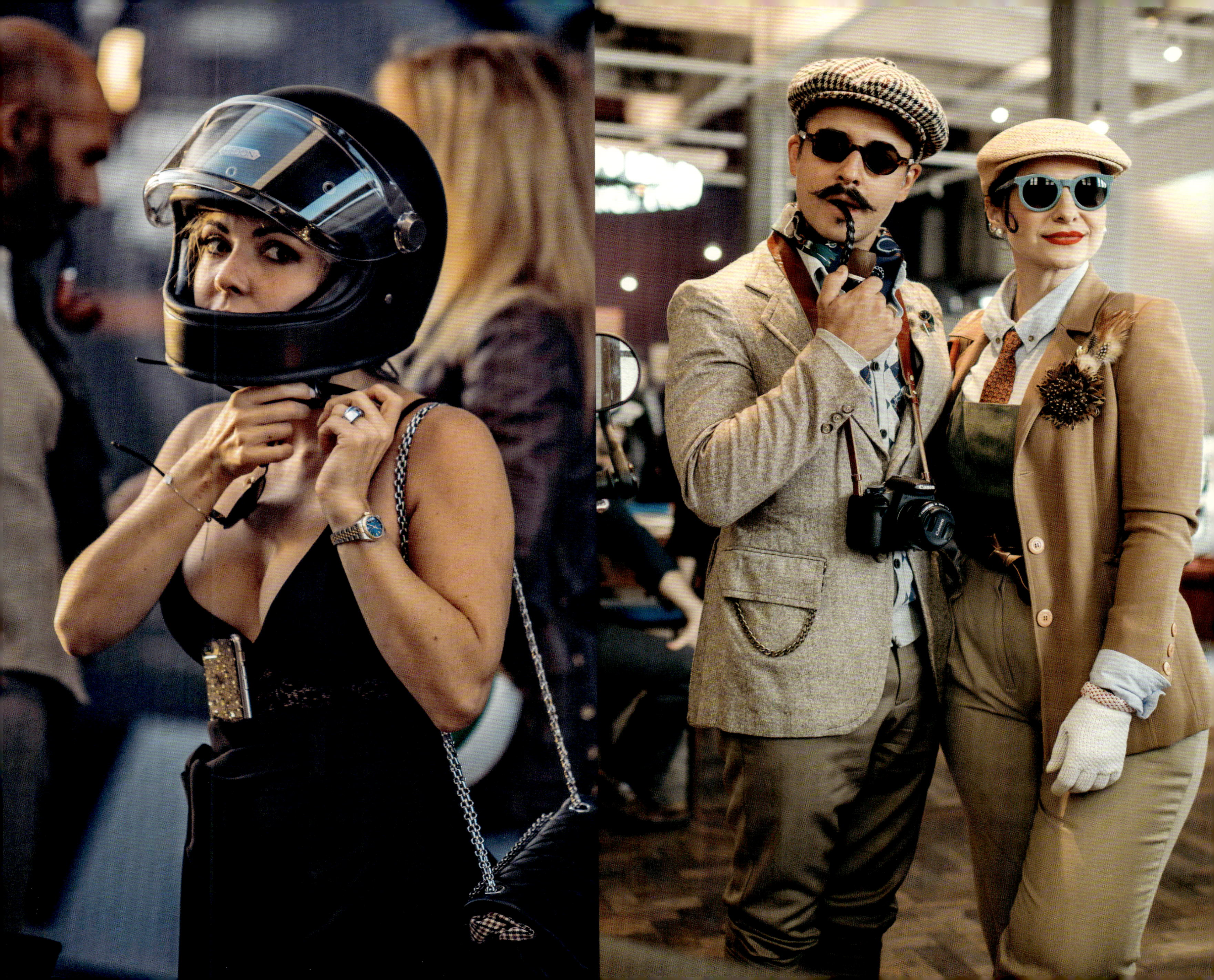

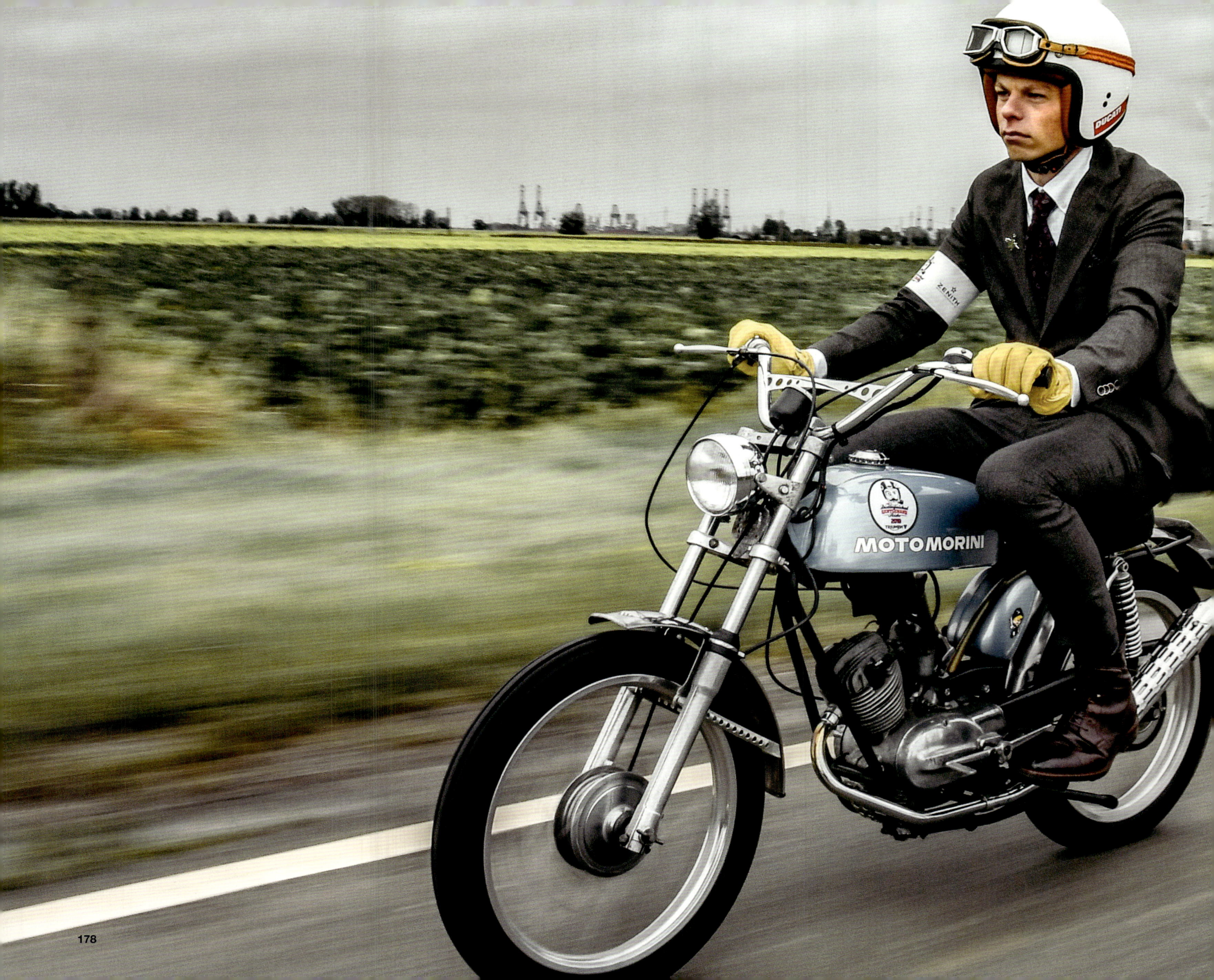

MOTOMORINI
ZENITH
DUCATI

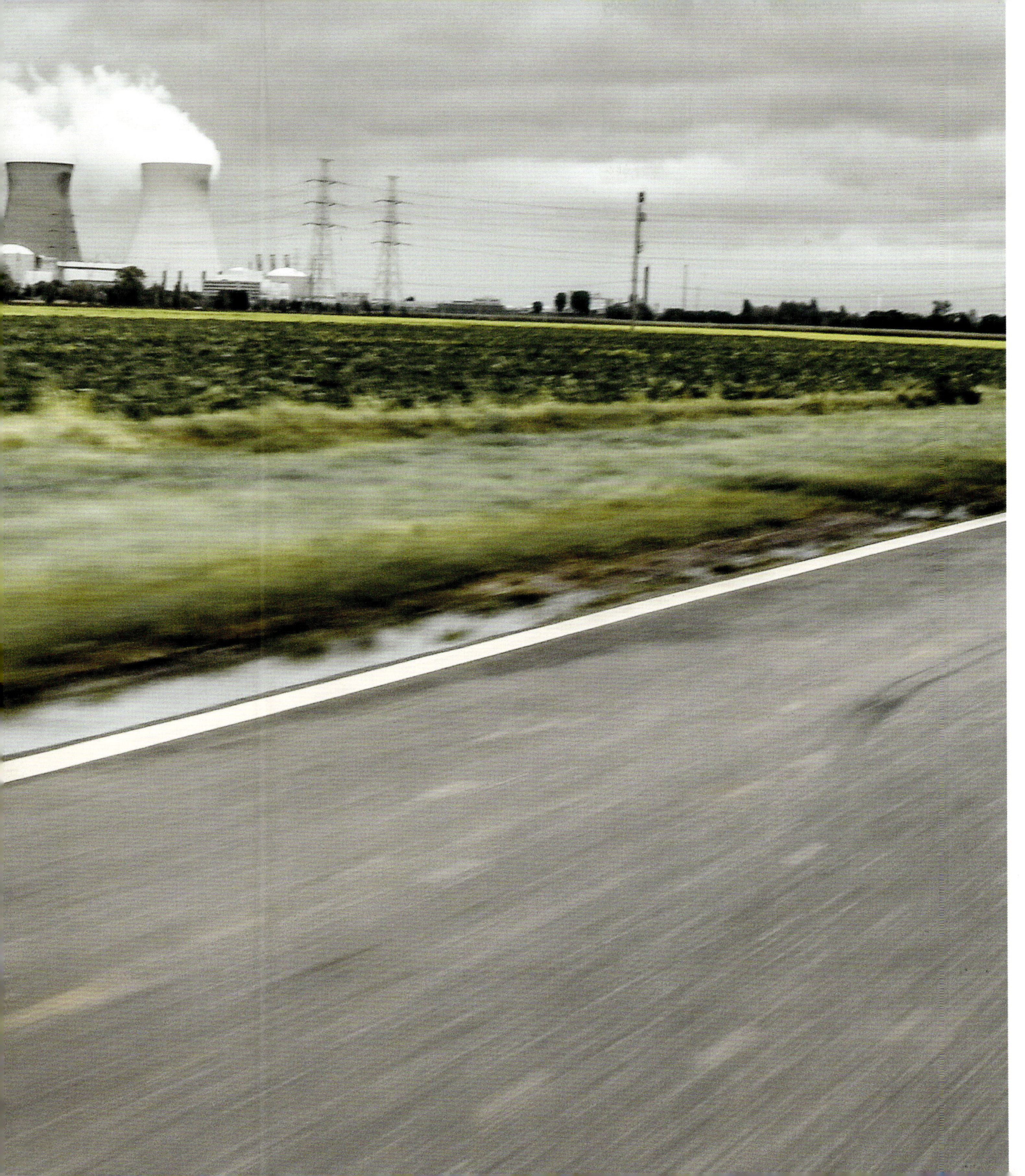

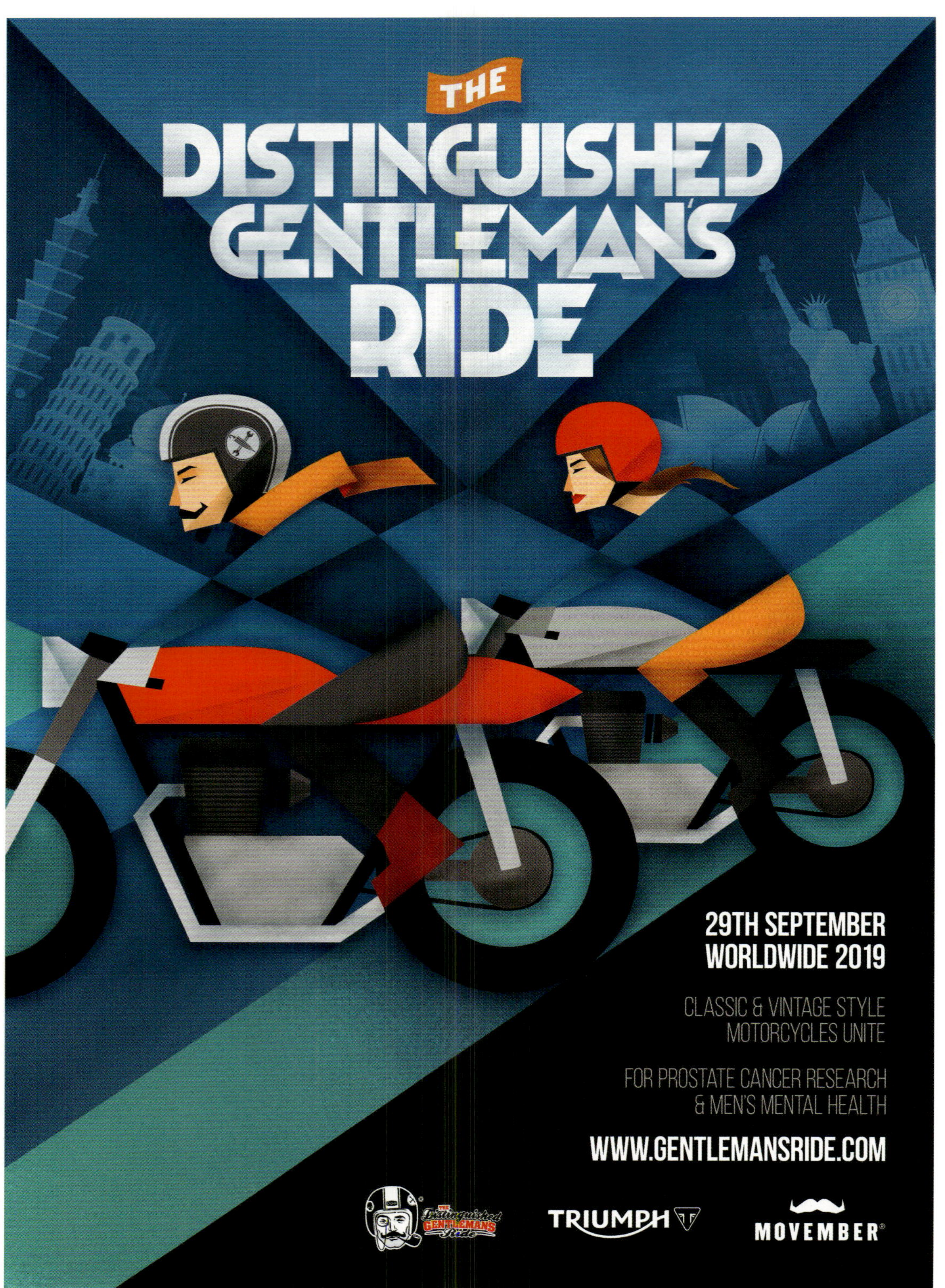

2019 Ride Poster

Designed by Tanya Koch

This year marked a return to the Art Deco style, but developed it even further using layers and textures to create a dynamic and angular design. It showed stylized depictions of both men and women riders amidst a range of local and international landmarks. By using both men and women, we reinforced the message that the causes DGR raises funds for and awareness of affects everyone because we all have men we love that we'd like to see live happier, healthier lives.

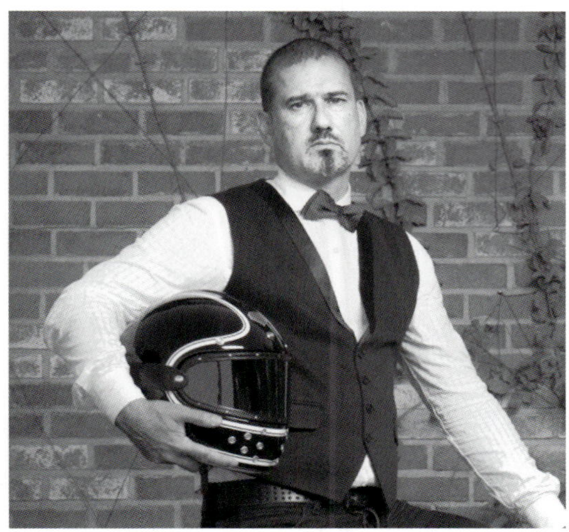

DGR PHOTOGRAPHER:
Rahoul Ghose

"Ten years of The Distinguished Gentleman's Ride have gone by in a flash. It's an event that strikes at my core, pairing moto interests and dapper fashion with a worthy cause.

In those early years, The Distinguished Gentleman's Ride became very personal when two close moto friends separately succumbed to cancer and suicide. I still think of them before the ride each year.

Shooting in NYC has given me an opportunity to capture the elements I so love about the city; its cultural diversity and gender inclusivity, its openness and its enthusiasm and heart in embracing this global phenomenon.

DGR has also afforded me the opportunity to work with some extremely talented photographers over the years to capture the breadth of a DGR ride day. I count many of those generous individuals as close friends now.

Causes aside, DGR really hits a chord. In a world full of uncertainty, the event makes the Earth seem a little closer together, if only for a day."

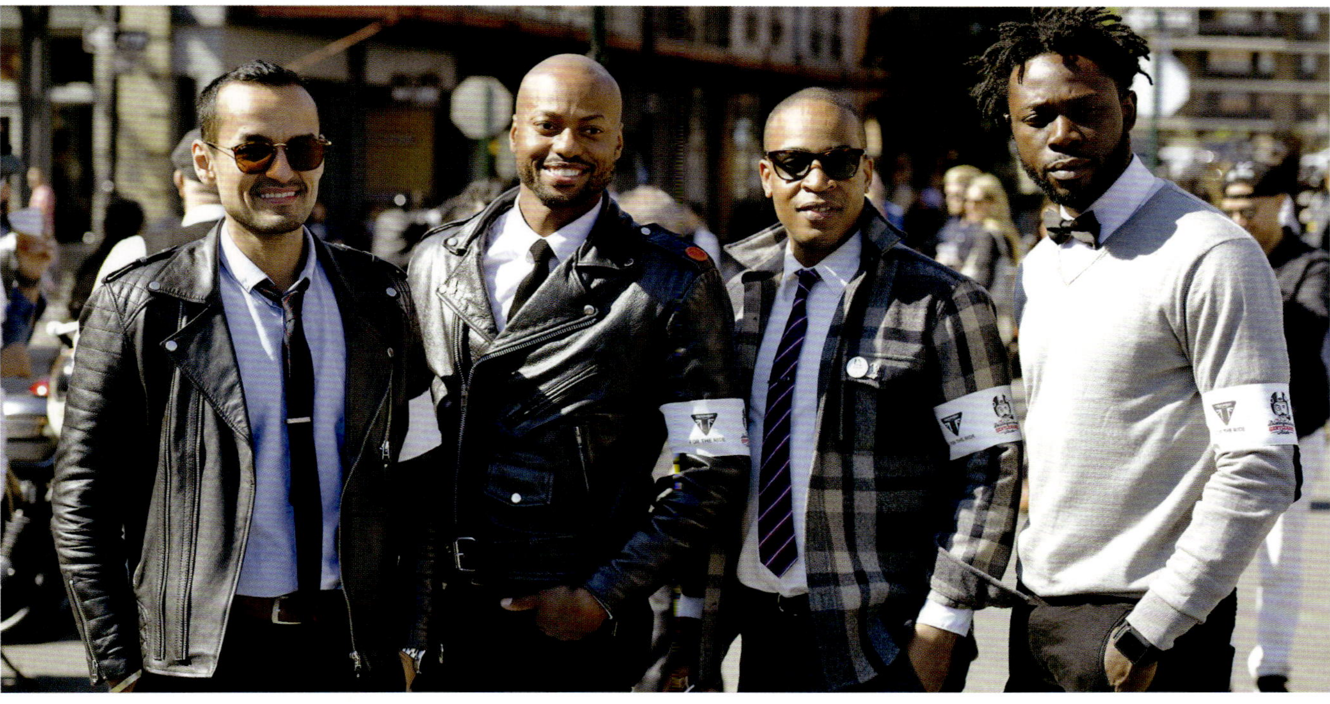

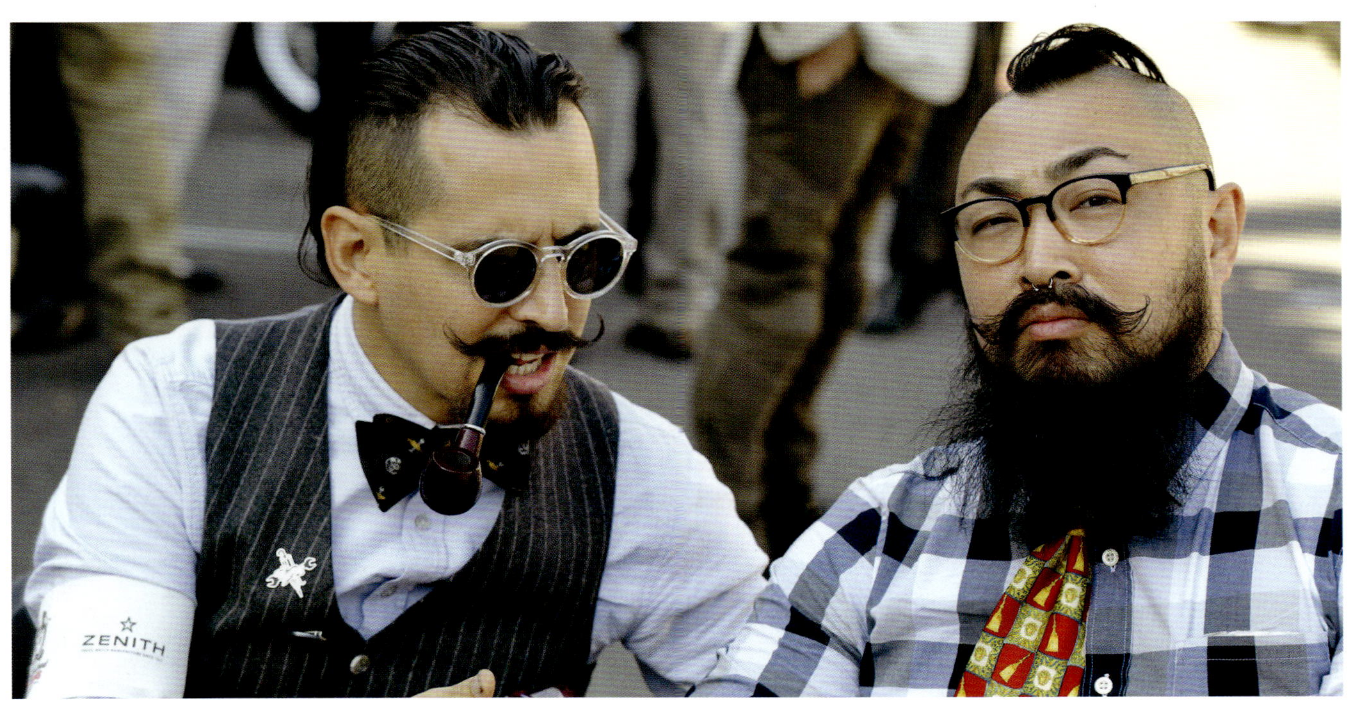

Hugo Eccles

"I was in the first DGR in 2012, and I've ridden in one every year since. London, Los Angeles, San Francisco—whatever city I'm in, I make a point of being involved. In those ten years, I've seen the DGR have a hugely positive effect both inside and outside the motorcycling community. It's brought people together and, in the process, nurtured the custom culture, from personal shed builds to professional customs.

It's also helped improve the perception of motorcycling and, by doing so, drawn new people into our community. As our community changes, so too does the DGR. Case in point, last year I rode an electric motorcycle. (It was certainly easier—maybe even more enjoyable? Heresy!—not having to worry about overheating an air-cooled engine or burning out a clutch!) As the Ride continues to grow, I expect we'll be seeing more electric motorcycles. I'm excited to see how DGR evolves to meet this exciting new era, and welcomes those new riders into our community."

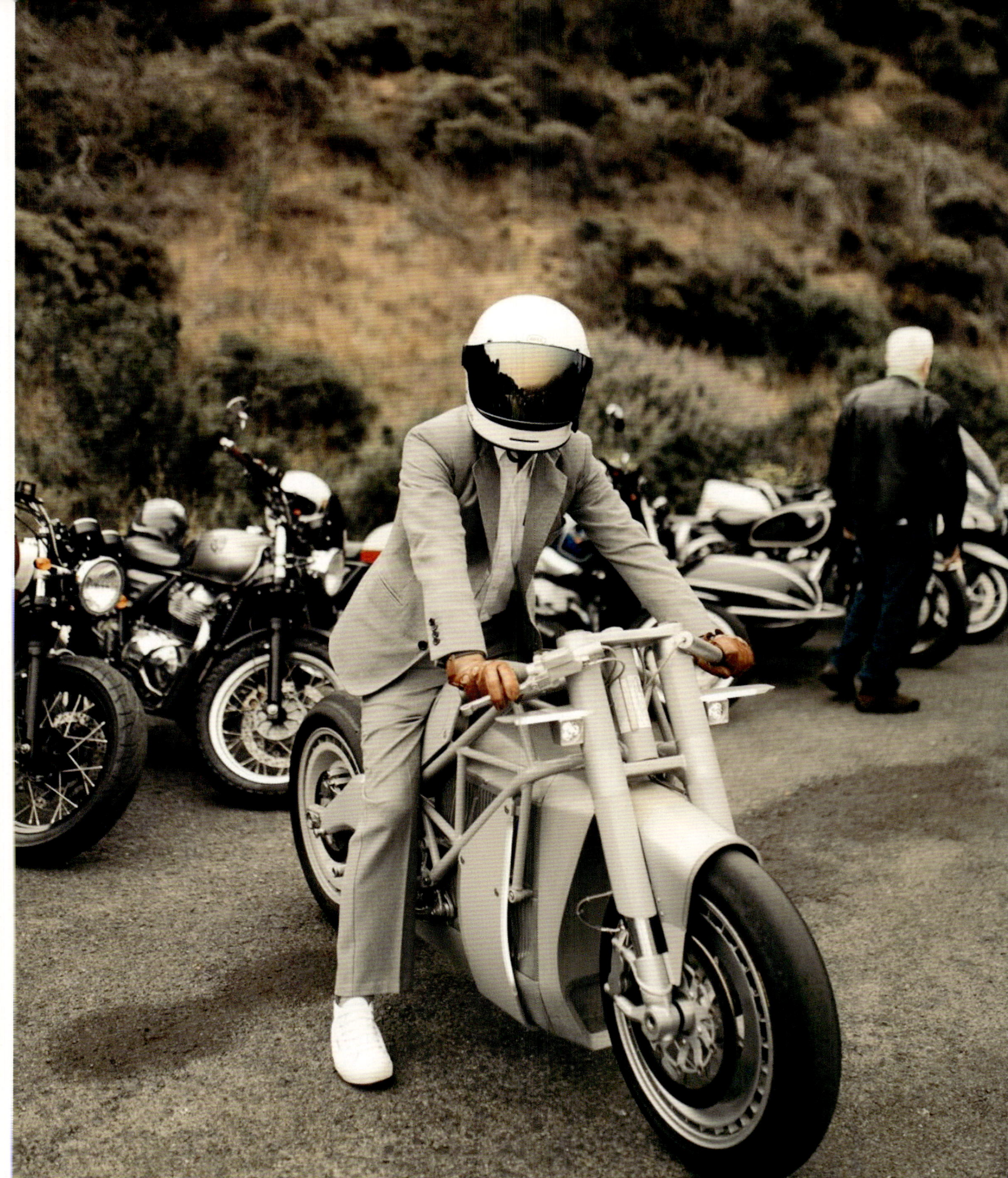

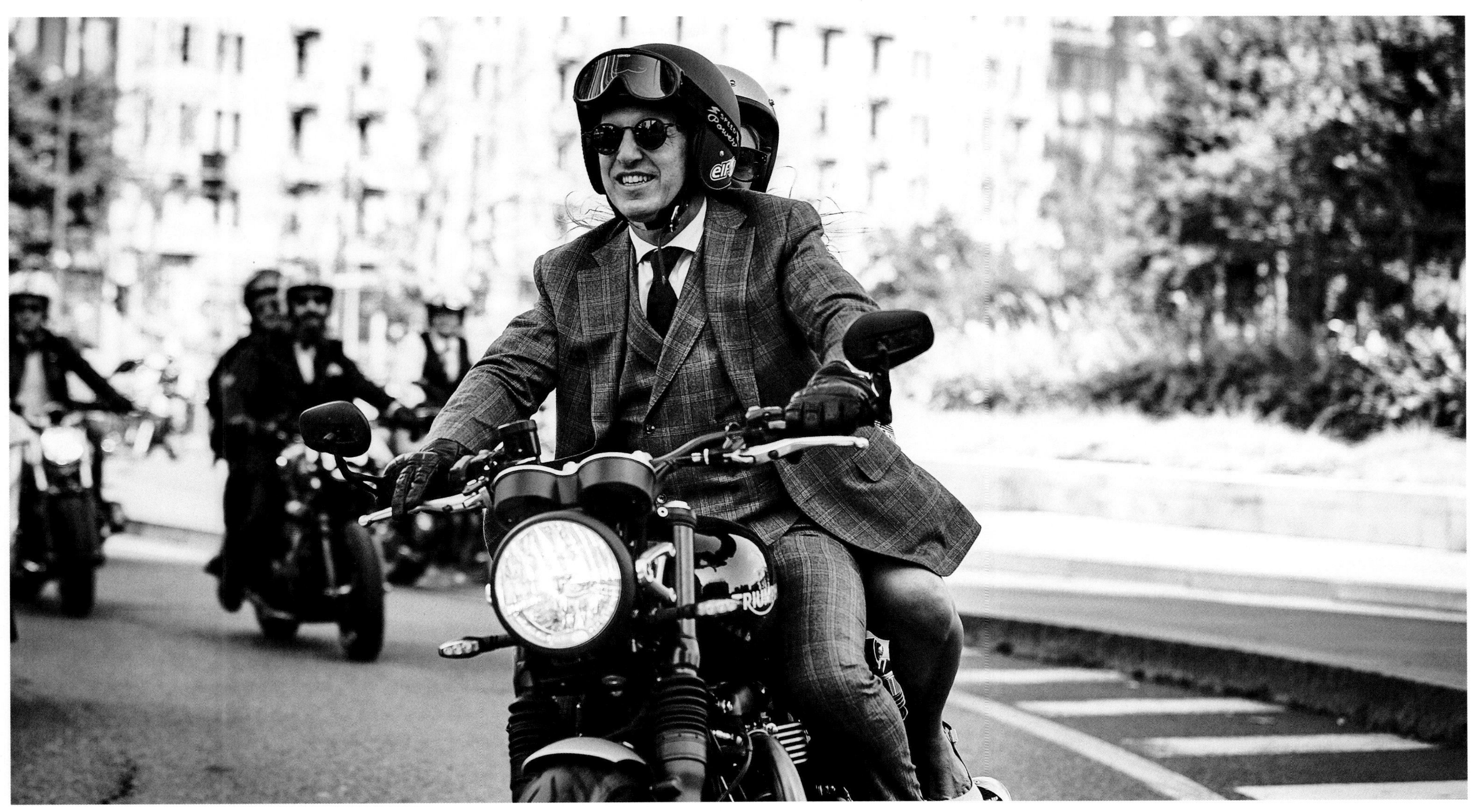

UN GENTILUOMO
A MILANO

Ride Host: **MATTEO ADREANI**
Location: **MILAN, ITALY**

I heard about DGR at the very beginning on some cafe racers group on Facebook. In 2012 and 2013, I had family matters (two newborn girls) and couldn't attend or host it.

Finally, in 2014 I could host my first DGR in Milano, which was an instant success. I love DGR because, while I work on it, I know that I am doing it for a great cause and, at the same time, I have a great time. To be honest, in the beginning, I was just looking at the fun side of the event, but soon I realized how important its cause is.

While gentleladies are always mindful of prevention, we men think we are invulnerable, and that unpleasant things only happen to others. This is why I think the DGR is so important: it reminds us how important prevention is to live better and longer. Thanks to DGR, many of my friends had a prostate checkup for the first time in their life.

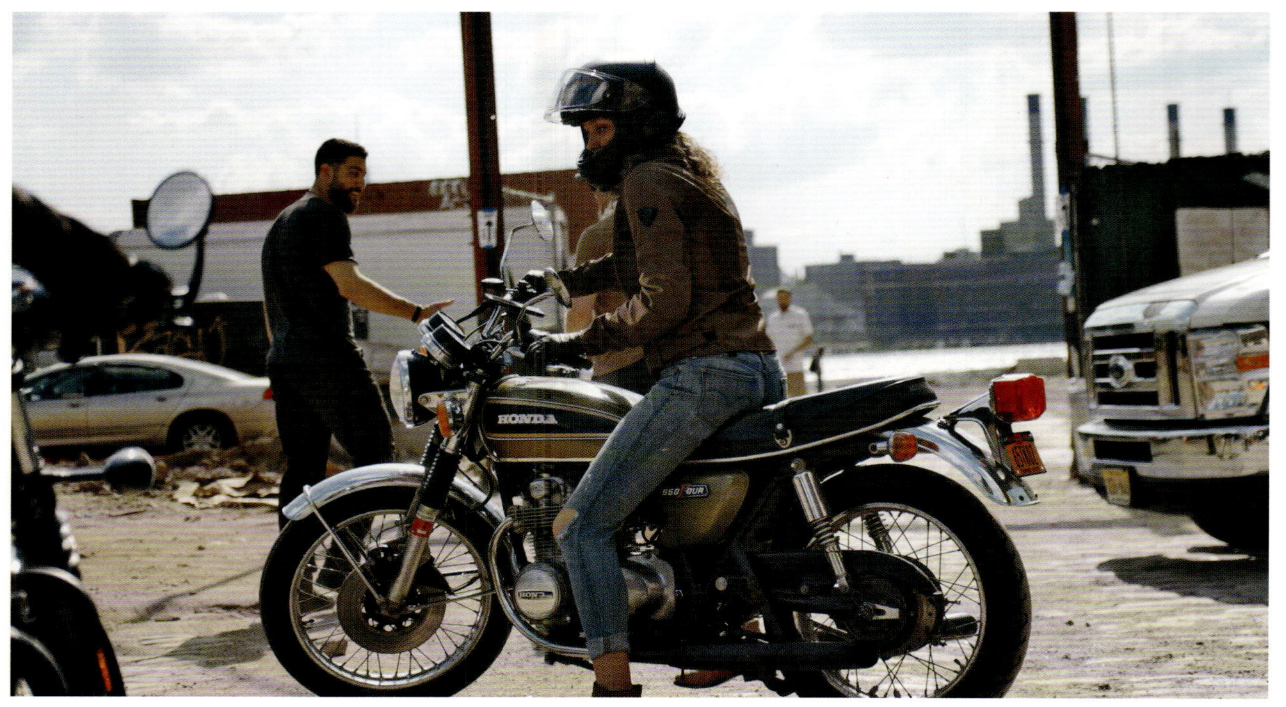

DGR DIRECTOR:
Cam Elkins

The stories I've filmed for DGR are, I would say, my most beloved. The ones I'm most proud of. Not only did the process of making each of these stories lift my craft in film-making and reiterate to me the power of film but also presented to me some of the most profound life experiences I've ever had. I thank DGR from the bottom of my heart for allowing me to create these films.

THE SEARCH - NEW YORK

Mark Hawwa introduced me to Kirsten, based in NYC at the time and one of the highest DGR group fundraisers in the US, as someone who was a force to be reckoned with. During my initial chats, I could tell she was fiercely driven by something very personal. She rode a mid-70s Honda CB550 Four and a Triumph Street Triple as her daily commuter, and she was just so helpful in making the shoot possible.

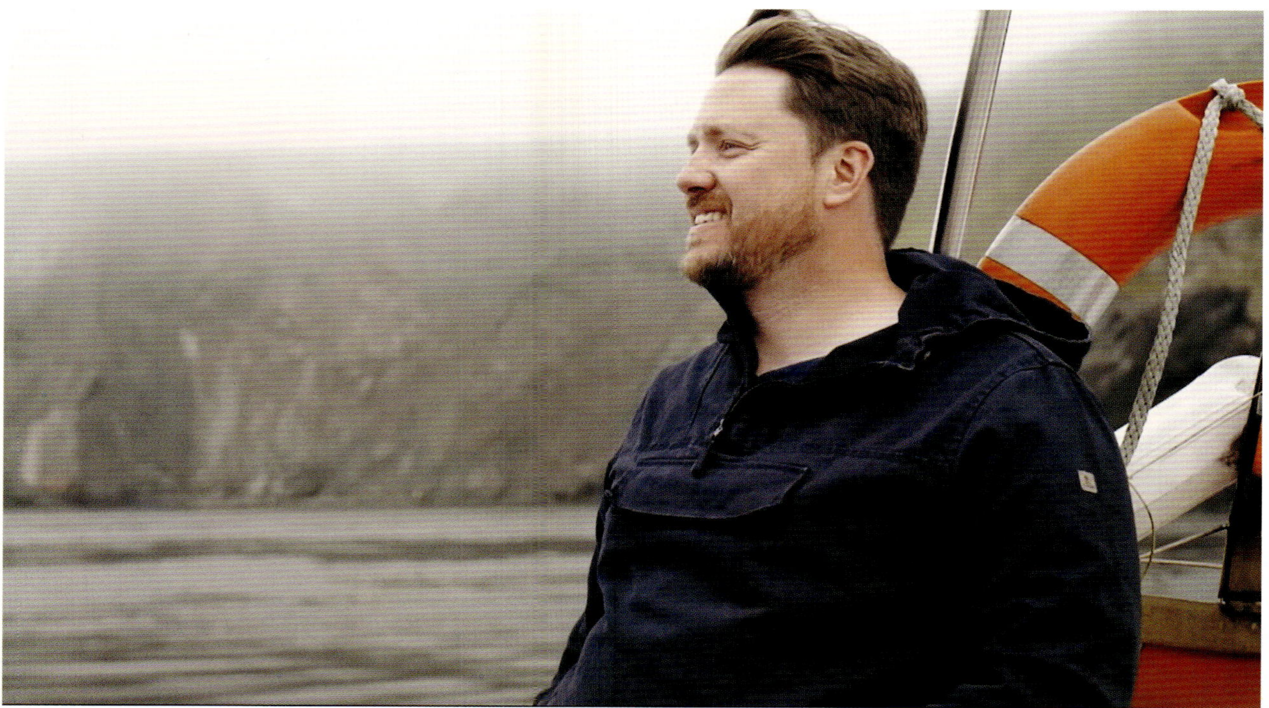

STRONGER - UK & WALES

The boys at DGR had introduced me to Chris and we spoke a couple of times at length before I met him at his home in the UK. His incredible story had already had a profound effect on me, and the moment I met him in person I just wanted to give him a big hug. The island in the piece was a perfect visual metaphor for someone suffering depression that I knew I would be incorporating into Chris's story.

SURVIVOR - TASMANIA

When the DGR boys suggested I do a story on Mark Atkinson, the older brother of my good friend Chris whose story "Romance" I had made a couple of years earlier, I was stoked. For one, we had tinnitus in common. I had the condition for most of my life and it's something that I can manage most of the time. For Mark, it's something that was the beginning of a tough personal journey.

COMING HOME - CONNECTICUT

This piece featured a story that focused on the positive effect DGR's fundraising has and how they work with Movember to identify programs that genuinely improve men's lives. One such program is "Resilience Grows Here" and their work with the local Valhalla motorcycle club. Led by veterans Ben and "Mad Dog," the two outfits work tirelessly to bring soldiers suffering from PTSD back from the brink.

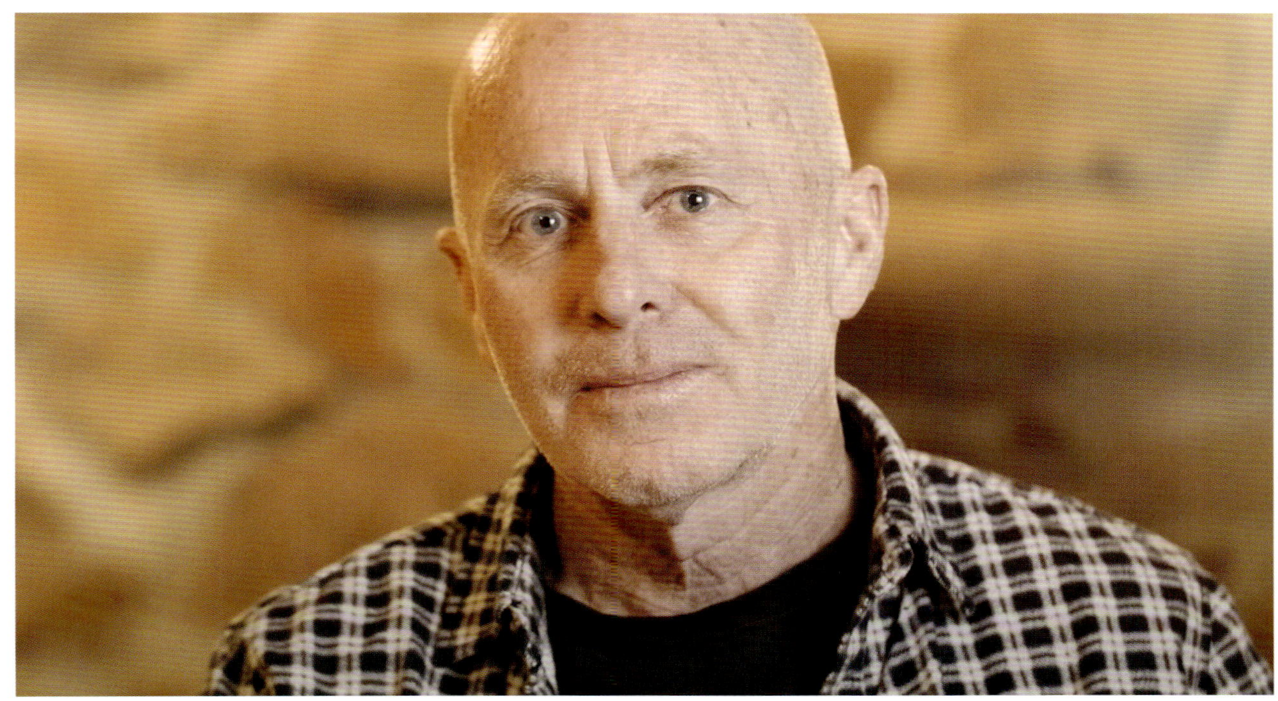

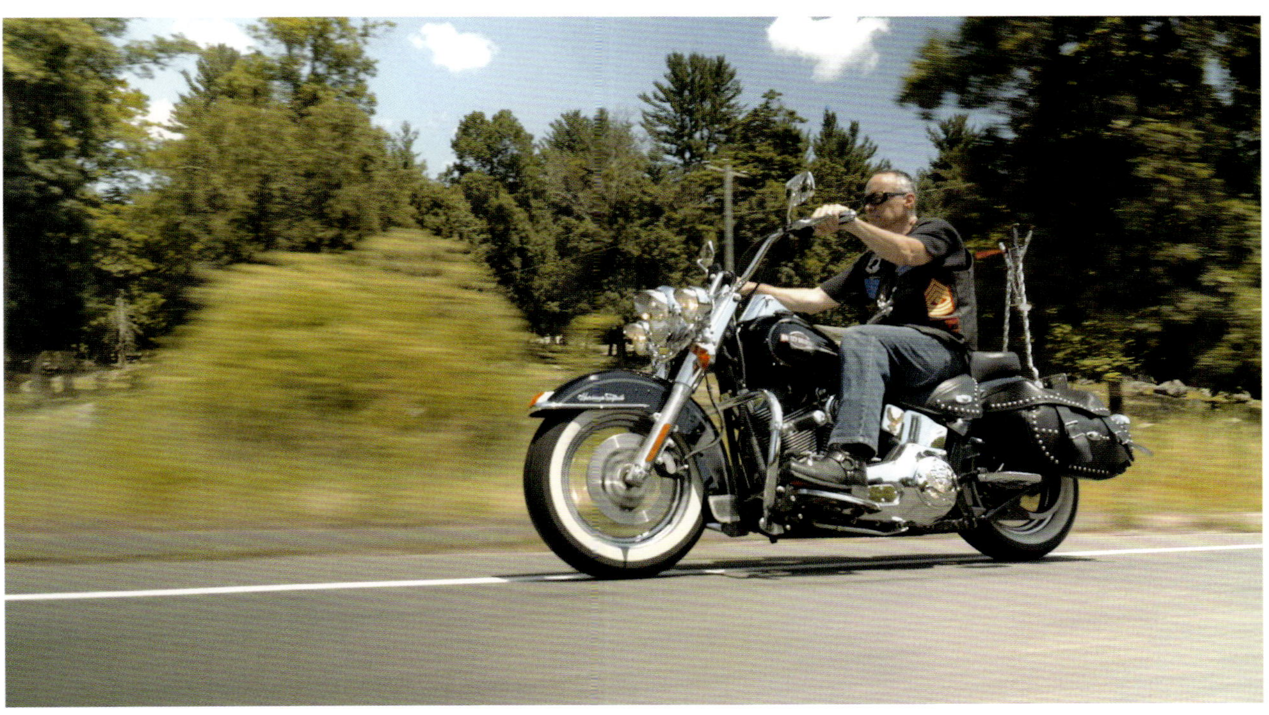

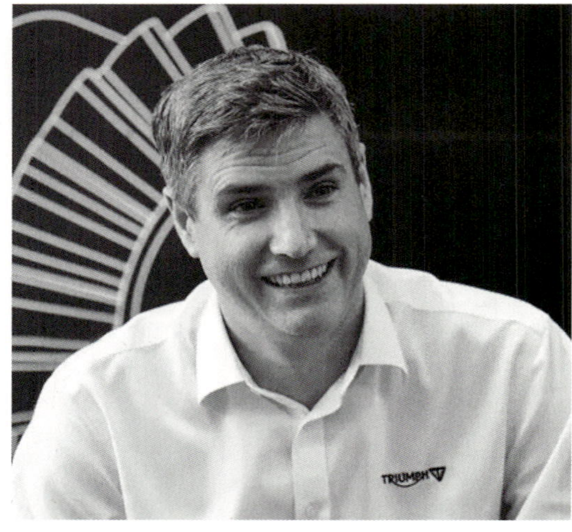

Nick Bloor

CEO, Triumph Motorcycles

"As the DGR's main partner, everyone at Triumph Motorcycles is incredibly proud to have played a role in helping this wonderful event and cause for good grow into the world-spanning activity and community that it is today.

Over the eight incredible years we've been involved, Triumph has worked hand-in-hand with the DGR, with the common goal of increasing the profile of the Distinguished Gentleman's Ride, to expand this amazing community of like-minded riders and ultimately increase the money raised to support the cause, which is to fund and raise awareness of prostate cancer research and men's mental health.

Together we have achieved many great things from rewarding riders who raise funds with the opportunity to win a brand new Triumph to building one-off custom bikes to highlight the event, and of course riding together 'dressed dapper' with thousands of like-minded bikers in some of the world's most amazing locations.

From our dealers to our staff, to Triumph fans and DGR riders globally it's easy to see how much passion there is for this significant cause, and I have no doubt that this passion will drive the DGR to reach even greater heights in fundraising and rides across the world – which is a journey that I am personally proud to be on together."

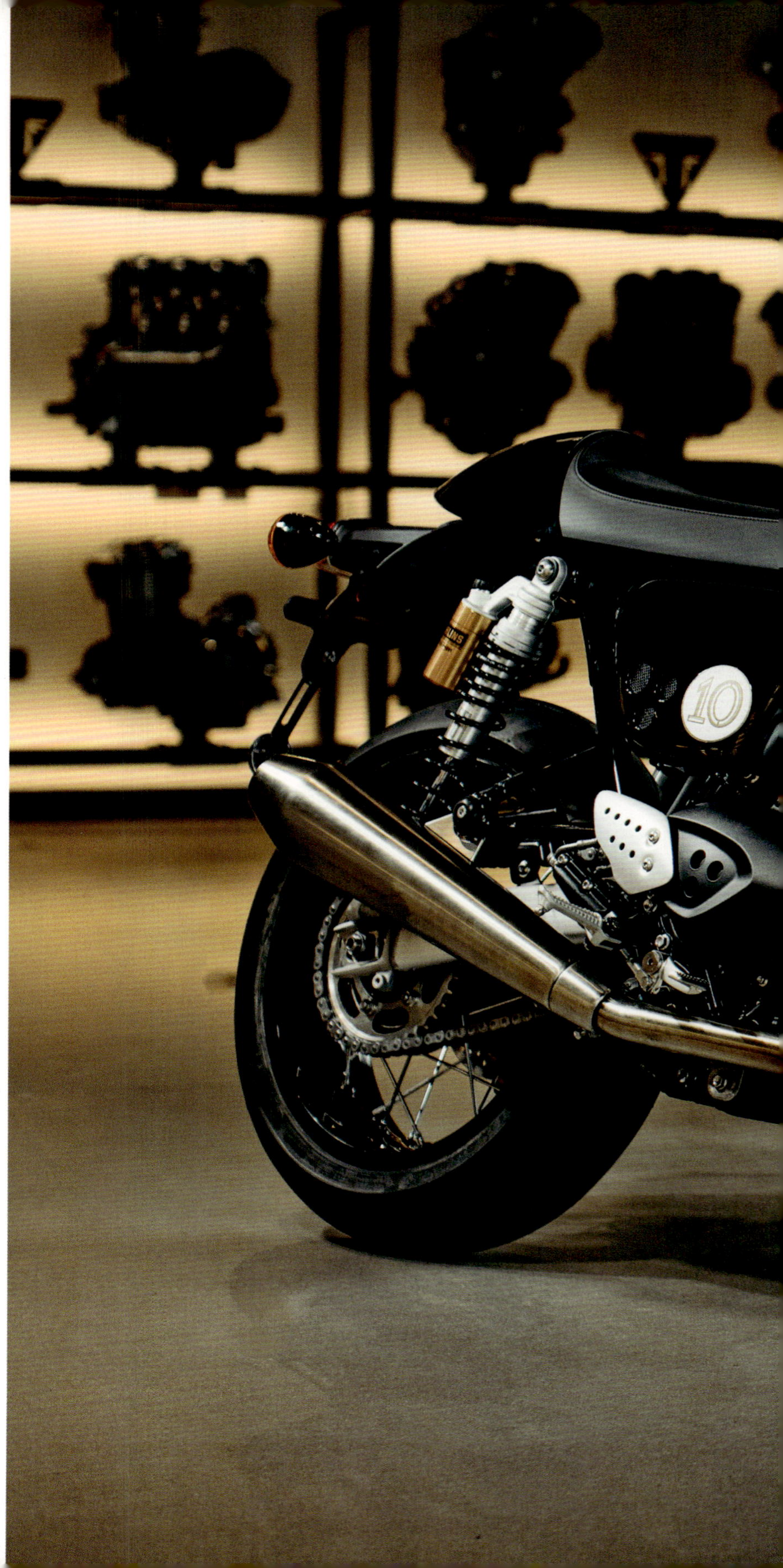

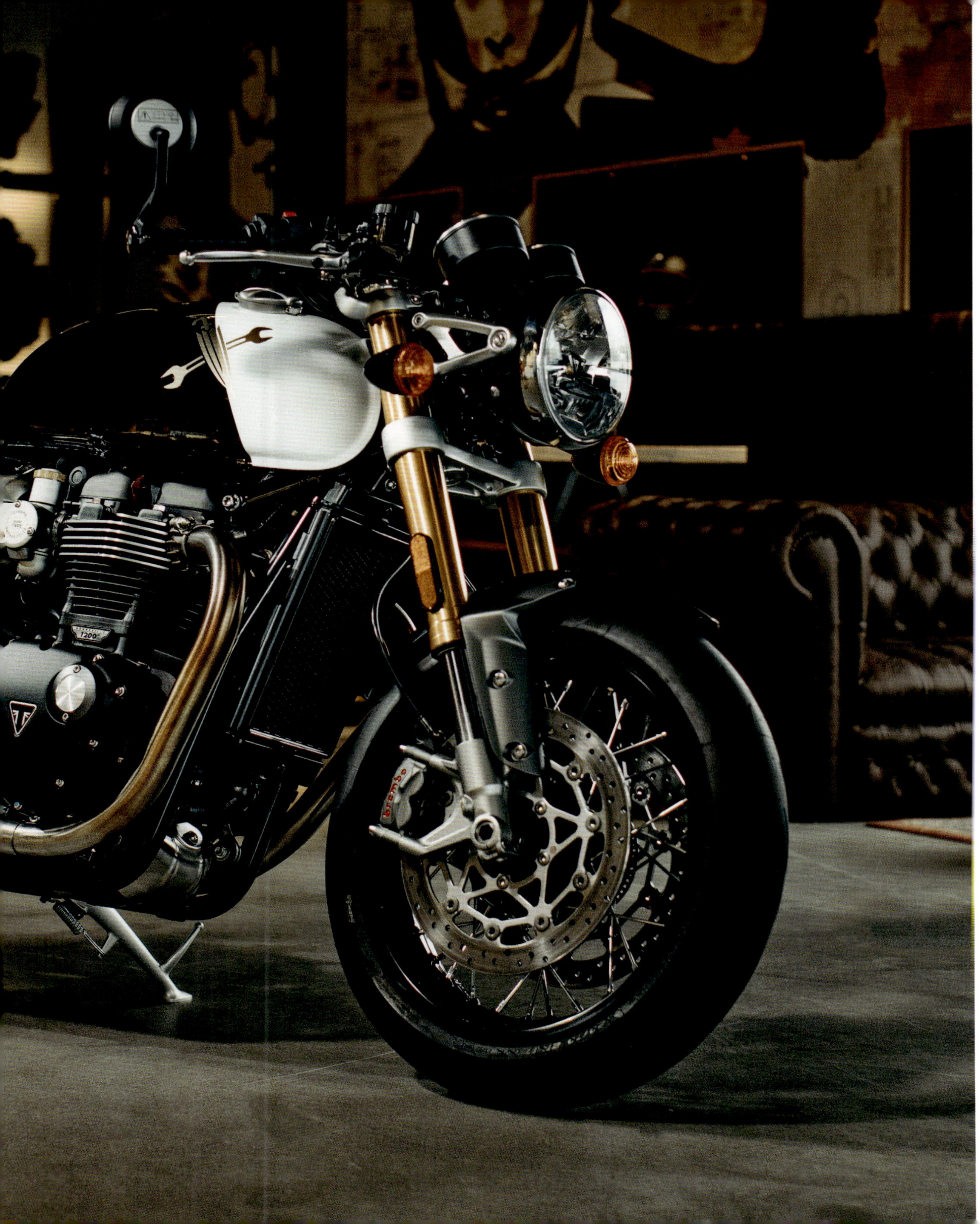

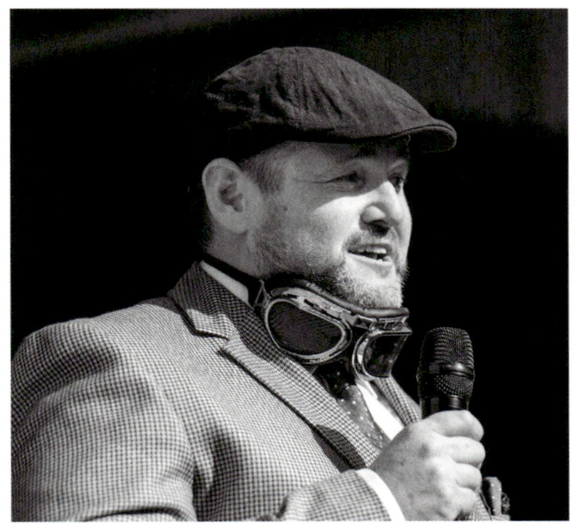

Miles Perkins
**Head of Brand Management,
Triumph Motorcycles**

*"For me, riding the DGR is incredibly important for
two reasons. One, it's such a fantastic event, being
surrounded by like-minded people riding with your
friends and family is such a joy.*

*But for me, it's so much more than just a day out be-
cause it's in support of a cause that is very close to my
heart as I lost my wonderful father to prostate cancer."*

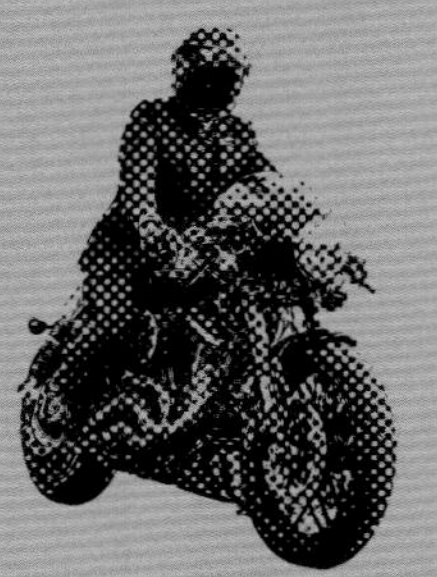

2020

- R I D E   N I N E -

WITH COVID-19 AFFECTING THE WORLD, WE LAUNCHED OUR RIDE SOLO TOGETHER CAMPAIGN, UNITING ON THE SAME DAY FOR MEN'S HEALTH. **56,000 RIDERS** AND **2,531 CITIES** WERE SOCIALLY DISTANCED BUT GLOBALLY CONNECTED FOR THE CAUSE.

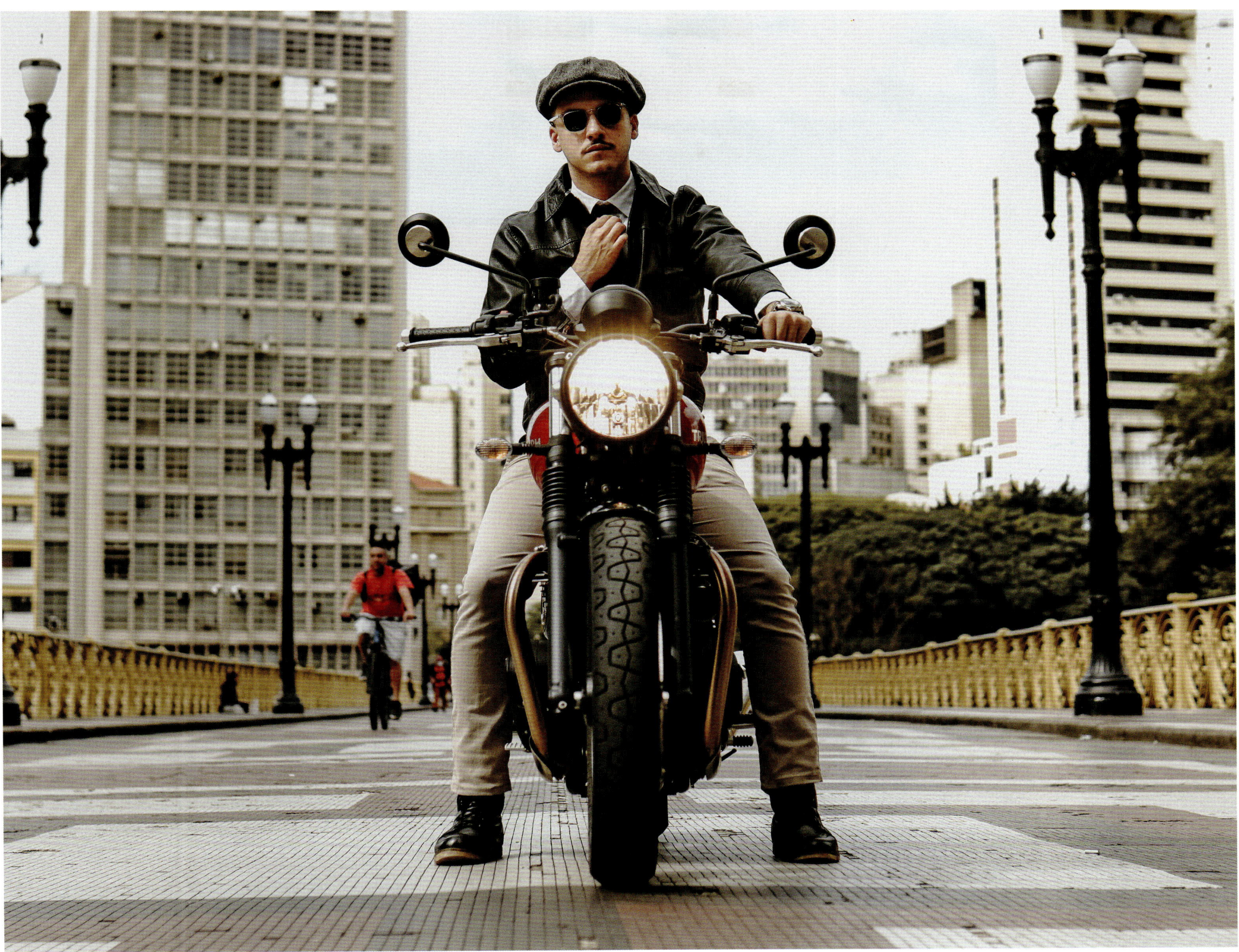

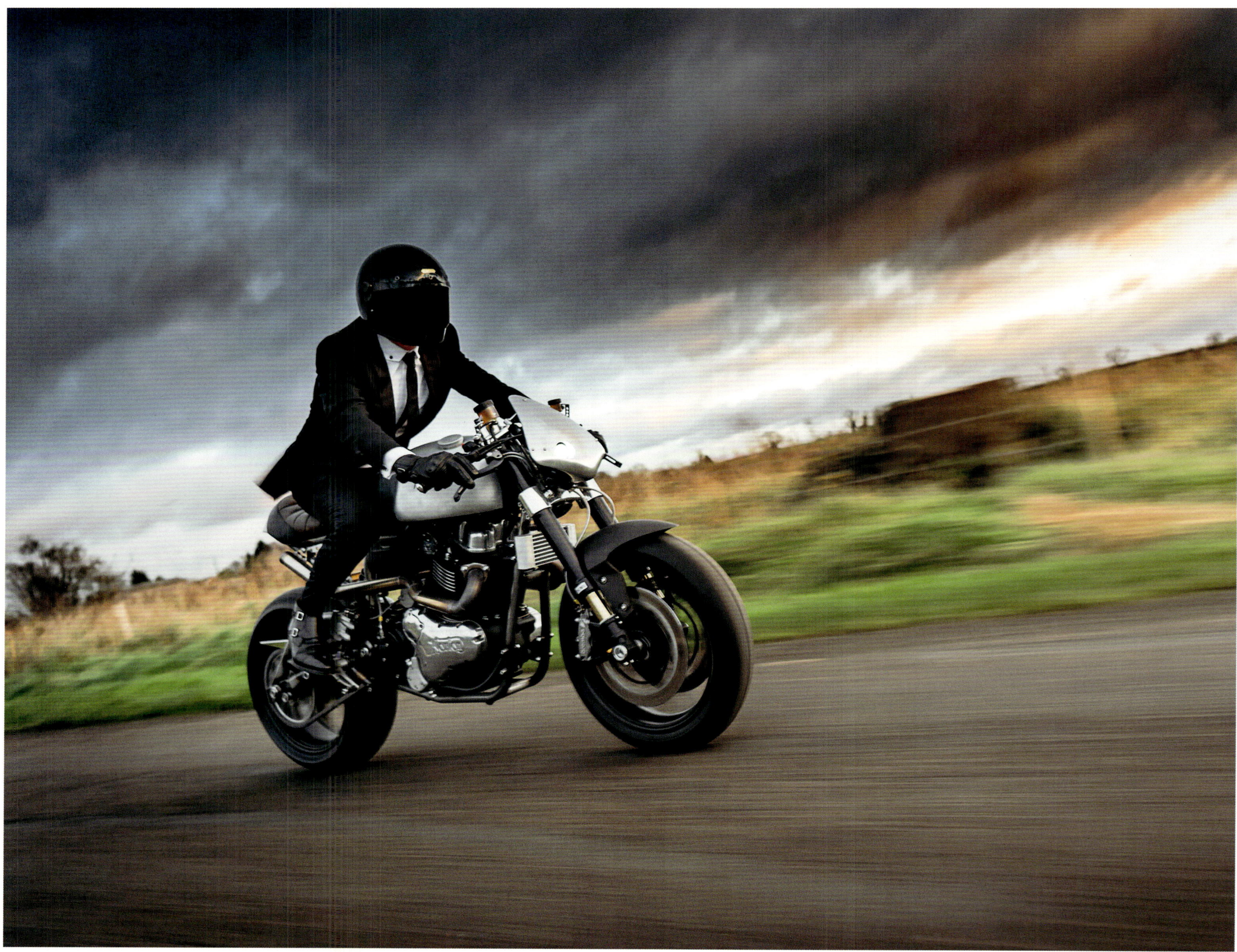

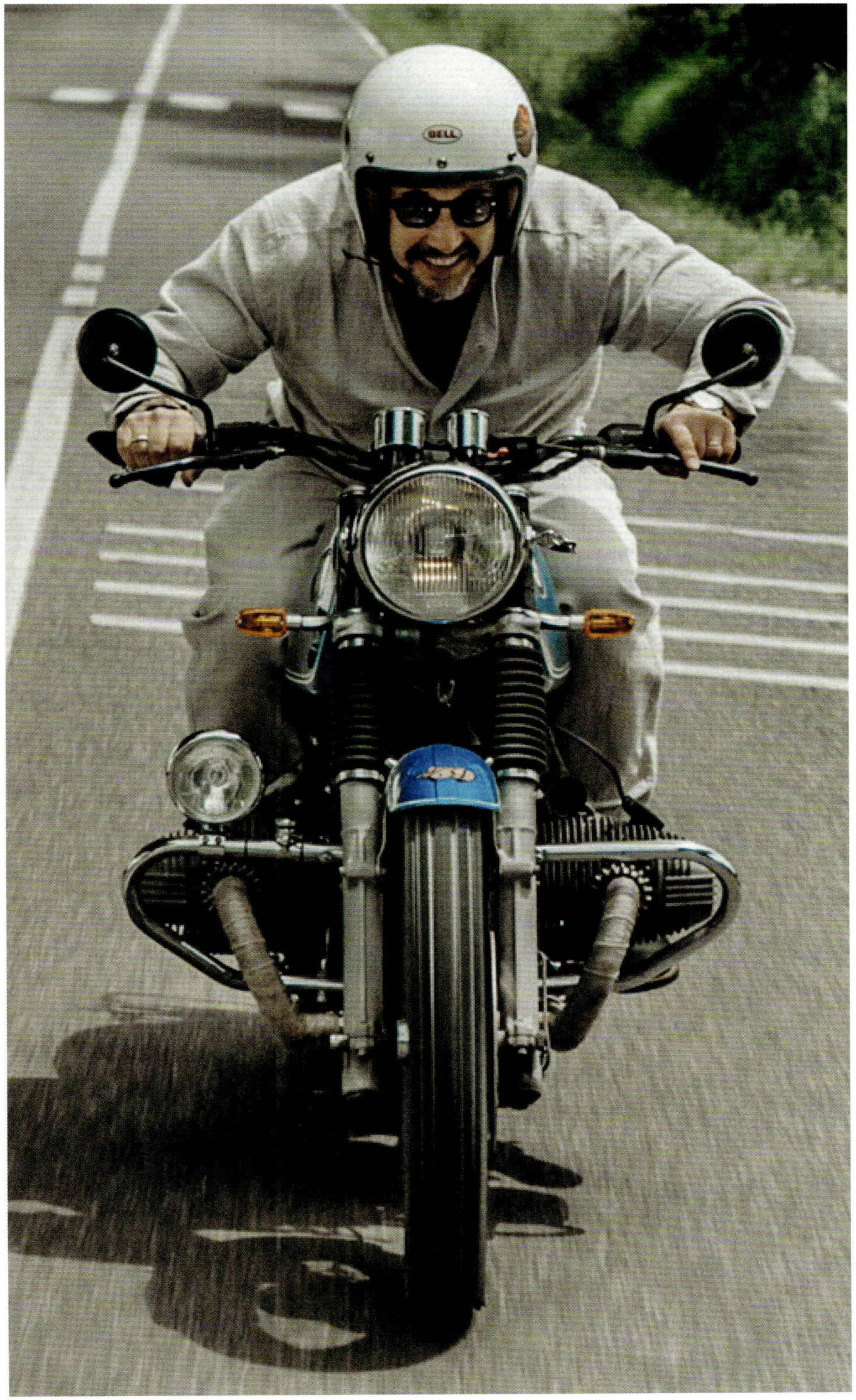

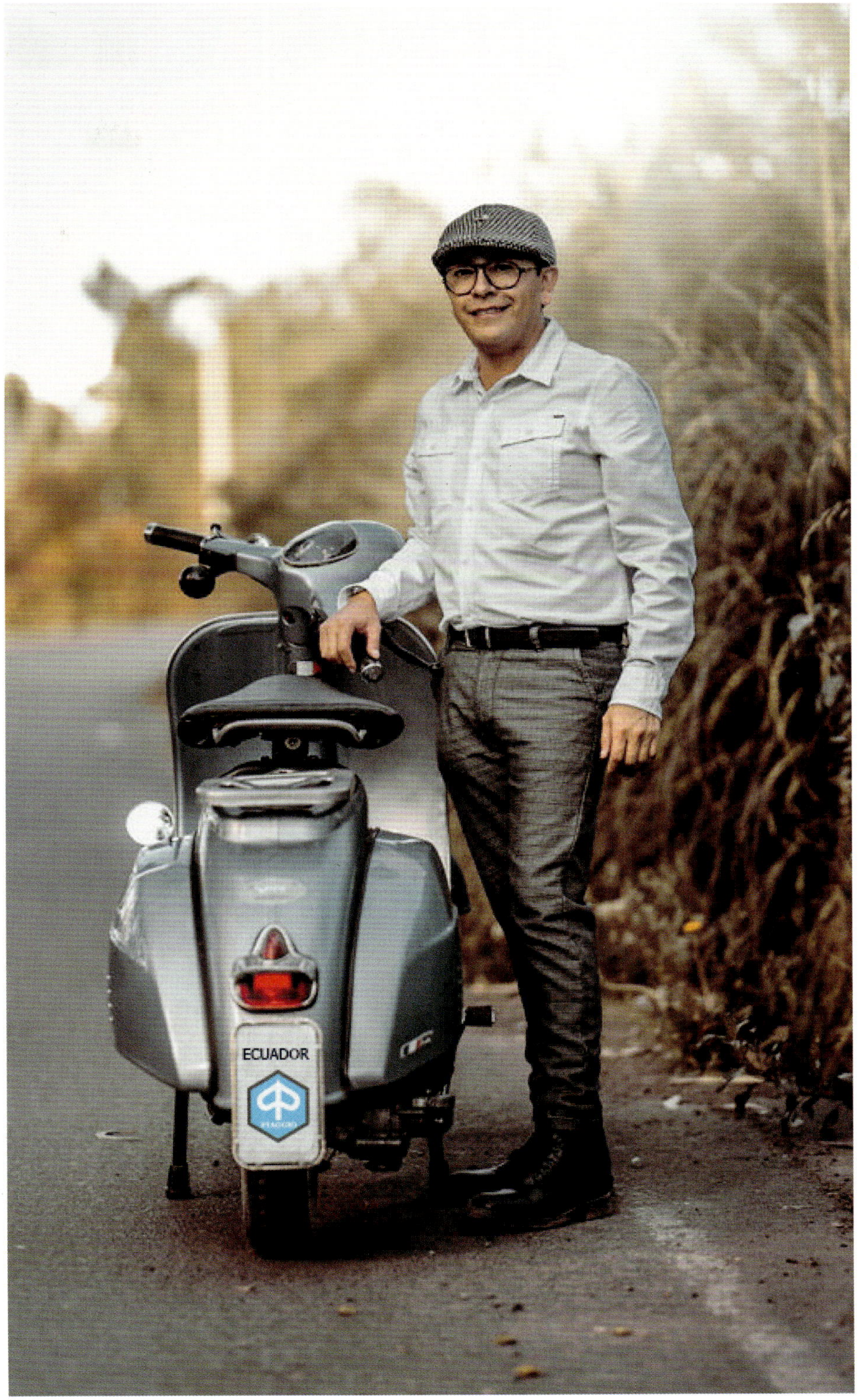

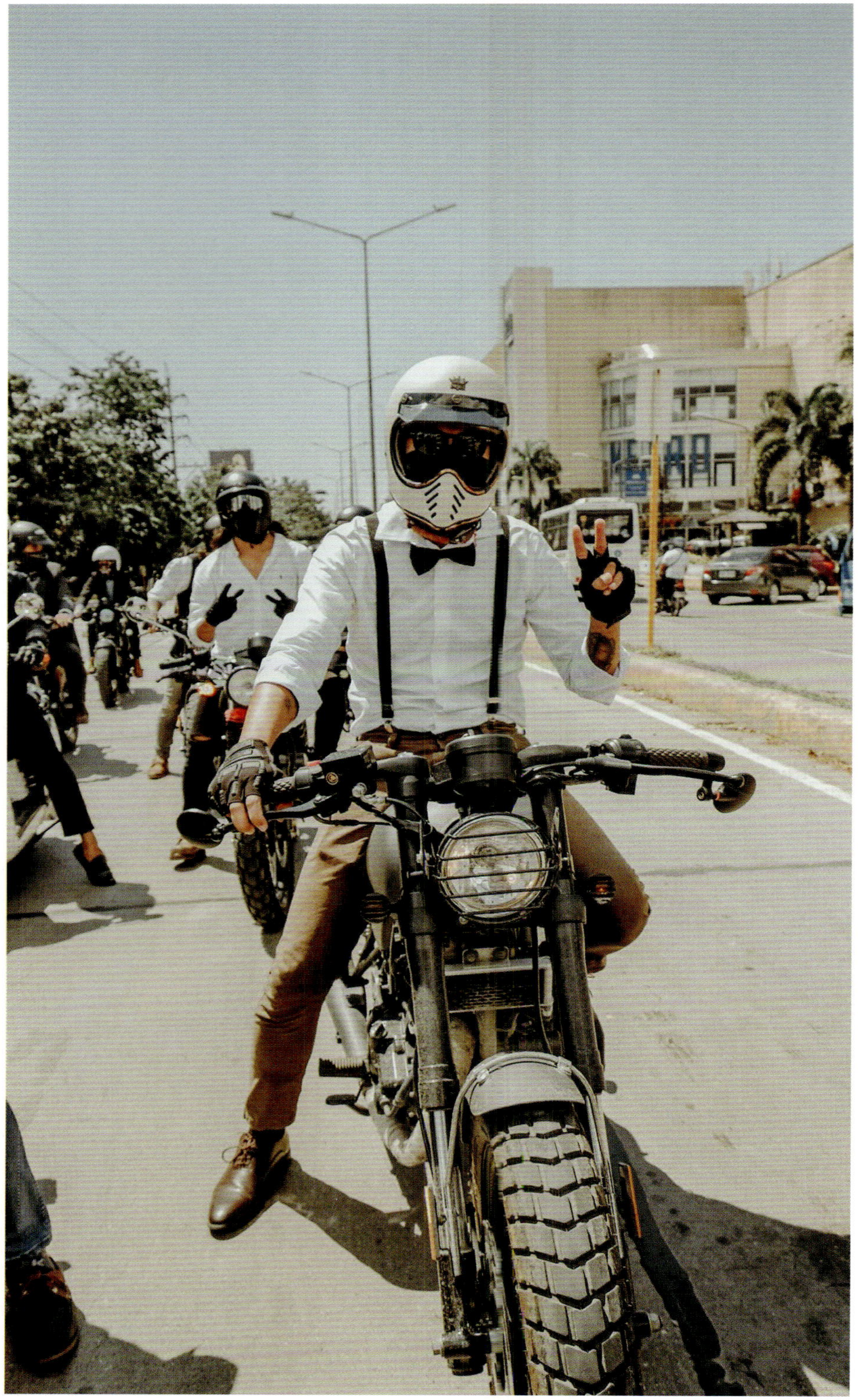

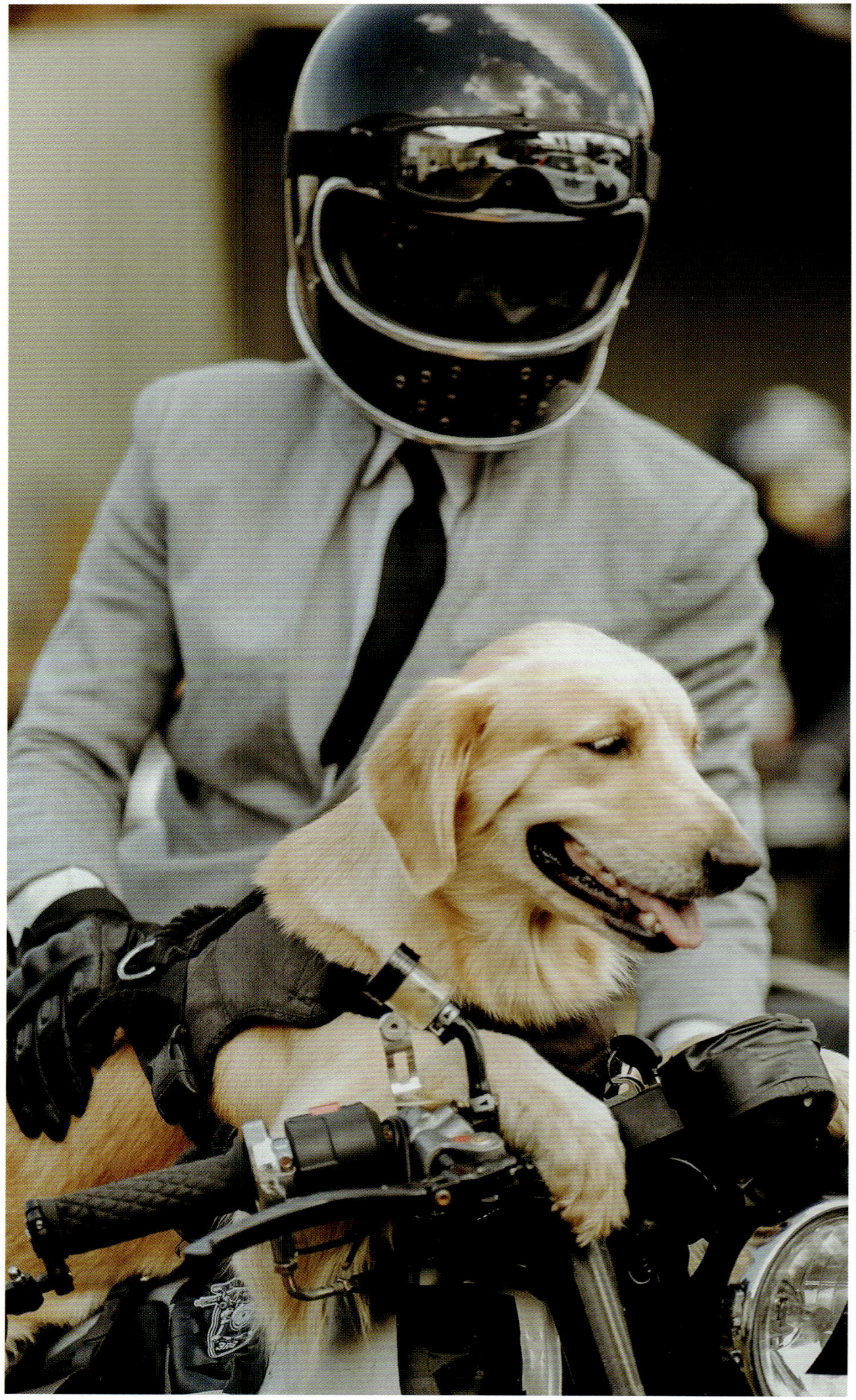

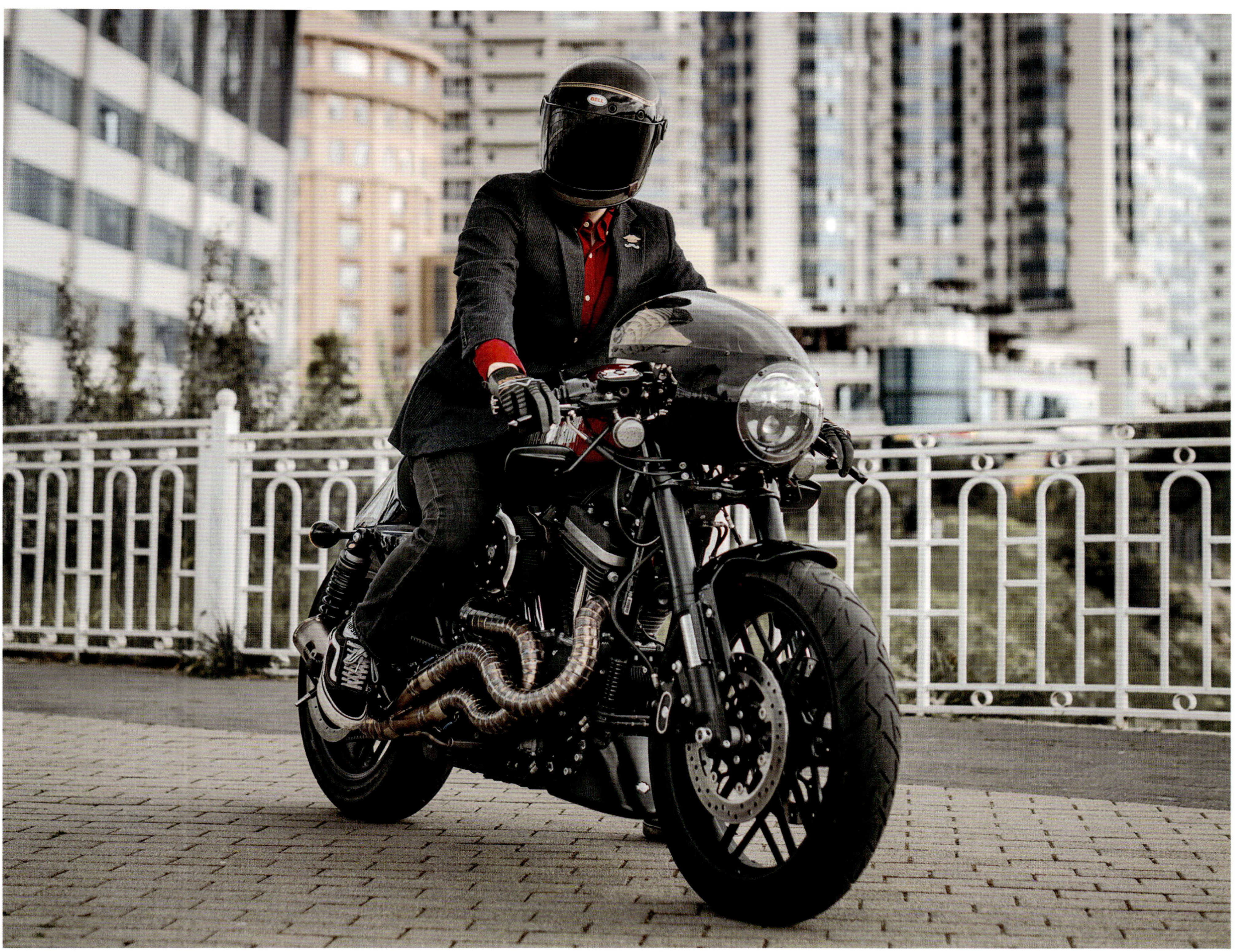

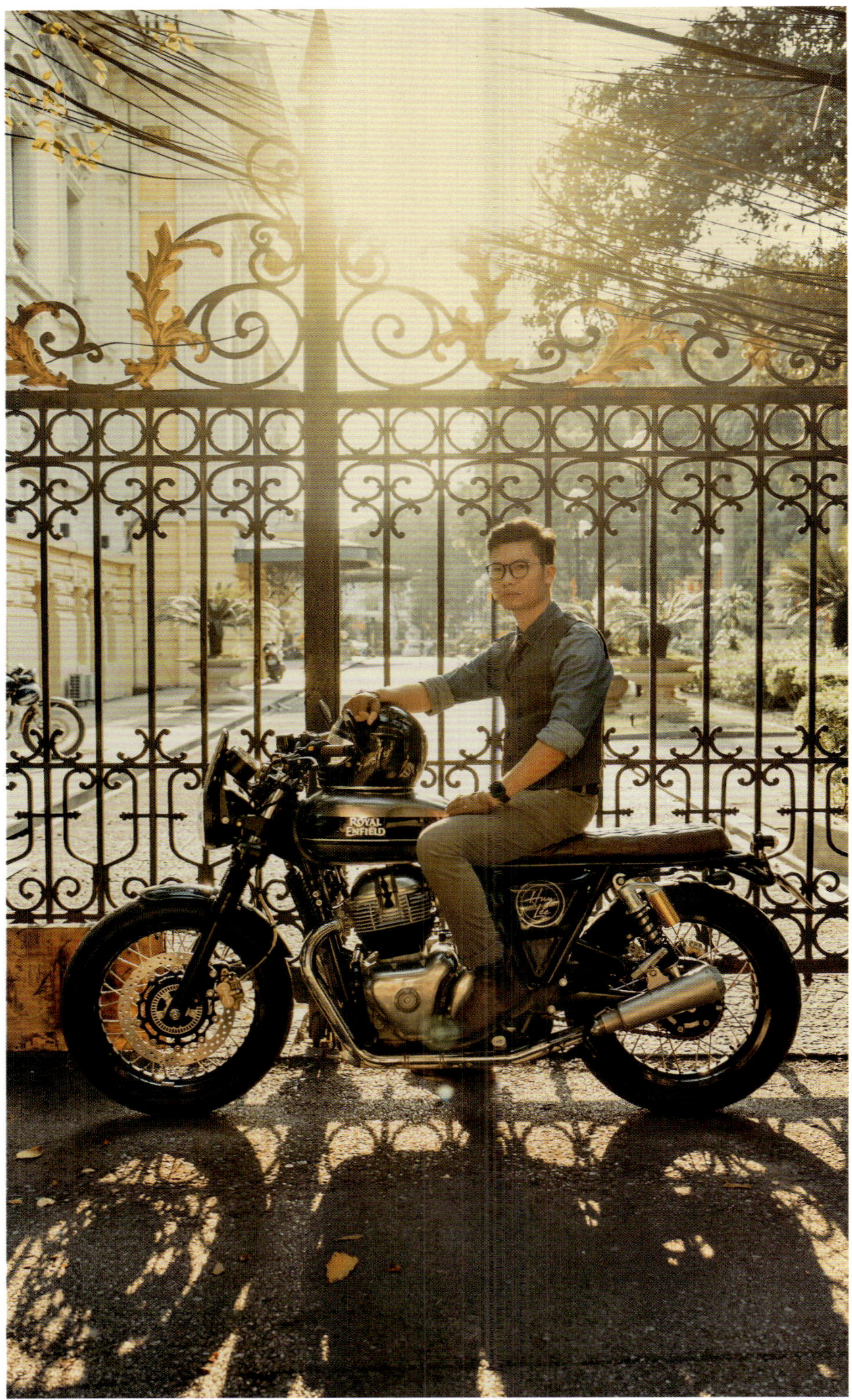

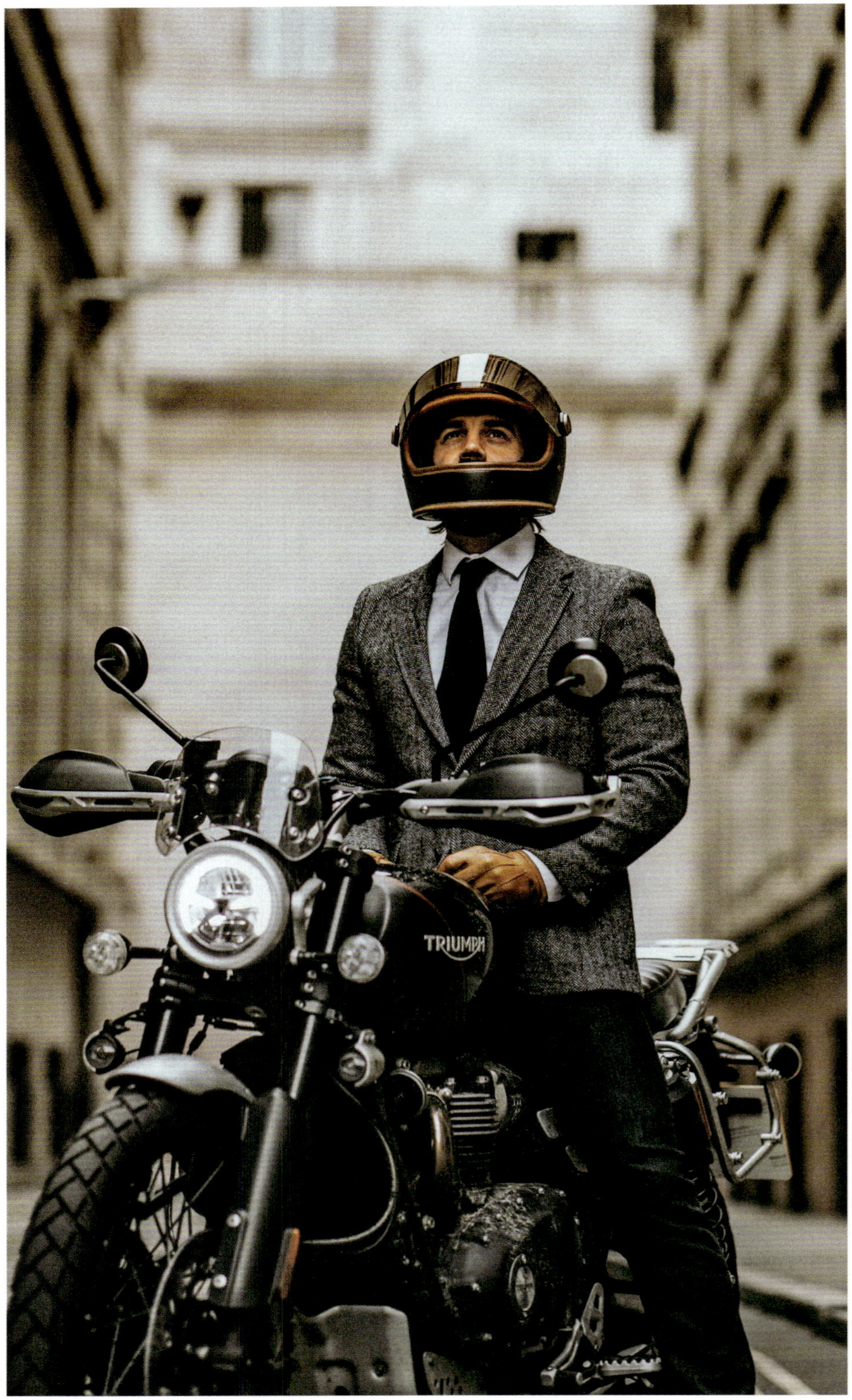

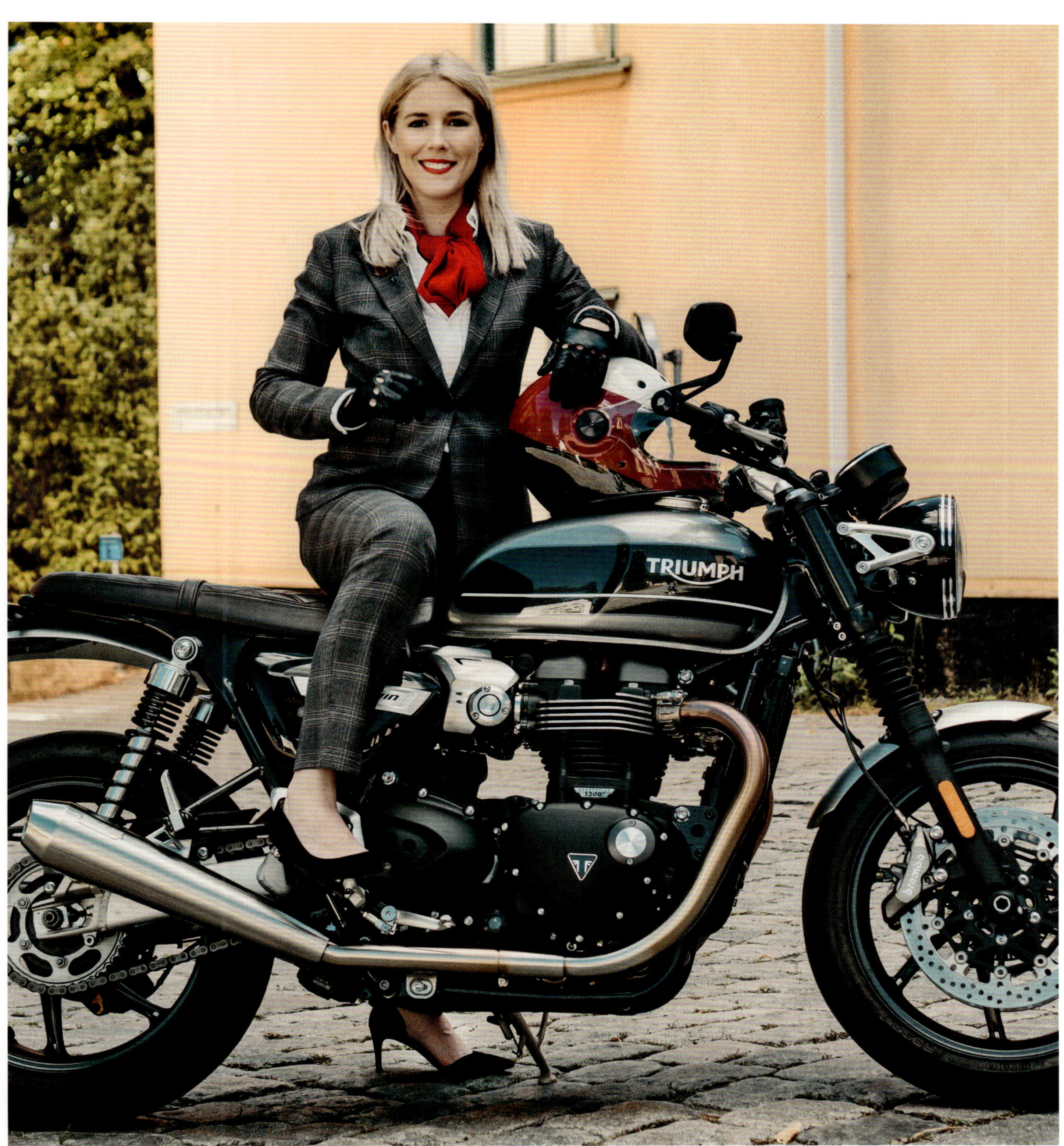

Hanna Johansson

Triumph and DGR Ambassador

"I've been a part of The Distinguished Gentleman's Ride for five years now and I love the whole atmosphere around it. In 2021, I rode a Triumph Bobber alongside my Dad in Stockholm in support of all the amazing men in my life."

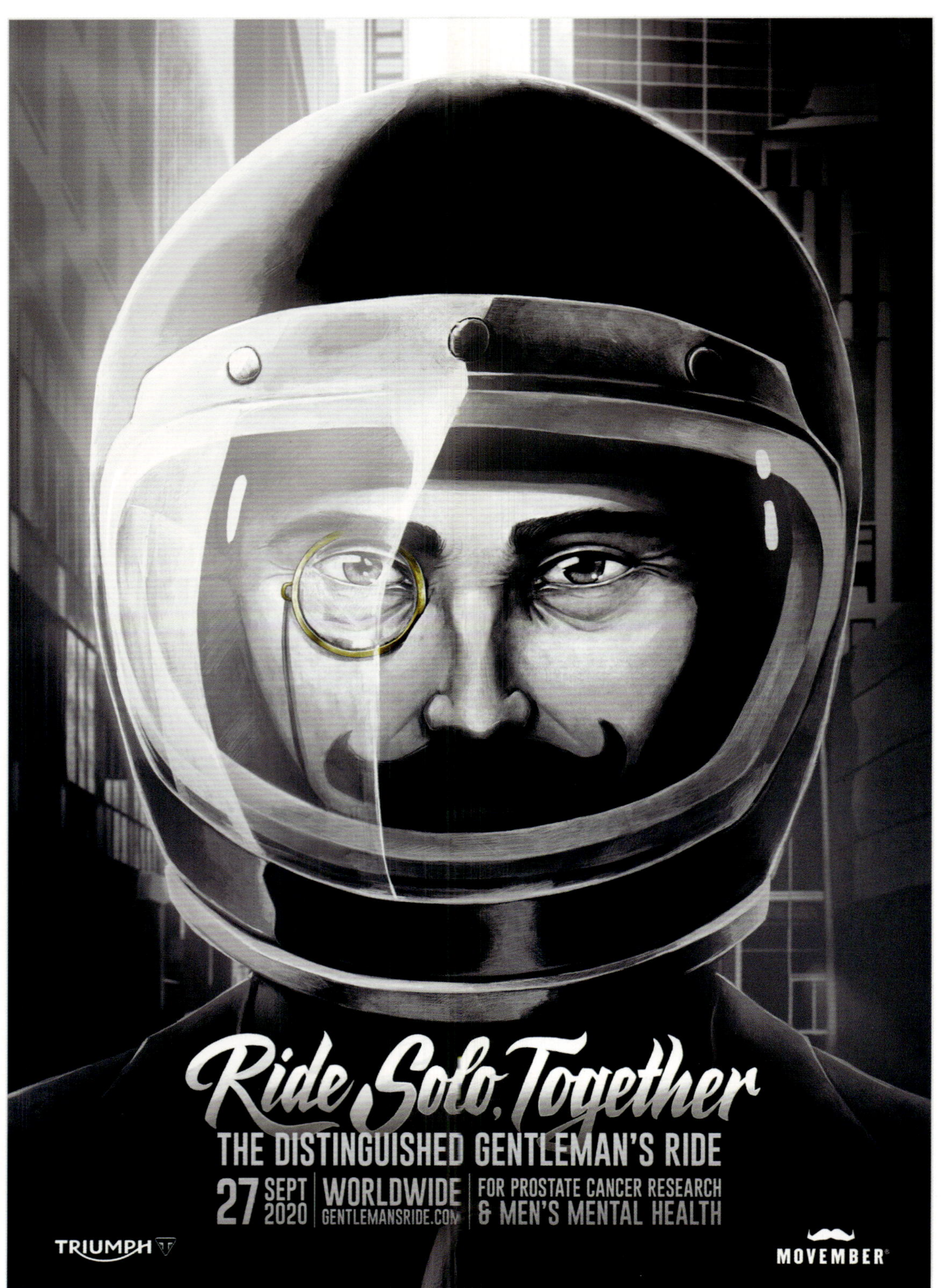

2020 Ride Poster

Designed by Tanya Koch
With the world reeling from the outbreak of COVID-19, DGR was determined to go ahead. This time, however, as a socially distanced ride encouraging riders to "Ride Solo, Together." It shows the classic mascot, Sir Silversteed, front and center and ready to ride. Depicted in a strong, painted style with his trademark monocle, Remington for the first time ever was represented wearing a full face helmet and visor—a gentle nod to keeping riders safe using protective masks.

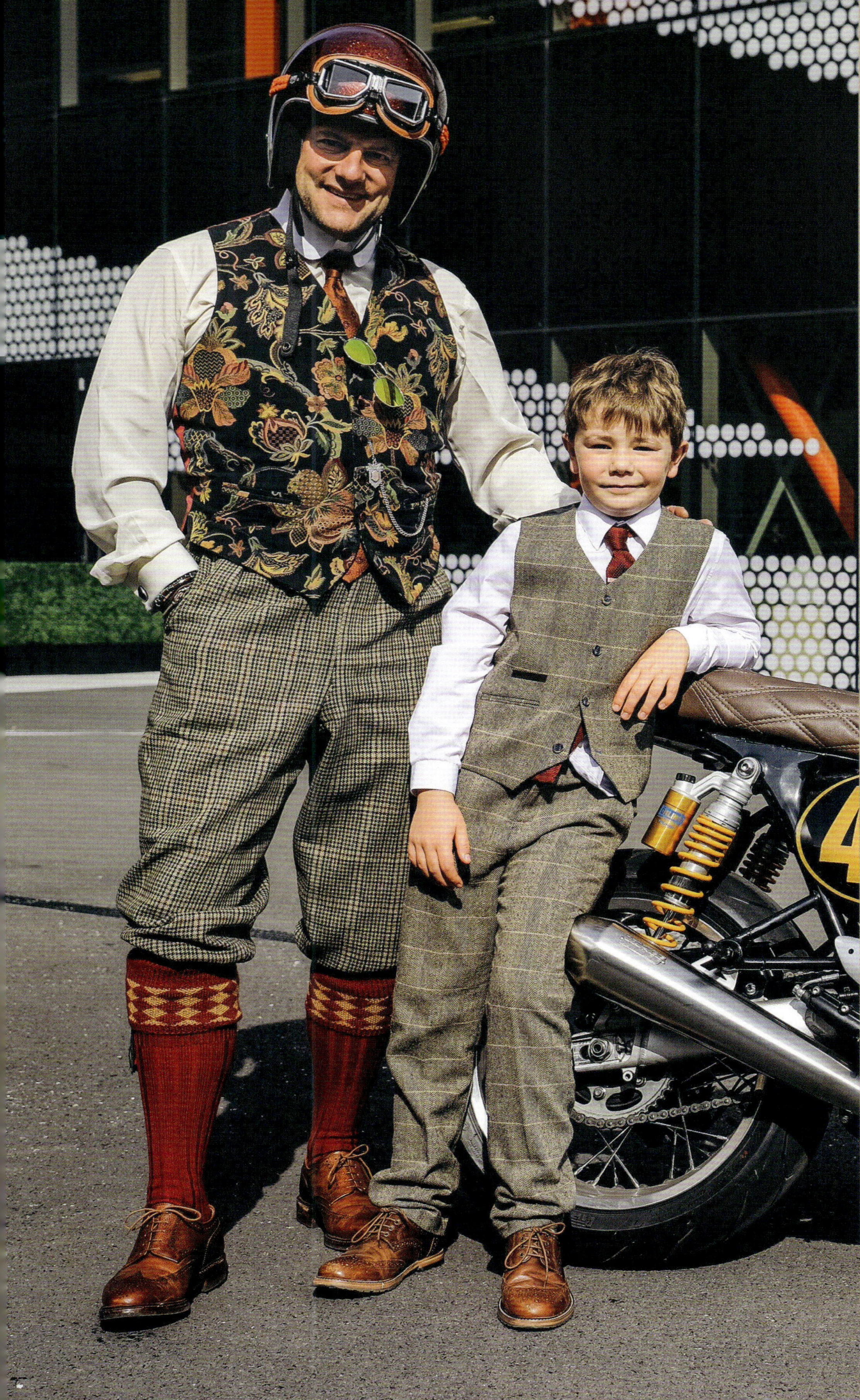

GAP3 Active Surveillance
A DGR-FUNDED PROJECT

Despite advances in prostate cancer detection in recent years, many men with slow-growing tumors have undergone active treatment, such as surgery, even though it was unlikely that their cancer would progress. This is known as "overdiagnosis" and "overtreatment." This group of men may experience significant side effects from overtreatment, such as incontinence and sexual dysfunction, that can impact their quality of life. In many cases, men with slow-growing tumors do not need active treatment and can instead be managed with regular monitoring of their disease. This type of management is known as Active Surveillance, a strategy designed to help avoid the side effects caused by overtreating prostate cancer.

The GAP3 Prostate Cancer Active Surveillance Consortium and Database aims to help improve how men living with slow-growing tumors are managed and avoid the burden of overtreatment. The project includes collection of clinical, MRI and genomics data, as well as Patient Reported Outcome Measures (PROMs), from 21,000 men who have chosen active surveillance instead of active treatment. Data has been collected from men attending 28 hospitals, medical research institutions and treatment centers across 16 countries. Analyzing this data enables researchers and clinicians to address critically important research questions that could lead to improvements in prostate cancer care.

This program is funded in Australasia (Australia, Korea, Singapore and Japan), Canada, UK, US, Europe (Netherlands, France, Finland, Italy, Ireland, Sweden, Switzerland, Germany and Spain).

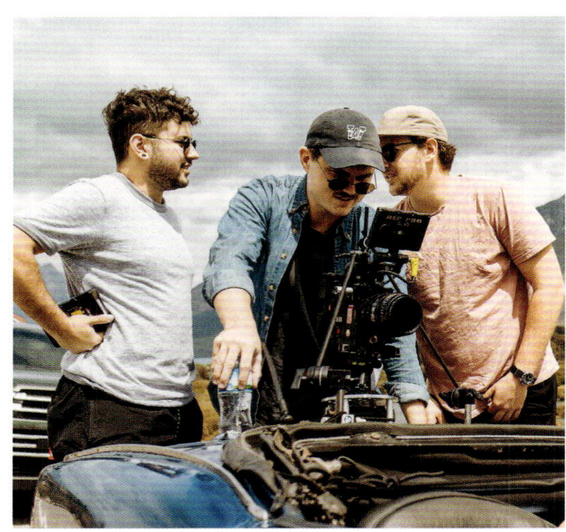

DGR PHOTOGRAPHER:
MY Media Sydney

"I first took part in DGR Sydney in 2013. I didn't actually shoot the ride that year, but from then on I did and I was stoked to be a part of the DGR family. I had met Mark through Sydney Cafe Racers that same year.

I've always got a long list of classic cars and bikes that I'm constantly working on. As I was trying to find inspiration and information on building an XS650, I had googled 'cafe racers in Sydney' and up popped Sydney Cafe Racers, so I joined the group.

Then Mark told me about DGR. I was hooked. Dressing up dapper has never been my thing, but seeing all the custom bikes that come out is a highlight. Every year, we see some of the most amazing builds; I think riding in a big group of cool bikes is the best part of it.

My crew and I have loved shooting the ride every year. It's pretty crazy to see how the last 10 years of motorcycling culture has changed, and to see it represented in so many cities around the world. We've been really proud to have been a part of that."

Mikki Young
Director, MY Media Sydney

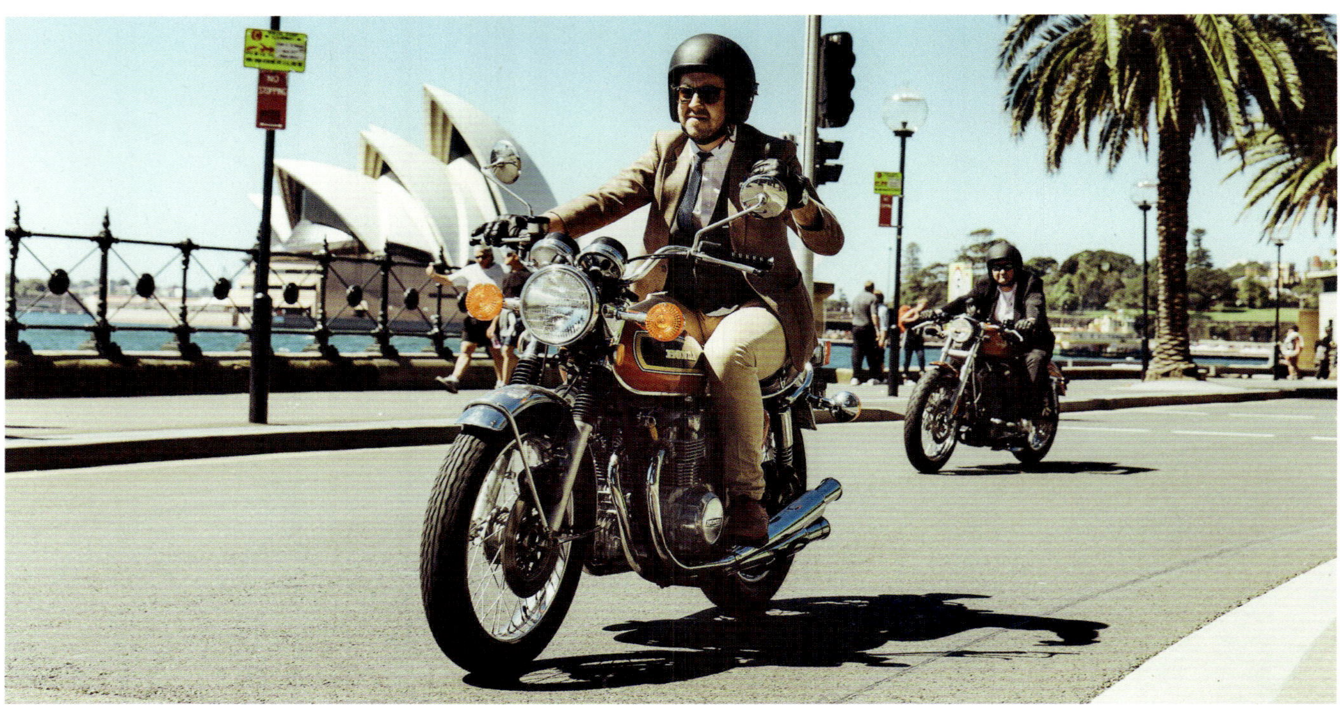

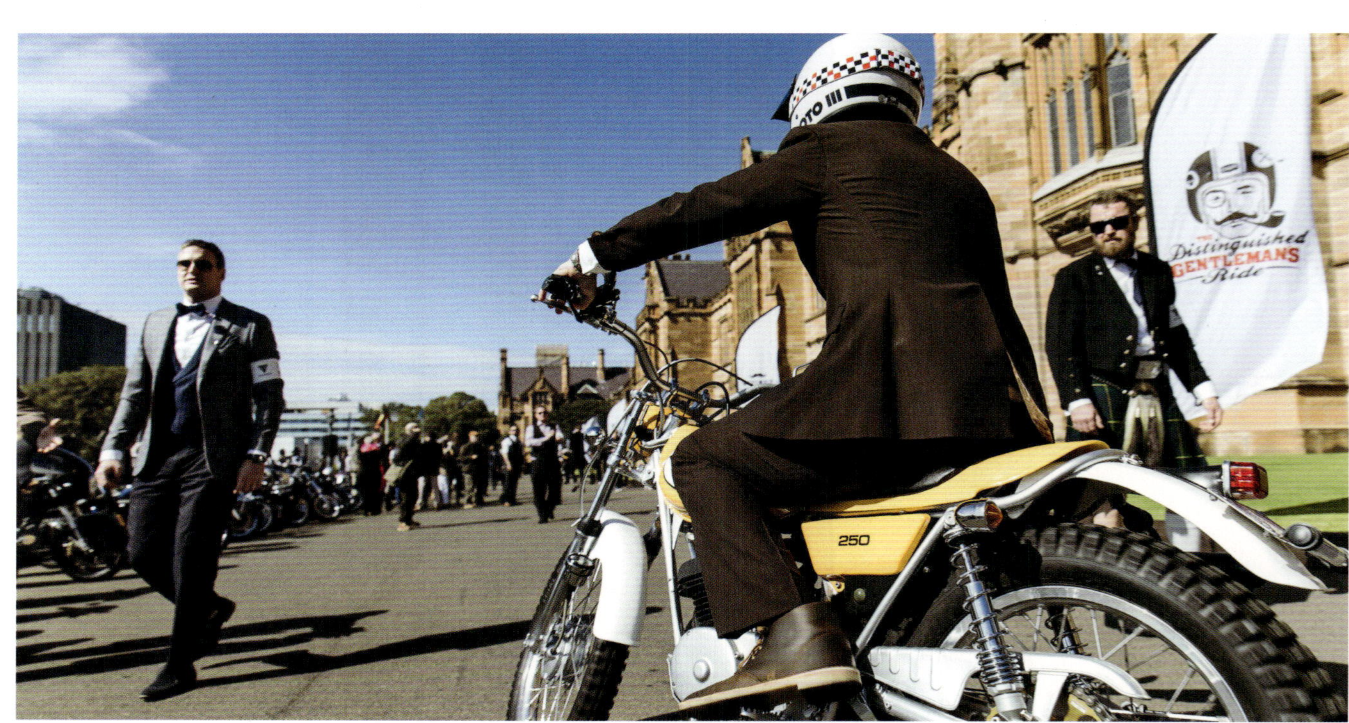

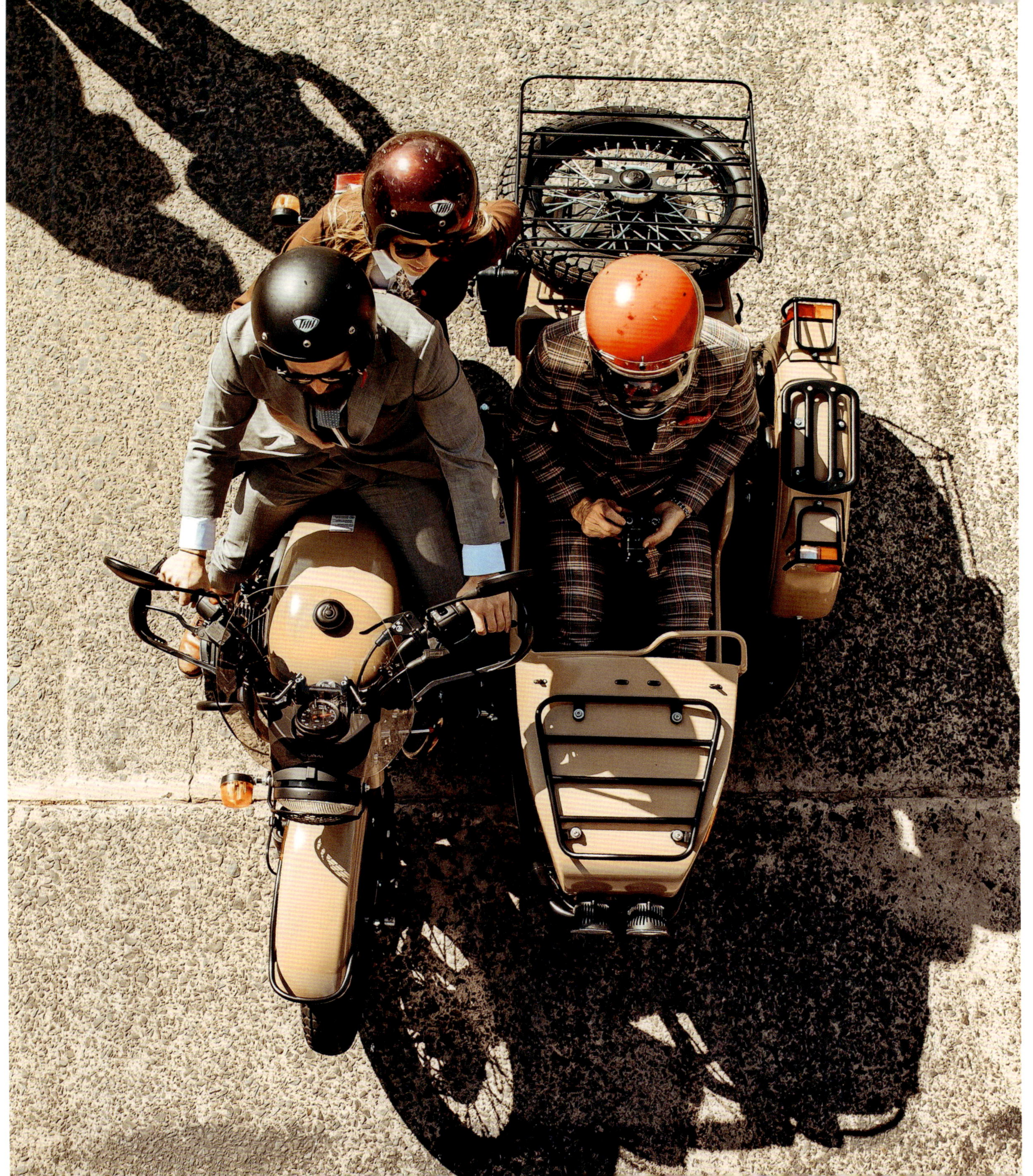

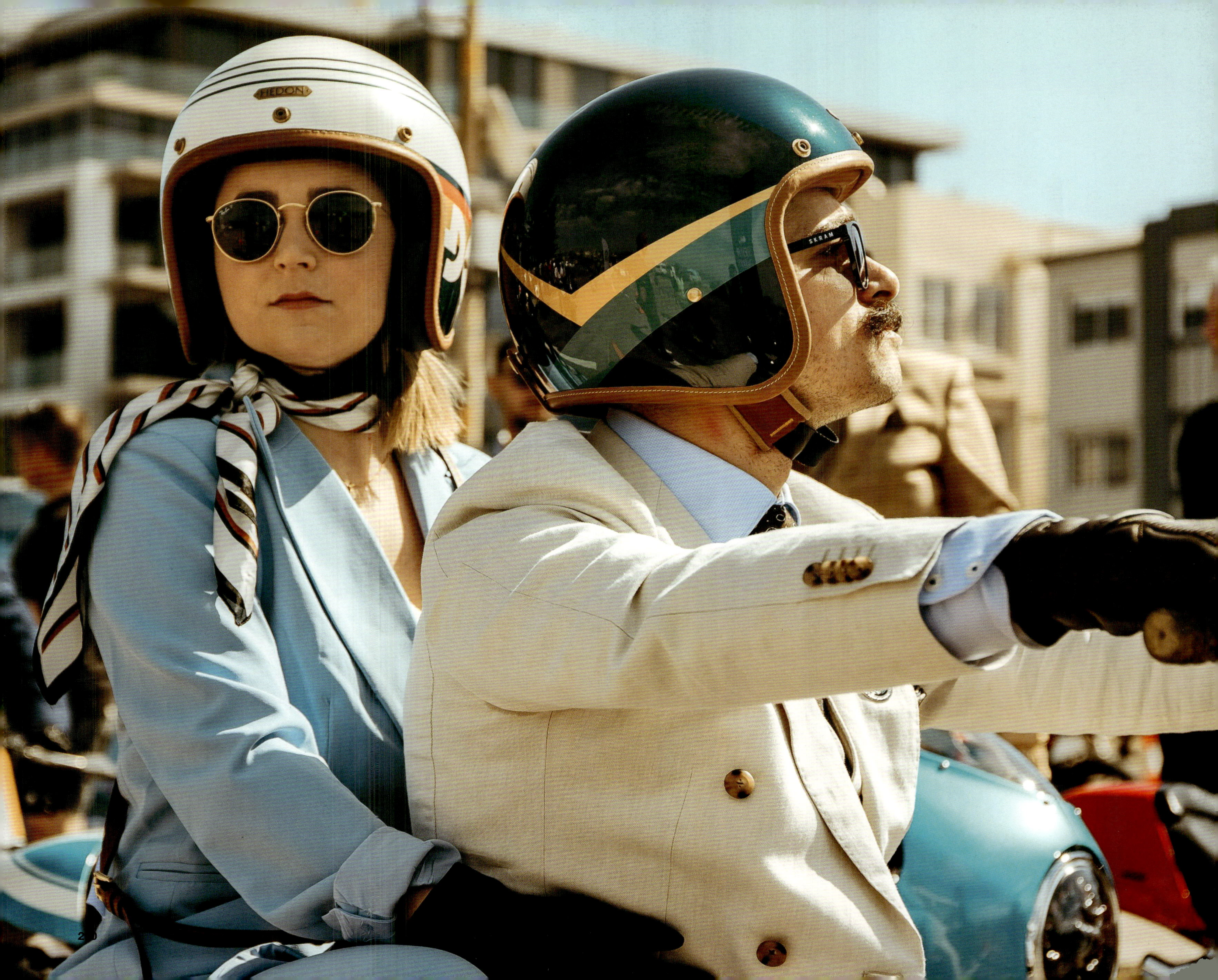

MODERN CLASSICS

A modern classic motorcycle is designed to look like it belongs to a long bygone era, but it also offers the rider the safety and reliability levels of a modern motorcycle. Put simply, it's old school style meets new school technology.

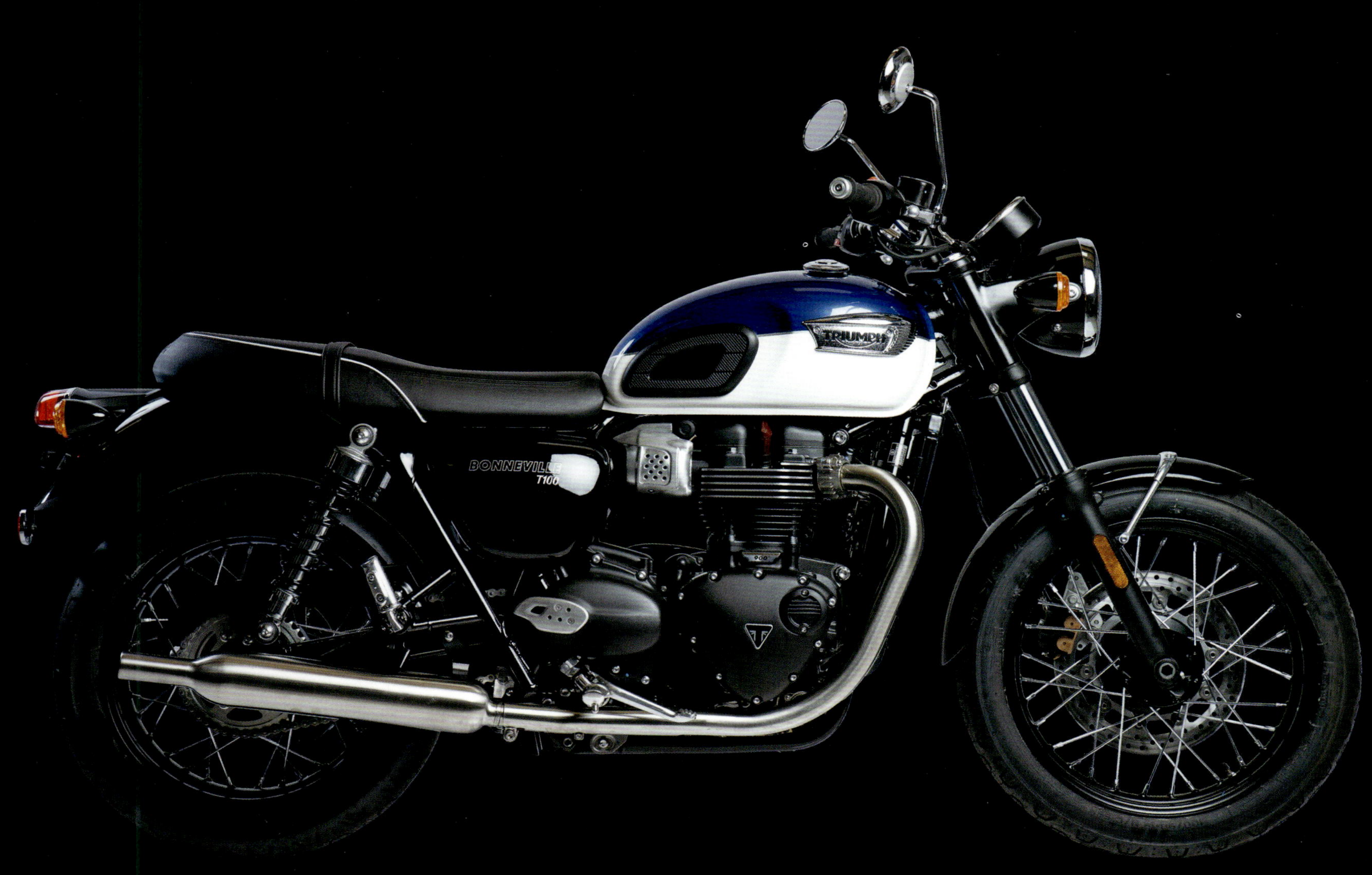

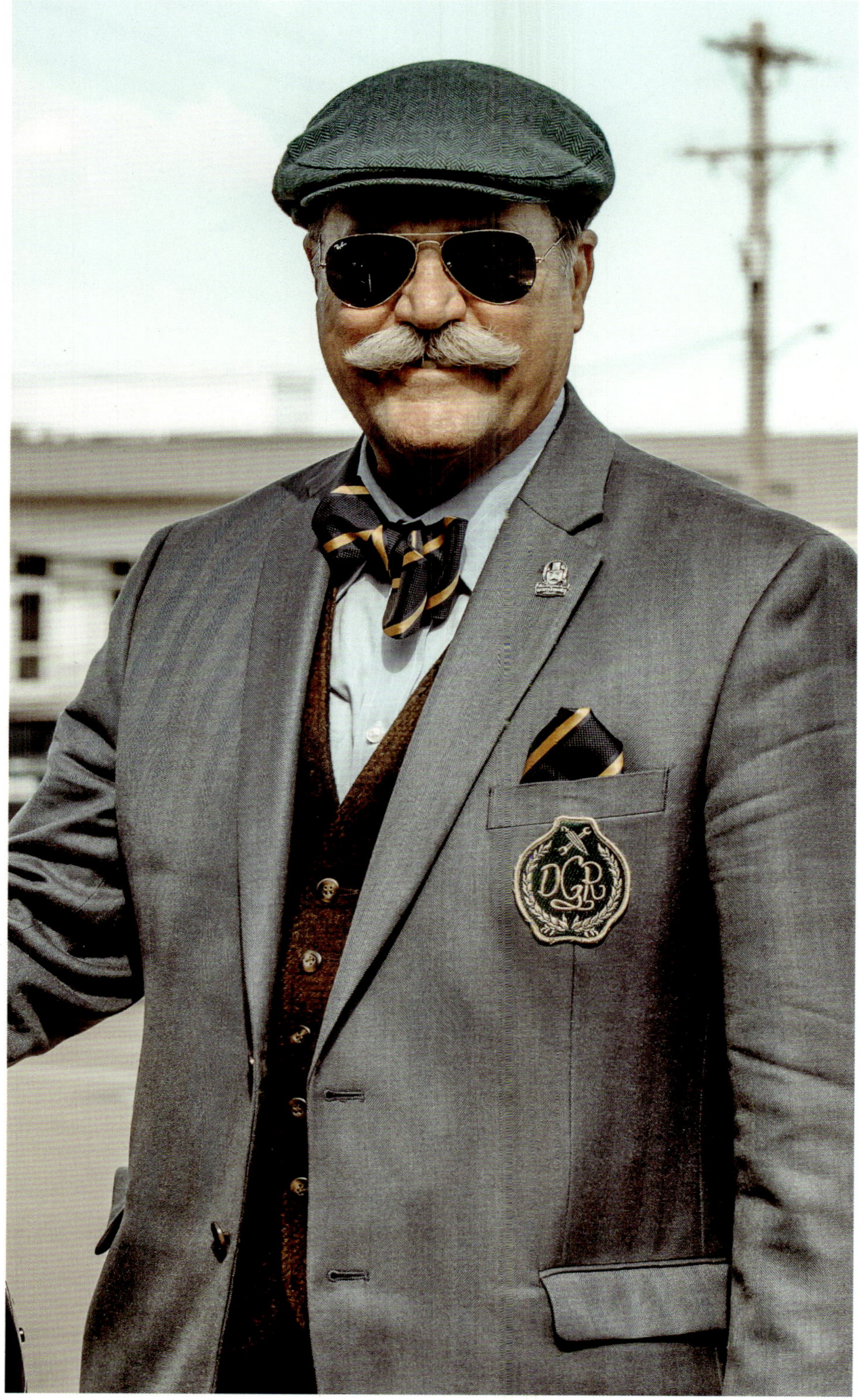

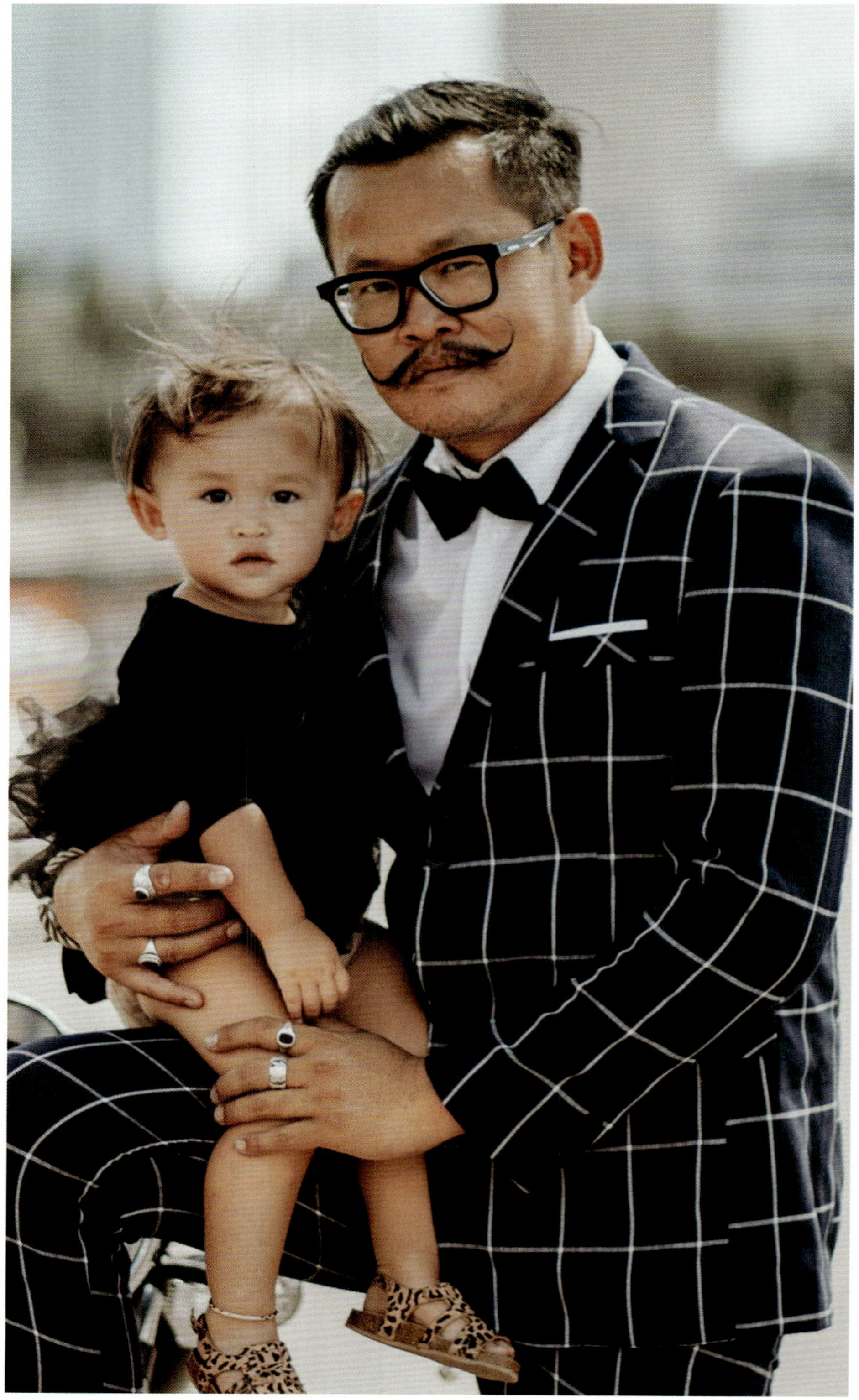

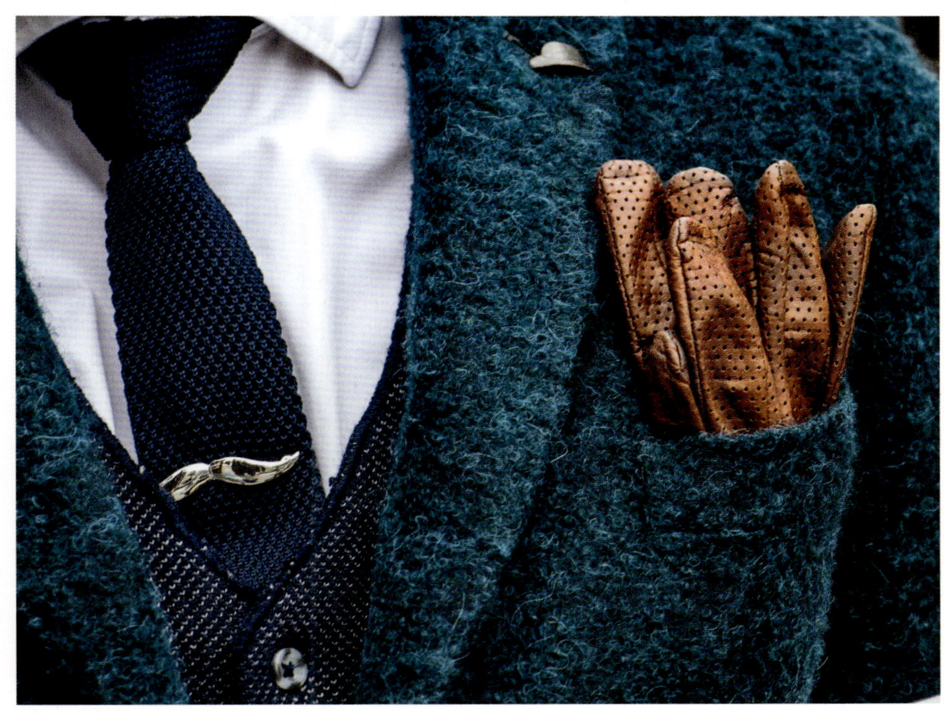
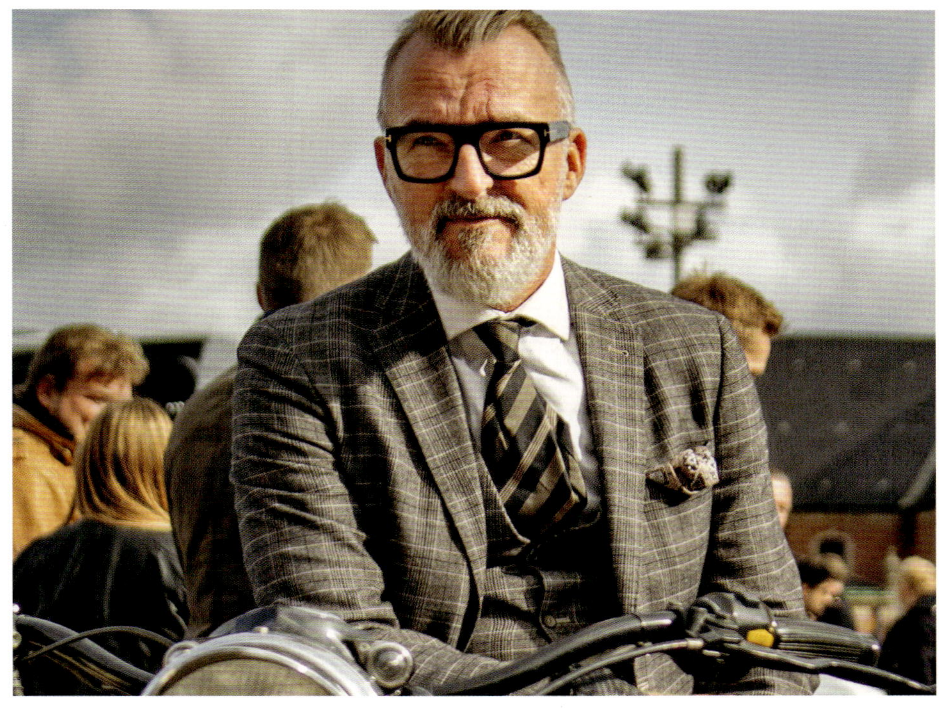
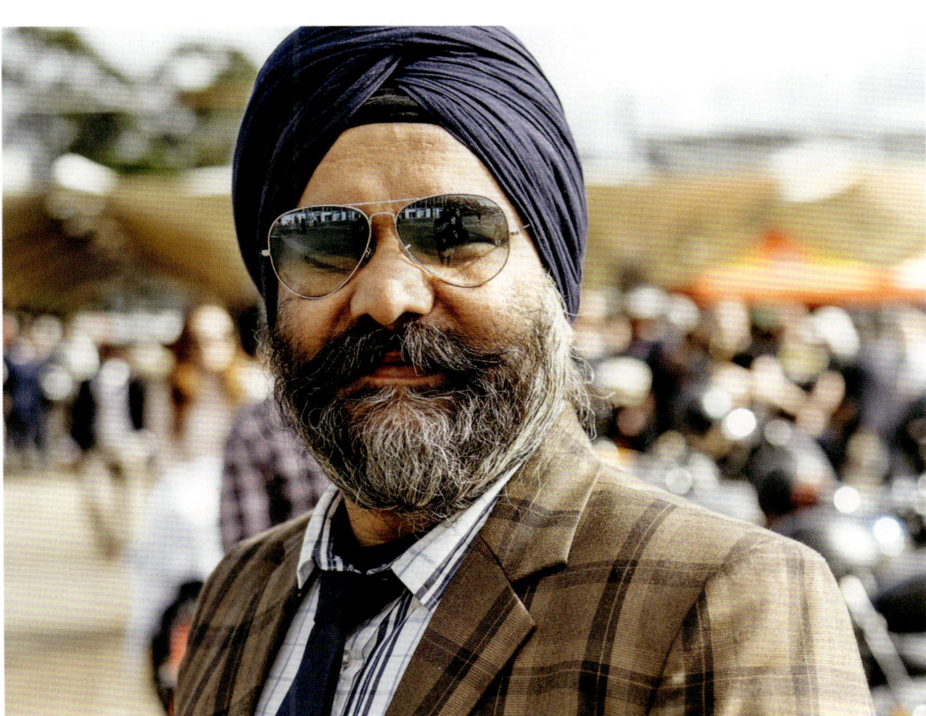
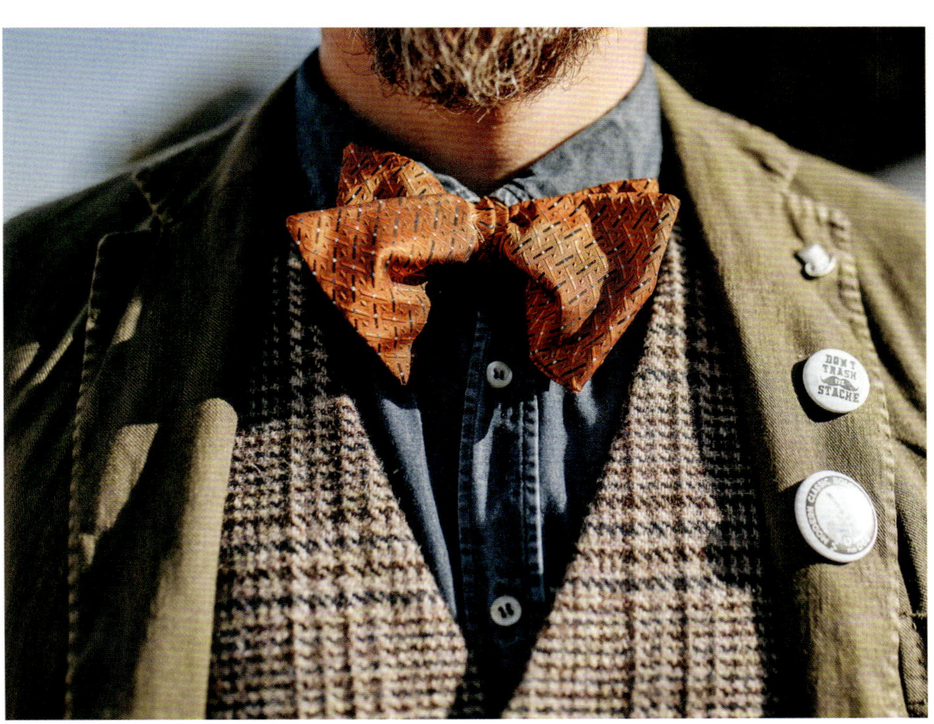

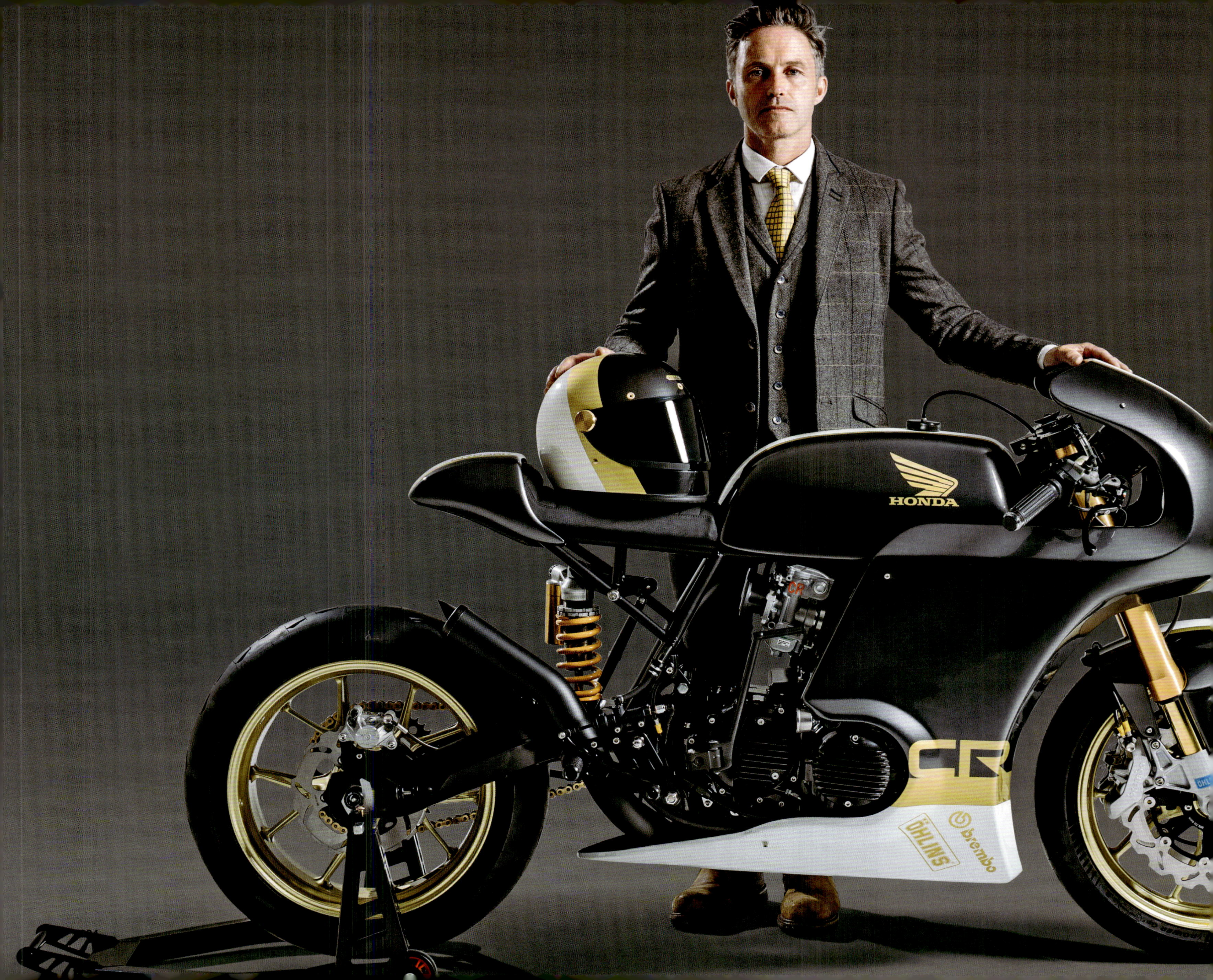

LIFE DRAWINGS

No one steers a steady ship, or at least not forever. I guess that's why the DGR resonates with me. I fear men are increasingly downtrodden and left confused by the shifting expectations of what it is to be a man.

Men are brought up to think one way and then they are told that it's no longer acceptable, or even required. Being a part of The Distinguished Gentleman's Ride means men get to share their life experiences, thoughts and the concerns that they may have been keeping under wraps. And they get to ride a motorbike for the day!

I'd done the ride once before and had high expectations of generating some reasonable fundraising from my friends and followers, but I immediately appreciated how pathetic it sounded to ask for a donation to basically have a fun day out! It's not like running a marathon, or swimming the channel. In fact, it's the exact opposite of a challenge or hardship, although bombing around the M25 at 6 am in a tweed jacket was bitterly cold!

So the first year was a little disappointing from a fundraising perspective for me. I felt like I had to do more, since that's the primary reason to do it, right?

In the run up to what I believe was the 2019 DGR, I tried to think of what I could do that was salable, scalable and would generate bigger numbers. It was clear I'd get bugger all with a heartfelt plea.

I've always drawn, and mostly sketched bikes and cars. It's the starting point of any idea and I'd got a fast and loose style that felt conceptual and free, but it was also pretty rapid. I put out the offer to sketch people's rides for £50 a pop! I didn't quite anticipate how many I'd end up doing!

Whether it's your car or your bike, the one thing we all like to do when we're not in or on them is to look at them; and a photo sometimes has too much of reality left in it. The rotten fence behind the bike or the oil patch leaking from under the car. A sketch tries to capture all the good stuff and isolate it, the line weight and freedom of the pen stroke liberates it and hopefully captures the spirit as well as the thing itself.

So I began and the orders came flooding in, I was drawing morning, noon and night, some requests were for direct copies, some were for their future build plans, and some were to visually complete a project that was half way though. To be honest I loved it and the breadth and character of rides were incredible. From 70's twin engined drag bikes to exotic Porsches, each one was unique and beautiful.

I'm not sure how many I did, I think it was around 170 and a couple of full-blown CAD visuals for more generous donations. I also donated my earnings from appearing on the TV series Goblin Works Garage as that was a bit of fun and I was pretty much doing the same thing for Anthony Partridge. It all seemed to coincide.

So that was that! I was spent, and I don't think I've touched the iPad since!

I'm proud of what we managed to raise and the generosity and spirit of the donations, and it's something I might attempt again in the future, who knows?

To the future of the DGR, and love to all my fellow riders!

Paul
AKA Ziggy Moto

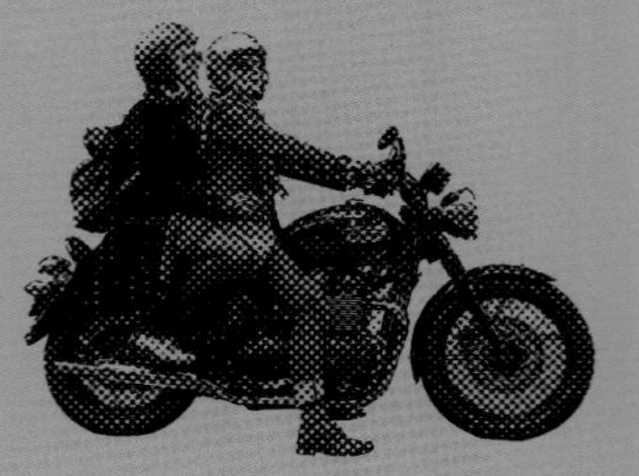

2021

- RIDE TEN -

TO CELEBRATE OUR DECADE OF DAPPER, COVID-19 WAS STILL LIMITING
DGR GROUP RIDES. WE OPENED THE EVENT TO THREE FORMATS
ALLOWING RIDERS TO TAKE PART TOGETHER OR INDIVIDUALLY.
56,000 RIDERS & **913 CITIES** TOOK UP THE CHALLENGE.

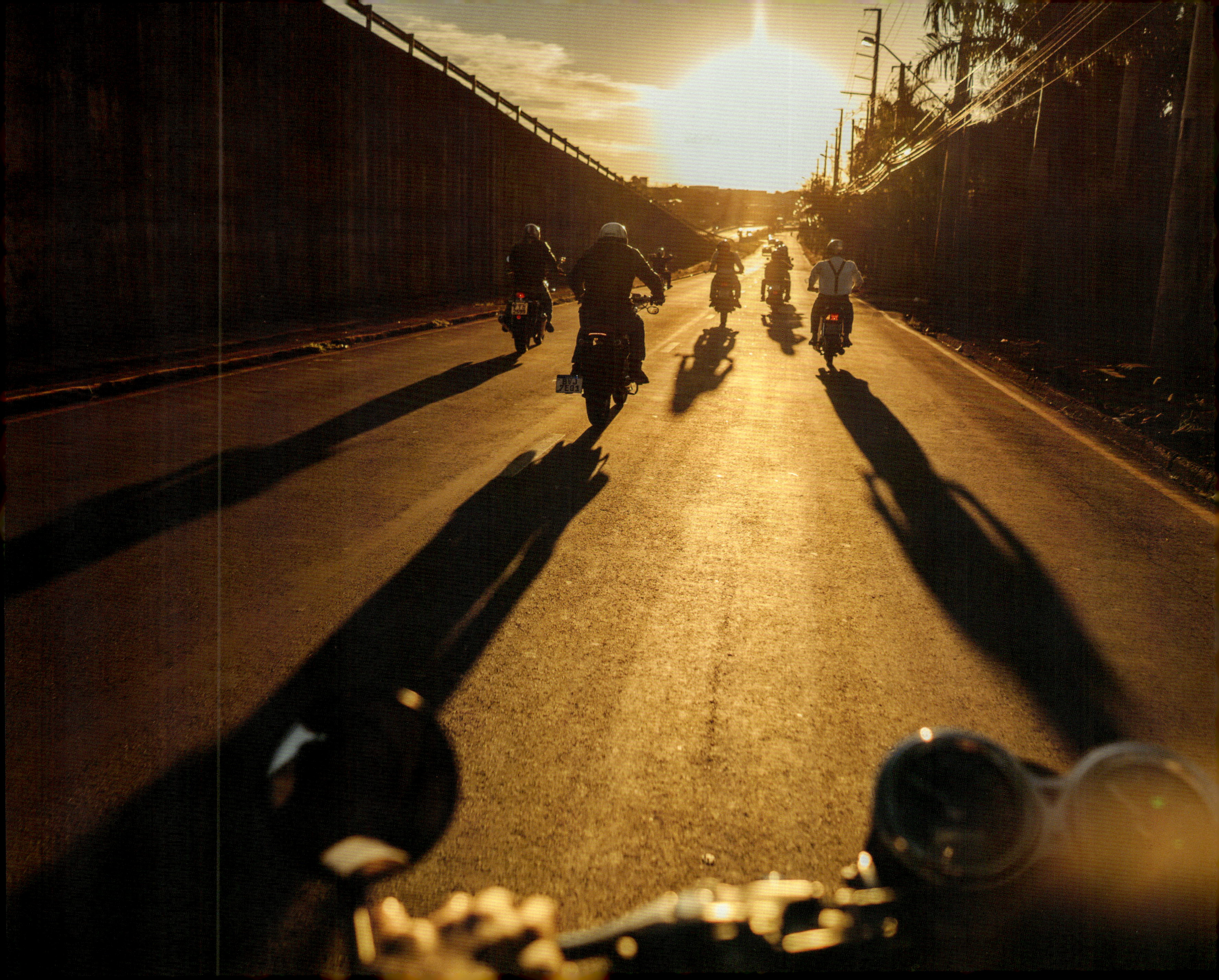

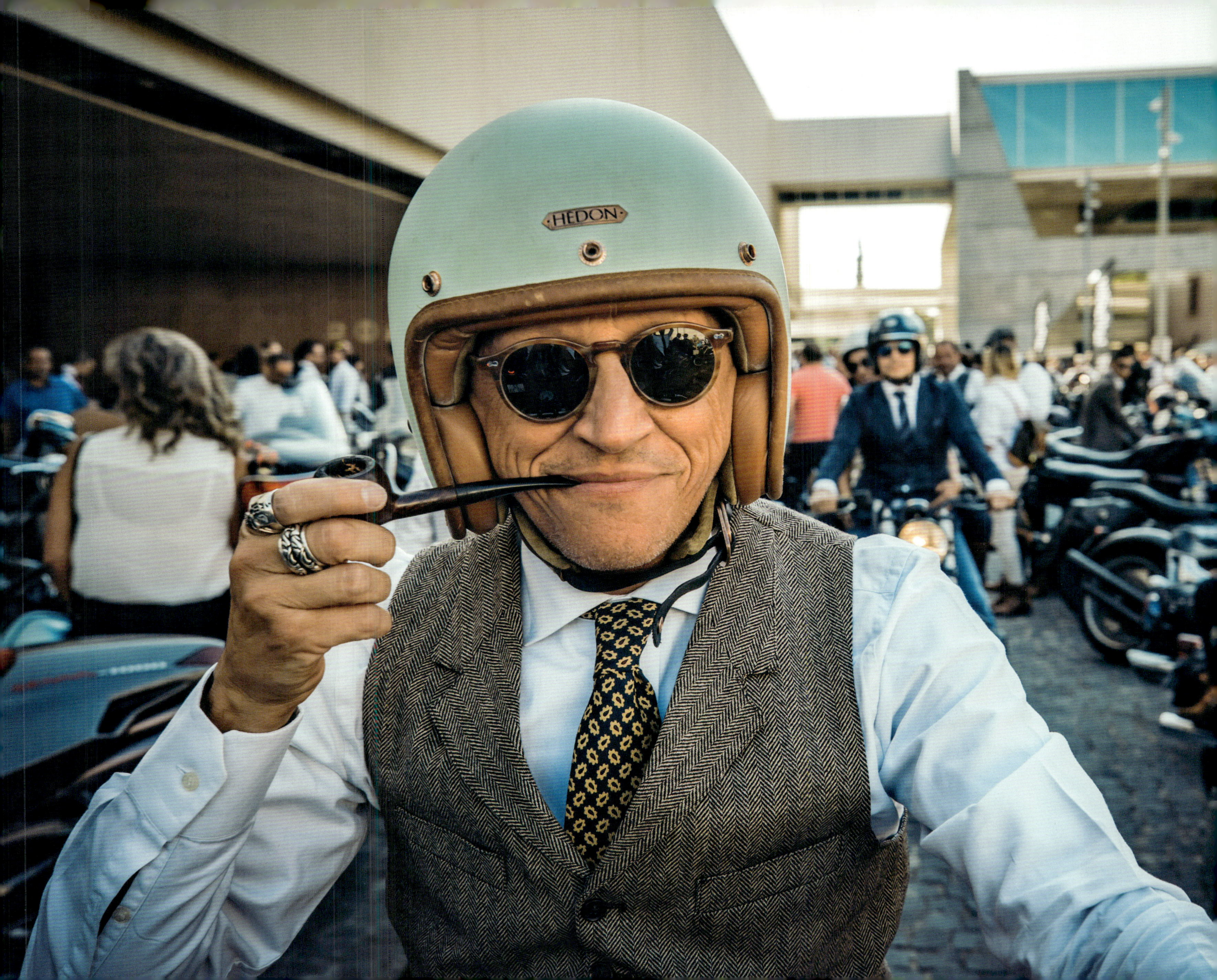
HEDON

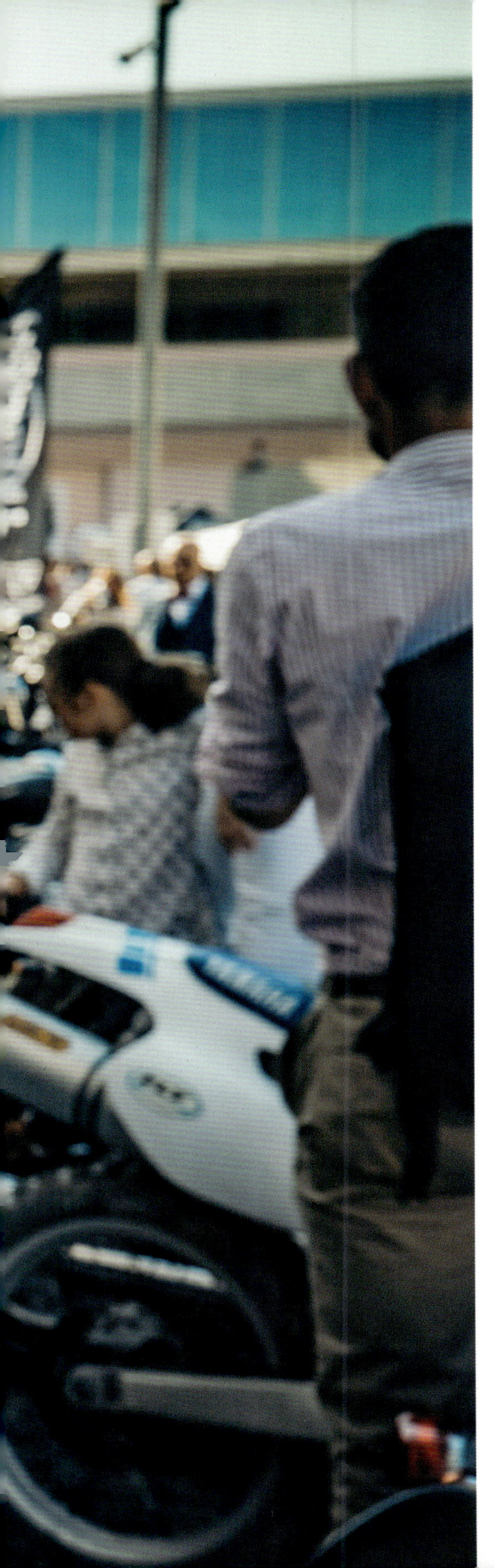

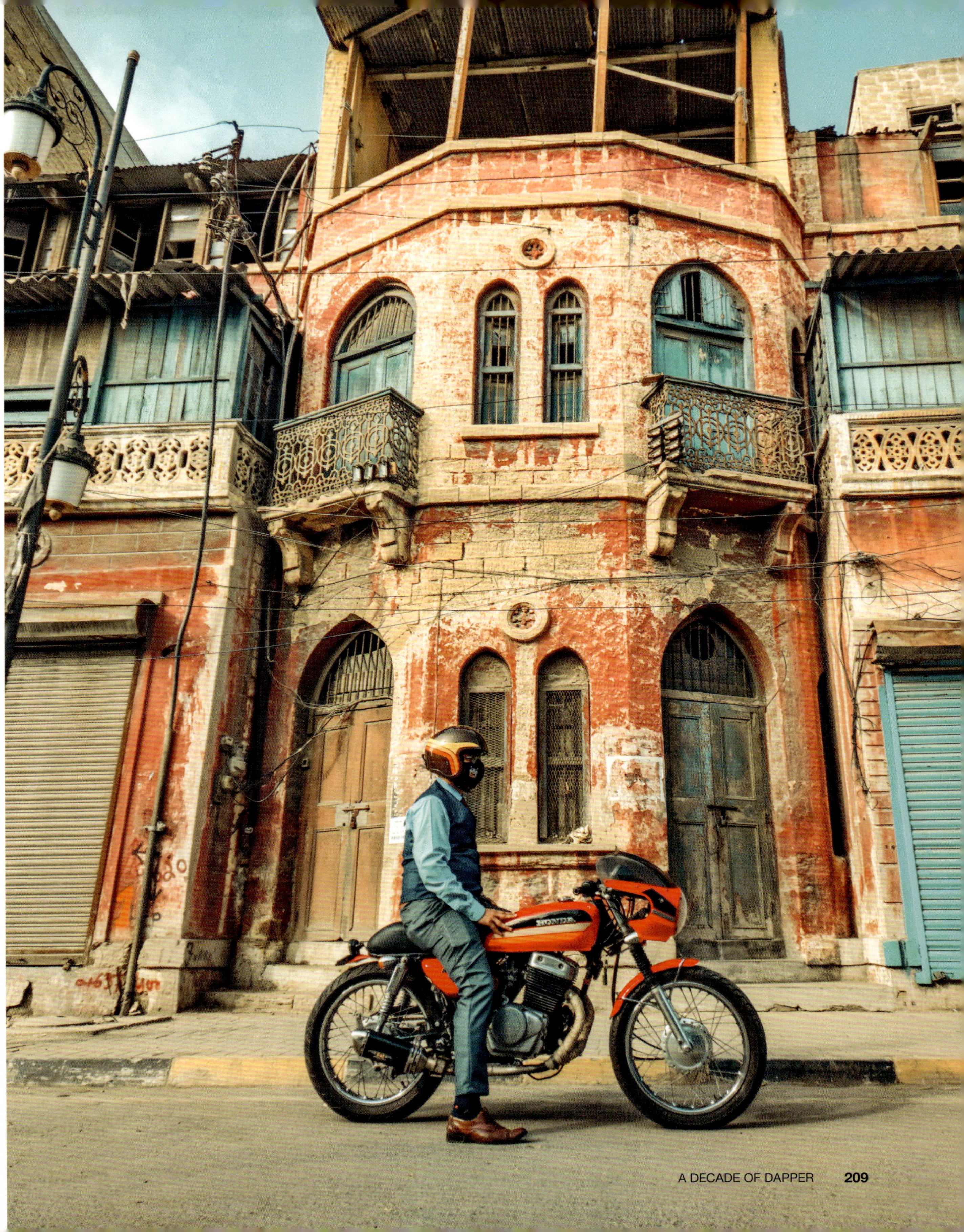

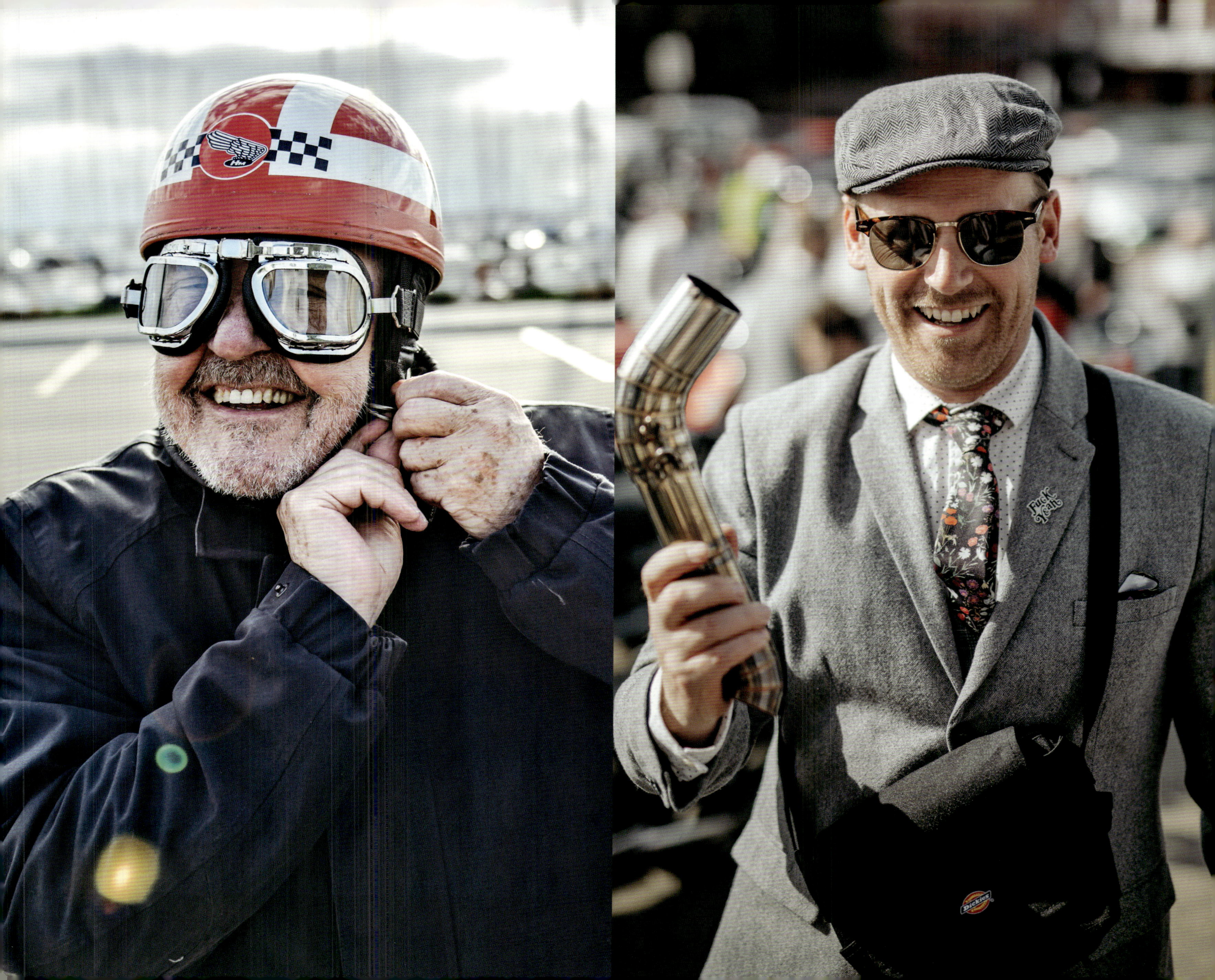

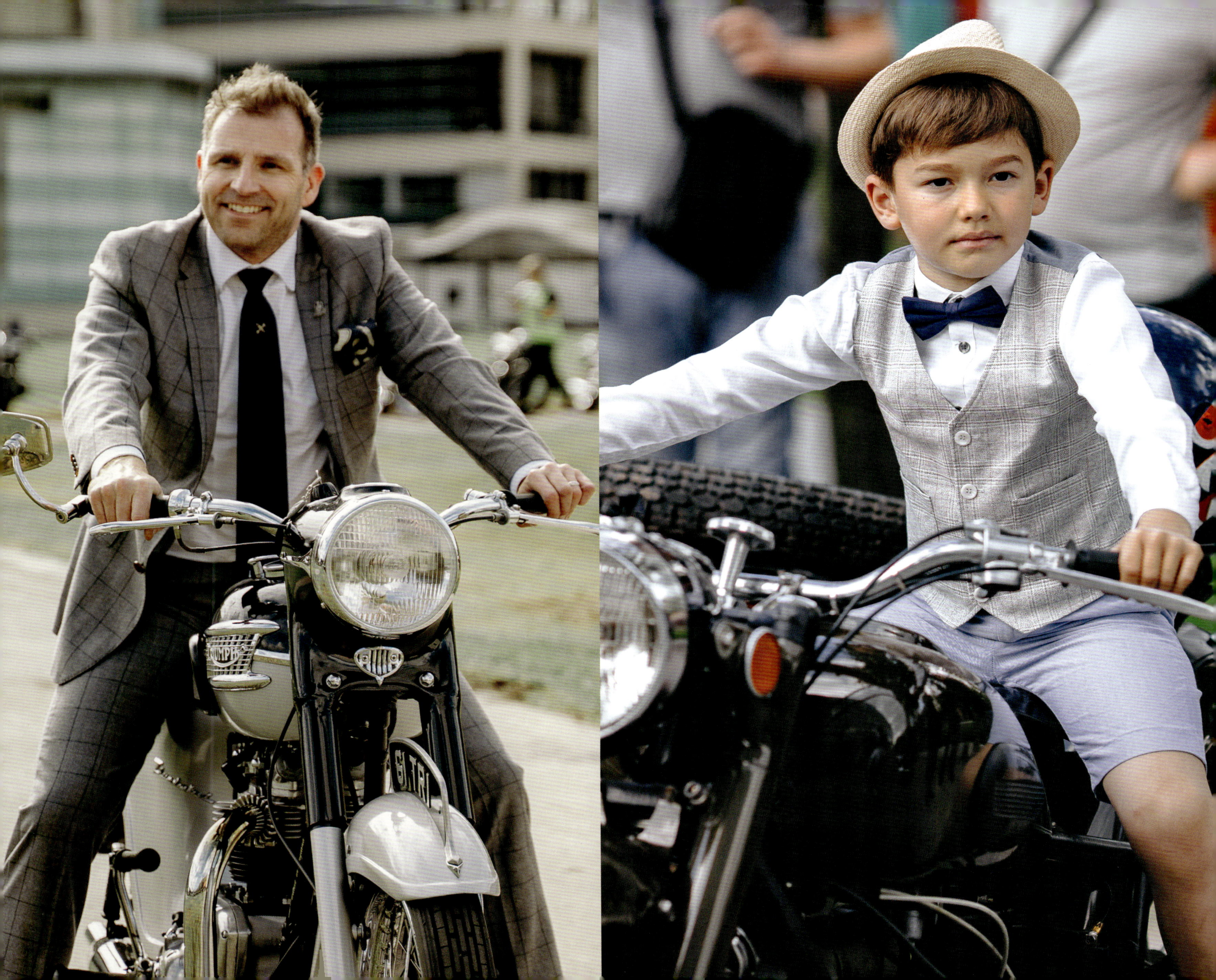

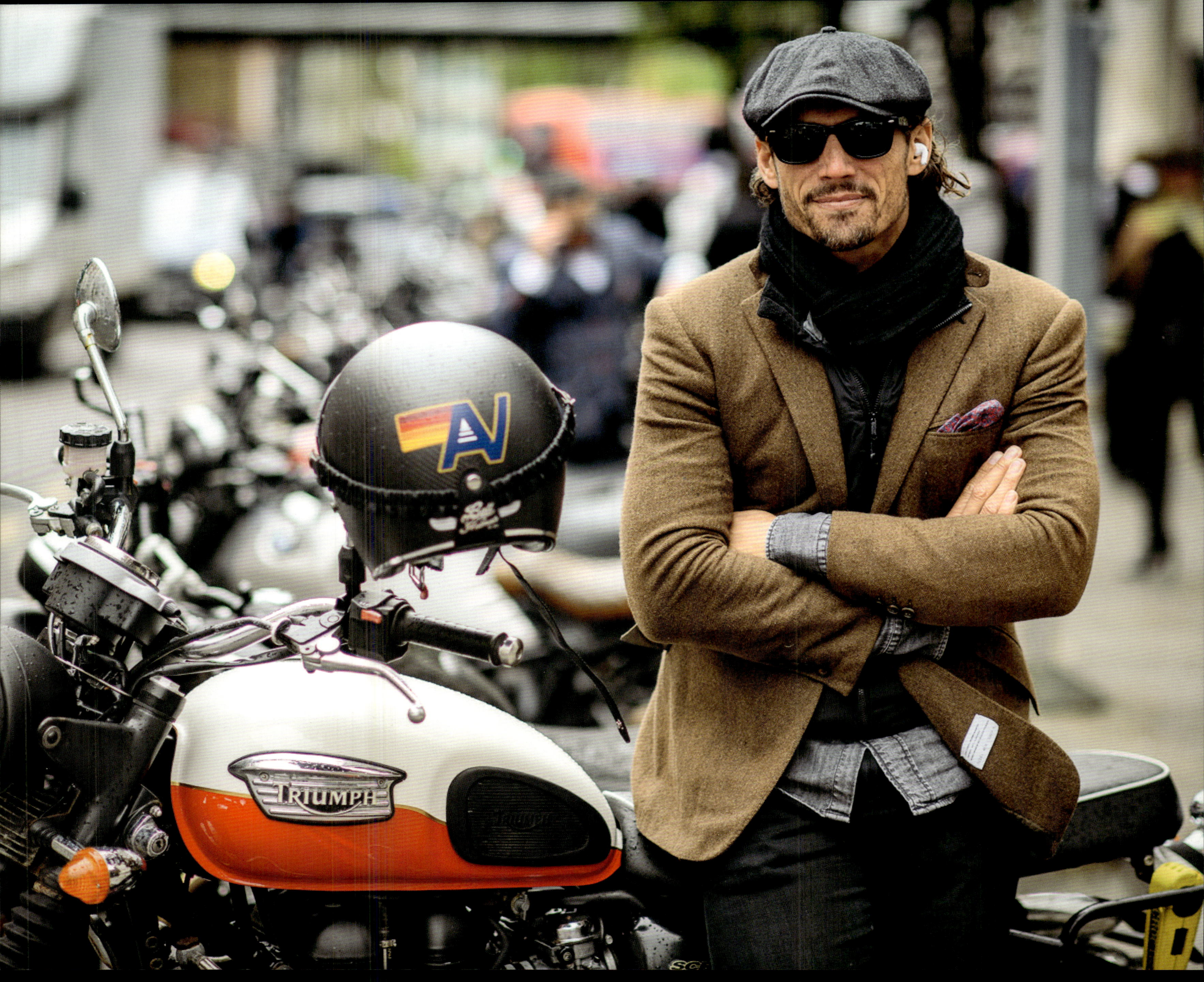

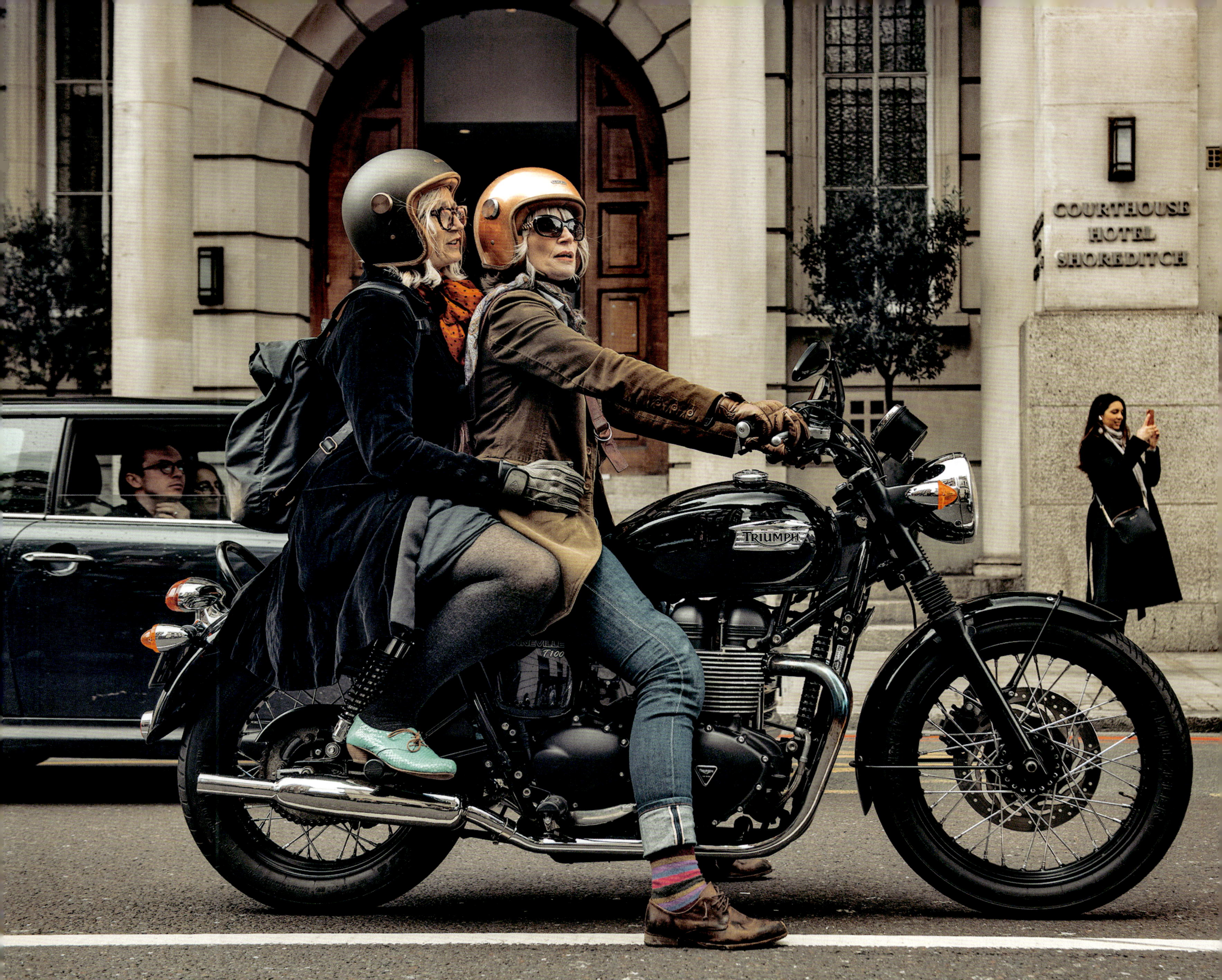
COURTHOUSE
HOTEL
SHOREDITCH
TRIUMPH
BONNEVILLE
T100

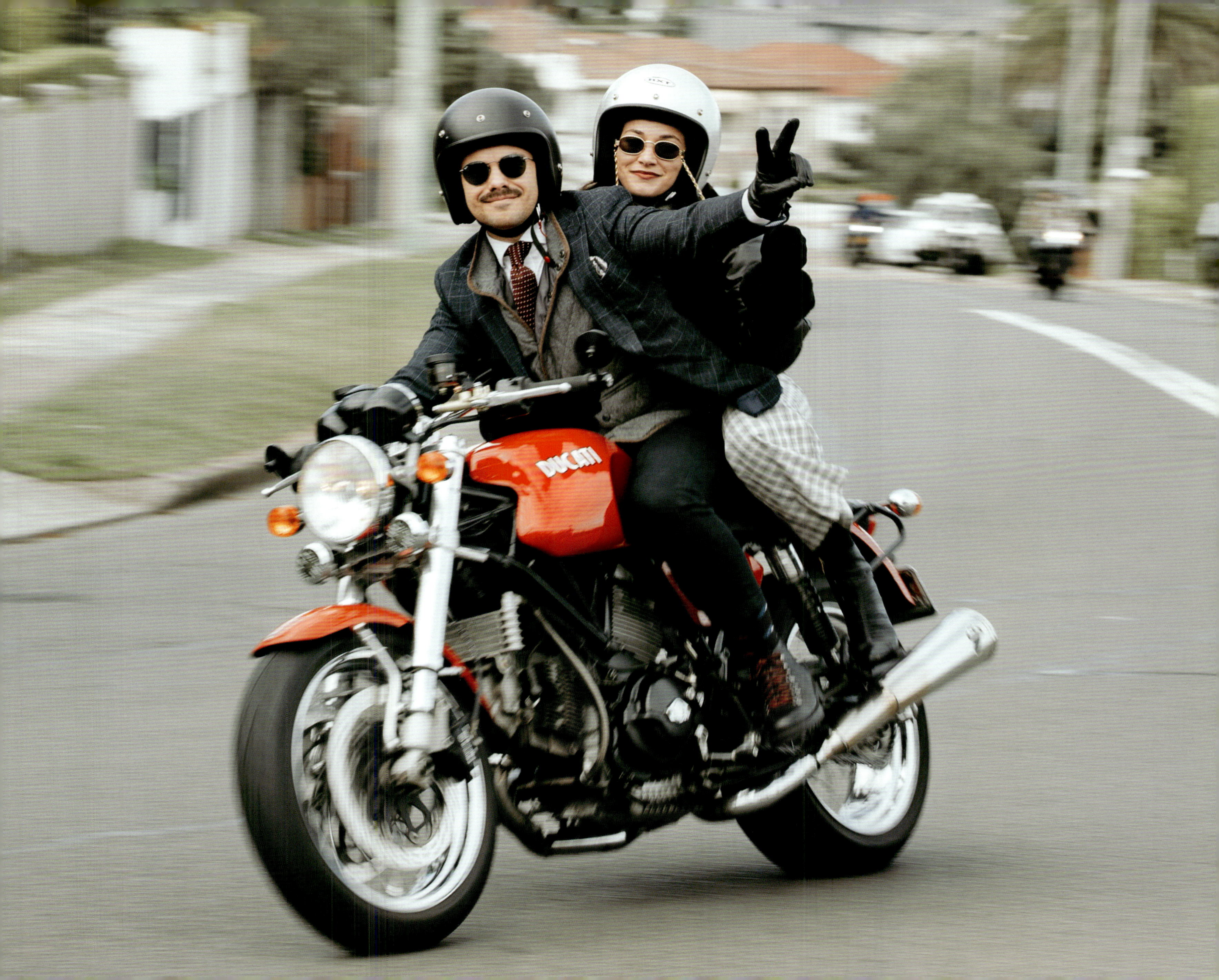

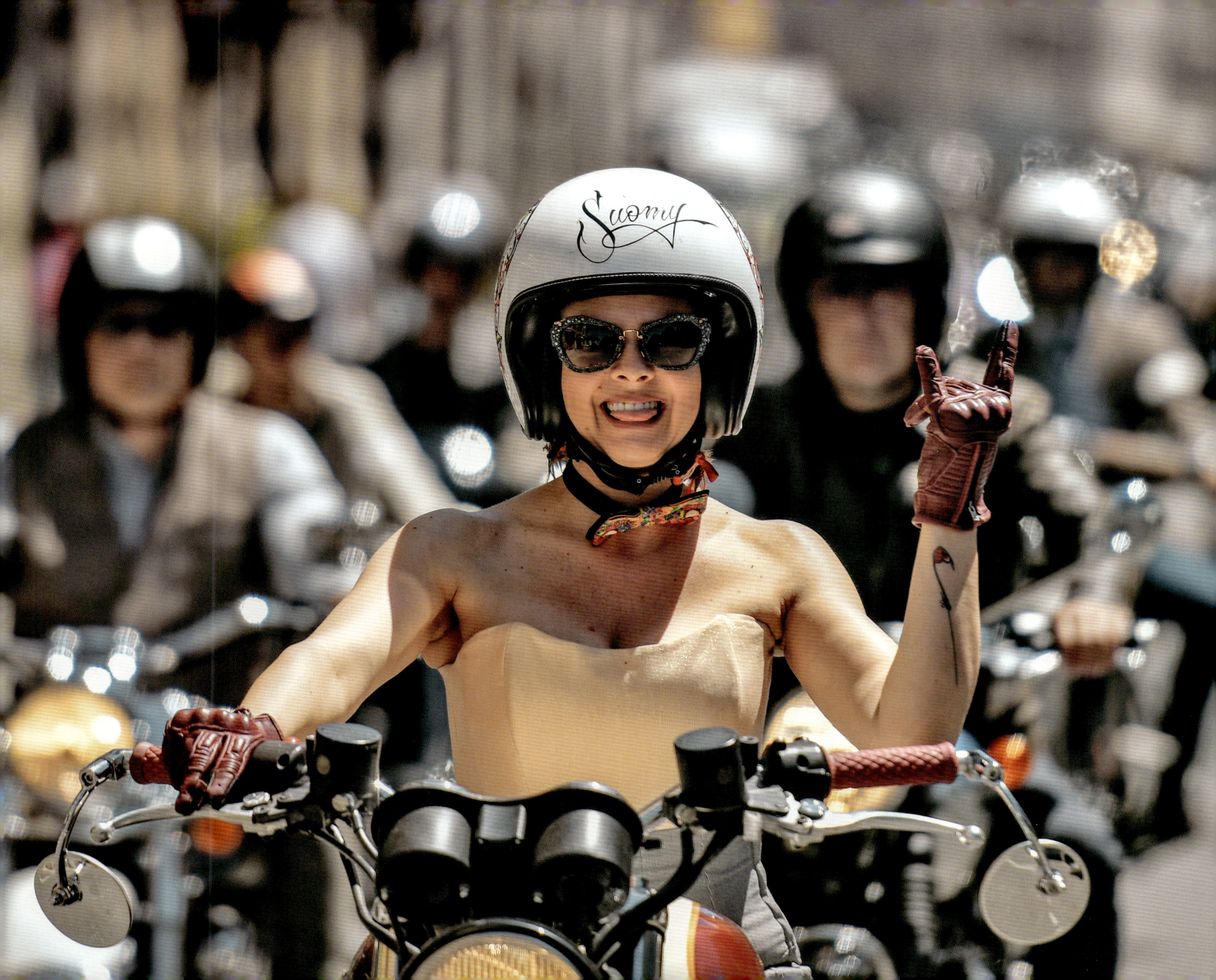

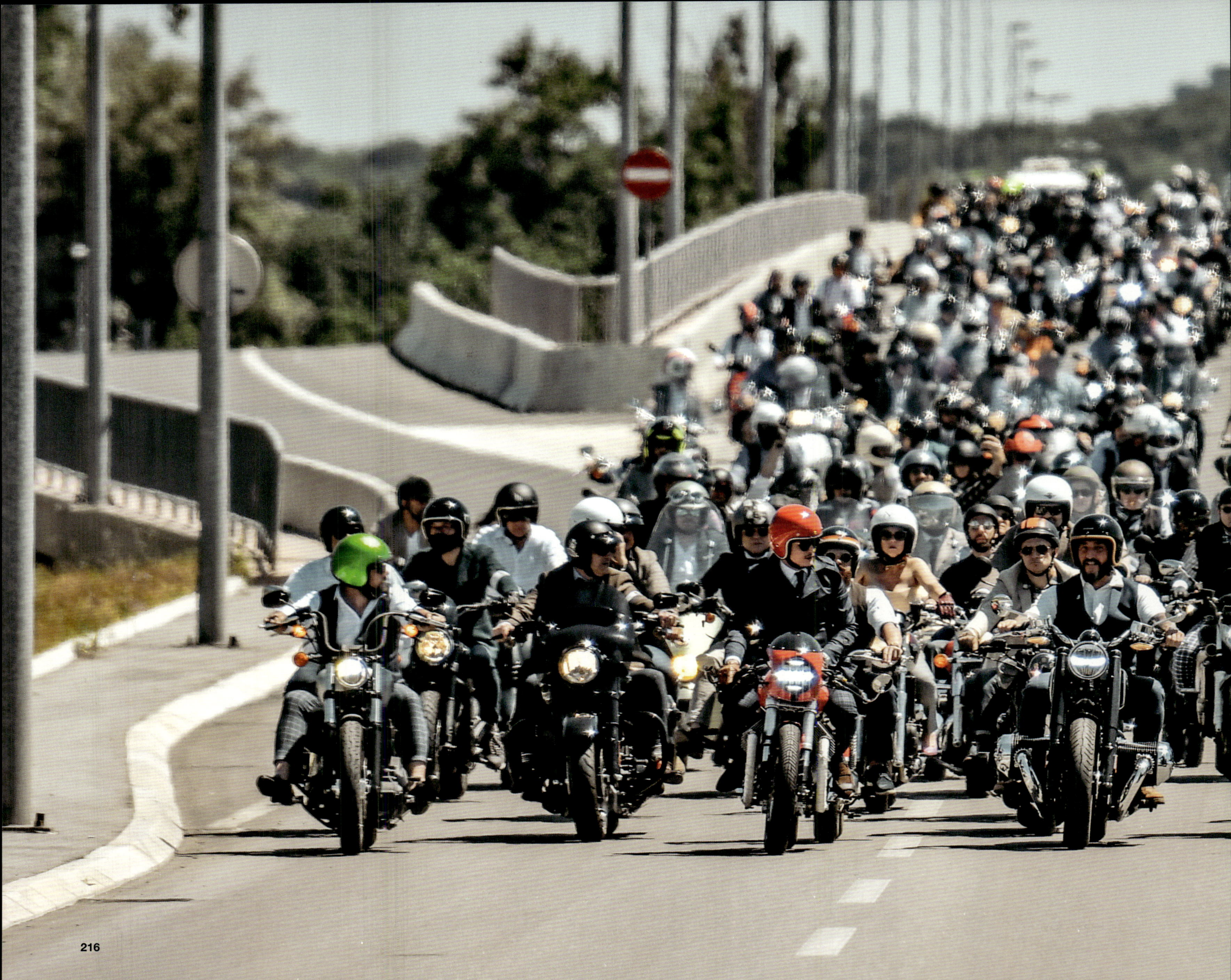

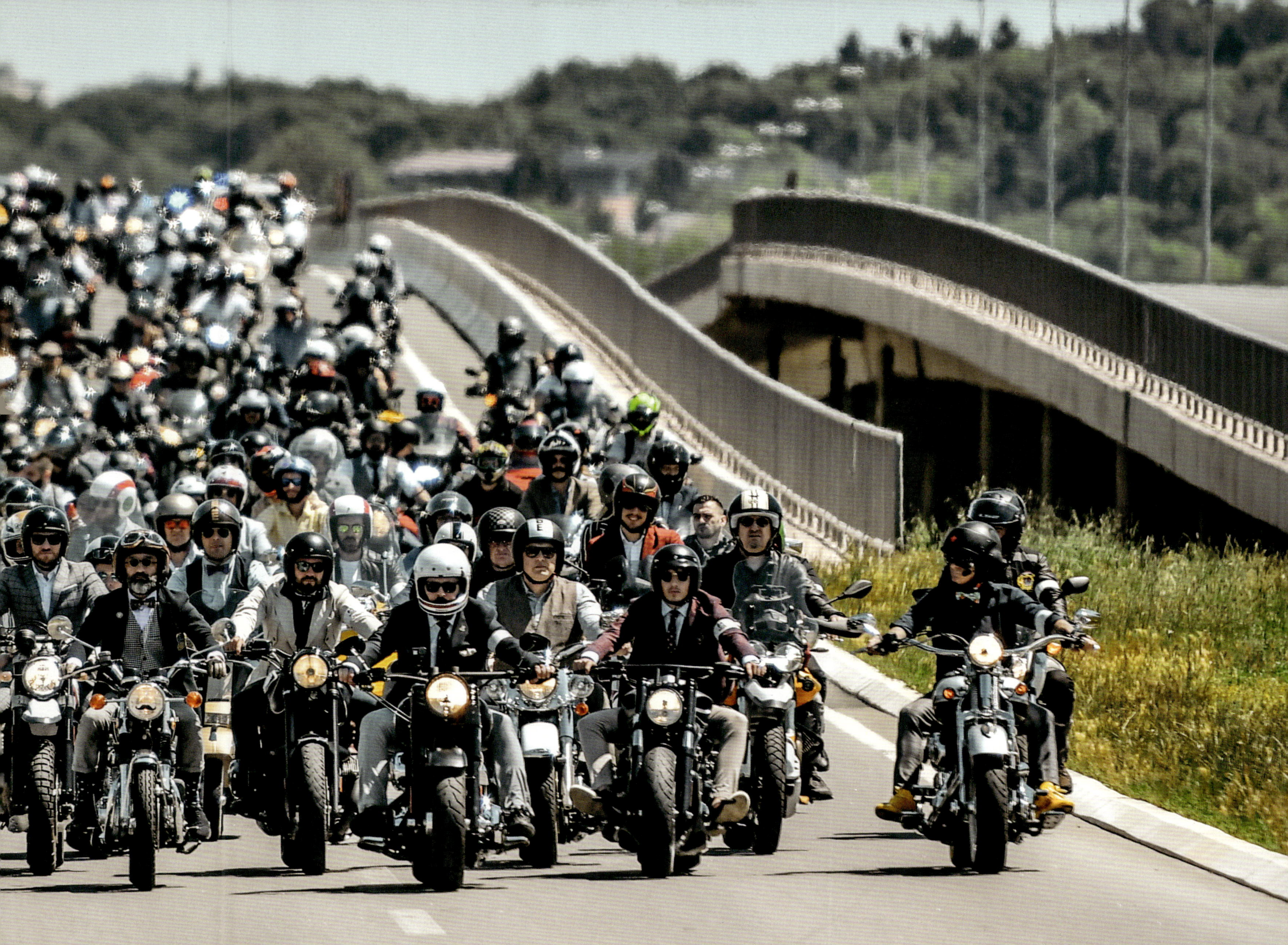

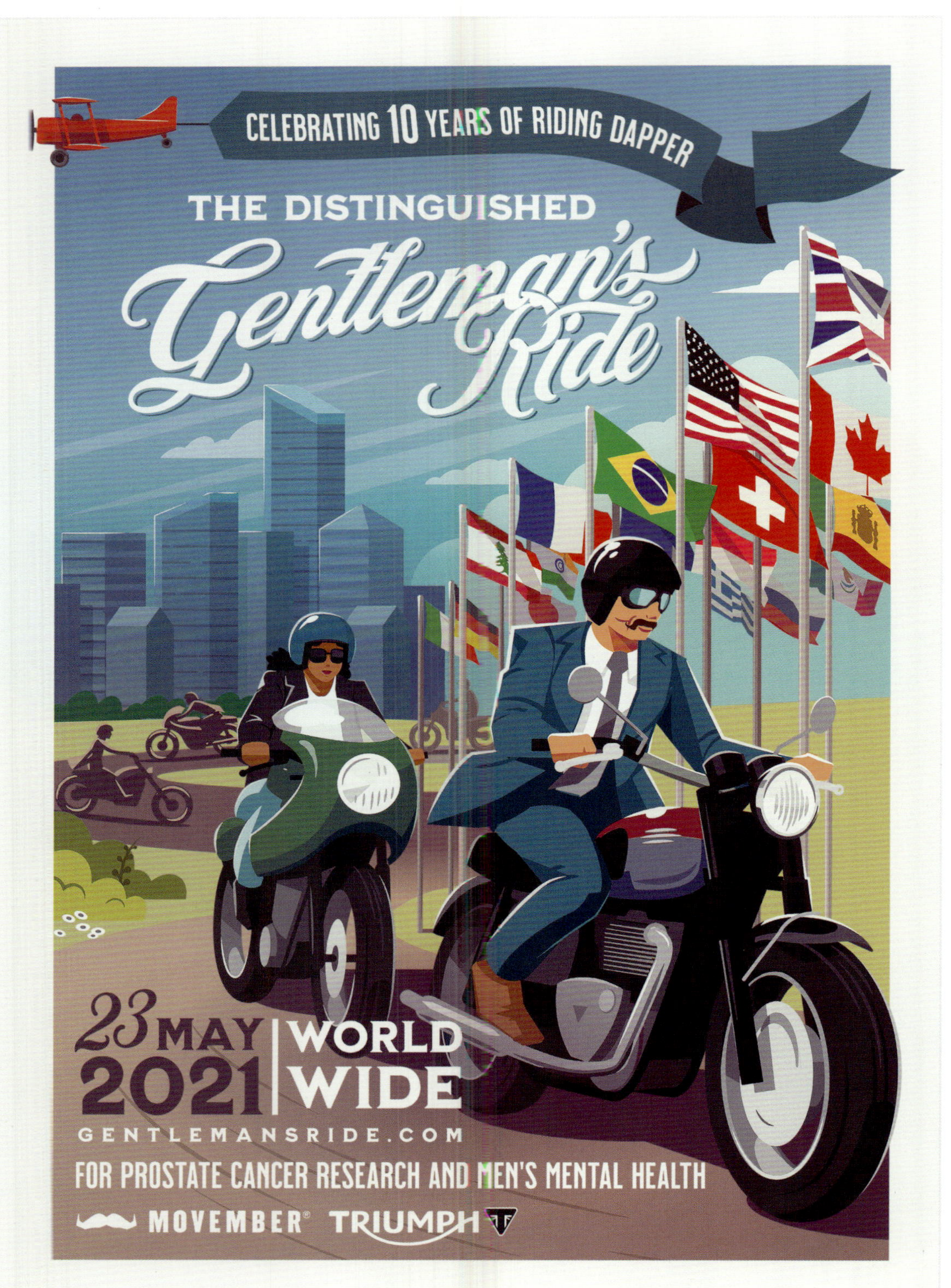

2021 Ride Poster

Designed by Andrew Rose
A return to the bright and colorful style after COVID-19, this year's poster embraced the event's international nature by proudly displaying flags from some of the 100+ participating countries, showing how widespread the event has become. The characters within the poster featured both men and women riding out of the city on classic Triumph motorcycles for the 10th anniversary of the first DGR event.

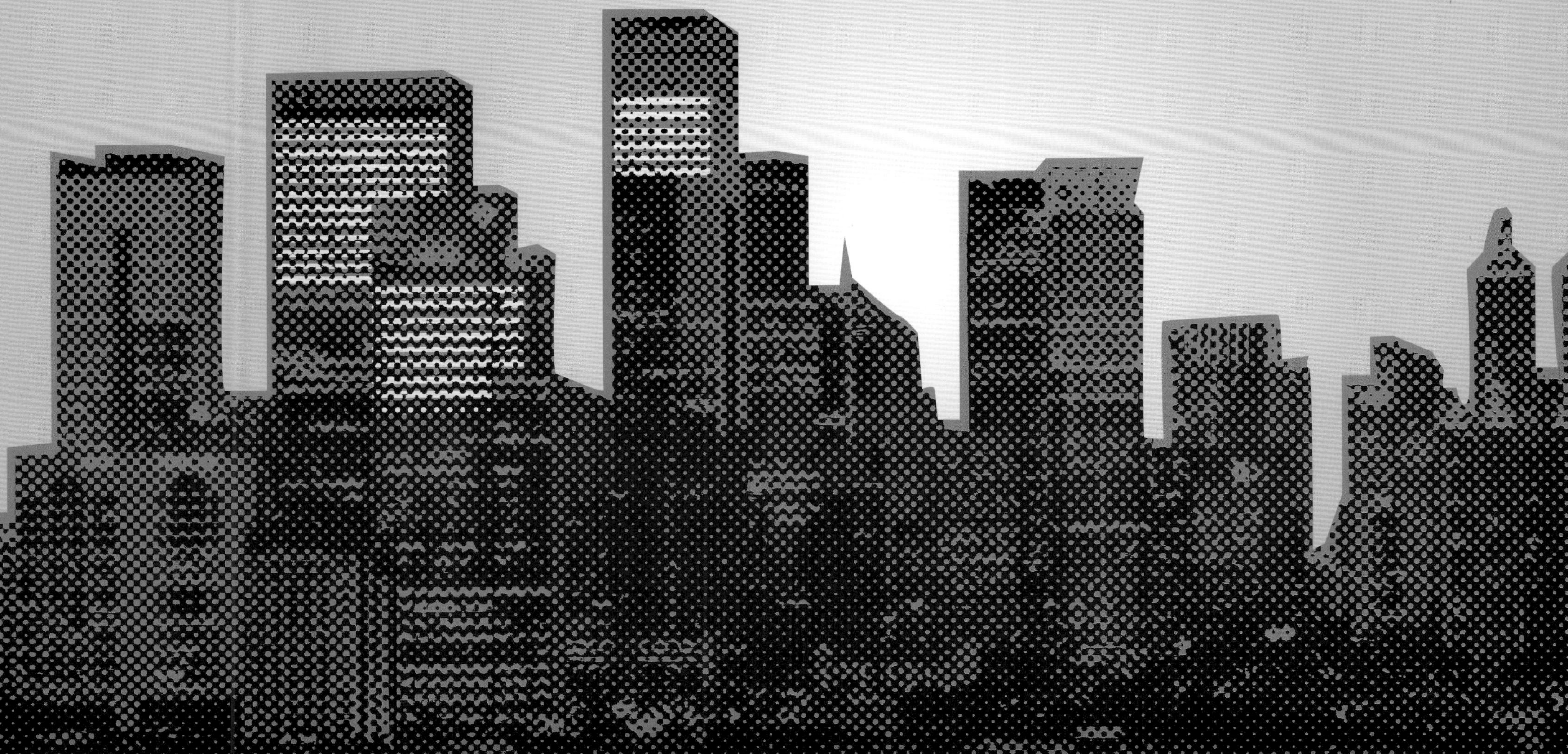

JAKARTA
FIRST RIDE: 2012
TOTAL PARTICIPANTS: 5,396
TOTAL RAISED: USD $11.4k
DGR CITIES

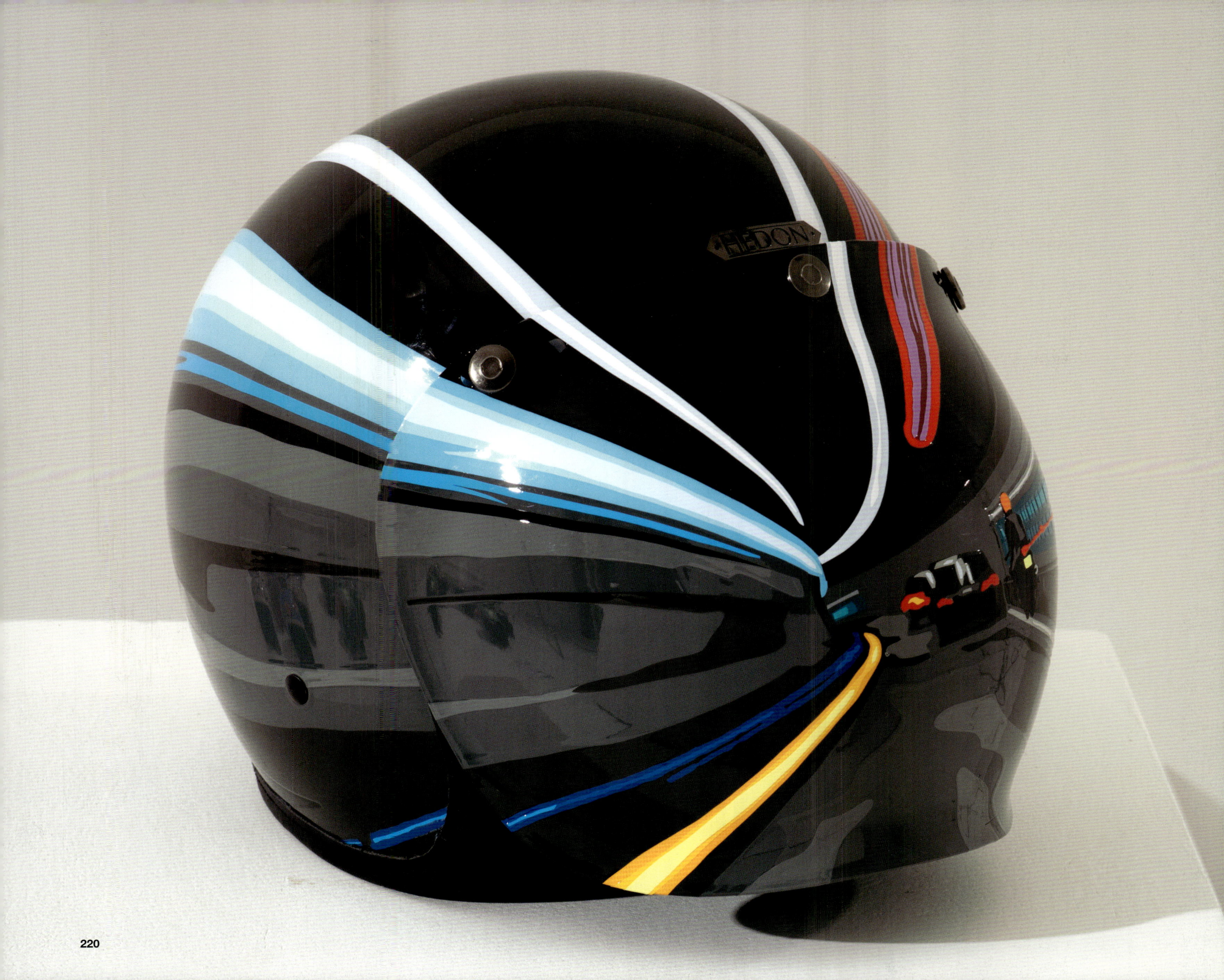

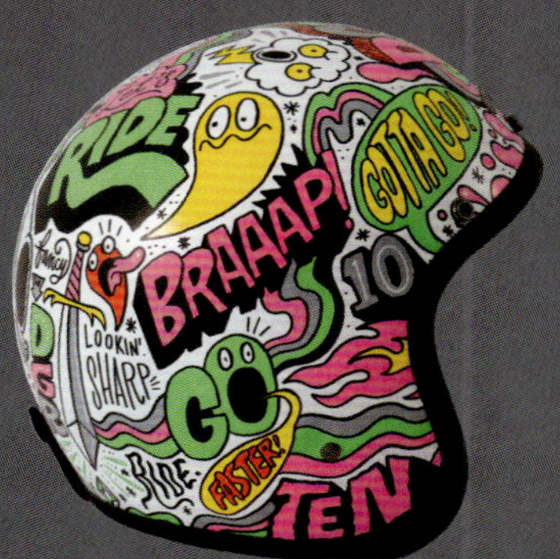

Chris Piascik

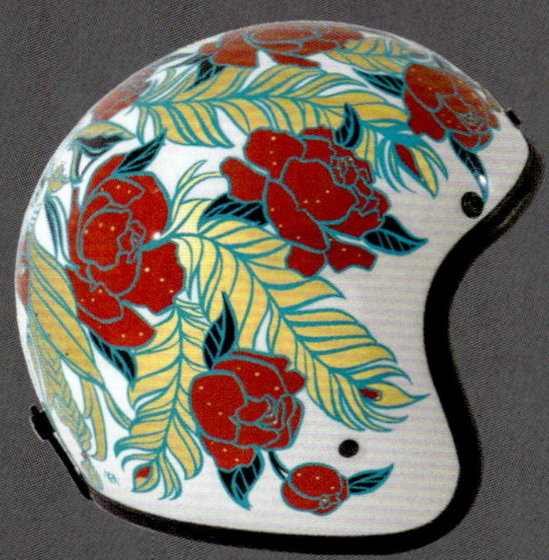

Kayla Koeune-Weisel

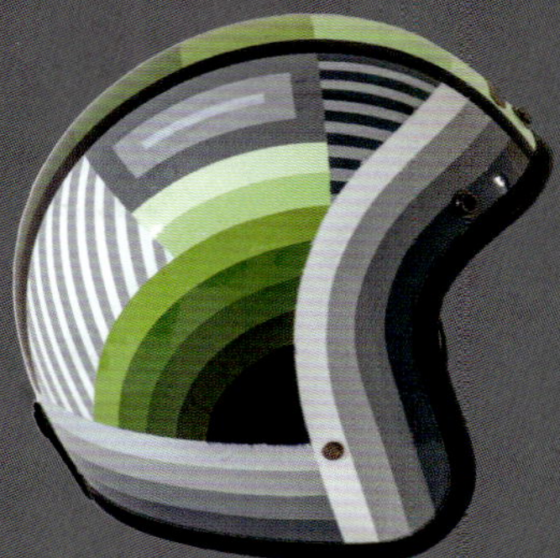

Bradley Eastman

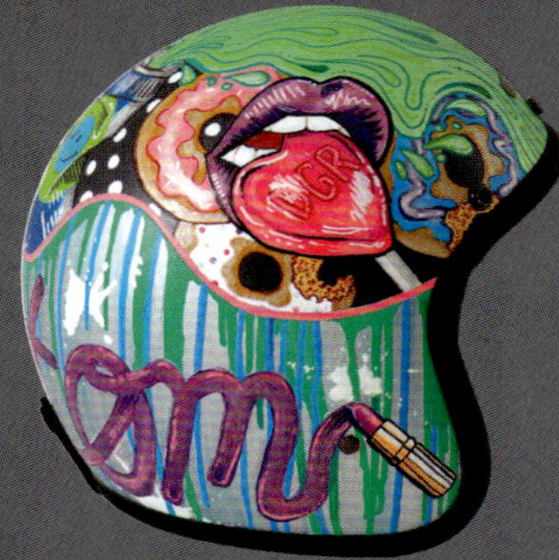

Helen Stanley

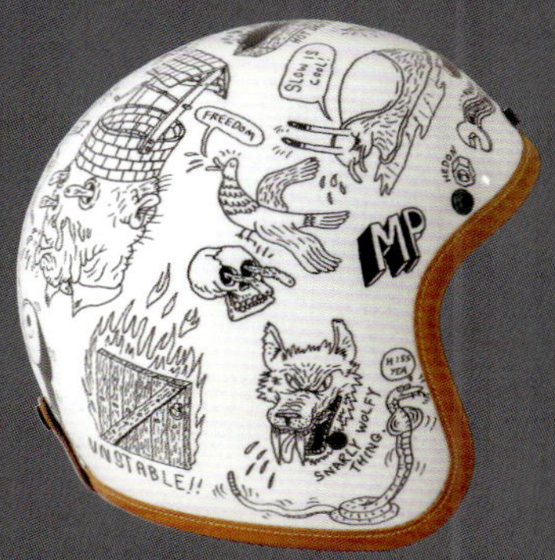

Maxwell Paternoster

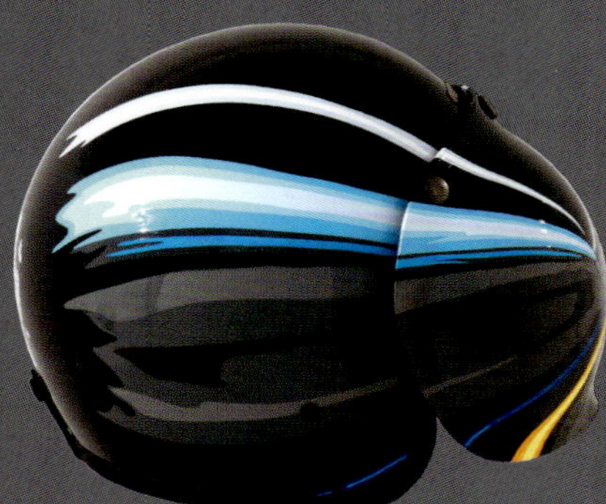

Joel Clark

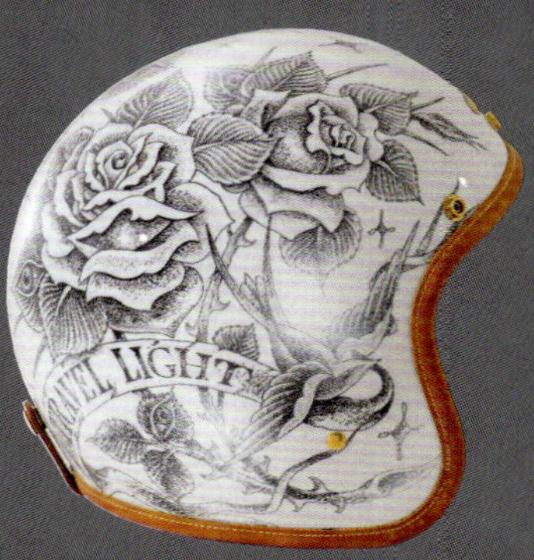

Luke Wessman

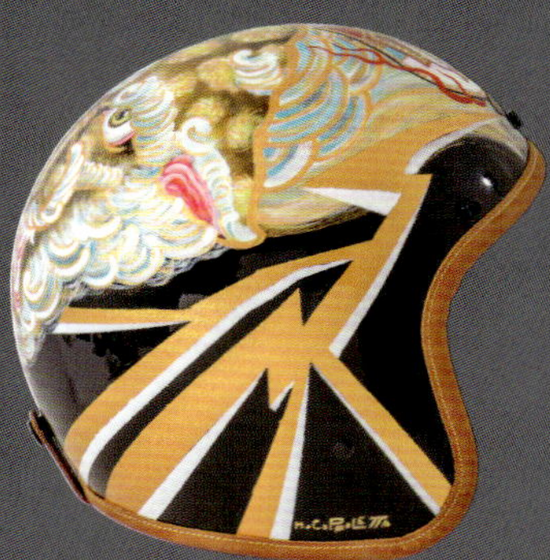

Mo Coppoletta

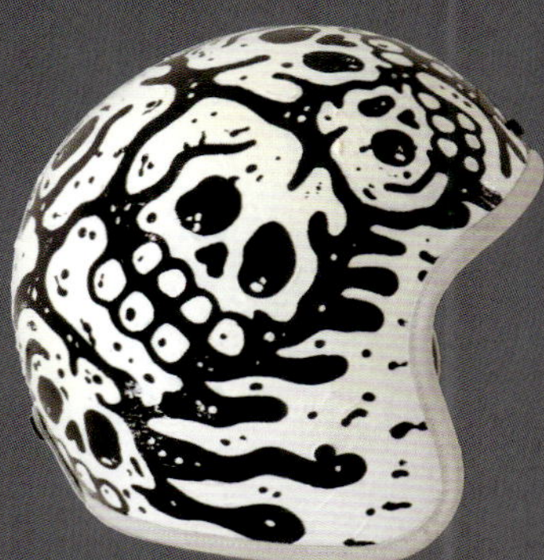

Sindy Sinn

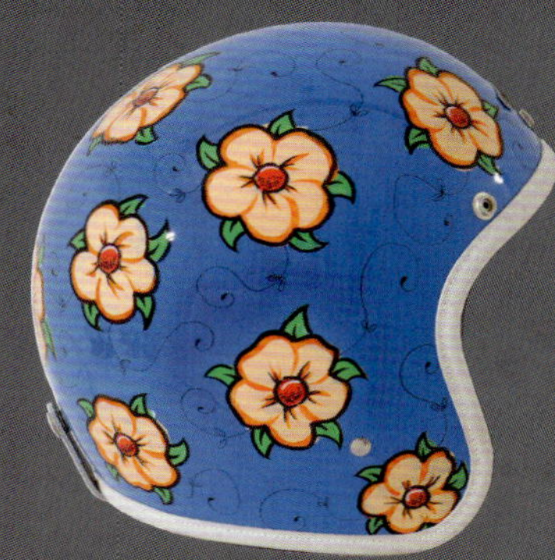

Steve Caballero

1O-YEAR HELMET AUCTION

To celebrate a decade of riding dapper for men's health, The Distinguished Gentleman's Ride and our helmet partner, Hedon, have brought together 10 artists from around the world to create 10 unique helmets to be auctioned off in 2021.

Each incredible artist was provided with a helmet shell and challenged to create a masterpiece of their choosing that expresses their artistic style on an unconventional canvas.

The auction raised a total of USD $17,950 for the cause, with all proceeds going directly to The Distinguished Gentleman's Ride's charity partner, Movember.

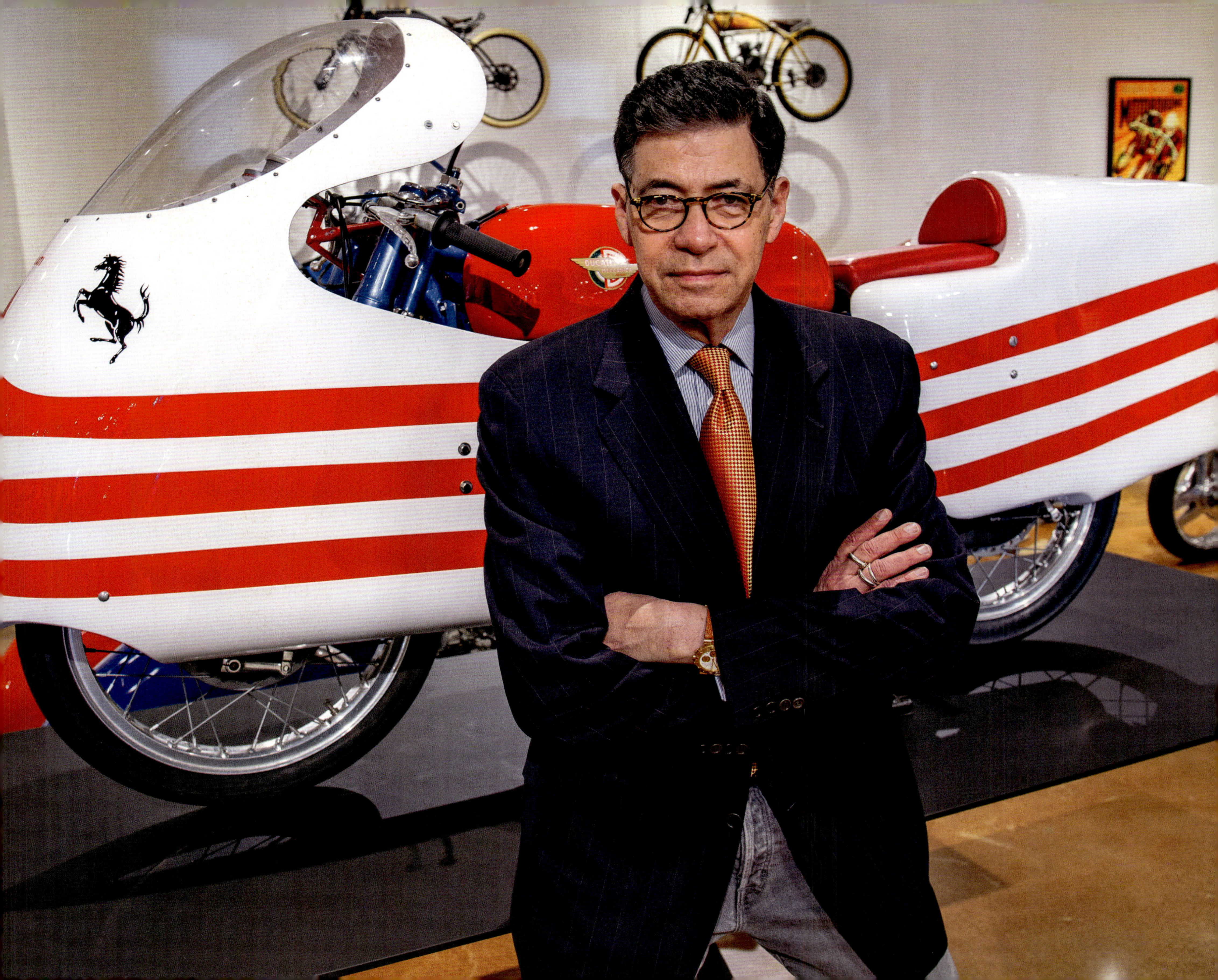

"I'VE OFTEN SAID THAT WHOEVER INVENTED LIFE
TWISTED THE KNOB OF DIFFICULTY ONE OR TWO
CLICKS TOO TIGHT.

WHEN WE HAVE A HANDFUL OF STRONG PERSONAL
CONNECTIONS OR ARE PART OF A GROUP WHO
HAS EXPERIENCED SIMILAR CHALLENGES, WE ARE
COMFORTED BY THE FACT THAT OUR CHALLENGES ARE
NOT UNIQUE TO US.

THOSE CHALLENGES AFFECT VIRTUALLY EVERYONE
ONCE WE DELVE BELOW THE SURFACE. DGR DELVES
BELOW THE SURFACE TO EXPOSE THE COMMONALITY
OF OUR CHALLENGES."

Bobby Haas
1947 - 2021

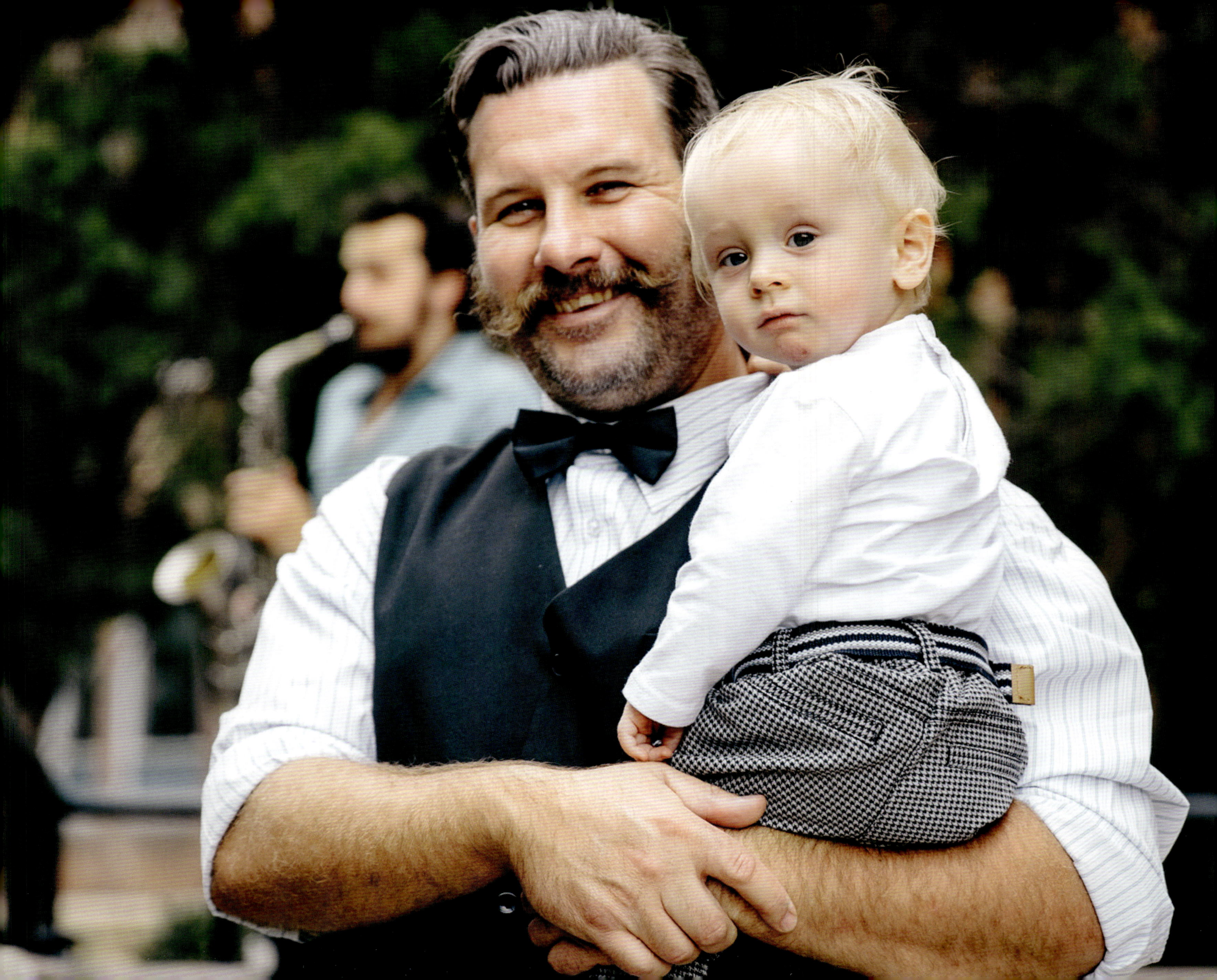

THE FUTURE OF DGR

Each year, we wonder if The Distinguished Gentleman's Ride has reached its peak. But each year without fail, we are blown away by the ever-increasing amount of dapper folk who join us to set new records. So, where do we go next?

The Distinguished Gentleman's Ride has been an amazing journey. In our wildest dreams we never quite realized how large it would grow. More importantly, we never realized how important the event would be. It's now bigger than any single person working on it. It's become an opportunity for men and women to connect, for friendships and relationships to grow and nourish. The event created an opportunity for those of us who didn't have a huge social network to meet people and connect.

Those friendships and relationships have ensured that we are happier, healthier and have others to share our passion and journey with. The future of DGR is always a tricky one to comprehend. When I started it, I thought its lifespan would be a decade, with charity fatigue, event fatigue, the changing environment of motorcycle emissions and difficulties riding in cities.

This is a big reason that we made the decision five years ago to carbon offset the entire event and all 100,000 motorcycles participating. With the transition into renewable energies, I believe the event will see a shift and a further acceptance of classic styled machines using electricity. There are brands already creating these styled machines with all manufacturers currently working on adding these to their stables.

Year on year we see more women joining us on this journey and supporting the men in their lives. We would love to see the event be attended by more folks other than men, showing support for the men in their lives who may be suffering from or succumbed to our cause areas. With the success of DGR, we also launched The Distinguished Gentleman's Drive. In its first year we had over 145 drives raising funds for the same cause. Held on separate dates, this event is also connecting people, breaking down the macho mentality of men and showing everyone it is okay to be vulnerable.

Prostate cancer is a hell of a disease, and if not caught early it can have devastating effects, even for those who survive it. Our future is motivating more men to get checked, funding more research, being there to support our friends mentally and connecting more throughout the year. Whether that is through motorcycles, cars or bicycles.

Mark Hawwa
DGR Founder

PHOTOGRAPHY INDEX

Pages **131** (L), **147** & **148** - photos by Bernardo Lucio.

Pages **79**, **104**, **105**, **186**, **187** & **197** - photos by Triumph Motorcycles.

Page **177** (R) - photo by Leca Novo. @lecanovo

Page **181** (L) - photo by Andre Pinces.

Page **37** - photo by Nathan McNeil - Set In Stone. setinstonemedia.com.au

Page **116** - photo by Boy Surminski. @boysurminski photography

Page **46** - photo by Ramon Wenger.

Pages **211** (L) & **214** - photos by James Macintyre. @jacintvre

Pages **156** (L) & **203** (TL) - photos by Miloš Muškinja.

Page **170** - photo by Robert Oliva Fotos. @robert.oliva.fotos

Page **193** - photo by Maksim Podtsepko. @foreigner611

Page **209** - photo by Efrah Shaukat.

Pages **24** & **83** - photos by Unfiltered Creative. unfilteredcreative.com

Page **93** - photo by Christopher Martin. @oppositepage

Pages **27** (R), **72**, **73**, **82**, **176** (L), **198**, **199**, **200** - photos by MY Media Sydney.

Page **115** (R) - photo by Nelson Oliveira. @no.photo.on.two.wheels

Pages **162** & **177** (L) - photos by Manuel Portugal. @manuelportugalphoto

Pages **2**, **66**, **67**, **69**, **70**, **71**, **109**, **110**, **111**, **120** & **230** - photos by Amy Shore.

Page **115** (L) - photo by Leandro Oscar Urizar. @redeyecollection

Page **90** - photo by David Marvier. @davidmarvier

Page **166** - photo by Steve Neilson. @valenmotors-photography

Page **32** - photo by Natalie Osburne.

Page **136** - photo by Jef Richaerts.

Pages **21**, **22** & **23** - photos by El Solitario.

Page **172** - photo by Juan Ventura Photography. juanstudio.com

Page **60** - photo by Hugh Miller Photography. hmillerphoto.com

Page **114** (L) - photo by Matthew Ng Photography. @matthewng.co

Pages **96** & **98** - photos by Jesse Allan Paul. jalanpaul.com

Page **102** - photo by Jared Rowe - Fotogenik Media. @fotogenikmedia

Page **152** (R) - photo by Mark Squitieri. @marks_nyc_moto

Page **156** (R) - photo by Veronica Verlan.

Pages **11**, **65** & **143** - photos by Chris Mitchell. @grouphomegarage

Page **150** - photo by Anam Anita Naz.

Page **160** - photo by Jake Pickle.

Pages **130** (R) & **202** (R) - photos by Mari Sabra. @marisabra photography

Page **203** (BL) - photo by Pat Stevenson. patstevenson.com

Page **169** - photo by Just Visual. @justvisual.it

Page **210** (L) - photo by Elias Moraga. @eliasmoraga

Pages **45**, **47**, **48** & **49** - photos by Laurent Nivalle.

Pages **27** (L), **62** & **74** - photos by Ana Pina.

Page **154** - photo by Frank Schulte Photography. schulte-photography.com

Pages **29**, **184** & **185** - photos by Storiesof Bike. @storiesofbike

Page **51** - photo by Tom Wall.

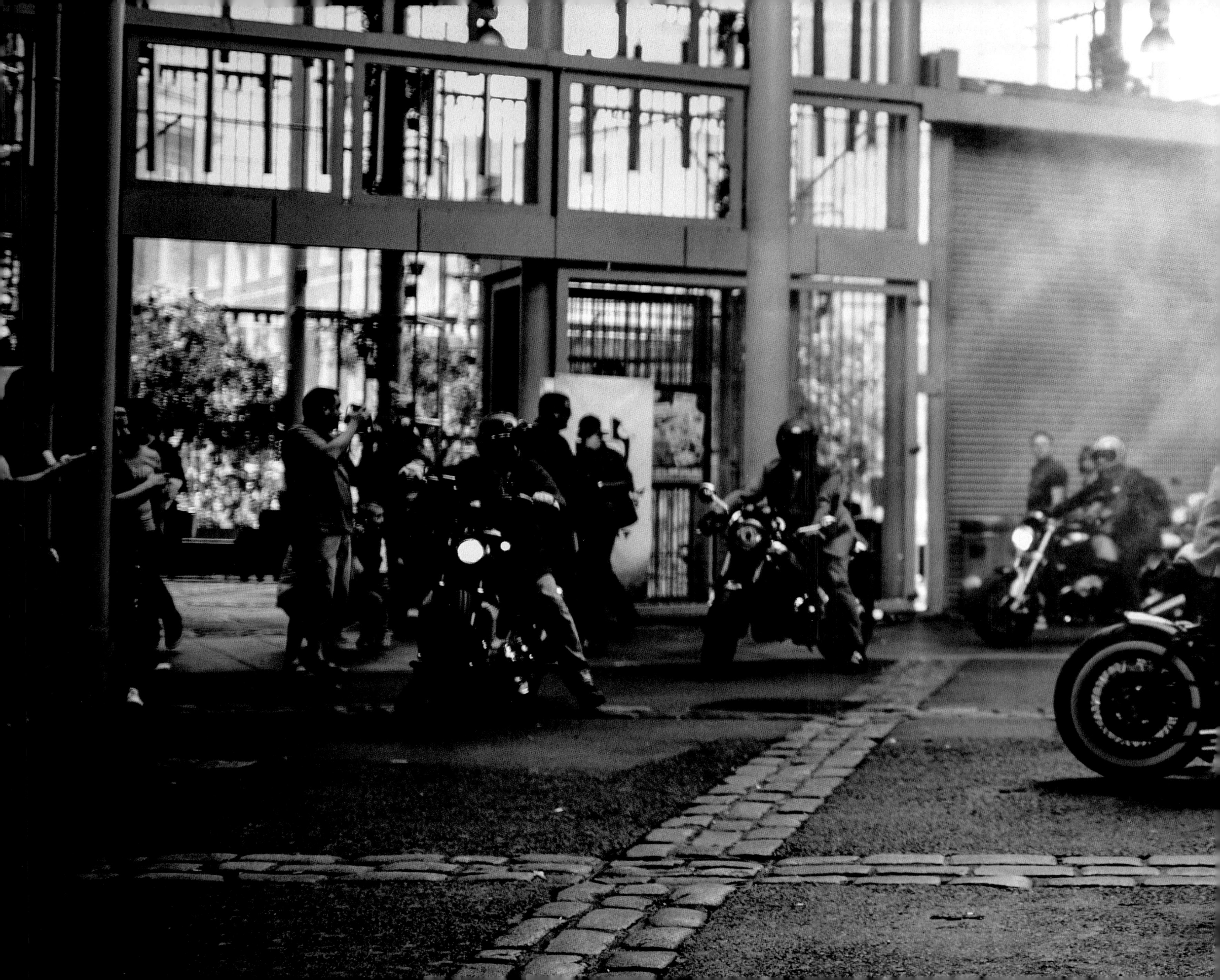

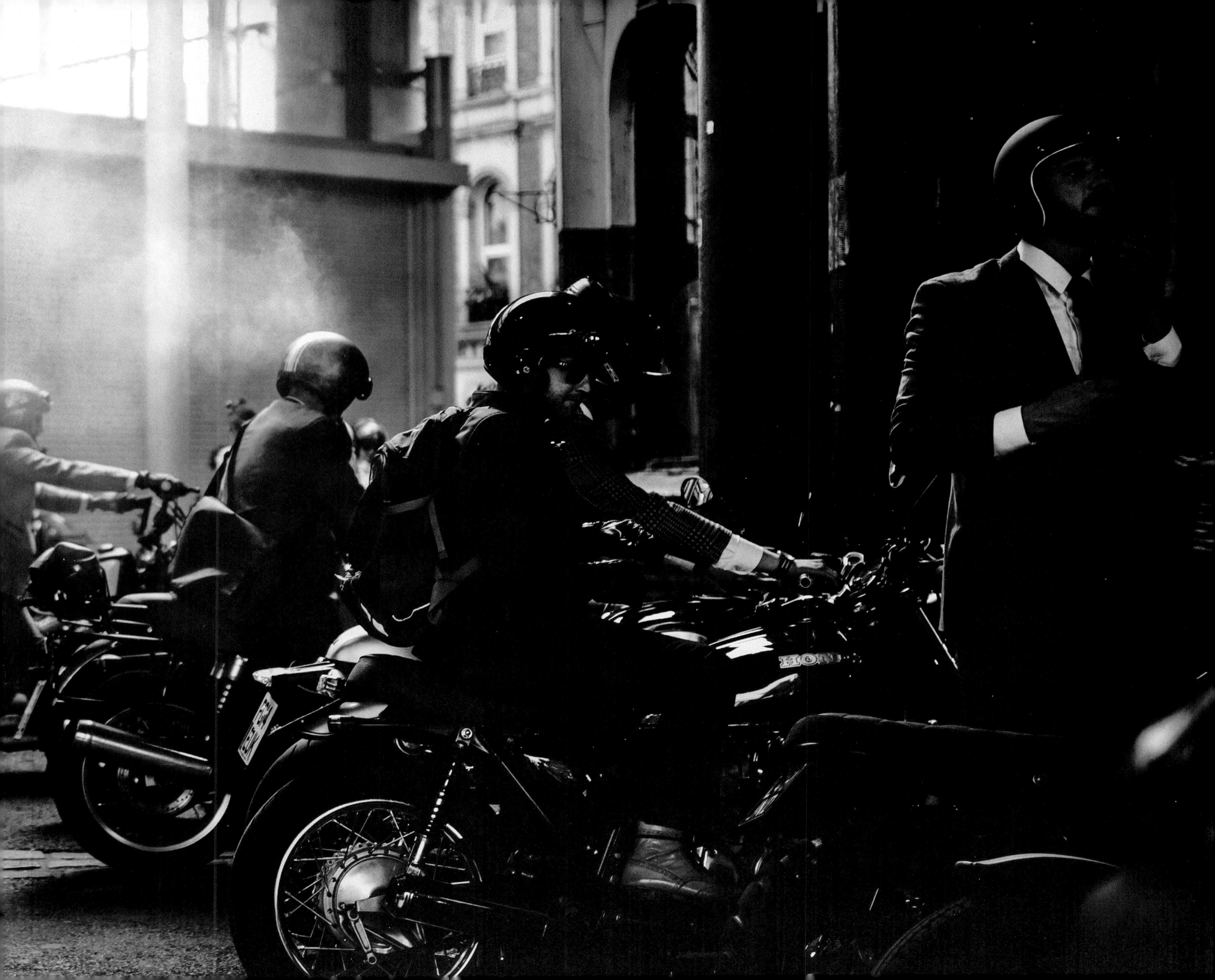

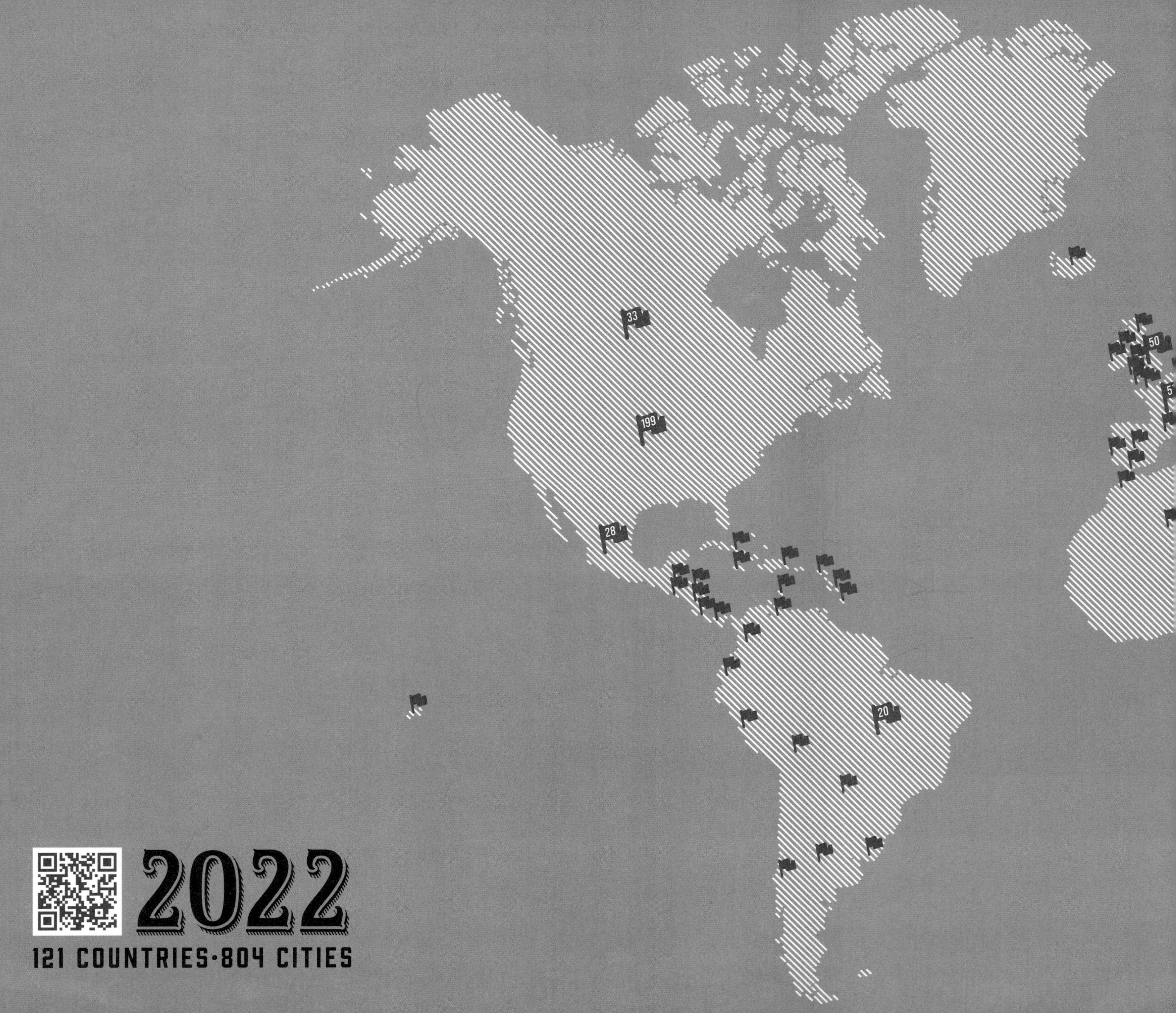
2022
121 COUNTRIES·804 CITIES
33
199
28
20
50
5